Computers in Applied Linguist
An International Perspective

Multilingual Matters

About Translation
   PETER NEWMARK
Code Mixing and Code Choice
   JOHN GIBBONS
Cultural Studies and Language Learning
   M. BYRAM, V. ESARTE-SARRIES and S. TAYLOR
Fluency *and* Accuracy
   HECTOR HAMMERLY
Foreign/Second Language Pedagogy Research
   R. PHILLIPSON, E. KELLERMAN, L. SELINKER,
   M. SHARWOOD SMITH and M. SWAIN (eds)
From Office to School: Special Language and Internationalization
   C. LAURÉN and M. NORDMAN
Individualizing the Assesment of Language Abilities
   JOHN H. A. L. de JONG and D. G. STEVENSON (eds)
Introspection in Second Language Research
   C. FÆRCH and G. KASPER
Investigating Cultural Studies in Foreign Language Teaching
   M. BYRAM and V. ESARTE-SARRIES
Language Acquisition: The Age Factor
   D. M. SINGLETON
Language, Culture and Cognition
   LILLIAM MALAVÉ and GEORGES DUQUETTE (eds)
Mediating Languages and Cultures
   D. BUTTJES and M. BYRAM (eds)
Methods in Dialectology
   ALAN R. THOMAS (ed.)
Second Language Acquisition - Foreign Language Learning
   B. VanPATTEN and J. F. LEE (eds)
Special Language: From Humans Thinking to Thinking Machines
   C. LAURÉN and M. NORDMAN (eds)
Teaching and Learning English Worldwide
   J. BRITTON, R. E. SHAFER and K. WATSON (eds)
Variation in Second Language Acquisition Vols I and II
   S. GASS, C. MADDEN, D. PRESTON and L. SELINKER (eds)

Please contact us for the latest book information:
Multilingual Matters Ltd,
Bank House, 8a Hill Road
Clevedon, Avon BS21 7HH
England

MULTILINGUAL MATTERS 75
Series Editor: Derrick Sharp

Computers in Applied Linguistics: An International Perspective

Edited by
Martha C. Pennington and Vance Stevens

MULTILINGUAL MATTERS LTD
Clevedon • Philadelphia • Adelaide

Library of Congress Cataloging in Publication Data

Computers in Applied Linguistics: An International Perspective/Edited by Martha C. Pennington and Vance Stevens.
p. cm. (Multilingual Matters: 75)
Includes bibliographical references and index.
1. Applied linguistics - Data processing. I. Pennington, Martha Carswell. II. Stevens, Vance. III. Series: Multilingual Matters (Series): 75.
P129.0885   1991
418'.00285   dc20

British Library Cataloguing in Publication Data

A CIP catalogue record for this book is available from the British Library.

ISBN 1-85359-120-3 (Hbk)
ISBN 1-85359-119-X (Pbk)

Multilingual Matters Ltd

UK: Bank House, 8a Hill Road, Clevedon, Avon BS21 7HH, England.
USA: 1900 Frost Road, Suite 101, Bristol, PA 19007, USA.
Australia: PO Box 6025, 83 Gilles Street, Adelaide, SA 5000, Australia.

Copyright © 1992 Martha C. Pennington, Vance Stevens and the authors of individual chapters.

All rights reserved. No part of this book may be reproduced in any form or by any means without permission in writing from the publisher.

Typeset by Editorial Enterprises, Torquay.
Printed and bound in Great Britain by Billing & Sons Ltd.

Contents

Preface vii

1. Introduction: Toward Appropriate Uses of Computers in
   Applied Linguistics 1

PART I: FRAMEWORKS FOR COMPUTER-ASSISTED LANGUAGE LEARNING IN THE 1990S

2. Humanism and CALL: A Coming of Age
   Vance Stevens 11

3. A Methodological Framework for CALL Courseware Development
   Philip Hubbard 39

4. Intelligence in Computer-Aided Language Learning
   Andrew Lian 66

PART II: RESEARCH ON APPLICATIONS OF COMPUTERS IN SECOND LANGUAGE ACQUISITION

5. Process and Product Approaches to Computer-Assisted Composition
   Martha C. Pennington and Mark N. Brock 79

6. Models of the Role of the Computer in Second Language Development
   Bernard Mohan 110

7. Computer Applications in Second Language Acquisition Research: Design, Description, and Discovery
   Catherine Doughty 127

8. Microcomputer Adventure Games and Second Language Acquisition: A Study of Hong Kong Tertiary Students
   Anthony Cheung and Colin Harrison 155

PART III: ANALYSIS TOOLS FOR A NEW GENERATION OF LANGUAGE APPLICATIONS

9. Analysed Corpora of English: A Consumer Guide
   Geoffrey Sampson 181

10. Computational Analysis of Language Acquisition Data
    Manfred Pienemann and Louise Jansen 201

11. Speech Technology Systems in Applied Linguistics Instruction
    John H. Esling 244

12. The Use of PC-Generated Speech Technology in the Development of an L2 Listening Comprehension Proficiency Test: A Prototype Design Effort
    Patricia Dunkel 273

13. Answer Analysis, Feedback, and On-Line Reference Help in CALL with Particular Reference to German
    Nic Witton 294

Indexes 319

Preface

This book grew out of an idea for a symposium entitled, 'Computers in Applied Linguistics: The Decade of the 1980s and Beyond', that we organised for the World Congress of the International Association of Applied Linguistics (AILA) at the University of Sydney, Sydney, Australia, in August 1987. Many of the papers represent second or third generation versions of papers read at the symposium or in other sessions at the Congress. Still others were solicited later, in order to round out the contents of the volume and to ensure representation of certain topics and areas of interest.

The development and editing of the papers was a major undertaking, requiring approximately two and a half years to complete. Besides a number of technical matters relating to the content of individual papers, it has been a huge task to edit so many papers at such great distances. Not only were the two editors situated approximately half way around the world from each other, but the contributors were spread out across Australia, Europe, and the United States. Looking back, we probably could not have conceived of a situation less conducive to good communication.

Though the process was slow and sometimes frustrating for us and the contributors, we did manage to communicate — via air mail, telephone, electronic mail, and personal travel. Each of the original papers has been extensively reworked based on two or more rounds of feedback from each of us. In their present versions, we feel that each paper represents a significant contribution to the burgeoning field of computers in applied linguistics, and we are pleased to have been able to support the development of this timely collection.

We wish to express our thanks to M. A. K. Halliday, whose encouragement to publish the papers from the AILA symposium led us to develop the present volume, and to Manfred Pienemann, who suggested Multilingual Matters as a potential publisher for the material. We also wish to express our thanks to all of our contributors for their interest in the project and willingness to work with us in bringing the volume to completion.

Martha C. Pennington   Vance Stevens
Hong Kong   *Sultanate of Oman*

1 Introduction: Toward Appropriate Uses of Computers in Applied Linguistics

Computers in Applied Linguistics: An International Perspective is a many-faceted volume which breaks new ground in at least four ways. First, it is the only edited collection on computers in applied linguistics that represents a truly international perspective, consolidating in one volume the insights of experts working in different countries spread across four continents. Second, it is the first attempt to bring the views of those working primarily as linguists together with those working primarily in applied fields such as education, applied linguistics, foreign language teaching, and English as a Second Language. Third, it is the only available volume treating both research and practice in use of computers in applied linguistics. Finally, the book is unique in its attempt not only to provide concrete information about specific computer tools and applications, but also to address certain important methodological and theoretical issues from a meta-perspective, looking at historical trends and conceptual directions for the field.

Many of the applications of computers in linguistics and related fields have exploited the basic capabilities of the medium to accomplish tasks that are difficult or impossible for humans to perform. Other applications have tended to exploit the novelty value of the medium, when used alone or when aligned with various peripheral devices, for commercial or educational purposes. In some of these cases, it has begun to be apparent that computers were pressed into service in inappropriate ways. In the last decade, developers have started to address the issue of appropriateness by systematically examining the ways in which the computer is being used in applied linguistics and by proposing new directions for computer applications based on a consideration not only of the medium's inherent capabilities, but also of the areas in research and practice which show the most promise for applications of the technology. The impetus for new developments in the use of computers in applied linguistics has thus come to be less a matter of understanding what is doable and more a matter of defining what is worth doing.

The authors of the papers in this volume are leading the way towards appropriate applications for computers in the decade of the 1990s and beyond, helping to clear the field of debris and staking out new areas for cultivation. Like pioneers who tame and settle the land, theirs is a struggle for control over the medium. These pioneers are discovering — as they expected — that once controlled, the medium is capable of nurturing rich environments for language learning and other applications to language research and practice.

The papers in this volume capture different aspects of the ongoing struggle to cultivate the computer medium to enrich language environments. The book is divided into three sections. The first of these (**Part I, Frameworks for Computer-Assisted Language Learning in the 1990s**) assesses goals and practices of computer-assisted language learning. The second section (**Part II, Research on Applications of Computers in Second Language Acquisition**) reports on research projects investigating various applications of computer-based tools. The third section (**Part III, Analysis Tools for a New Generation of Language Applications**) offers descriptions of some of the more promising computer-based tools for research and development.

Part I, Frameworks for Computer-Assisted Language Learning in the 1990s, seeks to define the place of Computer-Assisted Language Learning (CALL) in relation to the existing frameworks for educational practice and software development in the field of second language learning. This section of the book contains three articles, Vance Stevens' 'Humanism and CALL: A Coming of Age', Philip Hubbard's 'A Methodological Framework for CALL Courseware Development', and Andrew Lian's 'Intelligence in Computer-Aided Language Learning'.

Stevens begins by refocusing the development and assessment of language learning software away from behaviouristic models and towards humanistic educational principles. He discusses how humanistic courseware encourages exploratory interaction with the computer environment, promotes communication both by means of and in the vicinity of the computer, and motivates sustained use through problem-solving. The article also deals with the increasing use of productivity tools in language learning contexts, with recent attention to the effect of individual differences in computer use, and with improvements in interfaces that make software more natural to use.

Hubbard makes perhaps the most comprehensive effort in the literature to date to articulate a methodological framework for CALL. In his contribution

INTRODUCTION

to this volume, he focuses on courseware development, one component in a tripartite methodological framework that includes evaluation and implementation as well. Hubbard notes that 'many of the criticisms levelled at contemporary courseware are ultimately traceable to a lack of informed reflection' on the nature of language or of language learning. Hence, he proposes a framework for courseware development that follows the 'top-down' model of language teaching methodology elaborated by Richards & Rodgers (1982, 1986).

Lian's contribution builds on Hubbard's, as he reminds the reader at the outset that in intelligently implemented CALL, 'methodology is what matters the most'. His article reports on the nature of expert systems as they might be applied to computer-assisted language learning. The most ambitious projects, e.g. the *EXCALIBUR* or *Athena* projects, are still in a relatively early stage of development, though progress has been made in a number of the components that are required for their operation, e.g. in markup systems and in use of natural language databases for CALL. While Lian believes that short-sightedness is preventing software developers at present from sharing resources, he discusses conditions under which 'strategic intelligence' could result in systems capable of transporting, storing, and processing the huge databases that already exist in disparate locations throughout the world. Lian portrays conditions necessary for the computer medium to flourish in an educational setting, suggesting that for CALL to be implemented appropriately (i.e. intelligently), it may be necessary for educators to reconsider many current notions, such as that of 'lockstep' instruction.

The second section of the book, **Part II, Research on Applications of Computers in Second Language Acquisition**, consists of four articles with a research focus: Martha C. Pennington and Mark N. Brock's 'Process and Product Approaches to Computer-Assisted Composition', Bernard A. Mohan's 'Models of the Role of the Computer in Second Language Development', Catherine Doughty's 'Computer Applications in Second Language Acquisition Research: Design, Description, and Discovery', and Anthony Cheung and Colin Harrison's 'Microcomputer Adventure Games and Second Language Acquisition: A Study of Hong Kong Tertiary Students'.

In the first article of this section, Pennington and Brock provide insights into the appropriateness of computer software designed to assist writers. They test the effectiveness for students of English as a second language (ESL) of a computer-based text analysis program, IBM's *Critique*, finding that this type of software does not necessarily warrant claims made by its proponents. When compared with students receiving feedback that encourages a process approach to writing, students relying on only the text analyser for feedback produced fewer meaningful revisions, as opposed to students receiving process feedback, who made more meaningful revisions. The text analysis subjects also appeared to become increasingly dependent on feedback from the program, which casts doubt on claims that such programs promote self-monitoring and self-correction. Thus the results suggest that reliance on text analysis as the sole source of feedback in an ESL writing program is not an appropriate use of the computer, whereas word processing coupled with feedback appears to be an appropriate use.

Mohan's contribution further explores the issue of appropriate uses of computers, as he considers three models for computer use in language learning: (1) as a language teacher, (2) as a stimulus for talk, and (3) as a context for cognitive development. Each of these models is considered as to testability, consistency with research, and appropriacy as a use of computer resources. Mohan believes that the first model is defensible, and therefore probably appropriate, though one must distinguish the model itself from courseware which is inappropriate because it does not implement a viable instructional approach. Talk around computers is 'a natural side effect of computer use', and stimulation of such talk would seem intuitively to be an appropriate use of computers. However, in research carried out to test this effect on ESL students, Mohan discovers that talk around computers is not as rich as that which takes place in normal conversation; hence, in his view, using computers in this way is not appropriate. At the same time, he argues that computers may prove appropriate as means for developing cognitive–academic language proficiency.

Doughty successfully establishes several reasons for employing computers in research on second language acquisition. Doughty argues that it is pointless to examine whether computers are better teachers than teachers. Rather, computers are more appropriately exploited in research as environments for testing second language acquisition and as data collectors and analysers. She reports on a study in which the computer is used to control different instructional treatments on relative clause formation to which ESL students are exposed. In her study, computers are employed to monitor student interaction with the instructional program and then to evaluate the effect of each mode of instruction. It is found that both meaning-oriented and rule-oriented treatments produce greater improvement in relativisation ability than an exposure-only control treatment. The experiment also shows that subjects' improvement across all relativisation contexts is facilitated by a focus on one marked context.

Cheung and Harrison report on a two-phase experiment in which two groups of Chinese students are alternately exposed to an experimental treatment involving an English-language computer adventure game. In the first phase of the experiment, one group plays the adventure game while the other group learns word processing; in the second phase, the activities are reversed for each group. Both groups significantly increase their knowledge of program-specific vocabulary, though not of prepositions and conditionals. In questionnaire responses, subjects exhibit favourable attitudes toward the game and express the belief that it promotes their use of the target language, though the enthusiasm of the first group wanes during the period of the study in which they are no longer exposed to the game. Students' responses also indicate the desirability of making information about the nature of the game, its objectives, clues to its solution, and the meanings of some words readily available to players. Cheung and Harrison generalise their results to other 'move-based simulations' in which the computer responds to the user's decisions at different points, drawing conclusions for future research and courseware development.

Prerequisite to successful implementations of computer-based projects in applied linguistics is the development of powerful and flexible software tools capable of assisting the applied linguist in research and language study. Several of the contributors to this book have been instrumental in developing such tools, as described in **Part III, Analysis Tools for a New Generation of Language Applications**. This section comprises five articles: Geoffrey Sampson's 'Analysed Corpora of English: A Consumer Guide', Manfred Pienemann and Louise Jansen's 'Computational Analysis of Language Acquisition Data', John H. Esling's 'Speech Technology Systems in Applied Linguistics Instruction', Patricia A. Dunkel's 'The Use of PC-Generated Speech Technology in the Development of an L2 Listening Comprehension Proficiency Test: A Prototype Design Effort', and Nic Witton's 'Answer Analysis, Feedback, and On-Line Reference Help in CALL with Particular Reference to German'.

This section begins with Sampson's description of the available analysed corpora of English. The fact that this is an entirely appropriate use of computers in applied linguistics is obvious, as are the benefits to linguistic researchers of the availability of such databases. Analysed databases may also be a valuable source of content for designing computer-assisted language learning. These corpora were for the most part analysed by hand, though one, the Parsed LOB Corpus, was marked automatically using probabilistic techniques. Sampson points out that perhaps the most important reason for the creation of hand-analysed corpora is to provide the statistical data necessary for improving techniques in automatic parsing, which could in turn be applied to the automatic parsing of an even greater range of machine-readable corpora.

Developing software to do tedious and redundant, but vitally important, work such as parsing is one highly appropriate use of computers. Based on their work in acquisition of German, Pienemann and Jansen have developed a means of using a computer to assist in creating an analysed corpus for research on second language acquisition data. Their method of parsing is semi-automatic: they begin by manually coding the data to the point where the computer can continue the job automatically. Even in the manual marking stages, the computer program is designed so that marking becomes simply a matter of sorting words by a mouse-driven interface into the various possible categories; and where this job would be endlessly repetitive on paper, the machine is capable of instantly encoding all instances of identical items in the data. Once constituents have been identified and assigned values, the system uses relational databases and an ATN parser to complete the analysis. A database language is used to query the system for information pertinent to the research.

Esling has found appropriate ways to utilise databases comprising inventories of sounds in a wide variety of languages. He makes use of the computer's ability to store large amounts of linguistic data for near-instantaneous random access and to order this data in various ways. Esling's students can not only access in seconds a database of sounds that would be virtually impossible to amass themselves, but they can also manipulate and organise this data, hear it on demand, and see it in various graphic representations. What makes Esling's implementations compelling is that the computer is being used as Lian would envisage: as a way of getting students to make inductive leaps toward mastering the material at hand. While the computer provides an environment within which students can themselves extract focal items from authentic language data, one might also consider combining Esling's resources with Lian's conception of an expert system, whereby one could simply query the computer, 'Give me all the instances in your database of clicks in Xhosa'.

Dunkel describes the development of a computer-based system for testing proficiency in listening comprehension. Her description of this system illustrates two important features of computer applications. First, it is a humanistic development in testing, in that it is aimed at preventing learners from feeling 'frustrated and dissatisfied' by directing at them only questions appropriate to their proficiency level. Second, it is an appropriate use of technology in that it utilises the unique capabilities of the medium to standardise the testing process and the analysis of the results much more rigorously than could a human, given the human tendency to succumb to mood and fatigue. In a sense, the testing process developed by Dunkel is an expert system, in that it contains algorithms which make it function as would an experienced language tester operating under optimal conditions.

Witton's programs for acquisition of German adhere to most of Hubbard's recommendations for design criteria in providing hints of various types to lead students to correct answers, accepting alternative correct answers within the given context, offering explanations for why answers are incorrect, and anticipating incorrect answers and offering explanations concerning them. The key to Witton's programs is their refinement of what Hubbard calls 'anticipatory interaction', which, 'when done properly, ... can give students the ability to ask for and receive some of the same information they would in a face to face situation with teachers'. Accordingly, Witton's work essentially presents an expert system authoring package to allow students to gain greater insights into the linguistic features of German.

Witton's program includes an authoring system that requires teachers to specify constituent elements of the anticipated response sentences, with which information the computer can work out alternate acceptable responses. Sampson and Pienemann and Jansen have discussed how the creation of huge parsed corpora can be created automatically or semi-automatically. It is interesting to speculate on the possibilities of combining such tools whereby authentic target language materials can be parsed automatically and then incorporated into courseware utilising such databases. We can also imagine the possibility of combining the utilities of Dunkel's testing project with Esling's linguistic data in order to test the student's ability to discriminate the sounds of different languages, or to train or test other aspects of phonology, as suggested in Pennington (1989). In order for co-operative projects such as these to be feasible, we will need to heed Lian's advice on removing constraints to the assembly of shared tools and databases.

The articles in this book suggest that we are entering a stage of mature use of computers in applied linguistics. Implementations are being investigated which yield increasingly appropriate applications of computers for addressing particular tasks in linguistic research and language learning, in both specialised and mainstream uses. As Lian and Hubbard point out here, and has been previously pointed out by Dever and Pennington (1989), it is not necessary to wait for the next generation of artificially intelligent software: applied linguists can pursue a wide variety of options for making productive use of computers in their work right now.

References

DEVER, S. Y., & M. C. PENNINGTON (1989) Computer capabilities underlying computer-learner interaction. In M. C. PENNINGTON (ed.), *Teaching Languages With Computers: The State of the Art*. La Jolla, CA: Athelstan.

PENNINGTON, M. C. (1989) Applications of computers in the development of speaking and listening proficiency. In M. C. PENNINGTON (ed.), *Teaching Languages With Computers: The State of the Art*. La Jolla, CA: Athelstan.

RICHARDS, J. C. & T. S. RODGERS (1982) Method: Approach, design, and procedure *TESOL Quarterly*, 16: 2, 153–168.
RICHARDS, J. C. & T. S. RODGERS (1986) *Approaches and Methods in Language Teaching: A Description and Analysis.* Cambridge, UK: Cambridge University Press.]

Part I:
Frameworks for Computer-Assisted Language Learning in the 1990s

2 Humanism and CALL: A Coming of Age

VANCE STEVENS
Sultan Qaboos University, Sultanate of Oman

Introduction

This article attempts to put into perspective the coming-of-age of computer-assisted language learning (CALL), various aspects of which are documented in other parts of the volume. It is argued here that, in shaking off the influence of the early behaviourists, CALL is becoming more 'user-friendly', or humanistic. Whatever its precise manifestation, humanism in CALL means that courseware lends itself these days more to what students want it to be than what a particular program designer may have originally intended it to be. This watershed development has not only brought CALL more in line with current thinking about language teaching methodology, but also heralds the emergence of CALL as a versatile tool, as an aid to learning, and as an informant on language rather than a preceptor, task-master, or programmed instructor.

Before embarking on this topic, a few points should be made clear. First of all, it is not suggested here that CALL, or any learning for that matter, is not to some degree behaviouristic. Almost every human interaction — teaching in particular — is an attempt to modify behaviour. However, behaviourist psychologists have been restrictive in the transactions allowed in their models of how behaviour is modified, and it is the courseware evolving from such models that current CALL developers tend to reject.

A second point of clarification is that, in so far as no one theory succeeds in describing a mechanism as complex as how people learn — let alone how they learn languages, which themselves defy accurate description — this article does not intend to dogmatically espouse any particular theory of learning. It shows, rather, how recent developments in CALL exemplify humanist paradigms. Proponents of various learning theories (e.g. Skinner, 1974) generally acknowledge the limitations of their theories while arguing that the available evidence supports their view of how people learn. The view put forward here is that since we lack a means of either accurately describing or controlling what it is that we want people to learn, one major advantage of CALL is its flexibility in providing students with tools that utilise their demonstrated abilities to figure things out and so to learn according to their motivation and interest.

In its role as tool in language learning, CALL is not assumed to be the sole means of delivery of a course of language instruction. Therefore, certain objections to learner-directed modes of study (e.g. that they are inefficient because they rely on induction and leave the learner to wander aimlessly in a jungle of disordered linguistic data) could, if desired, be compensated for in other parts of a course. In this way, CALL can be integrated into the curriculum as a medium that allows students to experiment with concepts taught elsewhere. Conversely, CALL is also something that a student can employ on an *ad hoc* or self-access basis without its being part of a set course of study.

Changing Attitudes Toward the Way People Learn

It is widely recognised that mid-way through the present century, a convergence of behaviourist psychology and of structural linguistics led to a dominance of the audiolingual method in language instruction, and to interest in **programmed instruction** (PI) as a means of delivering instruction in general. Drill-and-practice CALL is in some respects reminiscent of the former, while PI lent itself particularly to the design of computer-assisted instructional programs (see Ahmad *et al.*, 1985, for a survey of this era of CALL development).

Eventually, as Brown puts it (1980: 242), 'language teachers were discovering that the ALM actually was not working! People were not learning the communicative functions of language.' A similar impression of programmed instruction is conveyed by Rivers (1981: 119), who notes that its tendency to 'preoccupation with the teaching of innumerable details about the language ... can distract attention from the real "terminal behavior", that is, the whole of language as it operates in an act of communication.' The problem with early CALL, as with the teaching practices it emulated, was that while both might have succeeded in teaching the surface forms of the language, neither promoted carry-over to spontaneously communicative contexts.

It was obvious to practitioners that either the model on which these methods were based or the interpretation of the these models in the creation of instructional algorithms was flawed. It may be unfair, as is often done, to lay the blame for these failures on 'behaviourism' as a whole; Carroll (1966: 104), in fact, attributes to the audiolingual habit theory 'a vague resemblance to an early version of a Thorndikean association theory'. Nevertheless, general dissatisfaction with lockstep teaching encouraged an interest in more humanistic approaches to learners and their individual strategies for learning.

Humanist approaches to learning are articulated in the psychology of Carl Rogers. Rogers (1961: 35) postulates an:

> urge which is evident in all organic and human life — to expand, extend, become autonomous, develop, mature — the tendency to express and activate all the capacities of the organism, to the extent that such activation enhances the organism or the self ... it is my belief that it exists in every individual, and awaits only the proper conditions to be released and expressed.

Hence the humanistic educator's interest in environments conducive to learning which favour this quest for self-actualisation. Such an approach is epitomised for computer-based learning in Papert (1980).

According to Graham (1986: 56), Rogerian therapy provides a threat-free environment 'in which the individual learns to be free. As such it is an educational process, one that Rogers believes can be as effective within the classroom as in the clinic' (Rogers, 1969) and which depends on the relationship between facilitator and client having three significant qualities. The first is what Rogers (1961: 33) calls 'a transparency on my part' and what Brown (1980: 77) interprets, in the area of language learning, as a focus:

> away from 'teaching' and toward 'learning'. The goal of education is the facilitation of change and learning. Learning how to learn is more important than being 'taught' something from the superior vantage point of a teacher who unilaterally decides what shall be taught.

This description anticipates the second significant quality of the therapist or teacher, which is 'unconditional positive regard for the client', while the third is empathetic understanding or genuine listening — a continuing desire to understand the feelings and personal meanings which the person is experiencing' (Graham, 1986: 55).

Rivers (1981: 89) characterises the influence of humanist psychology on language learning as follows:

> In practice, the humanistic approach has resulted in the inclusion in language-learning materials of vocabulary and activities for expressing one's feelings, for sharing one's values and viewpoints with others, and for developing a better understanding of others' feelings and needs. A language class is a particularly suitable environment for meeting affective needs,

because much of the activity can take the form of role playing, simulation games, and small-group discussions. The expressive arts ... require the student to seek the most appropriate forms in the new language to express nuances and meaning.

With this re-emphasis on individual worth and difference, language teachers became conscious of the fact that individual students prefer different modalities of learning ... they also learn at different rates and employ quite different strategies for understanding and retaining the material to be learned. With this new understanding, teachers were no longer satisfied with a monolithic 'what is good for one is good for all' approach.

Complaints concerning the inadequacy of CALL software have surfaced frequently in the literature, but are generally directed against the kind of software based on instructional algorithms rooted in PI and the pattern practice techniques associated with audiolingualism (Hubbard, this volume, chapter 3, cites several such complaints). But the situation is changing; we are now seeing improvements in CALL courseware in accordance with more recent shifts in approaches to the way people learn languages (Stevens, 1989a).

The present article attempts to show how these improvements have followed from humanistic approaches to language learning, as characterised above. First of all, it will be shown how present CALL courseware emphasises learning rather than teaching. Recent CALL development attempts to exploit an urge for self-actualization in learners through use of non-threatening learner-centred settings in which discovery learning, problem-solving, and tool-based activities figure prominently. Furthermore, in current CALL courseware, the role of teacher is diminished with respect to that of the student, in providing control over modalities for learning and in attempting to compensate for individual differences. Second, the article suggests that current CALL courseware displays 'positive regard' for students in so far as programmers have gone to great lengths in their consideration of the convenience of those using it. Finally, the article raises the question of communication both with and around computers — in particular, regarding activities in which students can 'express nuances and meaning' in the target language.

Focus on Learning as Opposed to Teaching

Humanism in language learning seeks ways to empower individuals to direct their own learning, rather than ceding control over learning to an authoritative entity, as in behaviourist models. Higgins (1983; 1988) expresses this notion in terms of his **pedagogue/magister** dichotomy. In his view, the magister is the instructor directing students unilaterally, while the pedagogue is a slave following a step behind, always ready with a clue or answer when asked. The pedagogue facilitates learning but does not control it. Higgins points out that magisters have their place in learning, but when 'magisterial thinking' predominates, learners may be discouraged from extending their learning through productive experiment.

Whereas it often serves the magister's purposes to customise the teaching environment, the pedagogue operates in the environment at large. Accordingly, and despite a dearth of corroborating evidence, many language teachers have found intuitively appealing Krashen's suggestion (1982) that grammatical competence will follow naturally from interesting, relevant, comprehensible, and unsequenced language input. More recently, parallel distributed processing (PDP) has emerged as a model of cognition which seeks to explain how humans learn without resort to explicitly expressed rules. Developers of PDP models have succeeded in simulating acquisition of past tense verb forms (Rumelhart & McClelland, 1986) by programming a computer to develop 'connection strengths which allow a network of simple units to act as *though* [emphasis in original] it knew rules' (McClelland *et al.*, 1986: 32). Such a model suggests a mechanism by which acquisition could conceivably occur solely through learner interaction with authentic language environments. The above paradigms lend theoretical support to use of materials for language learning which replicate an authentic target language environment.

The computer is coming to be regarded as a medium with significant potential for work with authentic materials. It is possible to store large databases containing natural language on computers and to provide students with means of accessing these more thoroughly and efficiently than is possible with other media. From a humanistic standpoint, interaction with the database is non-threatening and is prompted by learner interest, curiosity, and need in fulfilment of the urge to 'expand, extend, become autonomous, develop, mature'.

We look now at three genres of courseware promoting student autonomy in learning. Such software provides environments for (1) exploratory interaction, (2) problem solution, and (3) use of software tools to develop productivity skills contributing to greater maturity in language learning. Some evidence that students have favourable attitudes toward learning English using a battery of CALL software comprising these three genres has been presented by Stevens (1988b; 1989c).

Exploratory Interaction

One school of CALL development, pioneered for language learning by Higgins and Johns (1984), sees the computer as a repository of information, only parts of which are revealed at any given moment. Thus, students are led to supply the missing pieces according to their knowledge or intuition about how the target language operates. From the feedback received, students test their intuitions, strengthening or weakening them in a continual process. In so doing, students make discoveries about the target language. It is assumed that because they have to work things out according to logic and pattern, they are more likely to internalise and retain the fruits of their discoveries than with other media.

In diametric opposition to exploratory software is software following the programmed instruction approach. The PI approach utilises carefully prescribed steps incorporating a gradual build-up of knowledge, with checks on learning at each step, possibly including branching according to how well the student is doing. (Where one part of the instructional sequence must be mastered before the student proceeds to the next, this is more specifically referred to as **mastery learning** (see Jamison *et al.*, 1974, for an overview of research into PI and mastery learning).) With PI-based CALL, what is learned is largely controlled by the programmer. Exploratory software, on the other hand, provides tools enabling students to browse and manipulate a database. Access to information could be in almost any order, and its presentation is under the control of the student.

Both approaches have their advantages and disadvantages. The first approach is behaviourist-based and will result in language learning only if the programmer has an accurate model of all relevant aspects of the learning situation and can emulate this on the computer. For example, a model of the student would have to accommodate individual differences such as maturity level, proficiency in the target language, and preference for inductive or deductive approaches (addressed in greater detail below). The model of the material to be taught might be relatively simple, as in the case of verb forms in various languages, or complex, as in the case of how these same verbs might be used in discourse. The compelling thing about this approach is that it would work if — but only if — we understood and could control the relevant aspects of the learning (and linguistic) situation. The possibility of close control explains the popularity of such an approach at a time when behaviourists were fairly confident that steps in learning could be reduced to discrete elements, and when linguists felt that they were on the verge of developing productive grammatical models of living languages. However, those who take a more holistic approach regarding the interaction of the many complex and little understood cognitive and affective factors involved in language learning and who see little hope of devising truly accurate models of either languages or learners can never be reconciled to the PI approach as a way of developing competence in a language beyond the most rudimentary levels of proficiency.

It has been pointed out that one advantage to the exploratory approach is that students can be provided powerful means of systematically accessing data, and so can, in theory, learn by observing and manipulating more comprehensive and authentic databases of materials than they could using any other medium. While PI might actually limit student access to linguistic data, in so far as it restricts them to a prescribed program of learning, the exploratory approach broadens the field considerably and encourages student independence and curiosity. Another advantage to the latter approach is that, in purposely allowing flexibility, the materials developer does not require in advance full information on the targeted users or their learning situation.

Machine-readable authentic text is often available in the workplace in the form of materials that ESL instructors, or teachers in other disciplines, have created using word processors. Often, such texts are created for purposes other than CALL work – for example, course materials which students are studying concurrently with their courses at a language center, or even everyday correspondence. Students are thus able to work interactively with texts that are authentic and often of immediate relevance to them (see Stevens, 1988a, for a description of the use of such programs in a language learning setting).

Johns (1989) also notes the advantages of using relevant and authentic texts with language learners. His remarks are made with regard to concordancing, which is another example of exploratory language learning software. A concordance program will find every instance of the occurrence of a string in a given text and display the context surrounding each instance of that string. Sources for extensive corpora of such text are discussed by Sampson (this volume, Chapter 9). Long the domain of linguists and literature specialists, concordances are only recently finding their way into the second language classroom. Stevens (1989b) describes how concordance output can be directed toward creating relevant and authentic vocabulary exercises, including hands-on exercises whose purpose is to encourage ESL learners to gain insights into salient features of the target language by running their own concordances on samples of authentic discourse.

One of the most compelling applications of the exploratory principle is hypermedia (described more fully below) — for example, hypertext, which allows students to access facilitative information by opening 'windows' on individual words or chunks of text. The windows may themselves allow elaboration on text, so that the amount of information available can proceed to some depth. Two hindrances to development of this approach are the labour needed to prepare the elaborations to text and the memory needed to store these elaborations if help is to be global. The latter problem could be attenuated through use of CD-ROM, in which case storage memory is sufficient for dictionaries and similar resources to be made available for random access. The first problem then becomes one of developing algorithms to enlist the available resources in making possible elaboration on demand (see Lian, this volume, Chapter 4 for insights on such algorithms). The result is text which students can read (or videos they can explore, or a combination of these and other media) with the help of instant-access dictionaries, encyclopeadias, maps and atlases, diagrams, translations into various languages, or whatever on-line assistance has been built into the program. It is easy to imagine how placing a cursor over a troublesome lexical item and having the computer provide an animation, illustration, or information pertaining to that item would be an improvement over students' tediously consulting off-the-shelf resource materials when reading or writing, a process so cumbersome as to be underutilised by students and others.

Success with the exploratory approach requires that students be sufficiently motivated to search the database and that they do so in a systematic manner. Therefore, in practice, the success of exploratory CALL depends largely on the extent to which students are guided and motivated to work efficiently, as well as on the power and flexibility of the exploratory tool and on the scope and authenticity of the database (see Esling, this volume, Chapter 11 for a report on one such implementation).

Problem-Solving

The problem-solving format cuts across almost all aspects of CALL; accordingly, there are puzzle and problem-solving elements in many of the examples of software cited under other topics in this article. Still, this format is itself an important characteristic of humanistic software.

One type of software for exploring databases is that which permutes text, creating reconstruction puzzles which students then resolve. For example, sentences are put out of order, and students restore them; or sentences are encrypted and students decode them; or cloze passages are created, and students replace the missing words (e.g. Stevens & Millmore, 1987).

Another useful problem-solving genre is the adventure game. Computerised adventure games are based on algorithms that set up a 'maze' of possible outcomes which are accessed according to choices made by the player in pursuit of some goal; successful negotiation of the maze is the puzzle in need of solution. Cheung and Harrison (this volume, Chapter 8) discuss the motivating value of the adventure game format, which they refer to as 'move-based simulation'.

Surprisingly, few adventure games have emerged specifically for CALL. One such game is *LONDON ADVENTURE* (Hamilton, 1986), in which a traveller faces a day in London with a shopping list of last-minute gifts to buy and a plane to catch. Armed with a certain sum in foreign currency travellers cheques, the player must ask directions politely of passers-by in order to find an exchange bureau to get pounds. The player must then buy maps and guidebooks providing information on London transport and department stores in order to purchase the gift items before it is time to catch the plane home (the program sets a clock at the start of play). Other CALL adventure games include the interactive video programs discussed below, as well as *MYSTERY HOUSE*, adapted for ESL by Baltra (1984), and now in the public domain. The latter is one of many mystery and adventure games created originally for native speakers but capable of providing productive problem-solving contexts for language learning.

Another genre of software that has come to frequently employ a problem-solving format is tutorial software. Such software often operates in Presentation and Play modes; that is, there is one mode by which students receive instruction (sometimes by perusing a database) and another where they play games presenting challenges based on what has been learned. For example, there is a commercial software package which presents various facts on explorers of the New World during the Age of Discovery and then sets up problem-solving tasks which rely for their solution on associating the correct explorers with given facts (Neosoft, 1984). Other such commercially-available programs deal with subjects such as geography (*EUROPEAN NATIONS AND LOCATIONS*, 1985) and science (*FAMOUS SCIENTISTS*, 1985). In promoting reading skills in the target language (especially scanning and culling desired information from a text), and in providing settings for the discussion of facts and solutions to problems, such programs can provide fruitful contexts for language learning.

Increasingly, programs for teaching grammar, vocabulary, reading and writing incorporate games and puzzle elements; *ESSENTIAL IDIOMS* (Richardson & Wise, 1985), for example, teaches idioms in English via activities ranging from simple presentation of the material to a beat-the-clock mode. The latter activity is essentially a variation on fill-in-the-blanks, but its appeal to students is greatly enhanced by use of a game-board format, and by making the clock an integral part of the puzzle (see Stevens, 1987).

An interesting combination of adventure and tutorial formats, with value and appeal to ESL students, is found in *ROBOT ODYSSEY* (Wallace & Grimm, 1986). The game starts with a student alter ego getting out of bed and falling literally to the bottom of Robotropolis, to the sewer. The rest of the game is a quest to extract oneself step by step up through the six levels of Robotropolis and back to the light of day. In order to evade the strict but otherwise benign police robots and effect an escape, one must work through a series of tutorials to learn how to enter and rewire the robots. The tutorials teaching the skills required are computer counterparts to Total Physical Response (Asher, 1966); that is, they instruct students to move this, pick up that, put this there, etc. The student reads these instructions and learns by actually doing as instructed. Once a tutorial is completed, the student has the specialised skills necessary for escaping another level of the Robotropolis maze. Thus, the game proceeds with the student reading instructions, performing operations which at every step confirm comprehension of the instructions, and eventually using the newly acquired knowledge to resolve the current predicament toward the overall goal of escape from Robotropolis (Stevens, 1988c).

Other language learning puzzle games available for personal computers include interactive versions of popular board-format games such as *Scrabble* and *Trivial Pursuit*. Finally, the text manipulation programs mentioned earlier all rely on a human interest in puzzles as motivators for what might otherwise be relatively mundane text-based exercises. It is important to note that the effects of computer-based enhancements on such exercises would be impossible to achieve in any other medium.

Presenting language learning tasks in problem-solving format has its drawbacks, however. For one thing, puzzles do not appeal to all types of language learners; some may benefit from inductive (i.e. problem-solving, exploratory) modes of learning, even as others would prefer more directed and deductive modes (as discussed more fully below). Also, if students do not understand the underlying benefits to them of solving a particular puzzle, they may look upon the activity as a frivolous waste of time, or they may work the puzzles only as such and not approach the tasks in ways conducive to language learning. Care must be taken to ensure that puzzle activities are constructed so as to promote effective language learning strategies rather than allowing students to resort to puzzle-solving strategies that may actually be counterproductive for language learning.

There is little research on this aspect of CALL; however, Windeatt (1986) notes several ways that cloze exercises as they are typically implemented on computer may counter optimal reading strategies. For example, students working cloze exercises on a computer treat text locally rather than globally, as they rarely scroll past one screen (when the cloze was presented on paper, they tended to read over the entire text). Moreover, they tend to pursue solutions one blank at a time rather than considering other blanks which might provide clues to the solution of the original blank (students working on paper moved quickly from blank to blank).

Further evidence that the strategies students employ for solving puzzles may not involve strategies for language learning can be gleaned from observing students solving cryptograms. Cryptograms are puzzles in which each unique letter in a block of text has been changed to some other unique letter selected at random; for example, all the occurrences of *a* become *c*, all occurrences of *b* become *p*, and so on throughout the block of text. Interestingly, students solving cryptograms can complete a puzzle yet be oblivious to the message in the sentence elucidated. This is evident when the encrypted message carries instructions, and the students, on successfully decoding the message, fail to follow the instructions and profess later to have been unaware that any instructions were given. In other words, they seem to be capable of decoding an encrypted sentence without attending to its meaning. This may be isolated behaviour particular to certain students, and perhaps with certain texts, but it is worth being aware of possible limitations to the use of puzzles in effective CALL implementations.

In sum, problem solving can serve as an adjunct to language learning and can be more entertaining than explicitly instructional modes. However, development of appropriate language puzzles may require more study and effort on the part of materials developers and teachers than one might at first expect if the activity is to achieve the desired effects.

Using Software as a Flexible Tool for Productivity and Learning

One important reason for the increasingly common acceptance of computers as a viable medium for language learning is that computers have high face validity, in that they are perceived by both students and teachers as being important to learn to use. Phillips (1986: 4) points out that the computer is 'now part of mass consciousness and permeates social life at many different levels', and unlike the language lab is capable of 'being transplanted to the environment of the world outside'. In other words, computers have the unique advantage of being viable instructional tools, and at the same time of being devices that students want to use and to become more familiar with for reasons quite apart from language learning. Thus CALL presents a unique opportunity to provide learners with a rich environment of functional, communicative, and interactive materials in a given target language, and to do so by means of a delivery system that students are often predisposed to use.

Accordingly, a working knowledge of computer-based tools, the third kind of software promoting autonomous learning, is useful in its own right. Common examples of such software are word processors, desk top publishers, communications software, computer-based spreadsheets, database management programs, spelling checkers, syntax and style checkers, and programs dealing explicitly with various stages in the writing process. Learners using such software practice with language, both in learning to use and in actually using the software, and also experience a gain in *productivity skills* which can in turn be put to use in further enhancement of linguistic abilities.

Productivity skills enable the learner to use tools which enhance control over organisation and manipulation of data, largely by reducing what Kemmis *et al* (1977) called *inauthentic labour*, i.e. the energy one must expend to accomplish the authentic labour which is the true purpose of undertaking the task. An example of inauthentic labour (in Higgins, 1988) is retrieving a dictionary from among other books on a shelf, perusing the key words at the top of its pages, and finally searching the page itself for a particular word. The availability of an on-line dictionary reduces to a few key-presses such ancillary steps and helps ensure that most labour done is authentic — in this instance, the labour involved in discerning the meaning of the word in question (see Witton, this volume, Chapter 13 for an example of a similar implementation).

After surveying a number of CALL developers in the United States, Johnson (1985) concludes that the computer could be much better used 'as a tool to accomplish functional tasks' than as a vehicle for 'traditional or even communicative CALL'; and that the study of language when using computers should be a 'by-product' of instruction focusing on tasks related to social and academic success in school (pp. III-5 and III-6). Thus, software tools for improving productivity in work can be taught as foci for functional language learning activities. The communicative aspects are enhanced because the students have real reasons for seeking information directed at solving immediate problems and are motivated to learn the language they need in order to use the software for accomplishing specific tasks. Furthermore, foreign students at American universities and secondary schools, who often initially have difficulty making friends with native-speakers, can find native-speaking classmates willing to help them use the computers in student terminal rooms. Thus the chance of making contacts vital to assimilation into a foreign culture is enhanced by the need to seek help in utilising computers as productivity tools.

Several textbooks have appeared which teach computer-based productivity skills as CALL. For example, the text by Abdulaziz *et al.* (1985) teaches computer programming to ESL students. Similarly, Barlow (1987) has produced a book teaching skills such as typing, word processing, use of writing aids, and spreadsheet and database manipulation to advanced level non-native speakers. It is not difficult to envisage how such skills might be taught in a content-based language course. The focus would be on the computer-based productivity skill, but the target language would be the medium of instruction and of the materials used; and the students would meaningfully practice that language by interacting and communicating with other users of the skill in question (both novice and experienced) toward accomplishing tasks that utilise that skill.

Providing Control Over Modalities for Learning

The overriding importance of allowing the user rather than the program to control the progress of a lesson or activity is still not universally accepted in program design, as is evidenced by software still on the market which locks students into a sequence of steps dictated by the program (e.g. Rosen *et al.*, 1985). However, allowing learners control over the various aspects of their learning is an important consideration in humanistic CALL. In their essay on 'clarifying educational environments', which describes conditions especially conducive to learning, Moore & Anderson (1969) argue the importance of providing learners with several perspectives on learning, among which they can shift at will. Their remarks prompted a study by Stevens (1984) examining the benefits of letting students choose sequence of CALL delivery, with results suggesting that learning is enhanced when choice and control are in the hands of students.

Humanistic CALL programs provide not only a multiplicity of choices, but also quick and easy means of making them. For example, students should be able to move easily within (or out of) the program — there should be a clear means of escape from the program, either at once or by backing out through menus, and of escape from tasks, perhaps by 'passing' on to the next one. Students should be able to choose to receive hints or even answers to save them the frustration of getting stuck.

Software developers are increasingly displaying all options clearly on the screen, and usually in some consistently designated area so that the user knows where to look for them. Often, selection of options is accomplished by moving the cursor until the option is highlighted, and then pressing the Return or Enter keys, or clicking. Often, there is a space on the screen for a description of the purpose of the option currently highlighted, and this information changes as the cursor is guided back and forth over the options. The trend for current software is not only to provide more options for users, but to provide means within the programs themselves to ensure that users know what these options are.

Compensating for Individual Differences

It has long been acknowledged that individualisation of learning is one advantage of CALL over other media. Traditionally, individualisation has meant that the learner can choose to work in privacy and silence, or that the software will branch according to how well the student is doing with the content of the program. More recently, it has been suggested that individualisation in CALL could achieve greater sophistication than this.

In research considering a range of cognitive styles, abilities, and aptitudes in students undergoing a course in computer-managed instruction, Federico (1982) found a need for 'adapting instruction to individual differences in students' cognitive attributes' (p.17). Chapelle & Jamieson (1986), in research on ESL students using *PLATO*, decry the approach taken in those lessons as being 'notoriously "insensitive" to individual learner differences' (p.41) and suggest that this insensitivity may be a reason why field independent students disliked CALL implemented on the *PLATO* system. If field dependence or independence is indeed a factor in a student's appreciation of a certain exercise format, and if the computer can be programmed to judge a student's field dependence or independence, then it follows that students could be presented lessons in alternative formats commensurate with their cognitive styles.

This field of inquiry is a potentially burgeoning one for CALL. As Ellis notes (1985: 116):

> the existing research does not conclusively show that [cognitive style] is a major factor where [linguistic] success is concerned. There has been no research into the effects of cognitive style on route of acquisition.

Jamieson & Chapelle (1987) attribute this inconclusiveness to limitations in the methods of data collection employed for such research (observation and self-reporting). Because their data was collected on-line and analysed by the computer, Jamieson & Chapelle were able to show how the cognitive variables field dependence/independence and reflection/impulsivity are related to three learning strategies, and how the latter are predictors for TOEFL scores.

Not only do data collected on computer have a high level of integrity relative to the other means mentioned, but such data are in turn amenable to analysis by the computer (the data in the Jamieson & Chapelle study, for example, were rendered by means of a computer program to a format usable by the SPSS statistical software package). The ability of computers to control lesson delivery, scrupulously collect data on its use, and then analyse the results also made possible the studies by Doughty (this volume, Chapter 7) and van Els *et al.* (1988). The improvements in data collection and analysis made possible by computer-based research suggest techniques not previously available to researchers for probing the effects of cognitive style on the 'route' of second language acquisition.

The idea of testing for learner differences and then adjusting program delivery accordingly has occasionally been applied in CALL. For example, generative CALL lessons have been produced which individualise grammar materials based on error analyses of the students' first languages (Dalgish, 1989). Also Dunkel (this volume, Chapter 12) addresses the concept of tailoring CALL lesson difficulty according to learner proficiency.

Practically speaking, although we have the theoretical capability of catering to a wide spectrum of individual differences, and though work is in progress to actualise what is currently being imagined in theory, this area of CALL development is still much in the future. Consider, for example, the potential of bringing artificial intelligence and expert system techniques to bear on individualisation, as suggested by Liau (this volume, Chapter 4). Given the 'insensitivity' to individual differences of so much courseware in the past, the potential for improvement through greater individualisation of courseware is great.

Positive Regard for Students: Humanistic Interfaces

Current CALL courseware is programmed with 'positive regard' for students to the extent that it is considerate of their comfort and requirements when using it. This is evident in considering recent developments in interfaces to computer-based learning tools, whose power is increased in part through increased convenience of access made possible by improved interfaces.

Conceiving of interfaces is like delving into dreams, as this mental process can easily transcend the realm of reality. Evans, in *The Mighty Micro* (1979), imagined himself lying on his back in bed staring at a terminal fixed to his ceiling as he paged about the snippets of reading matter which he had just downloaded over phone lines from the central library database. When Evans wrote his book, the mouse had not been invented, but this would have allowed him, by moving his fingers over a device at his bedside table, to perform such tasks as opening windows, blocking text off, and clicking it in to save and read later, etc.

Hofstetter (1985) has pointed out how important it is that what people have to do to get the computer to function should not distract them from what is happening on the screen. The recumbent Evans, staring concentratedly at the effects of his prestidigital manipulations on the screen on his ceiling, was implicitly aware of this fact. Having to look up and down at a keyboard is distracting, whereas keeping eyes focused on a screen while using a touchscreen capability (as provided in the *PLATO* system), manipulating a mouse or a joystick, talking to the computer, or pointing at the screen is not. Peripheral devices are, however, not commonly available on student computers although such devices on personal computers in homes and offices are increasingly common.

Designers of interfaces seek to render non-purposeful (i.e. inauthentic) effort negligible. An example of an interface that significantly reduces the labour in marking linguistic data is reported in Pienemann and Jansen (this volume, Chapter 10). Similarly, Esling (this volume, Chapter 11) notes how using computers 'makes it possible to access many pertinent items of data that would otherwise be extremely difficult, or even impossible, to extract from an interfering matrix of irrelevant material'. What would make such a task impossible is of course the amount of inauthentic labour involved.

The interfaces that Esling describes involve the attachment of audio devices to the computer. Audio interfaces allowing the computer to speak or even to recognise speech have potential for reducing distraction in student interaction with machines (encouragingly, Dunkel, this volume, Chapter 12, notes that audio interfaces are becoming cheaper and more readily available).

Hypermedia, in conjunction with a variety of peripheral media, has recently caught the attention and imagination of CALL developers. The original hypermedium was hypertext, which allows computer users to indicate a word on the screen (by moving the cursor to it) and to get more information on that word, perhaps a definition or an example (usually by opening a window on the additional information). This basically entails embedding 'buttons' anywhere on the screen and making things happen when the buttons are 'clicked'. In the possibilities for making things happen, recent implementations of hypermedia have gone well beyond text.

In Underwood's (1989: 8) view, hypermedia implementations 'give the student power over the medium: the power to explore a body of information without being constrained by the author's view of how it all fits together, the power to follow an idea as far as one's imagination, and the medium, will allow.' In the implementation Underwood describes, the computer controls a videodisc player. The Main Menu is a picture of a room with objects in it, each of which is a HyperCard button. Clicking the preview button near the television set, for example, calls up a map of the story-line of the film on videodisc. 'The power of the map, however, is that it is alive: each of the icons representing the scenes is also a HyperCard button linked to a set of videodisc player commands' (Underwood, 1989: 16). Clicking any button causes a ten-second preview of the scene, after which the script of that scene in Spanish can be seen. Icons alongside the script allow students to play the whole scene or to see an English translation, and clicking on any line in the dialogue or its translation causes that line to be played from the videodisc. Other buttons present exercises, or allow the students to access the database of scripts. Thus, students can search for any word in the script, or for every occurrence of any word, as in a concordance program (except that here, they can also play the accompanying video segment on demand).

Another provocative example of hypermedia is Ashworth & Stelovsky's (1989) *KANJI CITY*. Students must read signs, maps, and business cards in order to negotiate the fictional Kanji City, and must finance their journey by passing quizzes at the school or winning at a grammar slot machine. In simulating social encounters, *KANJI CITY* provides opportunities for learning social behaviour as well as for improving language skills. Following yet another trend in recent CALL development, the program constitutes an integrated set of shell programs which will work on their own or with data sets designed to teach languages other than Japanese.

It is also possible, using only the standard keyboard, for software designers to ensure focused attention to the computer screen. This is accomplished when user input is restricted to the cursor movement keys, space bar, and Enter or Return key, all of which can usually be struck without having to look down. Encouragingly, software making imaginative use of these keys in user interfaces is becoming commonplace.

For example, the *LONDON ADVENTURE* game mentioned earlier allows display of options by using the arrow keys to present these in the manner of a revolving drum (where each option over-writes the last one in the same place on the screen, as if the options were written on a drum which, when turned, displays the next or previous option). Similarly, *SUPER CLOZE* (Millmore & Stevens, 1990) lists options on a screen with an arrow that runs up and down the list in response to the press of any of the following keys: the arrow keys, the space bar, the Enter key, or a number key corresponding to the number next to the item in the list — whichever the student finds most convenient. While the student peruses the options, an explanation of the one highlighted appears below the list in the manner of a revolving drum. As in the case of *LONDON ADVENTURE*, selection of any option is made by pressing the Enter key; it should therefore not be necessary for students to look down from the screen to rummage through the options and make a selection. Still other commercial programs in the adventure game format allow arrow keys to control movement of a figure around a screen layout representing rooms, stairs, a river (choosing a direction at a fork), and the like (Klug & Relf, 1984; McKinley & Ragan, 1984; Stine *et al.*, 1984).

As further accommodation to the way people generally prefer to use software, manuals (though often provided) are frequently not required to learn how to work the most recent software. Such software either has an on-line tutorial to help the user learn how to use it, or, as is often the case, menu screens that guide the user by suggesting options at obvious junctures. Recourse to manuals is further obviated by providing help on demand; and the help given at a particular moment might even refer specifically to the task or screen at hand, or even to the current cursor position. This is quite in keeping with the humanistic trend toward greater consideration for learners in making CALL software convenient to use.

Communication in and Around CALL

A final characteristic of a humanistic learning environment is that it encourages free expression of feelings and opinions and creates an atmosphere conducive to subtle nuance in communication.

Students engaged in computer-based activities often form groups around the computer. This is in part because computers promote brainstorming in resolving the outcome of interactional sequences, and in part because exploratory interaction creates opportunities for using language to discuss with teachers and peers the nature of discoveries made in the course of completing computer-based tasks. In addition to communicating with others while using computers, student interaction with the computer itself can be to some degree 'communicative'. Accordingly, two forms of communication prompted by computers can be distinguished: (1) that between language learners and others working in the computer-based interactive environment, and (2) that between language learners and the computer itself.

Communication Between Language Learners and Others in the Computer-using Environment

That computer-based activities can be an impetus for communication among students as well as between students and teachers has often been noted anecdotally (e. g. Dutra, 1985; Taylor, 1986) and is observable whenever two or more students engage in CALL at the same computer, or when students ask for help in using computers or in solving problems posed by the software. Rivers (1989) agrees that 'practical use has shown that [task-oriented games and simulations] provide for genuine communicative interaction when students work together in groups at the workstation, the challenges of the CALL activity stimulating them to lively discussions, disputes, and cooperative decision-making'.

In computer labs, students tend to form groups of two or three around a single computer, even when there are enough computers available for each student to use one individually. One reason for this may be that students using computers do not feel that they are being watched or judged; perhaps as a result they do not feel that the work they do on the computer is their own private property. When they do not regard computer-based activities as tests, they become relaxed about pooling information and seeking help from friends.

Brainstorming occurs when many minds are focused together on solving a problem. Everyone uses slightly different approaches and strategies when solving problems, and when learners work together in unravelling problems set by the computer, the contributions of different members in the group, each approaching the problem in a slightly different way, can help the group overcome obstacles. For example, in working on an adventure game, single players, using their limited repertoire of problem-solving strategies, can bog down, just as a driver stuck in sand might dig a car more and more deeply into a rut by persisting in the same strategy for trying to solve the problem. In the case of the driver, a passer-by may come along and suggest letting some air out of the tyres, or help gather wood or stones to put under the wheels. In the same way, one member of a student group will often suggest a move that is obvious to that person, but not to the others. Sometimes, the group will try it, and it works. One benefit of a group configuration is that members can eventually learn from each other alternate approaches to solving problems. Especially relevant to the discussion here, work at the computer puts students in situations where they seek advice and information from one another.

When using exploratory software, if the students are a homogeneous language group, they tend to use their own language in these groups; if instead their native languages are different, they will likely communicate with each other in the target language. Mohan (this volume, Chapter 6) provides insights into the kind of interaction that takes place in such heterogeneous groups. Leaving aside the exact nature of the communication that occurs, it is obvious that computers at least promote social aggregation, a vital prerequisite to communication. Other computer-based settings — e. g. electronic mail and computer bulletin boards — provide opportunities for communication in written form in the target language. The fact that computers seem to be a catalyst for human-to-human communication is worth exploring, and exploiting, in language learning.

Word processing is possibly the most universally used and at the same time the most universally underrated genre of communications software available today, although a survey by Johnson (1987) found word processors to be prevalent in ESL settings. Suggestions abound for using word processors as devices for teaching grammar and rhetoric. Schcolnik (1987) suggests a number of manipulations to writing that can be accomplished by means of word processors, such as garbling text with global search-and-replace commands and then having students put the text right by reversing the process. Daiute (1983) cogently examines how word processing facilitates writing, while Pennington and Brock (this volume, Chapter 5) provide evidence that word processing facilitates meaningful revision in a process approach to writing. Marcus (1983) notes how word processors can become catalysts for oral, in addition to written, communication. He describes an activity, for example, in which students exchange computer screens, so that one student can comment on the other's writing while the latter is composing it blind.

Daiute (1985) also suggests numerous applications of word processing to language learning — for example, having students produce yearbooks using word processors or desktop publishing tools. In an ESL course in which two separate heterogeneous groups of students were trained to use the same word processor, the present author observed the students to become more involved than usual in preparing (and more willing than usual in revising) writings for yearbooks in which they communicated their feelings about their language learning experience. Additionally, they had to communicate regarding editing and layout with each other and with the company that would print their yearbook. The students worked without access to desktop publishing software, but such software in conjunction with a publishing activity would add a further communicative dimension to the activity, as students negotiated with experts and with each other in learning and then manipulating the software.

Another configuration that promotes communication in a target language allows students to be in direct contact with each other (or with teachers, or even with unknown correspondents) through networks. For example, John Southworth (in *ad hoc* demonstrations at the University High School in Honolulu, Hawaii) has used *PLATO* to put his students in touch with peers across the ocean. Similarly, internationally played simulations sponsored by the International Simulation and Games Association are reported in Crookall *et al.* (1988) and Crookall and Oxford (1988).

The above examples show various ways that communication between humans can be promoted by CALL. We now turn to communication within CALL itself, that is, to having a student in simulated communication with the computer.

Communication between language learners and the computer itself

Before embarking on this discussion, we should consider carefully the notion of communication with computers. To say that people communicate with each other (whether or not around a computer) is to say that they desire to make themselves known to another communicator and to induce a response.

In communication, people exhibit verbal and written behaviours, the purpose of which is to invoke a response. The response desired could be phatic, informative, or motor. But more than that, it will likely be appropriate and empathic; that is, humans (at least when being polite) generally respond to other humans by doing more or less what is asked of them and by trying to appear willing to please (Grice, 1975). Above all, humans generally consider the feelings of others, and if they are unable to respond in the way expected, will frequently explain their reasons for not being able to do so.

Computers are able to communicate half-way — that is, they can prompt phatic, informative, and motor responses from students and can respond in kind to prompts; but they cannot do so with empathy. Being logical and mechanical, they could be programmed to perfectly emulate human verbal behaviour only if there existed an accurate model that could fully predict all such behaviour. Since none exists, nor is in the foreseeable future likely to exist, computers, even when programmed to be on their best and most civilised behaviour, inevitably respond to humans in ways that appear inappropriate and abrupt. Programmers are developing algorithms in the realm of artificial intelligence (AI) which are based on a variety of approximate models of human verbal behaviour, and these achieve varying degrees of success in attempting to communicate with humans. For example, highly communicative parsers are components of the expert-system CALL environments envisaged by Lian (this volume, Chapter 4).

Although there has been recent progress in AI-based CALL (e. g. Bailin & Thomson, 1988; Cook, 1988), the level of communication that users of present-day software can expect is limited. *ELIZA*, for instance, figures heavily in Underwood's (1984) book on communicative CALL in a chapter entitled 'The computer as a communicative environment'. *ELIZA* is a program designed to emulate an empathic listener. Not unexpectedly, however, *ELIZA* has no comprehension whatsoever of what the user tries to tell it, but works by locating key words in user input and fishing questions and statements from its database in reaction to these. Thus it is not really empathic, nor a listener in any sense at all.

Nevertheless, students have been known to communicate in good faith with an *ELIZA*-like program called *LUCY*. Stevens (1986) describes an incident in which a student tried to teach *LUCY* the name of the capital of Japan. The student began by asking the computer several times in succession what he thought was a simple question — 'What is the capital of Japan?' — to which the computer replied with a series of responses to incomprehensible questions; e. g. 'Why do you ask?', 'Does that question interest you?', etc. The student, a little annoyed, decided to inform the computer, by entering the information from the keyboard, that the capital of Japan was Tokyo, and then re-ask the same question. When the computer reacted with the same intransigence as before, the student called in the teacher, who explained what the program was doing. Two healthy outcomes stemmed from this incident: (1) the student learned that computers were mechanical, not communicative, as he had previously thought, and (2) the teacher realised that *LUCY* was eliciting real communication, if only for a few minutes, from at least one student.

Despite limitations in how students are presently able to communicate with computers, the medium is still capable of greater communicative interchange than is possible with any other educational medium, save another person. This is especially true when computers are used in conjunction with other media. Because of its ability to sustain interest and give the learner command over the medium, interactive video seems particularly able to achieve a high degree of simulated communication. Saint-Leon (1988) has suggested that using authentic materials on *videodisc* might be the next best thing to learning a language in a country where the target language is spoken. With the high degree of control learners have with computer-interfaced videodisc, interactive video could, for the period of time that it is used, be an even more productive learning environment than residency in a foreign country (see, for example, Underwood, 1989, and the discussion below).

MONTEVIDISCO (Gale, 1983; Schneider & Bennion, 1984) is remarkable among projects simulating communication using videodisc in its liberal use of absurdity and humour. *MONTEVIDISCO* was filmed in Mexico with native speakers of Spanish operating in their natural environment. Students constantly confront people who speak to them in Spanish, after which they are given multiple choice responses. Students can play the program 'straight', or they can indulge in the bizarre — e. g. they can accept a potion from the local pharmacist and see the glass tilt before their eyes and the pharmacy ceiling swim out of focus, blending into that of the hospital where they seemingly 'come to'. This option leads to a confrontation with a nurse, whom students can obey and so stay in the hospital, or elude and then find themselves on the street. Walking the streets in *MONTEVIDISCO*, it is possible to turn a corner and come face to face with a cigar-chomping Mexican motorcycle policeman for one of the most memorable confrontations in the program (the policeman is not an actor, but the genuine article). This may lead to a trip to jail, where students can attempt to bribe the local authorities. This results in even more trouble — or fun, as the case may be. But whatever the results, they come about as an effect of students simulating communication with characters in the program.

An even more ambitious effort involving interactive video is the Athena Project being carried out at the Massachusetts Institute of Technology (Kramsch *et al.*, 1985). The Athena Project aims to bring high technology — i.e. advanced parsing techniques and speech recognition, in addition to interactive video — to bear on authentic and language-rich learning materials. The umbrella project of Athena has spawned sub-projects, one of which is Furstenberg's (1987) *FRENCH VIDEODISC*. In this program, students assume the role of a resident of Paris who faces two challenges: (1) a deadline on a job and (2) the need to find a new place to live after falling out with a girlfriend. In accomplishing the latter task, students have access to on-line resources such as maps of Paris, newspaper advertisements, etc. One can also arrange a meeting with a real estate agent and receive a tour of a set of flats in various price ranges. Some of the flats are well beyond the hero's means, and the dialogue with the agent can become humorously sarcastic. For realism, the walking-tour was filmed in an actual Parisian neighbourhood and allows minute exploration; most if not all of the scenes were shot on location in Paris. Here again, students influence outcomes by communicating in the role of the main character.

Adventure games do not have to include sophisticated parsing in order to be communicative. *MONTEVIDISCO* communicates with the learner in natural and wholly contextualised Spanish, but the learner communicates with *MONTEVIDISCO* in single keypresses denoting multiple choice responses. Yet the impression of communication is such that the learner rarely feels constrained. *LONDON ADVENTURE* operates along the same lines, but without a video component. The student interacts with the computer by using arrow keys to view options comprising things to do and say; impolite and otherwise inappropriate utterances result in people turning away and going on about their business, while appropriately worded requests elicit positive responses and desired results. Although students do not actually compose utterances or even words in interacting with the program, they still control what is being said, and they constantly deal with the program's communications to them.

Although computers are not yet natural communicators, when programmed well, they are good at communicating with students, and often allow students to communicate in satisfying ways with them. Video by itself is able to communicate to a viewer; interfaced with a computer, video allows perhaps the ultimate in modern-day emulation of authentic communication.

Conclusion

Rivers (1989) expresses her impression of the present state of CALL in the following advice to developers:

> There is a real danger of a return to much drill and grammatical practice, with long explanations, which are relatively easy to program ... They may

provide the student with a more solid base of knowledge of the language but little opportunity to consolidate creative control for the expression of personal meanings.... It is essential ... that computer-assisted language learning set its sights much higher than the widespread drill-and-practice tutorials and grammar teaching, which in their common form, can be recognized as the strong influence of uncreative programmed instruction.... If CALL is to realize its professional potential, we must keep emphasizing the need for innovative thinking in the production of a diversity of materials that promote creative use of language by the learner.

In making courseware more humanistic, software developers are gradually removing the grounds for recently voiced dissatisfaction with CALL. In avoiding the rigid behaviourist-based approaches of earlier years, CALL is moving toward granting learners greater control over their own learning. It does this by providing exploratory environments for language learning, presenting problems in need of resolution, and providing tools for further work and learning. Present-day CALL seeks to provide multiple paths to learning and to cater more actively to individual differences than is possible with other media.

The future promises greater interactivity with computers in language learning. Exciting possibilities exist for interface with audio and video cassette recorders, as well as with CD-ROM and laser videodisc, especially when applying to all of these the greater potential for interactivity using artificial intelligence. Even today, CALL software developers are developing facilitatory techniques that make software more powerful by being more convenient and easier to use. More to the point — and exactly the point at which the behaviourist-based algorithms have largely failed — humanistic CALL software is designed to promote communication, either with the computer itself or with other students using the CALL program.

The case has been made here that these developments fit comfortably into a humanist paradigm. Of greatest importance, the shift away from behaviourist-based software and towards humanistic applications has brought CALL more into line with modern principles of language learning and teaching. As a result, CALL can now be more widely perceived as a welcome enhancement to contemporary language learning curricula.

Acknowledgements

I owe many thanks to Martha Pennington, whose meticulous feedback on the various drafts led to many improvements in this paper; also to Alan Beretta and Roger Griffiths, who constructively played Devil's Advocates.

References

ABDULAZIZ, M., W. SMALZER & H. ABDULAZIZ (1985) *The Computer Book: Programming and Language Skills for Students of ESL*. Englewood Cliffs, NJ: Prentice-Hall.

AHMAD, K., G. CORBETT, M. ROGERS & R. SUSSEX (1985) *Computers, Language Learning and Language Teaching*. Cambridge: Cambridge University Press.

ASHER, J. (1966) The learning strategy of the total physical response: A review, *Modern Language Journal*, 50, 79–84.

ASHWORTH, D. & J. STELOVSKY (1989) *KANJI CITY*: An exploration of hypermedia applications for CALL, *CALICO Journal*, 6: 4, 27–39.

BAILIN, A. & P. THOMSON (1988) The use of natural language processing in computer-assisted language instruction, *Computers and the Humanities*, 22, 99–110.

BALTRA, A. (1984) An EFL classroom in a mystery house, *TESOL Newsletter*, 18. 6, 15.

BARLOW, M. (1987) *Writing with Computers*. La Jolla, CA: Athelstan.

BROWN, H. D. (1980) *Principles of Language Learning and Teaching*. Englewood Cliffs, NJ: Prentice-Hall.

CARROLL, J. (1966) The contributions of psychological theory and educational research to the teaching of foreign languages. In A. VALDMAN (ed.), *Trends in Language Teaching*. New York: McGraw-Hill.

CHAPELLE, C. & J. JAMIESON (1986) Computer-assisted language learning as a predictor of success in acquiring English as a second language, *TESOL Quarterly*, 20: 1, 27–46.

COOK, V. (1988) Designing a BASIC parser for CALL, *CALICO Journal*, 6: 1, 50–67.

CROOKALL, D., A. CECCHINI, A. COOTE, D. SAUNDERS & A. DELLA PIANE (eds), (1988) *Simulation-gaming in Education and Training*. Oxford: Pergamon.

CROOKALL, D. A. & R. OXFORD (eds), (1988) *Language Learning Through Simulation*. Rowley, MA: Newbury House.

DAIUTE, C. (1983) The computer as stylus and audience, *College Composition and Communication*, 34, 134–145.

— (1985) *Writing and Computers*. Reading, MA: Addison-Wesley.

DALGISH, G. (1989) Error analysis and courseware design, *C. A. L. L. Digest*, 5: 5, 1–3.

DUTRA, I. (1985) Hypothesis-testing and problem-solving software for ESL students. Paper presented at the 19th Annual TESOL Conference, New York, April 8–14.

ELLIS, R. (1985) *Understanding Second Language Acquisition*. Oxford, UK: Oxford University Press.

EUROPEAN NATIONS AND LOCATIONS (1985) San Francisco, CA: DesignWare.

EVANS, C. (1979)*The Mighty Micro*. London: Victor Gollancz Ltd.

FAMOUS SCIENTISTS (1985) Dimondale, MD: Hartley Courseware, Inc.

FEDERICO, P. (1982) Individual differences in cognitive characteristics and computer-managed learning, *Journal of Computer-Based Instruction*, 9: 1, 10–18.

FURSTENBERG, G. (1987) A videodisc for teaching French: Work-in-progress report. Paper presented at the Fourth Annual CALICO Convention, Monterey, CA, April 6–10.

GALE, L. (1983) *MONTEVIDISCO:* An anecdotal history of an interactive videodisc, *CALICO Journal*, 1: 1, 42–46.

GRAHAM, H. (1986) *The Human Face of Psychology: Humanistic Psychology in its Historical Social and Cultural Context*. Milton Keynes, UK and Philadelphia, PA: Open University Press.

GRICE, M. (1975) Logic and conversation. In P. COLE and J. MORGAN (eds), *Syntax and Semantics*, Vol. 3, Speech Acts. New York: Academic Press.

HAMILTON, T. (1986) *LONDON ADVENTURE*. Cambridge, UK: The British Council in association with Cambridge University Press.
HIGGINS, J. (1983) Can computers teach?, *CALICO Journal*, 1: 2, 4–6.
— (1988) *Language, Learners and Computers: Human Intelligence and Artificial Unintelligence*. London and New York: Longman.
HIGGINS, J & T. JOHNS (1984) *Computers in Language Learning*. Reading, MA: Addison-Wesley.
HOFSTETTER, F. (1985) Perspectives on a decade of computer-based instruction, 1974–84, *Journal of Computer-Based Instruction*, 12: 1, 1–7.
JAMIESON, J. & C. CHAPELLE (1987) Working styles on computers as evidence of second language learning strategies, *Language Learning*, 37: 4, 523–544.
JAMISON, D., P. SUPPES & S. WELLS (1974) Alternative instructional media, *Review of Educational Research*, 44: 1, 1–67.
JOHNS, T. (1989) Whence and whither classroom concordancing? In T. BONGAERTS et al. (eds), *Computer Applications in Language Learning*. The Netherlands: Foris Publications.
JOHNSON, D. (1985) Using Computers to Promote the Development of English as a Second Language. A report to the Carnegie Corporation of New York.
JOHNSON, N. (1987) Current uses of computers in ESOL instruction in the U. S., *CALICO Journal*, 5: 2, 71–77.
KEMMIS, S. , R. ATKIN & E. WRIGHT (1977) *How do Students Learn?* Working papers on computer-assisted learning: UNCAL evaluation studies. Occasional Publications 5. Norwich, UK: University of East Anglia, Centre for Applied Research in Education.
KLUG, R. , & P. RELF (1984) *TALES OF ADVENTURE*. New York: Scholastic.
KRAMSCH, C. , D. MORGENSTERN & J. MURRAY (1985) An overview of the MIT Athena Language Learning Project, *CALICO Journal*, 2: 4, 31–34.
KRASHEN, S. (1982) *Principles and Practice in Second Language Acquisition*. New York: Pergamon Press.
MARCUS, S. (1983) Real-time gadgets with feedback: Special effects in computer-assisted instruction, *The Writing Instructor*, 2, 156–164.
MCCLELLAND, J. , D. RUMELHART & G. HINTON (1986) The appeal of parallel distributed processing. In D. RUMELHART, J. MCCLELLAND, & the PDP RESEARCH GROUP (eds), *Parallel Distributed Processing: Explorations in the Microstructures of Cognition*. Vol. I, Foundations. Cambridge, MA: MIT Press; pp. 3–44.
MCKINLEY, A. & A. RAGAN (1984) *TALES OF DISCOVERY*. New York: Scholastic.
MILLMORE, S. & V. STEVENS (1990) *SUPER CLOZE*. Shareware available from TESOL/CALL-IS MS-DOS User's Group.
MOORE, O. & A. ANDERSON (1969) Some principles for the design of clarifying educational environments. Reprinted in C. GREENBLAT & R. DUKE (eds), *Gaming-simulation: Rationale, Design, and Applications. A Text with Parallel Readings for Social Scientists, Educators, and Community Workers* (1975). New York: John Wiley and Sons.
NEOSOFT, INC. (1984) *THE SEA VOYAGERS*. Greenwich, CT: CBS Software.
PAPERT, S. (1980) *Mindstorms: Children, Computers, and Powerful Ideas*. New York: Basic Books.
PHILLIPS, M. (1986) CALL in its educational context. In G. LEECH & C. CANDLIN (eds), *Computers in English Language Teaching and Research*. London, New York: Longman.
RICHARDSON, W. & S. WISE (1985) *ESSENTIAL IDIOMS IN ENGLISH: CAI ADAPTATION*. New York: Regents/ALA.

RIVERS, W. (1981) *Teaching Foreign Language Skills*, second edition. Chicago, London: The University of Chicago Press.
— (1989) Interaction and communication in the language class in an age of technology. Plenary address at the Fortieth Meeting of the Georgetown Round Table on Languages and Linguistics.
ROGERS, C. (1961) *On Becoming a Person: A Therapist's View of Psychotherapy*. London: Constable.
— (1969) *Freedom to Learn*. Columbus, OH: Chas. E. Merrill Publishing Co.
ROSEN, M. , B. LOWERY & M. MERRILL (1985) *THE WRITING SERIES*, Disks 1 through 5. San Francisco, CA: EduWare.
RUMELHART, D. & J. MCCLELLAND (1986) On learning the past tenses of English verbs. In D. RUMELHART, J. MCCLELLAND, & the PDP RESEARCH GROUP (eds), *Parallel Distributed Processing: Explorations in the Microstructures of Cognition*. Vol. II, Psychological and biological models. Cambridge, MA: MIT Press.
SAINT-LEON, C. (1988) The case for authentic materials on videodisc, *CALICO Journal*, 6: 2, 27 40.
SCHCOLNIK, M. (1987) Re-word CAI: A method for practicing reading skills with the aid of a word processor. Paper presented at the Fourth Annual CALICO Convention, Monterey, California.
SCHNEIDER, E. & J. BENNION (1984) Veni, vidi, vici via videodisc: A simulator for instructional conversations. In D. WYATT (ed), *Computer-assisted Language Instruction*. Oxford, New York: Pergamon.
SKINNER, B. (1974) *About Behaviorism*. New York: Vintage Books edition, 1976.
STEVENS, V. (1984) Implications of research and theory concerning the influence of control on the effectiveness of CALL, *CALICO Journal*, 2: 1, 28–33, 48.
— (1986) Using *LUCY/ELIZA* as a means of facilitating communication in ESL, *TESOL Newsletter*, 20: 2, 13–14.
— (1987) Software review of CAI adaptation of Robert J. Dixson's *Essential Idioms in English*, *TESOL Quarterly*, 21: 3, 558–564.
— (1988a) Self-access language learning materials at Sultan Qaboos University, *The Journal of Educational Techniques and Technologies*, 21: 2/3, 2–4.
— (1988b) CALL in a self-access resource centre. Paper presented at the 22nd Annual TESOL Conference, Chicago.
— (1988c) Software review of *ROBOT ODYSSEY* 1, *CALL-IS Newsletter*, 5: 1, 8–10.
— (1989a) A direction for CALL: From behavioristic to humanistic courseware. In M. PENNINGTON (ed), *Teaching Languages with Computers: The State of the Art*. La Jolla, CA: Athelstan.
— (1989b) Classroom concordancing: Vocabulary materials derived from authentic, relevant text. *English for Special Purposes Journal*.
— (1989c) A study of student attitudes towards CALL in a self-access student resource centre. *System* 19, No. 2.
STEVENS V. & S. MILLMORE (1987) *TEXT TANGLERS*. Stony Brook, NY: Research Design Associates.
STINE, W. , M. STINE & R. KLUG (1984). *TALES OF MYSTERY*. New York: Scholastic.
TAYLOR, M. (1986) Software review of *PRESIDENTIAL CAMPAIGN*, *TESOL Newsletter*, 20: 4, 12.
UNDERWOOD, J. (1984) *Linguistics, Computers, and the Language Teacher: A Communicative Approach*. Rowley, MA: Newbury.
— (1989) HyperCard and interactive video, *CALICO Journal*, 6: 3, 7–20.
VAN ELS, T. , K. DE GRAAUW & M. STORTELDER (1988) Grammatical feedback in a

computer-based editing task. *Australian Review of Applied Linguistics*, 11, 176–188.

WALLACE, M. & L. GRIMM (1986) *ROBOT ODYSSEY* I. Menlo Park, CA: The Learning Company.

WINDEATT, S. (1986) Observing CALL in action. In G. LEECH & C. CANDLIN (eds), *Computers in English Language Teaching and Research*. London and New York: Longman.

3 A Methodological Framework for CALL Courseware Development

PHILIP HUBBARD
Stanford University, USA

Introduction

By the mid 1980s, microcomputers had been around long enough for many people to have had enough contact with them to recognise their potential as a tool for language teachers and learners. In addition, professional organisations devoted specifically to exploring the role of computers in language teaching had been formed, such as the CALL Interest Section of International TESOL (Teachers of English to Speakers of Other Languages); MUESLI, the microcomputer users groups of IATEFL (International Association of Teachers of English as a Foreign Language); and CALICO (Computer Assisted Language Learning and Instruction Consortium). CALL appeared to be on the ascendancy. But this period also saw the publication of a number of books and articles criticising the questionable effectiveness of commercially available materials. Ariew (1984), Baker (1984), Dalgish (1984), Holmes (1984), Pennington (1986), and Underwood (1984), among others, all argued that the current state of CALL was far from what it should and could be, and that the dominance of drill-and-practice software, often based centrally on behaviourist learning principles, was coupling the technology of the 1980s with the methodology of the 1960s.

Since that time, there has been some development in the areas of simulations, games, and grammar and reading tutorials, but the pedagogical value of much of the current software remains questionable. What is often overlooked in the criticisms, however, is the fact that we have been struggling to master a new technology that as a field language teaching was — and is still - unprepared to deal with. It should not, in fact, be surprising that CALL is still searching to find its place in language teaching, and that the initial uses of computers in this domain would be fairly obvious ones. Given the relative infancy of microcomputer-based CALL, we have probably just begun to develop its potential, a sentiment echoed in Phillips (1985) and Weible (1987). What we have is a case of technology in search of appropriate and effective methodology, and yet that search appears to have become stagnated and, where progress is apparently being made, fragmented.

If we are to see any kind of real progress in the development of pedagogically sound software for language learning, it is crucial to begin with the assumption that there is a great deal of growth potential in CALL, even given the limitations of today's machines, and that we do not need to wait for the Golden Age of Artificial Intelligence, whenever that may come, to descend upon us from corporate and university research laboratories. The question for current practitioners is how to go about realising that potential in a more systematic and expedient way than has so far been the case.

In the past few years, CALL has clearly established itself as a separate discipline within language learning: It has its own professional organisations, such as CALICO and the CALL Interest Section of TESOL, journals and newsletters, and a growing number of conferences, monographs and anthologies (including the present one) devoted to it. It does not, however, have a coherently defined methodology. Specifically, there is little in the way of agreement as to what elements are involved in applying the computer to the domain of language teaching and learning and even less in the way of working concepts or principles dealing with how this should be accomplished. This is not to say that there has been no methodological development in CALL: Several different conceptual models have been proposed, such as Underwood's (1984) communicative CALL and Higgins' (1983, 1988) magister/pedagogue model, but what has been missing has been a more comprehensive framework, one that would allow the concepts in these and other methodological orientations to be analysed, compared, and contrasted. More importantly, such a framework would provide for the principled design and production of new CALL courseware, for the evaluation of courseware relative to particular teachers and learners, and for the determination of effective implementation schemes for a piece of courseware in a given language learning situation. That is, instead of developing the field of CALL primarily from the bottom up, as has so far been the case, CALL practitioners — courseware developers, researchers, and teachers — could utilise such a model to work on developing the field from the top down as well.

This article begins by outlining in a general way a proposed comprehensive methodological framework for CALL, including discussions of both the fundamental principles guiding its construction and the advantages such a model has to offer. The remainder of the article explores in greater detail one of the three major components of the model, a framework for courseware development.

A Comprehensive Methodological Framework for CALL

Before introducing the proposed methodological framework, the use of the term *methodological* in this context deserves clarification. A *methodological framework* here means a framework for the description and analysis of methods, which are ultimately nothing more than a set of procedures applied in a consistent and reasoned fashion in the pursuit of a given goal, such as learning to speak and understand a foreign language. As will be seen in the next section, the underpinnings of 'a consistent and reasoned fashion' may involve a number of factors interrelating in complex ways, including various dimensions of the learner, the language, the teacher, the materials, and the learning situation.

Figure 3.1 illustrates the three major components — or modules — of the proposed comprehensive methodological framework: *courseware development, evaluation,* and *implementation.* Each specifies those characteristics of the teaching and learning process relevant for integrating the CALL courseware into a specific teaching/learning situation relative to the viewpoint — creator, evaluator and teacher/user, respectively — implied by its label. While the general progression for a given piece of courseware is from development to evaluation to implementation, the double headed arrows capture the fact that there are other directions for interaction. For instance, the development process as a whole may involve field testing of one or more versions of the courseware where information from evaluation or implementation is used to modify the courseware design. Similarly, a teacher evaluating a piece of courseware for possible purchase might have the opportunity to actually use it and then utilise the information

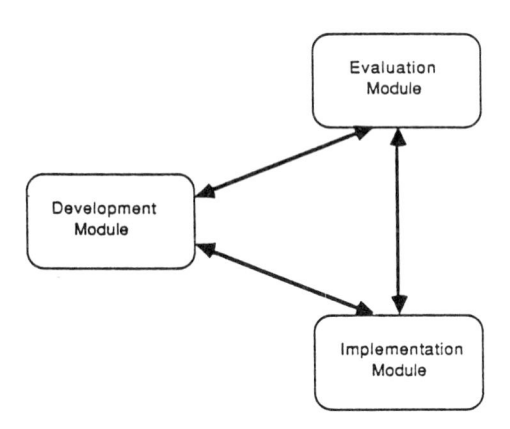

FIGURE 3.1 *CALL methodological framework*

gathered from that implementation of it in making the final decision of whether or not to buy it.

Besides being comprehensive, it is assumed here that a methodological framework should ideally be principled in the sense of having its form and content follow from a set of assumptions that have a high degree of face validity, either because they already represent widely held viewpoints or are natural extensions of them. Four such principles are offered below.

(1) The framework should be based to the degree possible on existing frameworks or views of methodology for language teaching and learning in general. This makes it easier to interpret and aids in integrating CALL into, rather than isolating it from, the language teaching profession at large.
(2) The framework should be non-dogmatic and flexible. It should not be tied to any single conception of the nature of language, language teaching, or language learning, nor any specific combination of hardware, nor any specifc language skill or mode of presentation. Rather, it should specify the logical relationships among learners, teachers, and computers in as neutral a way as possible.
(3) The framework should explicitly link the three facets of courseware development, evaluation, and implementation. It should characterise the close relationships of these three aspects of CALL in a consistent fashion, utilising the same terminology where appropriate.
(4) Finally, the framework should faithfully represent the nature of the multiple relationships among its components. More specifically, it should specify all the elements of the teaching/learning process and the nature of dependent and interdependent relationships among them, along with taxonomies or operational definitions for determining the contents of each component.

Before beginning the description of the development portion of the framework that will be the focus of this article, it is worth considering in more detail what the potential value of a methodological framework would be to individual courseware developers or teachers who make use of CALL materials and to the field as a whole. The principles above direct the framework's form and content, but they do not characterise its use. It is not immediately obvious how such a framework would necessarily lead to more effective CALL software: if anything, it might seem to be a limiting factor that would stifle innovation. It is argued here, however, that a properly constructed framework could yield the following benefits:

(1) As mentioned above, it would clarify the components of CALL and show how they interact. Previous frameworks, such as those in Curtin & Shinall (1987), Hubbard (1987), Phillips (1985), Underwood (1984), and Wyatt (1987), to name a few, have focused on only a part of the overall

methodological picture, failing to address the conditions specified in one or more of the preceding principles.

(2) By its comprehensiveness, the framework would provide an integrated and internally consistent metalanguage for discussion of issues in CALL, documentation of design decisions, and published reviews.

(3) It would provide a mechanism for suggesting possible areas for new courseware development through the consideration of various combinations of categories within its components.

(4) In a similar way, it would suggest specific new areas for research in CALL as well as provide a consistent base for interpreting existing research.

(5) It would provide an integrated set of evaluation criteria for determining the fit of software with the teacher's views, the learner's needs, and the syllabus goals and constraints.

(6) It would establish a foundation for determining the effective uses of a piece of courseware in a given situation, including scenarios which may not have been envisaged by the designer.

Assuming there is some value to such a framework, then, the next question is what would one look like? If a framework of the type suggested by Figure 3.1 is assumed, the interrelations of the development, evaluation and implementation modules are apparent, but there is no hint as to what their internal structures might be. The most common approach to discussing these areas in a coherent way has been to develop classification schemes and lists of components. This is the tactic taken by Phillips (1985), Wyatt (1987), and many other authors who have developed software evaluation checklists. In some cases, these frameworks consist of only an unordered set of questions covering the issues seen by the particular author as being central to a specific approach (e. g. Underwood, 1984, for communicative CALL), while in others, there is a hierarchical structure imposed. A second approach has been simply to discuss in a general way the issues involved: This is the direction taken by Weible (1987) in his discussion of methodology. While both of these approaches have their merits — the first for its explicitness and the second for its depth of analysis — neither captures adequately both the comprehensiveness and the complex interrelationships suggested by the preceding four principles.

Within the three modules of this framework, an entirely different approach is taken. The relationships among the components are specified as a *network*. As will be seen, using a network allows a more direct representation of the apparent multiple dependencies involved in each module than would be possible under either of the other two approaches. A network also has the advantage of laying out the components in a single, visual 'map', making it easier to see how they are integrated.

The present framework has been built on the earlier, more limited frameworks of Phillips (1985), which listed seven categories specifying typologies for software form, content and implementation, and Hubbard (1987), which focused on the relationship of language teaching approach to software design and evaluation. The goals of these earlier frameworks differed somewhat from those of the present one. The major thrust of Phillips' work was to show how a relatively small number of descriptive categories could be used both to account for differences among existing pieces of CALL courseware and to suggest new types. For instance, his category of *activity type* has subcategories including quiz, game, and text reconstruction, among others, while his category of *program focus* has language-based subcategories such as discourse, sentence, and lexis. By combining activity type and program focus in a matrix, pairs such as text reconstruction/discourse and text reconstruction/lexis emerge. The former pair describes cloze or storyboard programs involving the reconstruction of discourse level texts and the latter pair describes programs like hangman involving the reconstruction of a particular word. This use of a matrix foreshadows the network diagrams in the present framework, which also involve combining of categories, but in a more complex fashion. The goal of the framework in Hubbard (1987), on the other hand, was to focus attention on the assumptions about language and language learning manifested in a given piece of courseware: this turns out to be only one of the areas considered by the present framework. Taken together, the Phillips (1985) and Hubbard (1987) frameworks address many of the important considerations in the development, evaluation and implementation processes.

Principle 1 from the list above states that a CALL methodological framework should attempt to link itself with more general methodological frameworks for language teaching. In line with this principle, the foundation for the present framework is a model proposed by Richards & Rodgers (1982, 1986) for characterising and comparing language teaching methods according to their fundamental components. Their framework is designed to define any method in terms of three basic organisational levels: Approach, Design, and Procedure. Briefly, *Approach* represents the method's assumptions about the nature of language and language learning; *Design* represents the realisation of those assumptions in terms of curricular goals, learning tasks, and the roles of learner, teacher, and materials; and *Procedure* represents the implementation of those goals through specific learning and practice activities and feedback techniques.

In this section, a comprehensive methodological framework for CALL has been proposed, principles guiding its construction have been offered, its value to CALL practitioners has been discussed, and certain aspects of its form and content have been outlined. The remainder of this article will focus on a description of the development module of the proposed framework, detailing its components and their interrelationships.

A Methodological Framework for Courseware Development

As illustrated in Figure 3.2, which represents the development module of the present framework for CALL, the Richards & Rodgers model is adopted in a more dynamic way than originally intended by the authors: *Design* is the central component of the network with *Approach* and *Procedure* feeding into it. While liberties have been taken with the Richards and Rodgers framework to accommodate the special nature of CALL materials development, most of their core concepts remain.

Figure 3.2 also shows clearly the kinds of interconnections that a network diagram can capture. The arrows in the network are intended to represent the most significant dependency relationships; that is, the boxes at the tails of the arrows directly determine or limit the choices to be made in the boxes at the heads of the arrows. Note that, ultimately, all arrows converge on the box labeled 'Courseware Production'. This is meant to be interpreted in the following way: the results of all decisions leading to final courseware production should be consistent with one another to the greatest degree possible, given practical limitations.

It is beyond the scope of the present work to describe all that goes into the components represented by the boxes in Figure 3.2. However, relevant details of each component will be discussed below with the aim of clarifying its role in the courseware development framework. As the description progresses, it will be seen that different components have different types of internal structure. Some, such as *linguistic assumptions* and *learning assumptions* in the Approach section, involve a characterisation of a body of knowledge about a certain area. Others, such as *language difficulty* and program difficulty in the Design section, involve a subset of areas to consider which combine to represent that category. Still others, such as *program focus* in the Design section and *activity type* in the Procedure section are taxonomic in nature and present relatively fixed classification schemes.

Approach

The view of *Approach* taken here is essentially the same as that of Richards and Rodgers (1982) up to the point where the role of the computer is considered. The Approach section consists of the following components: *linguistic assumptions, learning assumptions, language teaching approach, computer delivery system,* and *approach-based design criteria*. This section of the framework is reproduced in Figure 3.3.

FIGURE 3.2 *Development module*

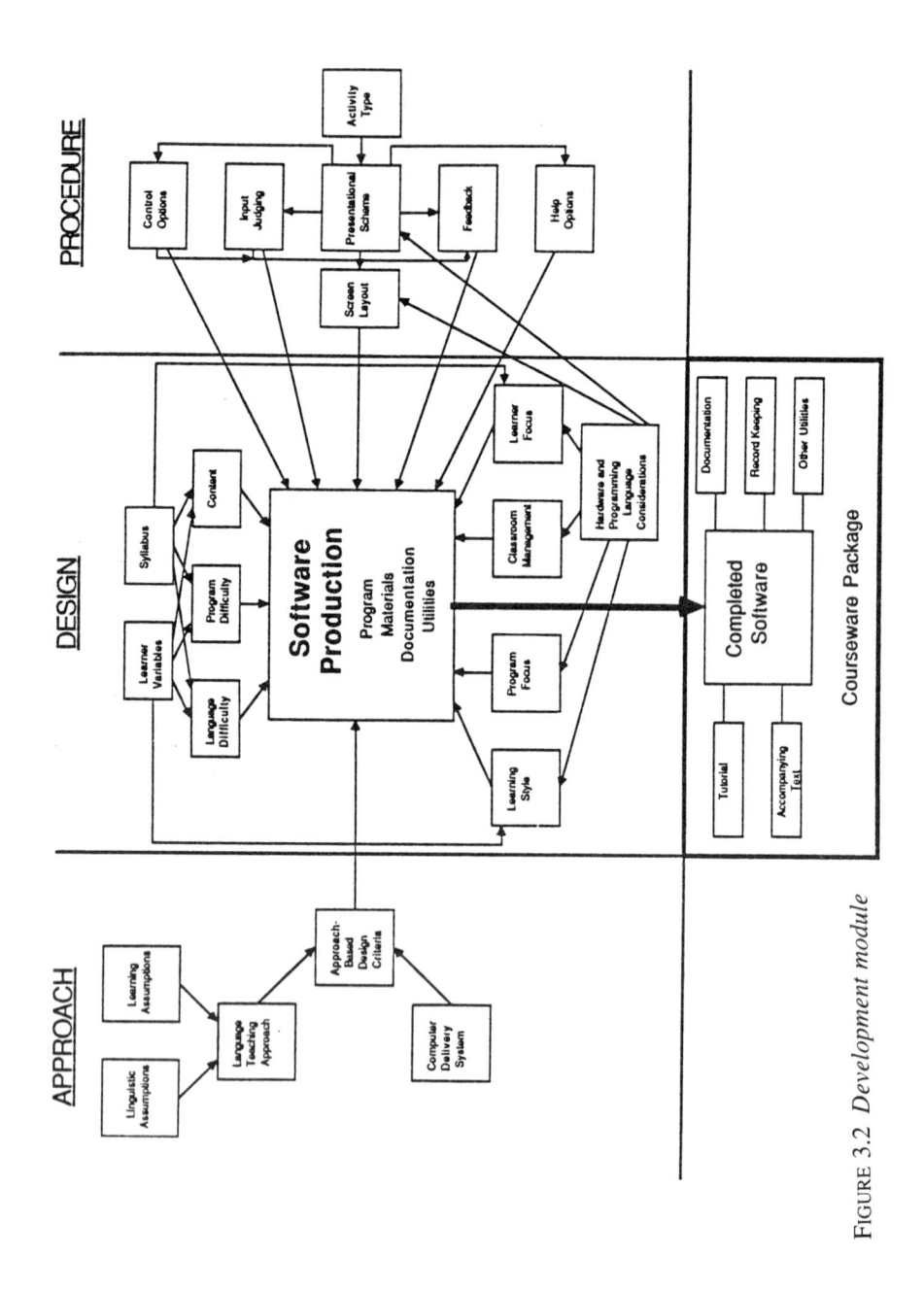

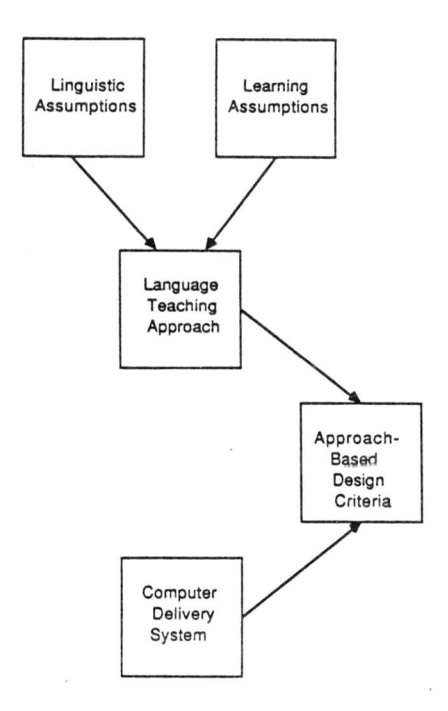

FIGURE 3.3 *Approach section*

Linguistic assumptions

First, Approach includes the developer's assumptions about the nature of language structure and function, ideally, but not necessarily, based on some linguistic theory or theories. It is incumbent upon developers to make these assumptions as explicit as possible, not only to themselves but also to the eventual users — both teachers and students — if we are to have principled language teaching programs that are internally consistent. Some of the questions to be considered at this stage include the following. Is the grammar of a language governed by patterns and analogy or by rules? Is language knowledge fundamentally structural, functional, or both? Is the sentence the fundamental unit of language, or are phrases and discourse structures fundamental? Are syntax, semantics, and lexicon separable components of a language or inseparable? These are just some of the basic questions which a designer should be prepared to address before embarking on a development project. It is of course not reasonable to expect definitive answers, since theoretical linguists have not reached consensus on many of these issues. Working assumptions can be made, nevertheless, and to the degree possible, explicitly justified. For specific skills, such as reading and writing, there are similar sets of questions to be answered.

Learning assumptions

Parallel to the developer's assumptions about the nature of language are those about the nature of language learning. This involves both assumptions about second language learning processes internal to the learner as well as assumptions about the role of the external environment in second language learning. It may also include assumptions about the relationship of language learning to other types of learning, in particular, a characterisation of the ways in which learning a language is similar to and different from learning anything else. Once again, the ideal here is to find a basis in theories or models of the language learning process that are empirically supported, and most importantly, consistent with the developer's views of the nature of language. Many of the criticisms levelled at contemporary courseware are ultimately traceable to a lack of informed reflection in this or the preceding area, though they may also involve a lack of understanding of the developer's assumptions on the user's part. For instance, some programs for teaching grammar and vocabulary have involved rather inconsistent blends of mechanistic behaviourism of the type described by Stevens (this volume, Chapter 1), and conscious, analytical learning.

Language teaching approach

Linguistic and learning assumptions form the basis for the developer's language teaching approach. Once again, the framework is consistent with Richards & Rodgers' conception except that *teaching* here is taken in the wider sense to mean not only direct instruction, but also the setting up and control of any environment where language learning or practice takes place (as in individual instruction via computer when a teacher is not present). There are any number of different approaches that have served as the foundation for classroom language teaching over the past few decades, but most can be classified into one of three general categories: behaviourist, explicit learning (or cognitive code), and acquisition (which here subsumes most communicative and humanistic approaches, as described in Hubbard, 1987). Behaviourist approaches are characterised by a view of language as a habit structure and grammar as patterns to be drilled to the point of overlearning. Explicit learning approaches are characterised by deductive learning of rules of grammar and usage. Acquisition approaches are characterised by exercises focusing on the communicative function of language, realistic interaction, and inductive learning. There are, of course, approaches which cut across these categories as well. Whatever the approach taken, it will determine to a great degree what the roles of the teacher and learner will be, what the role of the student's native language will be (if any), what form the syllabus will take, how language material will be presented and practiced, and how learner errors will be dealt with.

Computer delivery system

Perhaps the most intriguing aspect of CALL for courseware designers is the computer itself. A number of books and articles on CALL and CAI have focused on the strengths of the computer. We know it can be made effective as a text manipulator, answer judger (within certain limits), animator, timer, record keeper, and controller of audio and video devices. We know it is not at present much of a conversationalist. Given an understanding of these strengths and limitations the developer can then see how the computer can be used as a *delivery system* for materials for language instruction and practice relative to the assumptions of a particular approach to language teaching.

Another important consideration here involves taking into account the results of certain types of empirical research in CALL, particularly those types involving the response of students to the computer as a teacher or conversation partner. While it is true that much of the experimental work done to date has been either flawed or inconclusive — both in showing the superiority of CALL to other learning options and in dealing with issues internal to CALL, such as program vs. user control (Pederson, 1987) — it is clear that the research base will continue to grow both in quantity and sophistication. A developer needs to be familiar with the relevant research in order to be in a position to interpret it relative to the goals of the planned product.

Approach-based design criteria

By merging the developer's views of language teaching approach with the inherent strengths and limitations of the computer as the interactive delivery system of language material, then, it is possible to come up with a set of approach-based design criteria. Hubbard (1987; 1988a) presents such a list for courseware evaluation, and it is an easy task to rephrase these criteria for courseware development. A partial list of design criteria for contemporary explicit learning approaches, for instance, would be the following:

(1) Gives meaningful rather than mechanical practice, contextualised in a coherent discourse larger than a single sentence.
(2) Provides hints of various types to lead students to correct answers.
(3) Accepts alternative correct answers within the given context.
(4) Offers the option of explanations for why correct answers are correct.
(5) Anticipates incorrect answers and offers explanations concerning them.
    (See Hubbard, 1987, for additional criteria and justifications for these.)

The determination of a set of such design criteria should be among the first orders of business in a principled courseware development process. However, it should be noted that the design criteria — and the language teaching approach in general — is not necessarily fixed for all courseware that a developer may produce. Depending on the developer's assumptions about language learning, the selection of a specific set of criteria may be dependent on the learner variables discussed in the following section — e. g. if the developer sees some value in both acquisition-oriented and explicit learning approaches, an increasingly common position these days.

Design

The *Design* section of the framework includes the following components: *learner variables, syllabus orientation, language difficulty, program difficulty, content, learning style, program focus, classroom management, learner focus*, and *hardware and programming language considerations* — most of which are taken from Phillips (1985). The major determining factors here are the syllabus and the learner variables: Except for the hardware and programming language considerations all of the other components are determined by one or both of these factors. As Figure 3.4 shows, all of these other components in turn converge on the courseware production, which includes the programs, materials, documentation, and any accompanying utilities, such as those for authoring or record-keeping.

Learner variables

Any piece of courseware should be designed with a particular group of users in mind, though this group may be broadly or narrowly defined. There are a number of dimensions to be considered for the target learners as a group, including but not necessarily limited to the following:

(1) Age
(2) Native language
(3) Proficiency level
(4) Sex
(5) Learner needs
(6) Learner interests

Besides these there are individual cognitive styles and preferred learning strategies which courseware may be designed to fit, including but not limited to the following types of learners:

METHODOLOGICAL FRAMEWORK FOR CALL 51

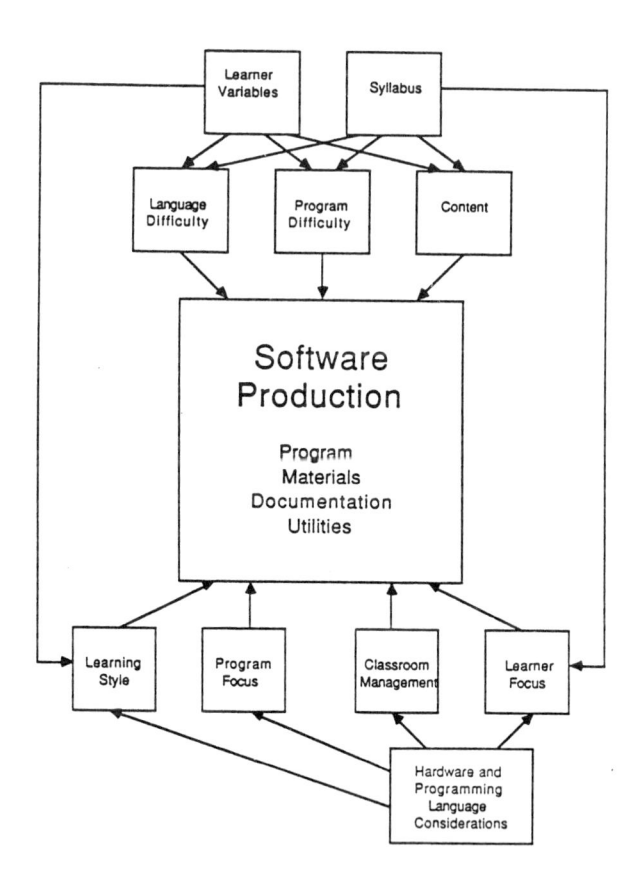

FIGURE 3.4 *Design section*

(1) Field dependent vs. independent
(2) Deductive vs. inductive
(3) Visual graphic, visual-textual, auditory, and kinesthetic learning-mode preferences
(4) Introverted vs. extroverted
(5) Ambiguity tolerant vs. intolerant
(6) Integratively vs. instrumentally motivated
(See Brown 1987 for a discussion of these and other learner variables.)

With reference to the last six categories, a few comments are in order. First, if CALL is ever to achieve the goal of true individualised instruction then courseware must be designed to address differences such as these, either by incorporating more options into a single courseware package or by developing different packages for specific learner varieties covering the same basic material. Chapelle & Jamieson (1986) discuss some of the issues involved in trying to develop software that will be sensitive to various cognitive and affective variables of the types given above and present evidence that even a learner's willingness to use computer materials is correlated with certain of these (e.g. field independence and motivational intensity). Second, certain poles of these dimensions have been correlated experimentally with greater success in language acquisition, e.g. tolerance of ambiguity (Brown, 1987: 90); thus one goal of CALL (and CAI in general) could be to develop programs that promote the development of these apparently more effective learning styles. Third these individual dimensions may correlate in some cases with the group variables above (age, native language, and learner interests in particular). For instance, young children are generally recognised as better inductive than deductive learners; a developer designing software for elementary school learners might want to take this information about children's learning style into account. Finally, as a note of caution, the degree to which these individual styles actually influence language learning is still unclear in many cases, and they may interact in subtle ways with other variables. Busch (1982) for example found that introversion rather than the expected extraversion correlated with success in learning English for a group of Japanese EFL students and suggested that cultural factors were involved.

Syllabus

There are several different types of *syllabus* that have been used commonly in language teaching, and it is important for a developer to determine the syllabus type which the courseware will be most consistent with. A structural syllabus, which much of the early software was designed for, is built around morphological and syntactic categories sequenced in a logical fashion along the dimensions of complexity, frequency, or both. A situational syllabus is designed around prototypical situations that the learners will be expected to encounter when they use the language. This type of syllabus is often integrated with a structural syllabus to provide contextualisation for grammatical points. A notional syllabus (Wilkins 1976) is based on semantic categories or so-called 'notions. ' In practice these notions are often combined with categories of language function to produce a notional–functional syllabus aimed at promoting communicative proficiency in the target language. Recently, the concept of a content-centred or content-based syllabus has become popular where the language learning focus is subordinated to the learning of some non-linguistic body of knowledge or skill. While there is not always a necessary correlation between the language teaching approach and the syllabus orientation, the possibilities for the latter are often determined by the former (see Hubbard 1987 for a discussion of these possibilities).

In dealing with particular skills, such as reading or writing, the syllabus may be oriented toward the learning and practicing of sub-skills and strategies for more effective processing and retention or production of the target language. In such a case, it may be structured around these skills and strategies rather than following the categories above.

Language difficulty

Language difficulty is the first of Phillips' (1985) categories to be discussed. This component represents a dimension determined to a large degree by design decisions made regarding the target learner's proficiency level and the requirements of the syllabus. Phillips proposes four areas of language difficulty, which he distinguishes with the terms *variety, transparency, familiarity*, and *length*. Other classification schemes for language difficulty are undoubtedly possible, for example traditional ones involving notions such as syntactic complexity, semantic concreteness/abstractness, and lexical frequency. What is important here from the CALL perspective as Phillips points out is that programs can be developed in which the student is allowed greater control over this dimension than is possible in a traditional classroom. In a text reconstruction program, such as one involving the cloze procedure for instance, a student may be able to select a text from a number of different ones representing a variety of reading levels. In such a case, any one of many formulas for determining reading difficulty might be included in the program to facilitate the student's selection.

Program difficulty

Demands placed on the learner in using the software that are not directly concerned with the linguistic point being learned or practiced are dealt with in the *program difficulty* component of Phillips' framework. As areas of program difficulty, he mentions redundancy, input, and timing: it is important to control these relative to the target group of learners so that program difficulty does not interfere unduly with the intended linguistic or communicative objective of the program. Besides these factors, the overall operational complexity of the program should be considered. For example, a lack of familiarity with the activity type (to be discussed in the Procedure section below) and the types of control decisions the program allows can add significantly to the difficulty of operating it appropriately. When a developer decides to produce courseware high in operational complexity for justifiable pedagogical reasons (maintaining learner interest through variety or giving the learner several control options for instance), then the addition of a tutorial to facilitate learning how to operate the program effectively may be advisable.

Content

Content is a problem area not just for a software developer, but for any language learning materials developer. As with the previous two categories, content is dependent on considerations of both the target learners and the assumed syllabus. While the language teaching approach will generally determine (or at least limit) what is considered appropriate content, material that is interesting and engages the attention — sometimes necessarily the *repeated* or *long term* attention — of the learners is a characteristic of most approaches and may make the difference between a learning task that is seriously attended to and one that is done in a perfunctory fashion.

While the topic area of the content (culture, literature, daily situations, etc.) is the most obvious consideration for a developer, there are other aspects of importance as well. Situational and linguistic realism have been proposed as factors having a significant influence on engaging the learner (Madsen & Bowen, 1978), and a developer who accepts that assumption would want to include content reflecting sociolinguistically valid language interaction. In an exercise involving reading, the degree of conceptual difficulty associated with the content of a text is a consideration: an assessment of the target learners' pre-existing knowledge of a topic is important here. A third area of content deals with any explicit instruction provided by the software. As in a textbook, such information must be as complete, accurate, and comprehensible as possible and should furthermore be geared toward effective presentation through the computer medium. Finally, there is the content of the material in the software's anticipatory interaction with the learner to consider, a point where the possibilities for CALL diverge considerably from those of a standard textbook (Hubbard, 1988b). *Anticipatory interaction* here refers to the materials developer's end of a 'conversation' in a communicative situation common in CALL where he or she must anticipate a learner action (e.g. specific responses the learner may input as part of the learning or practice task or specific information the learner may request) and prepare an appropriate response to be delivered by the program. Certain types of programs, particularly tutorials, allow the learners to ask for help or hints that will lead them to an acceptable answer to a question or solution to a problem. The programs may also provide explanations for anticipated right and wrong answers or solutions. When done properly, this can give students the ability to ask for and receive some of the same information they would in a face-to-face situation with a teacher.

At some stage in development, the considered input of a teacher experienced with the target learners is needed to ensure that the content of the software enhances rather than detracts from its effectiveness. This is particularly true in programs which involve anticipatory interaction.

Learning style

The category of *learning style* from Phillips' framework builds directly on a classification scheme proposed by Kemmis *et al.* (1977). It is distinguished from the *learner variables* component in that it focuses on varieties of learning task rather than varieties of learners. Kemmis proposes five general types of learning activities for CALL: recognition, recall, comprehension, experiential learning, and constructive understanding. Recognition and recall activities are relatively passive types: in the first, the learner only has to be able to identify previously learned material (e.g. noting which words in a list are spelled correctly), while in the second, the learner only needs to give a response to previously learned information (e.g. a definition of a word). In a comprehension activity, on the other hand, the learner must take a more active role, responding appropriately to new combinations of learned forms, as in a typical reading or listening comprehension exercise. Both experiential and constructive understanding activities are more exploratory and interactive. Experiential activities involve learning by doing, such as learning about word order and constituent structure from reconstructing a scrambled sentence. Constructive understanding activities involve using the computer as an experimental tool to discover new information, as in a conversational simulation such as *Chatterbox* (described in Phillips, 1985).

Wyatt (1987) has proposed a different classification for computer-learner interaction which may be relevant here. He distinguishes three categories of language learning programs: instructional, collaborative, and facilitative. In instructional programs (e.g. drills and most tutorials), students are responders rather than initiators and students learn from the computer. In collaborative programs (e.g. simulations and adventure games), the students are initiators and discoverers, taking more responsibility for determining their own learning paths. In facilitative programs (e.g. word processors), learning takes place as a result of the students' use of the computer as a tool for authentic labour.

Program focus

Phillips defines the *program focus* as the linguistic objective of the activity, arranged from higher-level to lower-level elements as follows: discourse/text, syntax, lexis, morphology, and graphology/phonology. As these categories are very general, a developer would need to go beyond them to consider, for example, *which* syntactic structures or lexical items a given program would involve. The hierarchical structure of these categories is such that practice at a higher level automatically involves practice at a lower level. A reading exercise focusing on the level of text, for instance, would also provide practice in syntax, lexis, morphology, and graphology.

Classroom management

Classroom management in Phillips' system refers to the grouping of students for a particular CALL activity. Most software is designed for the individual learner, but some types, particularly games, can easily allow for two or more users as part of the design. While most classroom management decisions involving more than two at a screen are generally made by the user rather than the designer (e.g. when a teacher organises whole class or small group activities when computer access is limited), it may be helpful for the designer to anticipate uses other than by individuals or pairs and, with such uses in mind, to build more flexibility into the program.

Another consideration of the designer in classroom management has to do with record keeping. If there appears to be value in keeping track of student records of any sort relating to the use of the program, building that option in for the teacher should be considered.

It is possible to see classroom management additionally as one of the major areas of interface between the development and implementation modules of the comprehensive methodological framework mentioned earlier. While it is beyond the scope of this paper to give a detailed description of the implementation module of the CALL framework proposed in Figure 3.1, it is worthwhile for the developer to devote some time during development of the software to thinking about its eventual implementation, i.e. about the various ways in which the learners and their supervising instructors may be able to exploit the software for language learning. It is possible for relatively minor programming changes to significantly impact on the range of possible implementation schemes for a given program or courseware package.

Learner focus

Another of Phillips' categories is *learner focus*, which he defines as the language skill area on which the software concentrates. His initial subdivisions for this are the traditional four skills of listening, speaking, reading, and writing. As he notes, these categories could do with further refinement: one way to accomplish this would be to set up lists of sub-skills for each of the major classifications, such as those for reading presented in Grellet (1981).

There has been a movement away from a sub-skills approach to these language areas in recent years. Thus, another possible orientation for the category of learner focus is that of conscious learner strategies, which was not mentioned by Phillips. The act of skimming in reading, for instance, may be viewed as a set of specific strategies, or procedures, for getting information about the content and structure of a text: reading the title, reading the first and last paragraphs, reading the first line of each paragraph, searching for key words and transitions, etc. If the goal of a developer is to teach such strategies, then they may appropriately become the learner focus of a given piece of software (see Hubbard, 1987, for a discussion of design and evaluation criteria for strategy-oriented software).

Hardware and programming language considerations

Considerations of hardware and programming language comprise another component left implicit in Phillips' system that is explicit in the current one. Ultimately, software designers are 'prisoners' of the available hardware, but within the restrictions imposed by the hardware, there is often a fair amount of choice possible. Areas of choice include the medium of presentation and response, which will impact on the Procedure section to be discussed below. Besides a basic monochrome Text mode, there are possibilities for use of colour, sound, and graphics for many systems, as well as the potential for linking to printers and audio or video output devices of various sorts. Input options are varied as well. Besides a keyboard, there may be a joystick, mouse, touch screen, or other device. Networking options may also be possible. While a number of these decisions may be predetermined for the designer, it is important for a comprehensive design framework to integrate this component, so that where options do exist, they may be selected in a principled way to be consistent with the rest of the design considerations.

The programming language is another non-trivial component of the design framework. As discussed in Wyatt (1983, 1987), there are choices to be made here with respect to machine or assembly language for a specific computer, general purpose languages, such as Pascal, BASIC, and C, authoring languages such as PILOT and authoring systems, such as MacLang (Frommer, 1987). One important consideration here is transportability: some languages (or 'dialects' of those languages) are more transportable to different machines than others.

Procedure

The components of the *Procedure* section of the network, reproduced in Figure 3.5, are the focus of most of the actual programming decisions. These

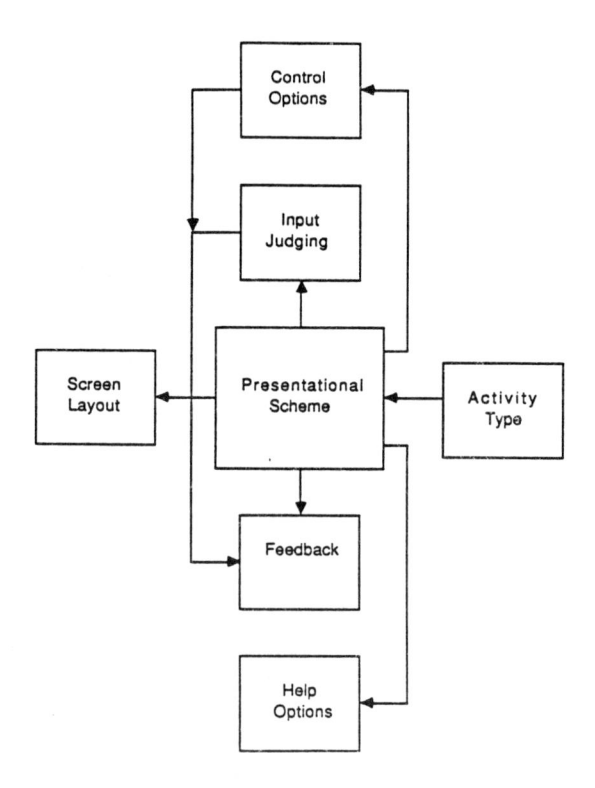

FIGURE 3.5 *Procedure section*

include the *activity type, presentational scheme, input judging, feedback, control options, Help options,* and *screen layout*. While these necessarily depend on considerations from the Approach and Design sections for their ultimate realisation in a given piece of software, the network has been laid out to have them *fit* those decisions, rather than be determined by them. This order of decision-making seems to more realistically capture the nature of the design process: drawing from a bank of existing techniques or developing variants of them rather than creating techniques solely in response to approach and design decisions.

Activity type

The most fundamental decision made in the Procedure section of the framework involves the selection of the *activity type*. This is the last component of Phillips' framework to be discussed. He offers seven types of activity in his

METHODOLOGICAL FRAMEWORK FOR CALL

description of this component — game, quiz, text construction, text reconstruction, simulation, problem solving, and exploratory activities — but notes that this is a productive category and that further developments in CALL may lead to new activity types. Historically in CALL there have been other classification schemes for activity types, one of the most common of which includes drill and practice programs and tutorials along with two of the categories Phillips recognised — simulations and games. In general, Phillips' seven categories make finer distinctions than this more traditional division, but it seems reasonable to add drill-and-practice and tutorial to the list even at the risk of overlapping with Phillips' *quiz* category because the terms have become so widely established.

Presentational scheme

The *presentational scheme* is the logical realisation of the choice of activity types and offers a wide range of possibilities to the designer in achieving that realisation. For a text reconstruction activity, for example, there are a number of possible presentational schemes. Cloze exercises, where certain items are deleted from a text, 'storyboard' exercises, where the entire text is deleted, and jigsaw readings, where the sentences or phrases in a paragraph are scrambled and the learner has to unscramble them, are representative of the range of possibilities.

While there are some commonly used and easily described presentational schemes such as the three mentioned above, some may be relatively complex and describable only in terms of the program in which they operate. This is clearly a highly productive category, both because of the potential for entirely new schemes and because of the ease with which new variations can be produced for existing ones.

One of the most significant decisions to be made here is what the communicative modality of both the computer's output and the learner's input will be. While both are often linguistic, one or the other may be non-linguistic as well. For instance, computer output might be textual, with learner input being only the movement of objects depicted with graphics; or the input might be textual, with output in graphic form. Note the importance of hardware considerations, too: In Figure 3.2 the dependency of the presentational scheme on the hardware (colour, graphics, sound, etc.) is explicitly indicated.

As Figure 3.5 illustrates, the presentational scheme is the central component of the Procedure section of the framework. The control options, input judging, feedback, Help options, and screen layout are all determined by it. This component necessarily involves some of the decisions about timing and branching as well, although these may also be determined to varying degrees within the other Procedural components discussed below.

Input Judging

Once the presentational scheme has determined the form of input the computer will accept from the learner, decisions must be made regarding how to judge that input. In the majority of programs to date, *input judging* has been limited to answer judging (of an implicit or explicit question posed by the program), but the program may also be designed to handle input that is not strictly speaking an answer. In fact, in some simulations and games, the learner's input itself may take the form of a question for the computer to answer.

In general terms, the aim of a developer is to anticipate learner input relative to the goals of the exercise and to develop appropriate responses on that basis. What is deemed appropriate for any given exercise is dependent on a number of factors (e.g. language teaching approach, proficiency level and age of the student, etc.), and there is no simple typology that can be laid out here as a guideline. In addition to the universal requirement that the program not crash as a result of inappropriate or unanticipated input, some basic considerations for instructional software in particular may include the following:

(1) Is there only one acceptable answer to an item, or more than one?
(2) If the input takes the form of a word or phrase, how are misspellings and inflectional/derivational errors dealt with? (See Pusack, 1983, for a discussion of the options available here.)
(3) If the input takes the form of a sentence, how are grammatical errors dealt with?
(4) How are other anticipated errors (e.g. word choice) dealt with?

Once decisions are made regarding what type of input to recognise and respond to, the form of the response, or feedback, needs to be determined.

Feedback

Feedback here is taken in the broadest sense to include any information the program communicates in response to specific input. The range of appropriate feedback types for a given piece of software will be determined to a large degree by the developer's approach-based design criteria, as mentioned above in the Approach section. There are several common types. First, a program may simply indicate whether a learner's response to some exercise item is correct or incorrect, through words, graphics, sound, or some combination of these types of output. It is also possible to offer some commentary concerning correct responses or incorrect ones that have been flagged during the input judging procedure. A third type of feedback is scoring, which can be used as a measure of success for a given item (e.g. more points for a faster correct response) or for an entire exercise. Scoring or other records, such as response patterns that have been calculated based on an analysis of cumulative input, can be used for a further type of feedback which directs a learner to a specific exercise for review. Such feedback may also be 'internal' if it is used by the program without the learner's intervention, as in cases where an item answered incorrectly is flagged by the input judging routine for some type of automatic review later in the program.

Besides the direct forms of feedback noted above, a developer may choose to provide indirect feedback. In a multiple choice format, for example, the program's response to an incorrect answer may simply be to eliminate that distractor and allow selection from the remaining choices. In experiential and exploratory types of software, such as adventure games and simulations, this indirect feedback will often consist of changes in the physical or communicative situation, which the user then reflects on relative to his or her expectations.

Control options

The notion of *control* is a complex one that has been a concern of both researchers and developers for some time. Higgins (1983) laid out the opposing philosophies of control for CALL by distinguishing programs that are *magisters*, or drillmasters under the automatic control imposed by the developer, from *pedagogues*, or programs that are under the control of — and hence subservient to — the learner, arguing that learners are best served by the latter. Some research has shown positive results for student control (e.g. Stevens, 1984), some research has shown negative results (e.g. Pederson, 1987: 102), and some research has discussed the problems of turning control over to students without sufficient training and psychological preparation (e.g. Hubbard et al., 1986). Besides control by the program or the user, there is the additional possibility for the developer to allow the teacher to exert intervening control of the software by enabling or disabling specific options for the student.

In principle, virtually any of the components in the Procedure section may be subject to the control of the learner, but there are a few areas that seem to be particularly open to learner control. Among others, these include choosing the activity type, the presentational scheme, and/or the materials for a given activity, exiting an activity or moving around within it at will rather than following a set sequence, selecting the rate at which information will appear and/or the amount of time it will remain on the screen, and requesting feedback and/or hints (see Help options below) rather than having them appear automatically.

Help options

Help options, defined here as any pieces of information which lead the user to success in a computer-based activity, fall into two basic categories: review and hints. One type of review option is a review of instructions, which normally allows the user to exit the activity temporarily, view all or part of the operating instructions on the screen, and then return to the activity at the point of exit. A second type of review is related to the learning activity itself and may involve a review of, for example, linguistic rules or cultural conventions that the activity is based on or a look at previous items in an exercise. These may be distinguished from hints or clues, which typically provide information specifically geared toward leading a user to correct responses for a given item in a learning exercise. As with the case of feedback (which in some respects overlaps with this category), the determination of what types of hints to include in an activity depends not only on the presentational scheme, but to a large degree on the language learning theory assumed by the developer.

Screen layout

The *screen layout*, the final component of the procedure section, is heavily dependent on the presentational scheme selected. However, given a particular presentational scheme, there are still certain areas of consideration open to the developer. The areas for decision-making include such aspects of presentation as print size, spacing, balance, use of colour, presence and quality of graphics, relative positions of graphics and text, presence and quality of animation, and undoubtedly a number of other possible considerations. In the case of interactive video, several additional dimensions become relevant, such as the quality of the video, the form and location of integrated text and graphics and the size and location of video windows. In the present framework, screen layout is taken to include the role of audio (both speech and non-speech) in connection with the visual image, but a case could be made for considering audio as a separate component.

Completed software

As noted in Figure 3.2, the development process ideally results in a convergence of Approach and Design considerations that are in harmony with Procedural decisions. Put simply, this means that the developer aims to produce software, be it a single exercise or an entire courseware package, that:

(1) Is based on the developer's informed assumptions about language and language learning.
(2) Is targeted toward a particular (even if broadly defined) audience of learners with particular learning objectives consistent with (1).
(3) Embodies computer-based learning activities whose form and content are consistent with (1) and (2).

The box in the centre of Figure 3.2 represents the proposed form of the software, including the program and materials together with any on-screen documentation or integrated utilities. The result of all these decisions, coupled with the non-trivial task of realising the design through creating the actual program, developing the materials, and refining both, is the completed software. The software, depending on additional development decisions, may be accompanied by a separate tutorial, an accompanying text, hard copy documentation, general record-keeping utilities, and any other utilities (such as an authoring program) in a complete courseware package.

Conclusion

This article has presented a framework for courseware development as one module of a comprehensive methodological framework for CALL. At the outset, four principles were suggested as the foundation for its design, and an attempt was made to adhere to those principles. Now that the components of the framework have been outlined and their interaction has been described, it is worth briefly clarifying just what the framework is and is not.

The framework does not represent methods nor does it create methods; it does not represent nor create courseware. The framework is a tool engineered to aid the developer in the courseware development process. While it does not specify a procedure for designing, programming, and producing materials for CALL, it does provide specific areas of consideration in CALL development by describing the relevant components recognisd as important in the areas of language teaching methodology and second language acquisition research, and illustrating the significant dependency relationships among them.

The goal of the original Richards & Rodgers (1982) framework was to provide a means of comparing and contrasting whole methods. It has been assumed here that the considerations which must be taken into account in describing a language teaching method are in essence the same ones that must be taken into account in creating language learning software. As long as improving language proficiency is the goal of a piece of software, the considerations described in this article are relevant to the developer and ought to be addressed. They are relevant regardless of whether:

(1) The software represents a whole course with a variety of instruction and practice activities, a single exercise, or something in between.
(2) The software is commercially published and aimed at a wide range of possible users and learning situations or is a customised lesson developed by a teacher for a specific group of students.
(3) The software will be used independently by the student or presented by the teacher to an entire class.

(4) The software is being used for instruction, drill, or communicative practice.

While there is clearly room for refinement, the network presented here offers software developers a principled framework for addressing the array of relevant considerations thoughtfully and thoroughly.

References

ARIEW, R. (1984) Computer-assisted foreign language materials: Advantages and limitations, *CALICO Journal* 2: 1, 43–47.

BAKER, R. (1984) Foreign language software: The state of the art, or pick a card, any (flash) card, *CALICO Journal* 2: 2, 6–10, 27.

BROWN, H. D. (1987) *Principles of Language Teaching and Learning*. Englewood Cliffs, NJ: Prentice-Hall.

BUSCH, D. (1982) Introversion–extraversion and the EFL proficiency of Japanese students, *Language Learning*, 32: 2.

CHAPELLE, C. & J. JAMIESON (1986) Computer-assisted language learning as a predictor of success in acquiring English as a second language, *TESOL Quarterly*, 20: 1, 27–46.

CURTIN, C. & S. SHINALL (1987) Teacher training for CALL and its implications. In W. FLINT SMITH (ed), *Modern Media in Foreign Language Education: Theory and Implementation*. Lincolnwood, IL: National Textbook.

DALGISH, G. (1984) *Microcomputers and Teaching English as a Second Language: Issues and Some CUNY Applications*. New York: Instructional Resource Center, City University of New York.

FROMMER, J. (1987) *MacLang*. Santa Barbara, CA: Kinko's Academic Courseware Exchange.

GRELLET, F. (1981) *Developing Reading Skills: A Practical Guide to Reading Comprehension Exercises*. New York: Cambridge University Press.

HIGGINS, J. (1983) Can computers teach?, *CALICO Journal*, 1: 2, 4–6

— (1988) *Language, Learners, and Computers*. London: Longman.

HOLMES, G. (1984) The computer and its limitations, *Foreign Language Annals*, 17:3 413–14.

HUBBARD, P. (1987) Language teaching approaches, the evaluation of CALL software, and design implications. In W. FLINT SMITH (ed.), *Modern Media in Foreign Language Education: Theory and Implementation*. Lincolnwood, IL: National Textbook Company.

— (1988a) An integrated framework for CALL courseware evaluation, *CALICO Journal*, 6: 2, 51–72.

— (1988b) The teacher in the machine, *CATESOL Newsletter*, 19: 6, 5–6.

HUBBARD, P., J. COADY, J. GRANEY, K. MOKHTARI & J. MAGOTO (1986) Report on a pilot study of the relationship of high frequency vocabulary knowledge and reading proficiency in ESL learners, *Ohio University Working Papers in Linguistics and Language Teaching*, 8, 48–57.

KEMMIS, S., R. ATKIN & E. WRIGHT (1977) How do students learn?, *Working Papers on Computer-Assisted Learning, UNCAL Evaluation Studies*, No. 5. Norwich, UK: Centre for Applied Research in Education.

MADSEN, H. S. & J. D. BOWEN (1978) *Adaptation in Language Teaching*. Rowley, MA: Newbury House.

PEDERSON, K. (1987) Research on CALL. In W. FLINT SMITH (ed), *Modern Media in Foreign Language Education: Theory and Implementation*. Lincolnwood, IL: National Textbook Company.

PENNINGTON, M. C. (1986) The development of effective CAI: Problems and prospects, *TESOL CALL-IS Newsletter*, 3, 6–8.

PHILLIPS, M. (1985) Logical possibilities and classroom scenarios for the development of CALL. In C. BRUMFIT, M. PHILLIPS & P. SKEHAN (eds), *Computers in English Language Teaching*. New York: Pergamon.

PUSACK, J. (1983) Answer-processing and error correction in foreign language CAI, *System*, 11: 1, 53–64.

RICHARDS, J. & T. RODGERS (1982) Method: Approach, design, and procedure, *TESOL Quarterly*, 16: 2, 153–168.

— (1986) *Approaches and Methods in Language Teaching: A Description and Analysis*. New York: Cambridge University Press.

STEVENS, V. (1984) Implications of research and theory concerning the influence of control on the effectiveness of CALL, *CALICO Journal*, 2: 1, 28–33, 48.

UNDERWOOD, J. (1984) *Linguistics, Computers, and the Language Teacher: A Communicative Approach*. Rowley, MA: Newbury House.

WEIBLE, D. (1987) Towards a media-specific methodology for CALL. In W. FLINT SMITH (ed.), *Modern Media in Foreign Language Education: Theory and Implementation*. Lincolnwood, IL: National Textbook Company.

WILKINS, D. (1976) *Notional Syllabuses*. New York: Oxford University Press.

WYATT, D. (1983) Three major approaches to developing computer-assisted language learning materials for microcomputers, *CALICO Journal*, 1: 2, 34–38.

— (1987) Applying pedagogical principles to CALL courseware development. In W. FLINT SMITH (ed.), *Modern Media in Foreign Language Education: Theory and Implementation*. Lincolnwood, IL: National Textbook Company.

4 Intelligence in Computer-Aided Language Learning[1]

ANDREW LIAN
Bond University, Gold Coast, Australia

Introduction

The development of Computer-Aided Language Learning (CALL) systems at the University of Queensland and at Bond University in Australia has its origins in the desire to discover or create optimal foreign and second language learning environments for adults. Although methodological issues will not be discussed in great detail in this paper, comments upon intelligence in CALL will inevitably be driven by assumptions as to the likely shapes of the learning environments in which CALL will be found. An attempt will therefore be made to try to sketch out very rapidly some of the assumptions which underpin the author's thinking on the matter.

Perhaps the most obvious feature of this general approach is the belief that language learning methodology is what matters the most. The computer is only a tool for effective learning. As for the environment in which the computer will be used, it is envisaged as an open, negotiable and negotiated, highly task-oriented, resource-based learning network where people progress at their own pace in a relatively asynchronous fashion. This view is in contrast with many of the current institutional practices where students are all 'expected to learn in the same way, at and in the same time, all in lock-stepped synchrony' (Lian, 1987). In other words, one is looking for a learning space where heterogeneity in the learner population can be seen as a blessing to be exploited rather than as a curse to be suffered.

Such a framework is, moreover, necessarily based on the assumption that the learner fundamentally wishes to satisfy a range of personal motivations together with the accompanying conscious or unconscious needs (for further details, see Lian, 1987). Under ideal circumstances, the language-learning environment will help to automatically extract these motivations and needs and adapt to them in a flexible, effective, self-regulating manner. An approach which attempts to provide such an environment has been developed in the University of Queensland's Department of French by Mestre and Lian under the name of *macrosimulation* (see Lian & Mestre, 1985; Mestre & Lian, 1983).

This CALL framework and the assumptions on which it is based raise questions about the traditional institutional notion of 'course'. One cannot help wondering whether the only way to actualise the principles outlined above might not be to create a completely new environment rather than struggling hopelessly to try to modify an institutional structure which finds its origins in outdated pedagogical principles and which, moreover, tends to be self-perpetuating.

The Notion of Intelligence in CALL

Typically, intelligence in CALL is thought of as synonymous with the implementation of highly complex programs which simulate human intelligence or which perform tasks that would require intelligence if performed by human beings. In other words, these sorts of programs are based on techniques of Artificial Intelligence (AI). Again typically, the sort of program which the notion of intelligence in CALL evokes in the minds of language teachers is a program which understands spoken natural language, is capable of responding appropriately through a voice synthesis device with an impeccable accent in a variety of registers, and at the same time contains the distilled essences of all the best language teachers in the world.

Although such devices may actually become available some day, we are still a long way from seeing them in our local supermarkets or even in our university computer and/or language learning centres. There are, however, a number of significantly more realistic ambitions which are already more or less within our reach. Perhaps the most complex yet promising of these is the development of expert system-based computer-aided learning (EXCAL). The aim here is to provide learners and course designers/authors with an environment for managing learning activity in a multitude of unpredictable ways. One such project currently underway in Australia is the *EXCALIBUR* project (T. J. Richards, La Trobe University, Director), which has brought together researchers from La Trobe University, the University of Melbourne, and Chisholm Institute of Technology.

The EXCALIBUR Project

EXCALIBUR is intended to be an intelligent, general-purpose computer environment that will provide a favourable development and delivery framework for computer-aided learning (CAL). Briefly, the *EXCALIBUR* project will consist of:

(1) A *domain expert system* consisting of a knowledge base and an appropriate reasoning system;
(2) A *student model* for each student, i.e. a representational map, or network diagram, of their cognitive abilities together with a map of their subject knowledge;
(3) A *teaching expert* which contains both general and subject-specific pedagogical knowledge;
(4) A *natural language interface* to parse and interpret (i.e. analyse) user input and to deparse and encode (i.e. synthesise) system output into natural language;
(5) A *reasoning system* capable of operating not just from knowledge in one of the above knowledge bases but also from the student's knowledge in order to construct a dialogue with him or her.

Further, the system will provide a development and authoring infrastructure together with the high level management routines required for implementation of the features just described, as shown in Figure 4.1.

The importance of good delivery and administration systems should not be underestimated by anyone involved in any kind of CAL. Indeed, it is likely that the level of sophistication in these types of systems will become the single most important factor in the next stage of CAL: the development rather than the present pioneering stage. One of the characteristics of this phase will be the realisation that it is no longer enough to make a set of good quality lessons available on a personal computer (PC), but that multi-tasking ability and sophisticated user management as well as access to a multitude of resources and records is essential. Such goals will begin to be realised once lesson developers overcome their blind enthusiasm for the potential of small, stand-alone machines and become more ambitious in attempting to apply intelligently the product of research into language learning methodology to a computing environment.

In fact, these new directions for CAL have already begun to be implemented by at least two of the current leaders in the CAL field: Carnegie-Mellon University and the Athena Project at Massachusetts Institute of Technology (MIT). Carnegie-Mellon, for instance, has developed a high-quality, high-speed environment, called Andrew+, which will allow transparent communication between a range of very high-powered workstations (Trowbridge, 1985). The

INTELLIGENCE IN CALL

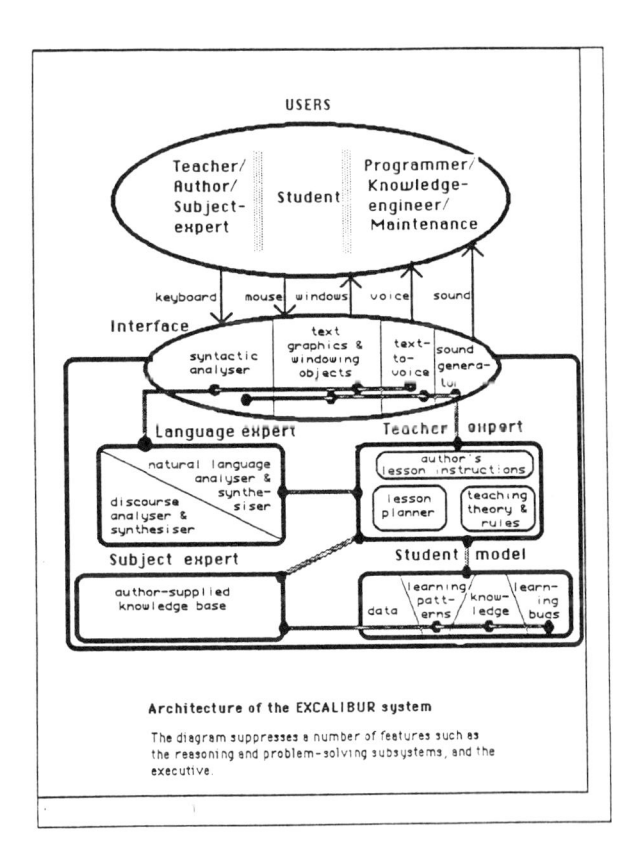

Architecture of the EXCALIBUR system

The diagram suppresses a number of features such as the reasoning and problem-solving subsystems, and the executive.

FIGURE 4.1

common factor which makes such communication possible is the UNIX 4.2/4.3 BSD operating system chosen to underpin this massive development.

From a different perspective, and certainly on a much smaller scale, the University of Queensland's HCRU[2] and the Language Centre at Bond University have developed a student administration system, Computerised Line Access Monitor (CLAM) (Deschamps, 1988), again under the UNIX operating system, which provides students with easy access to relevant information as well as the ability to manipulate information at no risk to themselves or to the system. It also offers electronic mail and bulletin board facilities for the dissemination of information and communication between teachers and students. A *reservation system* ensures smooth queuing of students through the system and guarantees that everyone is given a fair share of the available time, with easy access to materials appropriate to their levels of competence and to their needs. Error-logging and other facilities produce constantly up-to-date records of the computer system's status.

Intelligent Systems for Specific Purposes

So far we have been looking at systems which sit more or less intelligently on top of lessons and which are responsible for providing management and authoring support of one kind or another. Another form of development is likely to be in the area of high-powered intelligent systems created for specific purposes. These systems — possibly based on expert system technology — are likely to contain reasoning mechanisms in the form of inference engines driven by rules and domain-specific knowledge.

One such project (funded by an Australian Research Grants Scheme award) is currently underway under the author's direction. It relates to the creation of a natural language database for use in a generative approach to CALL. In its final form, the database will be suitable for the generation of authentic-like dialogues in a foreign language (Joy & Lian, 1983) as well as for use as a sophisticated information retrieval system. Computationally, the architecture will be based on a series of linked micro expert systems, which are to be managed in a multitude of ways by a frame description language in order to produce the desired results. The final product should be able to answer requests ranging from the simple to the quite complex: e.g. in the case of someone inquiring about French language and cultural practices, from a simple 'How do I greet my French boss?' to 'Show me a day in the life of a young Parisian executive.'. An important feature of the system will be the ability to justify its choices so that users can ask the machine such questions as 'Why did you say *bonjour* in line 3?' The single ability of being able to answer that sort of self-referential question places the system in a different category from most current CALL software (Lian, 1986).

Smart Subsystems

The systems described so far have all been self-contained. Some of them are still only on the drawing-board or in the relatively early stages of implementation. However, their components are becoming gradually available for use in what is commonly known as a *toolkit* approach to CALL. Indeed, one of the important purposes of systems such as *EXCALIBUR*, Andrew+, or even CLAM is to hold together smaller, perhaps more manageable, subsystems. The 'intelligence', if there is any, may well lie in the ways in which these subsystems — which, individually, are of great value — can be related to one another.

Thus, a lesson could, through judicious linking of subsystems, be generated as students are working at terminals. Such a possibility assumes, of course, that the computer's operating system allows such transactions and that there is enough storage space and processing power to perform all of the necessary tasks with minimal delays for the waiting learners. Unfortunately, this is often far from being the normal state of affairs. However, appropriate subsystems, three of which are outlined in what follows, do exist.

The first of these subsystems is the Domain Analysis Based Instruction System (*DABIS*), developed by G. Webb of Deakin University in Australia (Webb, 1986). DABIS consists of a relatively simple knowledge representation scheme which can be used for representing word classes in English and which appears capable of representing other kinds of knowledge as well. The most significant feature of the system is that after presentation of a series of problems, the system is capable of diagnosing errors in the user's understanding of the various features of the network. This feature makes it an enormously powerful subsystem which could be incorporated into a variety of types of software requiring accurate diagnosis of error. For examples of the kinds of diagnosis performed, see the sample analysis in Figure 4.2 (adapted from Webb, 1986: 82). At the moment, consideration is being given to the implementation of a computer-aided listening skills toolkit based on DABIS-like systems.

The second system of interest relates to the use of the computer as a resource base and/or as a manager of resources. If the computer is to be used as a resource or support system, then it seems important for it to have the capability of responding to such questions as: 'Where can I find examples of two persons insulting each other in French?' The computer should be able to respond with such statements as 'Consult dialogue generator 2a', or 'Look at videodisc X from frame A to frame B', and so on. Such a database is currently being designed and prototyped by J. C. Lacherez of the French Department at the University of Queensland, Australia. Similar projects will include the development of databases of authentic documents to be stored on CD-ROM by scanning original documents. These would then be retrieved for on-screen examination and/or dumped to a laser printer for distribution to students.

Perhaps less impressively intelligent is the development of relatively simple yet highly informative feedback mechanisms. Of particular interest are markup systems which allow students to make responses which increasingly match the courseware author's expectations. One such system, *ENGTUTE*,

Analysis of performance at the DETERMINER-TYPE-FC feature choice:
The student does not understand this feature choice.

Analysis of performance at the NOUN-TYPE feature choice:
The student understands this feature choice.

Analysis of performance at the TRANSITIVITY-FC feature choice:
The feature DI-TRANSITIVE is correctly understood.
The feature COPULA is not comprehended.
The feature TRANSITIVE is over-generalised.
The feature INTRANSITIVE is over-generalised.

Analysis of performance at the WORD-TYPE feature choice:
The feature VERB is correctly understood.
The feature NOUN is correctly understood.
The feature PREPOSITION is correctly understood.
The feature ADJECTIVE is correctly understood.
The feature PRONOUN is over-generalised.
The feature DETERMINER is under-generalised.

FIFURE 4.2 *A sample analysis produced by the DABIS analysis system.*

(Lian, 1984) has been devised at the University of Queensland and at Bond University, where it is routinely used for CALL. Currently, it provides feedback on typed input and is capable of selecting responses on the basis of exact matches, keyword or partial matches, word order, predicted wrong components and totally unrecognised components. It is not an intelligent system in the conventional sense, but merely provides information that relies on the users' intelligence to reduce the field of inference for their guesses. The system takes a student's response — i.e. a personal and individual production — as its starting point and then helps the learner to adjust it appropriately (Lian, 1984). This seems to be a powerful mode of interaction which, in principle, can be applied to many different kinds of activities, ranging from the development of listening comprehension lessons to the scanning of written texts for undesirable features (Lian, 1983).

As this last example shows, intelligence in CALL does not necessarily imply extraordinary programming complexity, with the machine doing all of the work. Furthermore, the development of probabilistic approaches to pattern matching and answer evaluation will greatly enhance such systems. For the time being, answer evaluation is being investigated at Bond University and the University of Queensland at two levels:

(1) At a first level, answer evaluation takes place through the processing of students' actual input, e.g. through an instantaneous interactive spelling checker.
(2) Answer evaluation also occurs in the attempt to abstract or infer propositional information from a learner's interaction with the system. This does not necessarily mean 'understanding' the student's input, but rather inferring from a series of keyword checks and/or menu selections the kinds of objectives which the student may have in mind.

Ultimately, it is hoped that this work will lead to the development of answer negotiation rather than answer evaluation systems, i.e., to systems where computer and learner will 'agree' on a response and where changes may occur not only in the learner's behaviour but also in the computer system itself and in its behaviour when dealing with specific learners' responses.

The Human Factor

Learners

In the discussion of intelligence in CALL so far, there is one factor which has been assumed but not clearly mentioned: the human factor. Although the discussion has been focused up to this point on computer programs, there is no doubt that human beings must occupy the central role and must be the ultimate beneficiaries of any intelligent programming.

Ultimately, the most important human beneficiary is the learner, whose own intelligence can be developed with computer assistance. Whatever programs are written, they will all necessarily draw and act upon the learners' intellectual processes if they are to be at all effective. We as teachers must teach our students to use their intelligence to interact effectively with machines and not to expect the machine to do everything for them.

For instance, the development of learners' skills in interpreting error feedback has two important effects. First of all, learners' reasoning and analytic processes are developed, leading to the establishment of a desirable level of autonomy for effective learning. Second, from a programming point of view, the task of developing high quality CALL materials is made significantly easier when learners improve their ability to interpret feedback. From this perspective, relatively simple systems can be used to good effect, as indeed they already are. In this and in other applications, it is not necessary to keep waiting for miracles in CALL to occur. A considerable number of small yet effective contributions can be made right now.

Teachers

The human being as teacher or course designer faces a very different set of problems from those faced by the learner. Perhaps the biggest of these is how to bring about change in a pre-determined world, for it is currently the lot of the CAL author/manager to shoulder a considerable part of the responsibility for change. The ability to inform and convince administrators that CALL can bring about benefits to teachers, learners, and administrators alike is undoubtedly an area where intelligence — at least, strategic intelligence — must play an important role. Once the battle for credibility has been won, teachers are faced with other pressing needs. These include:

(1) The restructuring of ordinary courses to maximise the benefits of the CALL component;
(2) The capability to make improvements in the degree and the quality of human support made available to learners, through trouble-shooting workshops or communication via electronic mail or computer-based news system;
(3) The ability to make the most of the available software, i.e. to know how to recognise the value of software even though it cannot do all that might otherwise be required of it in an ideal world;
(4) The strength to resist the temptation to use off-the-shelf software which is methodologically outdated and, instead, to set about developing their own computer programs.

As in the case of developing original software, exploiting the available software maximally might require having access to some sort of 'guidance' environment which is not itself an integral part of the program. As in other cases, the importance of surrounding programs with high quality management environments is clear.

The facilities for achieving these kinds of objectives are available now in various forms. Yet these objectives are often not implemented because educators are either unwilling or unable to envisage medium-to-long-term developmental efforts to solve problems. Important issues which are often seriously confronted include such matters as: portability of code and data files;

limitations in processing power; availability of record-keeping facilities for purposes of research and user administration; the large amounts of disk storage needed for rapid common access to databases and other materials; and the need for high- and low-speed communications to facilitate fast file transfer, national and international electronic mail communications, and rapid and transparent communication with remote hosts in order to access their resources.

Whether we like it or not and whether we think that yet another wonderful PC is just around the corner, intelligence should indicate that a stable and sophisticated computational environment is required for any serious long-term development and distribution of CALL. Current thinking on the matter, as exemplified by the Carnegie-Mellon and Athena projects, seems to indicate that the wisest course of action is standardisation on the UNIX operating system, particularly in its BSD versions. This potential solution is further echoed by the proliferation of UNIX systems on the newer generation of 32-bit microcomputers.

Conclusion

The question of intelligence in CALL is clearly not a simple one. It brings into play a multitude of technical and human factors. It seems, however, that the tasks required for intelligent implementations go beyond the capabilities of any single person or small group of persons — even those endowed with great visions and an unbreakable pioneering spirit.

Considering the limitations of individual efforts, a concerted effort needs to occur both nationally and internationally to provide support for soundly-based research and development on a small as well as on a large scale. Greater support is also required for teacher education and CALL literacy programs. In order for these objectives of support to be attained, the establishment of well-organised and co-ordinated national and regional CALL centres networked to their counterparts in other countries now appears to have become a necessity, if we are to progress intelligently into the future of CALL.

Notes to Chapter 4

1. The research reported here was partially supported by an Australian Research Grants Scheme Award and by University of Queensland Special Projects Grants. The author acknowledges this support with gratitude.
2. The term HCRU stands for the Humanities Computing Resource Unit.

References

DESCHAMPS, G. (1986) *Computerized Line Access Monitor (CLAM)* (User administration and management package). Humanities Computing Resource Unit. University of Queensland, Brisbane, Australia.

JOY, B. K. & A. LIAN (1983) The butcher, the baker, the candlestick maker: Some uses of dialogue generators in computer-assisted foreign language learning, *Australian Review of Applied Linguistics*, 6: 2, 60–71.

LIAN, A. (1983) Using scanners in the computer-assisted development of the writing skill in a foreign language. In R. M. RUSSELL, G. M. HARRIS, A. LIAN & B. W. CARSS (eds), *Proceedings of the 1st Conference on Computer-Aided Learning in Tertiary Education (CALITE)*. University of Queensland, Brisbane, Australia.

— (1984) Aspects of answer-evaluation in traditional computer-assisted language learning. In R. M. RUSSELL (ed.), *Proceedings of the 2nd Congress on Computer-Aided Learning in Tertiary Education (CALITE)*. University of Queensland, Brisbane, Australia.

— (1986) Generative computer-aided language learning: The University of Queensland CALL project and EXCALIBUR. In R. A. GIRLE (ed), *Report of the First Round Table Conference: Australian Educational Expert System Project*. Project EXCALIBUR Publications, University of Queensland, Brisbane, Australia.

— (1987) Awareness, autonomy and achievement in foreign language learning. Paper presented at the VIIème Colloque International SGAV, Brussels, 1986. Appeared in *Revue de Phonétique Appliquée*, 82–4, 167–84 (pre-published in *The SGAV Review*).

LIAN, A. & M. C. MESTRE (1985) Goal-directed communicative interaction and macrosimulation, *Revue de Phonétique Appliquée*, 73–5, 185–210.

MESTRE, M. C. & A. LIAN (1983) Toward genuine individualisation in language course development, *Australian Review of Applied Linguistics*, 6: 2, 1–19.

TROWBRIDGE, D. (1985) *Using Andrew for Development of Educational Applications*. Center for Design of Educational Computing, Carnegie-Mellon University, Pittsburgh, PA.

WEBB, G. I. (1986) *Knowledge representation in computer-aided learning: The theory and practice of knowledge-based student evaluation and flow of control*. Department of Computer Science, Technical Report, No.7. La Trobe University, Melbourne, Australia.

Part II:
Research on Applications of Computers in Second Language Acquisition

5 Process and Product Approaches to Computer-Assisted Composition

MARTHA C. PENNINGTON
and
MARK N. BROCK
City Polytechnic of Hong Kong, Hong Kong

Introduction

In recent years, computer-based writing aids have been increasingly incorporated into educational curricula at every level. In kindergartens and elementary schools in the United States, some children are taking their first steps towards literacy on computer (Hoot & Silvern, 1989). Students at secondary and tertiary levels who have previously found writing to be fearsome or tiresome may be encouraged by the anonymity, the patience, and the flexibility of the computer as a writing medium; most immediately recognise the benefits of drafting term papers and writing reports on the computer (Hawisher, 1987; Wresch, 1987). At Gallaudet College, hearing-impaired students have blurred the distinction between spoken and written language by using word processing programs on networked computers as a medium of communication with other students (Peyton & Batson, 1986).

The utility of the computer in generating written language is unquestioned. Yet many questions remain about its utility in writing instruction and the ways it can best be applied in a writing curriculum. To help practitioners decide on the most effective and appropriate uses of computers in the writing curriculum, carefully designed studies which compare different applications of computer-assisted instruction to the teaching of composition need to be conducted. There has been only a small amount of research to date which systematically examines use of the computer in comparison to some other approach to writing. The majority of these studies compare word processing to the use of ordinary, nontechnological writing aids (for representative studies and discussion, see Harris, 1985; Daiute, 1986; Lutz, 1987; Phinney, 1989). The number of studies which involve ESL students is quite small (for individual studies, see Reid *et al.*, 1983; Reid, 1986; Piper, 1987; for an overview, see Phinney, 1989), as is the number of studies comparing more than one approach to computer-assisted instruction (Daiute, 1986; Wresch, 1987). Research comparing two or more different approaches to computer-assisted writing instruction in university-level ESL has not yet appeared in the literature.

This paper reports on research comparing two different approaches to the individualised use of computers as supplements to university-level ESL writing courses. One of these focused on use of word processing in conjunction with the IBM text analysis program, *Critique*, while the other focused on use of word processing without the addition of text analysis. The study was designed to involve tutorials in which the writing of students who worked with *Critique* was guided primarily by the computer-generated feedback, while the writing of other students who used only the word processing program was guided by interaction with the tutor in a process approach. The paper examines student attitudes, written products, and the types of revisions made under the two different conditions. It contains four major sections, in addition to a concluding section. The first of these offers background on writing research. The second section describes the study in detail. The third and fourth sections describe and discuss the findings of the study. The concluding section summarises the main findings and lines of discussion.

Background to the Study

Though computer-based writing aids in general, and word processing in particular, have received accolades from numerous teachers and students alike, the findings of research to date have not always supported an overwhelmingly positive evaluation of the effectiveness of computer-assisted writing. Kiefer (1987) decries the lack of good research on computers and writing, warning that computer-assisted writing cannot be heralded unquestioningly as the panacea for student's composing problems. Piper (1987), in contrast, asserts that students using computer-based writing aids move almost effortlessly through the various stages of the writing process until arriving in a natural way at the finished product. At the same time, Piper (1987) notes that in an intermediate ESL class which met in a microcomputer lab, some students preferred to work alone — without the computer — rather than to be forced to work in a group in order to gain access to a terminal. An overview of the research to date indicates that the effectiveness of computer-based writing aids may depend on the particular use to which the computer is put, the circumstances of use, and the type of student working at the computer.

Much of the research conducted on the use of computer-based writing aids has focused on the amount and kinds of revision encouraged by word processing. Daiute (1984) found that writers who used word processing to compose made more changes than those using pen and paper. No difference in the quality of writing of writers using either technique was detected, however. The results in studies by Collier (1983) and Lutz (1987) are similar. Research by Harris (1985) and Daiute (1986) uncovered negative results: writers using word processing in their studies revised less than writers using traditional means.

Researchers generally agree that the act of revision itself is facilitated by word processing, as 'writers can insert, delete, and substitute text with an ease hitherto unknown' (Hawisher, 1987: 145). In the reported studies where word processing did not result in increased revision, it may be that the subjects did not have sufficient exposure to the computer during the course of the research to have learned to take full advantage of the potential of the medium or that they were not sufficiently aware of the various ways in which it could aid in their revising behaviour. As Phinney (1989: 87) notes, 'without specific instruction in using the computer to facilitate the writing process, from prewriting to revision, the computer alone appears to have little effect in changing writing behavior in naive writers'.

In a comprehensive overview of previous research on the effects of word processing in the writing curriculum, Phinney (1989) cites over a dozen studies which show positive effects of word processing on the writing process. In particular, these studies, taken as a group, indicate that word processing:

— made revision easier, resulting in more and different types of revisions;
— altered revision behaviour and increased time spent writing;
— overcame blocking and allowed students to be objective about their writing; and
— improved attitudes toward writing. (Phinney, 1989: 84)

There is also general agreement about certain attitudinal benefits of word processing over traditional approaches to composition. From her overview of the literature, Phinney (1989: 87) concludes:

> Improvement in the affective factors of attitudes toward English and toward writing, motivation to write, time spent writing, and perceptions about one's writing behavior appear to be the major benefits of computer-assisted writing. For second language students, the computer also appears to reduce the fear of errors and to reduce worries about legibility.

Thus, it seems uncontroversial to state that word processing provides benefits which are consistent with, and which may help to implement, a process approach to composition.

A more surface- or product-oriented computerised writing aid that has attracted some interest and initial research is computer-based text analysis. Computer-based text analysis, or text analysis software, uses the special attributes of the computer and some sophisticated programming routines to analyse the frequency and the distribution of certain items in a text and to provide advice to the user for improvement. Ten years ago, only a few such text analysers had been developed. McDaniel's 1987 bibliography of computer-based writing aids (McDaniel, 1987) lists over two dozen such programs which are now widely available. The sophistication of these programs ranges from rudimentary — providing the writer with little more than a report of the number of words, sentences, and paragraphs in a text — to the more sophisticated type of program, or set of programs — providing an analysis of natural language in terms of grammar, punctuation, word choice, and other elements of a text. *Critique*, a new program developed by IBM and the most advanced type of text analyser available at the time of this study, even parses sentences, detailing which parts of speech are filled by the words that occur in a given sentence.

The bulk of research exploring computer-based text analysis has focused on the use at Colorado State University of a set of programs called *Writer's Workbench*. Developed at Bell Laboratories and originally intended for use by technical writers, Writer's Workbench has been modified to make it better suited for university English courses at Colorado State. The Workbench programs are grouped into three principal components: Proofreading, Style, and Organisation (Cherry *et al.*, 1983). The Proofreading component is actually 'five separate programs that check for spelling errors, consecutive occurrences of the same word, punctuation errors, faulty phrasing, and split infinitives' (Cherry *et al.*, 1983: 11). The Style programs provide a great deal of statistical analysis, much of which is based on readability indices. It also underlines all forms of 'be' verbs, as 'be' occurs with passives, nominalizations, and expletives — constructions which, according to the advice given by the program, writers may want to eliminate. The Style program highlights abstract words, comparing the words in a text to a dictionary of abstract words. The Organisation program provides an overview of the content and structure of a piece of writing by deleting everything but headings and the first and last sentences of each paragraph.

Research at Colorado State University has focused on the implementation of *Writer's Workbench* as an integral part of the English composition program. That research has championed several positive claims as to the utility of computer-based text analysis for both first and second language writers (Kiefer &

Smith, 1983; Reid, 1986). One general argument in favour of computer-based text analysis has been the reactions of students and faculty members, which Cherry *et al.* (1983) document as overwhelmingly positive. In addition to these attitudinal factors, the Colorado State researchers have investigated the important question of the effectiveness of *Writer's Workbench* in improving student's writing skills. Early studies at Bell Laboratories had indicated that writers 'using Writer's Workbench not only edit more thoroughly but also learn to edit on their own' (Gingrich *et al.*, 1981: 201). Evaluation of the programs at Colorado State with native writers suggests that 'textual analysis with computers intrigues college writers and speeds learning of editing skills by offering immediate, reliable, and consistent attention to surface features' (Kiefer & Smith, 1983: 202).

Though computer-based text analysis is inherently a late-stage, surface-level or product-oriented approach to assisting composition, Kiefer (1987: 25) claims that there is some evidence that the use of computer-based text analysis prompts writers to go beyond surface-level editing to make content revisions, such as changes in meaning, focus and voice. Her claims are weakened, however, by the fact that the subjects in her study revised their computer-analysed compositions with the assistance and input of an instructor. The computer analysis was used as a point of departure rather than as the focus for revision. It is impossible, as Kiefer admits, to attribute exclusively to computer-based text analysis the 'deeper' level content revisions which her subjects made.

The only published studies to date examining the effect of computer-based text analysis on ESL writers were also conducted at Colorado State University in connection with *Writer's Workbench* (Reid *et al.*, 1983; Reid, 1986). In the most recently published study (Reid, 1986), the progress of ESL students enrolled in a non-credit English composition course who used *Writer's Workbench* was tracked and compared with that of a comparison group that did not use the Workbench. Results indicate that ESL writers using the Workbench programs 'improved their editing and writing skills significantly, whereas students who did not have access to the WWB [Writer's Workbench] did not improve their skills' (Reid, 1986: 179). However, variables other than computer-based text analysis, such as teacher student conferences, classroom discussion of compositions, and motivational factors — for which the researcher did not control — may have affected the outcomes.

The results of studies investigating computer-based text analysis are unclear because of the numerous variables affecting their outcome. The studies cited for *Writer's Workbench* involved students enrolled in English composition classes who received feedback of one sort from the computer as well as other sorts of feedback from instructors and/or peers. Isolating the effect of the computer-based text analysis on the subjects' writing in these studies is difficult, if not impossible — a fact that the researchers themselves admit (Kiefer, 1987: 25; Reid, 1986: 173). Before claims can be made as to the utility of computer-based text analysis, research must be conducted that attempts to isolate the exact effects of computer-based text analysis and to set them in sharper relief as against any effects that may be due to the nature of word processing or to process-oriented aspects of the writing curriculum. The study described in the next section is a first attempt to isolate these effects.

The Investigation

Method

A study was conducted which examined the effects of two different computer-based approaches to individualised work in ESL composition. The first approach centred on use of *Critique*, an experimental text analysis program developed at IBM's Thomas J. Watson Research Center and recently made available to the English Department of the University of Hawaii at Manoa. Though *Critique* provides many of the same types of statistical analysis as *Writer's Workbench* and similar programs, it represents an advance beyond first generation text analysers, since it is the 'first [text analysis] program that can cope with ill-formed sentences' (Creed & Kau, 1988: 62). *Critique* accomplishes its analysis through a 'highly sophisticated, mainframe-based natural language parser and an algorithm for handling ungrammatical sentences: it relaxes its grammar rules one by one until it achieves a successful parse, then determines grammatical errors by noting which rules have been relaxed' (Creed & Kau, 1988: 63). According to Creed & Kau (1988), this parser is unique in its ability to deal with ungrammatical sentences and to provide assistance in correcting them.

For their initial evaluation of *Critique*, the English Department at the University of Hawaii at Manoa designated two Spring 1988 freshman English composition classes for experimental use of the program. Forty disks, or 'places', were reserved on the university's IBM 3081 mainframe computer, and four IBM XT terminals connected by cable to the mainframe were provided in another building for student use. Two of the reserved places were vacated early in the semester after two students dropped the course, presenting an opportunity for research with two ESL writers. The authors decided to investigate the use of *Critique* by these two students through a comparison study that would also involve two writers using word processing alone. The investigation was designed so that the *Critique* students (A Subjects), who can be viewed as the focal subjects of the study, received strictly product-oriented, surface-level tutorial input matching the emphasis of the *Critique* program and centring on the machine-generated feedback. In sharp contrast, the word processing only students (B Subjects), who functioned as comparison subjects, received strictly process-oriented tutorial input. Individualised tutorial assistance at the computer terminal was provided for each subject on a weekly basis by the second author. A detailed preliminary report of the findings of this study appears in Brock (1988).

All subjects used the same word processing program to generate text, and all were exposed to tutorial sessions of approximately equal length with the same person. For all subjects, the tutorial input was designed to reinforce the primary variable in the study, which was the type of approach taken to generation and revision of text by means of the word processing program. In the case of the A Subjects, the tutorial approach centred on text analysis, while in the case of the B Subjects, the tutorial approach centred on the process approach to writing. The difference in the A and B Subjects can be represented as shown in Figure 5.1.

The study set out to test effectiveness claims that had been made in the literature about text analysis (specifically, about *Writer's Workbench*) to see to what extent they would be applicable to *Critique* when used outside of other types of instruction or input to ESL students on their writing. At the same time, the study sought to assess the use of word processing with ESL student writers in a consistently process-oriented approach to composition. The *Critique*-based approach was considered to be a non-standard mode of composition instruction undertaken for the purpose of experimentation. The process-oriented approach was considered to be a relatively standard mode of instruction in composition

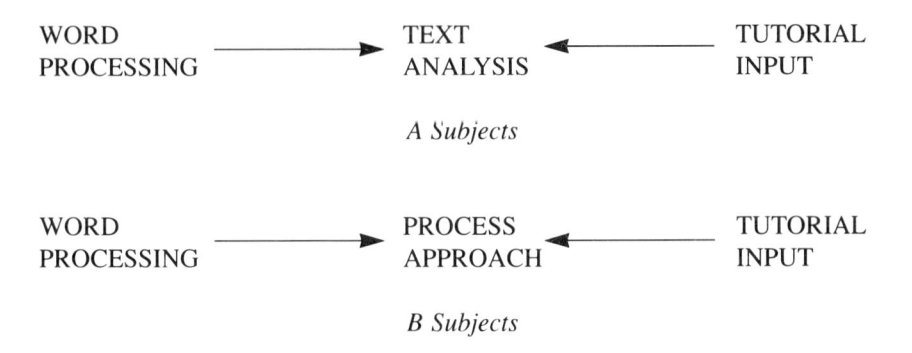

```
WORD                    TEXT                    TUTORIAL
PROCESSING  ─────────▶  ANALYSIS   ◀─────────   INPUT

                       A Subjects


WORD                    PROCESS                 TUTORIAL
PROCESSING  ─────────▶  APPROACH   ◀─────────   INPUT

                       B Subjects
```

FIGURE 5.1 *Contrast in treatments of the groups of subjects.*

which could serve as a basis for comparison of results for the subjects using *Critique*.

The study was designed to compare student attitudes, writing products and revisions encouraged by the text analysis program as compared with the process-oriented tutorial approach. The specific research questions of the study were:

(1) Do the drafts made by the A Subjects differ in length or overall structure from those made by the B Subjects?
(2) How do the revisions made by the A Subjects compare with the revisions made by the B Subjects? Specific questions of interest drawn from previous research with text analysis programs are the following:
   (a) Do the subjects exposed to text analysis (A Subjects) edit more thoroughly than those not exposed to the type of feedback provided by the text analysis program (B Subjects)?
   (b) Do the A Subjects increase their independence in editing through use of the text analysis program?
   (c) Do the A Subjects go beyond surface-level editing to make revisions affecting meaning?
(3) What attitudes are exhibited by the A and B Subjects towards their experiences in the investigation?

Subjects

Four students in an ESL section of freshman composition volunteered for the study after learning that it would involve writing with a computer. The subjects were two Korean males and two Chinese males. The subjects were randomly placed into two groups so that each contained one Korean and one Chinese. Subject 1, a Korean immigrant who had lived in Hawaii for six years, was placed in the group using *Critique* (A Subjects), along with Subject 2, a Chinese immigrant from Vietnam who had lived in Hawaii for five years. Subject 3, a Korean immigrant who came to Hawaii five years before, and Subject 4, a Chinese student from Hong Kong who had been in Hawaii for one year and who had lived in Canada for the two previous years, were placed in the process-oriented group (B Subjects). As shown in Table 5.1, which lists the subjects' writing scores on the University of Hawaii Writing Test (an analytic scoring instrument administered just prior to the period of the study), along with TOEFL scores of two of the subjects, all of the subjects had achieved a relatively advanced level of academic proficiency in English at the time of the study.

TABLE 5.1 *Subjects' placement test scores*

	Years in English-speaking country	Writing placement Test Score*	TOEFL Score	TOEFL Writing Test Score
A Subjects				
Subject 1	6	65	**	**
Subject 2	5	68	567	52
B Subjects				
Subject 3	5	70	**	**
Subject 4	3	69	550	50

* Out of 100 possible points
** Had not taken TOEFL

Materials

All of the subjects were proficient in word processing at the beginning of the study, though each was familiar with a different type of program and a different type of computer. In order to have all subjects writing with the same word processing program and to create compositions which would be compatible with the IBM-based *Critique*, the subjects all used the same IBM-based word processing program, *PFS: Write*, during the investigation. *PFS: Write* is a program noted for its simplicity and ease of use. Subjects all received a two-hour orientation and training session on *PFS: Write* which covered the basic features of the program that would be useful for writing compositions, such as deleting text, inserting text, moving text, and saving completed work. At the conclusion of training, each subject expressed confidence in his ability to use the program.

In addition to training in the use of *PFS: Write*, orientation for the A Subjects included an introduction to *Critique*. These subjects were familiarised with the procedure of uploading text from the terminal to the mainframe for analysis by *Critique*. They were then instructed in the *Critique* analyses. When the program detects an error in a text, it places a one- or two-word message underneath the word or sentence analysed as ungrammatical (see Appendix A for a sample analysis). For example, if the writer has joined two independent clauses with a conjunction but has failed to separate the two with a comma, the message 'MISSING COMMA' appears beneath the conjunction. If the user needs more specific information about the program's analysis, the designated function key, SHOW, is pressed, and additional information is provided in the form of a one- or two-sentence explanation of the analysis. A more extensive explanation, similar to that found in a writing textbook, is provided by pressing the SHOW key again. If the user decides to accept the analysis and to make the suggested changes, the program then re-analyses the sentence. If no error message is detected in the second parse, no error message will appear on the screen.

The A Subjects were instructed in techniques for implementing the revisions suggested by the *Critique* analysis and in procedures for downloading a revised composition, along with the analysis provided by the program, from the mainframe computer to an individual terminal. Procedures for saving the revised compositions and the *Critique* analysis on a computer diskette were also demonstrated.

An attitudinal questionnaire was developed to assess the reaction of subjects to the computer-assisted instruction in terms of ease of use, helpfulness, perceived improvement in writing, and recommendations for future use. The questionnaire, which was written in two slightly different versions, each with the wording adjusted to apply exclusively to either one group or the other, included eight questions to be answered on a five-point Likert scale and six questions to be answered by open-ended response. The questionnaire given to the A Subjects is included as Appendix B.

Procedures

Subjects wrote three compositions, each based on a subtopic of the general theme, 'World Problems and Solutions'. Each composition was completed in a series of three sequential drafts over a three-week period. The preparation sheet given to the subjects for the theme and the individual topics is shown in Appendix D. Each subject met individually for one to one-and-a-half hours with a tutor, the second author, at a convenient time once a week for the nine-week period of the study. Though the time spent with individual students in tutorial sessions varied somewhat, depending on the time needed to complete that week's draft, the total tutorial time over the nine-week period was controlled to be approximately equal for each student. All drafts were written using *PFS: Write* during the sessions with the tutor. The majority of these meetings were tape-recorded.

The tutorial sessions were in addition to the regular instruction which subjects received in their daily ESL writing class. The study was purposely designed to be essentially unrelated to the subjects' class work, though there was undoubtedly some overlap in the type of feedback received on assignments from the tutor and the classroom teacher. Since the investigators worked entirely independently of the classroom instructor and since all subjects received the same classroom input, this variable was not considered in the design of the study or the analysis of results.

In order to sharply distinguish between the subjects using *Critique* and those receiving process-oriented input, a set of contrasting tutoring protocols was developed based on the types of feedback provided by *Critique* and by process approaches to composition as advocated by such authors as Murray (1980), Taylor (1981), Zamel (1982), and Raimes (1983). These protocols, shown in Appendix C, were rigorously followed in the sessions with subjects and provided antithetical treatments for the two groups.

While each subject in the *Critique* group was writing his first draft, the tutor served mainly as an observer. When the first draft was completed, the subject was assisted in using the computer terminal for accessing *Critique*. Each A Subject used the computer analysis to revise the first draft and afterwards was given the opportunity of making other revisions with *PFS: Write*. The second draft was then analysed by *Critique*. In this process, the role played by the tutor was one of technical facilitator, allowing the text analysis feedback to be the primary intervention strategy used to create second and third drafts from a first draft. After completion of the third draft, the process was begun again with another composition written on the general theme.

The B Subjects used *PFS: Write* as a means to generate text on the same general themes as the experimental group. Unlike the A Subjects, however, these subjects interacted with and received feedback from the tutor from the beginning of the writing process to the end (see Tutoring Protocol, Appendix C). The focus was on the process of writing: that is, the act of writing itself was viewed as a way of discovering meaning (Murray, 1980). Before writing, each subject discussed ideas for his composition with the tutor. The tutor asked questions to help clarify and explore ideas (Carnicelli, 1980; Sommers, 1982). The subject was then encouraged to write a first draft, paying little attention in the early stages to organisation, and concentrating instead on exploring ideas. As the subject worked from the first to the second to the final draft, this process of discovering and focusing ideas was repeated.

Attitudes were assessed at the beginning of the study and throughout the nine weeks by discussion and observation of the subjects by the tutor, and by analysis of the tape recordings of sessions. In addition, written responses were solicited on the attitude questionnaire at the end of the study.

Analysis of drafts

Each draft was saved on a computer disk and later printed out for hand-coded analysis. Revisions between drafts were highlighted and coded according to categories adapted from Raimes (1985) and developed by the authors. The second author performed the initial analysis, which was fine-tuned in discussion with the first author, who helped to decide questionable cases. As shown in Figure 5.2, the categories for coding revisions are of two major types, *surface-level editing*, i.e. changes not affecting meaning, and *deep-level revision*, i.e. changes affecting meaning. Individual changes classified as *addition*, *deletion*, and *substitution* might be instances of either surface-level editing or deep-level revisions affecting meaning. The following are examples of changes in these categories which were tallied as surface-level editing not affecting meaning:

Substitution

I am ⟶ I'm
kind of ⟶ somewhat

Addition

lets imagine ⟶ let us imagine
four steps to be successful ⟶ four steps in order to be successful

Deletion

class, and eventually ... ⟶ class; eventually ...

Other categories of change are exclusively either surface-level editing — viz., *spelling, word form, punctuation, verb form or tense*, and *sentence structure* — or deep-level revisions — viz., *reorganisation* and *combination*.

In addition to the analysis performed by hand, a *Critique* summary analysis was performed on each of the drafts in both groups (see 'Summary' section of the sample analysis in Appendix A). Table 5.2 compares the characteristics of each composition draft in the categories of: (1) number of paragraphs, sentences, and words; and (2) number and ratio of long and short sentences.

Findings

Comparison of Critique summary analysis

A comparison of the summary analyses provided by Critique, as shown in Table 5.2, uncovers a striking difference in length of drafts between the A and B Subjects. Second and third drafts show the B Subjects increasing the length of

Surface-level editing	Deep-level revisions
a addition[1]	a addition
del deletion[2]	del deletion
sub substitution[3]	sub substitution
sp spelling	r reorganisation[6]
wf word form[4]	c combination[7]
p punctuation	
v verb form or tense	
ss sentence structure[5]	

(Adapted from Raimes, 1985)

[1] Refers to addition of a word [a(w)], phrase [a(phr)], or sentence [a(s)]. These coding symbols are used for cases of surface-level editing and for cases of deep-level revision affecting meaning.
[2] Refers to deletion of a word [del(w)], phrase [del(phr)], or sentence [del(s)]. These coding symbols are used for cases of surface-level editing and for cases of deep-level revision affecting meaning.
[3] Refers to substituting a word [sub(w)], phrase [sub(phr)], or sentence [sub(s)], for a previously used word, phrase, or sentence. These coding symbols are used for cases of surface-level editing and for cases of deep-level revision affecting meaning.
[4] Refers to a change in word form which does not affect meaning.
[5] Refers to a change in sentence structure which does not affect meaning.
[6] Refers to a major reorganisation within a paragraph or across paragraphs which alters meaning.
[7] Refers to the combination of two sentences or paragraphs.

FIGURE 5.2 *Coding categories*

their compositions substantially, while no such increase is seen in the compositions of the A Subjects. The compositions of Subject 3 increased an average of 398 words from first to third drafts. Subject 4, a more reluctant reviser, increased by an average of 110 words the length of his compositions from first to third drafts. This increase, though much less than that observed for Subject 3, is still much greater than that of either of the A Subjects, whose compositions increased by only eleven words or fewer from the first to the third drafts. Half of the compositions written with *Critique* were actually shorter on the third draft

TABLE 5.2 *Comparisons of length measures across drafts*

Compositions 1–3	Draft 1	Draft 2	Draft 2
A Subjects:			
Total number of paragraphs	4.7	4.7	4.7
Total number of sentences	32.3	32.5	34.0
Total number of words	533.7	535.7	532.0
Total number of short sentences*	6.7	7.2	7.8
Total number of long sentences**	3.8	4.0	3.3
Ratio of short to long sentences	1.8	1.8	2.4
B Subjects:			
Total number of paragraphs	4.3	4.7	4.7
Total number of sentences	24.2	32.0	36.5
Total number of words	490.8	657.3	744.7
Total number of short sentences*	1.2	1.8	2.7
Total number of long sentences**	7.0	9.0	10.2
Ratio of short to long sentences	0.2	0.2	0.3

* Sentences of 10 words or less
** Sentences of 25 words or more

than on the first. The average change for Subject 1 from first to third drafts was a decrease of 7 words, while for Subject 2 it was an increase of 4 words.

With the exception of Subject 3, subjects showed a small increase or a slight decrease in the number of sentences from one draft to the next; Subject 3 showed a larger increase in number of sentences across drafts matching the comparably larger increase in number of words. In 88% (21/24) of the cases, the number of paragraphs remained unchanged across second and third drafts of each composition (6 per subject). The increase in number of words in the compositions of the B Subjects is therefore not in general reflected in a greater number of paragraphs. Rather, the net result of the increase in words was that the B Subjects produced longer paragraphs.

Analysis of types of revisions

The types of revisions made by subjects in the two groups is an area of substantial difference. Table 5.3 summarises the kinds of changes made by subjects

PROCESS AND PRODUCT APPROACHES 93

TABLE 5.3 Total number and types of changes

	Surface-level editing	% of total	Deep-level revisions	% of total	Grand total
A Subjects					
Subject 1	72	85	13	15	85
Subject 2	140	97	4	3	144
B Subjects					
Subject 3	64	42	88	58	152
Subject 4	28	41	41	59	69

in both groups. Subject 3, a process writer, made the most changes of the four writers. Of the 152 changes made by Subject 3 in going from the first draft to the third, 64 (42%) were surface-level editing changes, that is, changes classified as not affecting meaning. 88 (58%) were deep-level revisions, that is, changes classified as affecting meaning. Although the fewest changes between drafts were effected by Subject 4, the other process writer, the percentages of the two major categories of changes are almost identical to those of Subject 3. Out of a total of 69 changes, 28 (41%) were surface-level editing changes, and 41 (59%) were changes affecting meaning.

A much higher proportion — more than double the percentage for the B Subjects — of changes made by the A Subjects were of the surface-level editing type. The compositions of Subject 2 contained the second greatest number of changes, of which 97% (140 out of 144) were surface-level editing changes and only 3% were deep-level revisions. Only 18 (13%) of the changes made by Subject 2 were changes not prompted by *Critique*. Of those 18, only two were revisions which altered meaning. The compositions of Subject 1, the other member of the *Critique* group, contained a total of 85 changes, 72 (85%) of which were surface-level editing changes and 13 (15%) of which were deep-level revisions. 26 (31%) of the changes made by Subject 1 were not prompted by *Critique*. Of these, only five altered meaning.

The report of subjects' revising behaviour would not be complete without a description of the analyses offered by *Critique* that were ignored by subjects using the program and of subjects' behaviour in the cases where the program's analyses were incorrect. The most frequent analyses offered by *Critique* which were not acted on by subjects using the program included: SENTENCE MAY BE UNCLEAR, SENTENCE IS TOO LONG, SENTENCE IS TOO DIFFICULT TO PROCESS, PARAGRAPH IS TOO LONG, and READABILITY

LEVEL IS TOO HIGH. Unlike other *Critique*-generated analyses which suggest, for example, the correct verb form or the position in which to place a comma, the analyses listed above do not offer the writer specific guidance about how to correct the indicated problem. It was in these cases that the A Subjects were most likely to make no changes at all.

Critique, though accurate in most of its analyses, parses incorrectly on occasion and then provides incorrect advice to the user. Dr. Robert Chandler, whose composition classes at the University of Hawaii used *Critique* during Spring semester 1988, estimates that the program is 75% to 85% accurate in its analyses (personal communication, 1988). *Critique*'s analyses of compositions written by subjects using the program for this study yielded a total of 240 suggestions for revision, many of which were incorrect or questionable. 98 out of the 240 (41%) were 'UNRECOGNISED WORD' messages; the other 142 were of various types. Even if we exclude from these 240 the incorrect analyses of spelling, as when a rare word or brand name not included in the program's dictionary was deemed an error, and some questionable cases in which the analysis was based on statistical data alone, there is still a remainder of 18 (7.5%) incorrect suggestions provided by the program. Of these 18 incorrect suggestions, half were accepted by the A Subjects and incorporated into their compositions.

Attitudes

The tutor's observations during the tutoring sessions and the analysis of tape recordings of tutoring sessions revealed that the initial reaction of subjects using *Critique* was similar to that reported by Kiefer & Smith (1983). They were intrigued, even amazed, at the program's ability to parse their sentences and highlight misspellings, ungrammatical constructions, and subject–verb disagreement. Both of the A Subjects learned to use the program quickly, though Subject 2 seemed much more tentative when using the program in the beginning than did Subject 1. However, he became much more relaxed and confident in his ability to use the program with experience and exhibited favourable attitudes towards the program at the conclusion of the nine-week period of the study, commenting: 'I like using Critique Because I can correct my writing error with out penalty'. The initial enthusiasm of Subject 1 waned somewhat during the course of the study, as comments he made to the tutor during the nine weeks indicated. Although he indicated in response to the questionnaire that *Critique* had been only somewhat useful in improving his writing, his attitude toward the program was still positive in his open-ended written responses, commenting: 'I think it is fascinating how it corrects sentences' and 'It helped me to think and put down your own ideas on the screen and let the computer correct the mistakes'.

The B Subjects expressed how easy it was to make changes in their compositions with the computer as compared to more traditional modes of writing. When asked if the time spent with the computer and receiving feedback from the tutor had proved helpful, both B Subjects responded positively. Subject 3 replied that he 'used to write a paragraph and stop' without making further changes. In contrast, he stated that 'now I have to go back and write more, add more ideas and make my writing clear'. Subject 4, a more reluctant reviser than Subject 3, stated that the experience had caused him to be more conscious of the reader. He said that the time spent writing on the computer and receiving feedback from the tutor had helped him to 'think about what the reader of my paper will think when he reads'.

Discussion of Findings

Since *Critique* is not designed to deal with the writing process as a whole but rather with late-stage editing concerns, it is surface-oriented, emphasising sentence structure and mechanics. This inherent emphasis of the text analysis program was reinforced by the tutor throughout the study with the A Subjects. In contrast, tutorial feedback for the B Subjects was structured so that a semantic focus — one centred on generating, organising, and developing ideas — was paramount. Revision in such an approach is an integral part of the process of discovering and refining meaning. Taylor (1981: 3) notes that writing itself can serve as a 'facilitator of thought and help to shape and refine ideas which are not fully formed'. Such an approach mitigates against the use of revision only for editing mechanical features. Revision instead becomes a powerful, integral tool in the act of generating text through writing.

The two groups in this study showed some differences in behaviour which may be attributable to the two different treatments they received. The difference in overall length of first to third drafts is a main result. The increased length of compositions from first to third drafts of the B Subjects perhaps represents an effect of word processing in the context of the process approach, which encourages experimentation with language, elaboration of ideas, and generation of content in a train-of-thought process. The general increase in the size of paragraphs across the drafts of the B Subjects can be taken to be a rough indicator of an increase in the amount of information per paragraph. Although the quality and content of drafts was not assessed in the present study, an increase in the size of these discourse units and in overall length of compositions can be viewed as progress in development of ideas through the elaboration of material already generated in previous drafts. This result is particularly intriguing in light of evidence, as cited in Wresch (1987: 16), that words-per-paragraph and words-per-composition ratios may correlate positively with independent assessments of essay quality.

The lack of increase in number of words and paragraphs from first to third drafts of the A Subjects can be interpreted as indicating that the amount of information in their compositions remained essentially constant from one draft to the next. This interpretation is reinforced by the observation of the tutor that the A Subjects did not revise through a process of elaboration but rather through a process of editing content already generated. If it can be concluded from the longer paragraphs in non-initial drafts of the B Subjects that the combination of word processing and process-oriented conferencing enhanced their creative revision process, then it also appears that the use of *Critique* in combination with word processing inhibited creative revision for the A Subjects.

Critique is dubbed an 'interactive' program, implying that there is a kind of give-and-take conversation between the program and the user. Though the analogy is not completely accurate, Subject 2 did carry on a kind of conversation with himself when using the program, as documented by the tape recordings of his sessions with *Critique* in the presence of the tutor. Sometimes when viewing the analysis provided by *Critique*, he would ask, 'What's wrong with that?' After pushing the SHOW key and receiving an explanation of the analysis, he would often exclaim, 'Oh, yeah', as if a light of understanding had been turned on in his mind. This behaviour pattern could be taken to be a sign of a self-monitoring facility developing on the basis of feedback from *Critique*. The general pattern, however, was of the A Subjects becoming increasingly dependent on *Critique*. On the basis of the behaviour of these two subjects, therefore, it cannot be concluded that *Critique* promotes self-monitoring and self-correction of surface-level errors.

One of the criticisms aimed at computer-based text analysis has been that such programs may encourage writers to do little more than tailor their writing to fit the suggestions prompted by the program (Wresch, 1987: 67). This criticism is particularly apt in those cases where the program's analysis is wrong, yet the writer makes the changes suggested in the analysis. Both of the A Subjects in fact had difficulty distinguishing those cases where the analysis provided by *Critique* was wrong from those where it was correct. Though repeatedly alerted to the fact that the program was sometimes wrong in its analyses, both students tended to make whatever change was suggested by *Critique*. Both appeared more interested in satisfying *Critique* and having it parse their sentence as 'correct' — i.e. having a sentence reanalysed by *Critique* after a change had been made and then having no error message appear —than they were in examining the validity of the program's suggestions. Subject 2 seemed to take particular satisfaction in making changes suggested by the program and then seeing the sentence re-parsed and found free of error.

Such reliance on the program as judge and jury —particularly when an analysis has not done justice to a text — is counterproductive, and possibly harmful, for the student who needs to develop an internal 'error monitor'. Like other non-proficient writers, subjects in the present study who revised with *Critique* appeared to become 'trapped within the sentence ... worried about accuracy ... concerned with vocabulary and not with concepts' (Raimes, 1983: 83). Rather than writing for meaning, the A Subjects wrote to meet the standards of the computer program. Focusing on the analysis offered by *Critique*, they made superficial repairs to sentences and left meaning unattended.

The A Subjects relied on an external monitor, the computer-based text analysis program, for assistance in revision, while the B Subjects were steered toward dependence on their own internal monitor. During the course of the study, the B Subjects seemed to have internalised many of the tenets of the process approach, focusing to a large extent, on meaning. It is interesting to note, however, that even though the tutor never called attention to surface-level problems, the B Subjects gave attention to this kind of editing. The majority of the changes made by these subjects were revisions affecting meaning, but at the same time a large proportion of changes involved surface-level editing. This result is inconsistent with the contention that surface editing will go unattended when the focus is primarily on writing as a process of discovering meaning. The types of changes made by subjects revising with *Critique*, however, do not support the converse of this argument, i.e. the claim (e.g. by Kiefer, 1987) that use of text analysis programs promotes 'deep' editing.

Although the A Subjects maintained favourable attitudes overall, the reaction of Subject 1 to his experience was not wholly positive throughout the study. Subject 1 seemed particularly deflated to learn that there were some grammar problems which the program overlooked and times when the program's analysis was simply incorrect. He seemed disappointed that the program was not an infallible guide, and so grew increasingly sceptical of the its ability to improve his writing skills. It is possible that this subject would have had a more positive experience overall if he had had more guidance from the tutor in distinguishing correct and incorrect analyses. The consistently positive attitudes of the B Subjects appear to stem from the combined effects of word processing and the process-oriented feedback offered by the tutor. Without the tutor, it is doubtful that the B Subjects would have exploited the word processing program in the same manner and to the same extent as they did in this particular investigation. Conversely, it would appear that the A Subjects were inhibited by the focus on the text analysis feedback from fully exploiting the potential of word processing in their work.

Conclusion

This study has contributed to the investigation of the application of computers in ESL composition, comparing the effects of two types of computer-assisted tutorials using word processing, one of which centred on computer-generated text analysis and the other of which centred on a human-facilitated process approach. The findings of the study are summarised below with reference to each of the research questions.

(1) Do the drafts made by the A Subjects differ in length or overall structure from those made by the B Subjects?

The A Subjects, who used IBM's *Critique* as a focus for their revision, wrote shorter drafts and shorter paragraphs than did the B Subjects, who received process-oriented tutorial assistance as a focus for their work.

(2) How do the revisions made by the A Subjects compare with the revisions made by the B Subjects? Specific questions of interest drawn from previous research with text analysis programs are the following:
   (a) Do the subjects exposed to text analysis (A Subjects) edit more thoroughly than those not exposed to the type of feedback provided by the text analysis program (B Subjects)?
   (b) Do the A Subjects increase their independence in editing through use of the text analysis program?
   (c) Do the A Subjects go beyond surface-level editing to make revisions affecting meaning?

In reference to point (a), no clear result emerges as to the thoroughness of editing. There was no trend differentiating the two groups of subjects in terms of number of revisions; each group contained one subject who made a substantially larger number of revisions than the other subject in the same group. Subjects in both groups made surface-level editing changes, although the proportion of such changes was much greater in the writing of the A Subjects than in that of the B Subjects. In reference to point (b), it appears that the A Subjects tended to become less independent in their editing, relying increasingly on the *Critique* analyses for guidance. In reference to point (c), the A Subjects made fewer revisions affecting meaning than did the subjects in the comparison group.

(3) What attitudes are exhibited the A and B Subjects towards their experiences in the investigation?

The A Subjects believed that *Critique* improved their writing, though one of two subjects became less enthusiastic in this belief as the study progressed. The B Subjects had positive attitudes and expressed the view that word processing and conferencing facilitated revision.

The results of this small-scale study suggest that word processing coupled with conferencing may help to promote in a relatively short period of time some of the aims of the process approach to writing, such as development of an internal monitor, favourable attitudes towards writing and revising, and meaningful and extensive revision of written drafts. At the same time, they indicate that reliance on word processing and text analysis will not produce comparable effects in written drafts in a comparable period of time and that initial confidence in the usefulness of this type of program may diminish over time. The results further suggest that use of a text analysis program such as *Critique* could be counterproductive for non-native writers if employed as a main source of feedback for revision. If such a resource is to be added to an ESL composition program, clear guidelines will need to be developed for its effective use by teachers and students.

The results of this study thus advise caution in any wholesale endorsement of computer-based text analysis as a writing aid for ESL students. The optimism expressed for computer-based text analysis in previous studies may need to be tempered by a careful examination of how this composition tool can best be exploited in an ESL context. Further study that involves a larger number of subjects, in individualised and non-individualised modes of instruction, must be completed before any definitive answers can be given to questions concerning what place different kinds of computer-assistance might have in the ESL writing curriculum.

IBM's *Critique* marks the advent of a new generation of computer-based text analysis programs which are capable of dealing with natural language and of analysing syntactic structure with a high degree of sophistication. There may well be a role for computer-based text analysis as an editing tool for non-initial drafts in which surface-level problems are the primary focus. Programs such as *Critique* may prove especially beneficial if coupled with process-oriented guidance and if used not in the introspective, 'internal' phase of drafting, but saved for an 'external' phase of writing in which considerations of audience become primary (Murray, 1980). As text analysis programs become more and more accurate in analysing syntax, such a role may prove plausible, and computer-based text analysis could become a valuable tool for ESL writers.

As this technology develops, more and more ESL teachers will be offered the opportunity to incorporate computer-based text analysis and word processing into their writing programs. While some focus on surface-level concerns is essential in ESL, as in native-speaker writing programs, the evidence does not clearly suggest that text analysers, in and of themselves, improve the writing of ESL students. At the same time, use of word processing alone will not automatically produce more or better writing than pencil-and-paper means. As in all other aspects of the curriculum, in the area of ESL composition decisions must be made about how best to use the available tools and techniques to achieve the goals of the institution and to meet the needs of the students served by that institution.

Neither text analysers nor word processors are the 'be-all and end-all' of the ESL writing course, that is, neither one provides a stand-alone medium for learning to write in a second language. Yet it seems that they may both have value if used in certain ways and for certain populations in a carefully designed writing program. However, before investing the time, the money and the energy to develop a computer-assisted component of a writing course, the classroom teacher or curriculum developer will naturally want to have an idea of the ways in which the computer medium can be used and the type of instruction which is likely to prove most beneficial in a given setting. Controlled studies and comparative research such as that described here will help to build up the research base from which the practitioner can glean useful information for making decisions about the most appropriate place for computers in an ESL writing curriculum.

Appendix A

Sample analysis generated by *Critique*

```
        One of the major problems we face in United State is
Aids.   What is AIDS anyway?  AIDS is a virus that attacts the
                                                 <1 SPELL>
immune system in our body.   Why is that we Americans make big
                          <2 FRAGMENT?
issue of AIDS?  Is it because AIDS have great impact on
                   2>
everyone?   Yes because it is matter of life and death for
those who has AIDS and for those who doesn't have AIDS. This
overhelming disease has no mercy for AIDS victims.   It not
<3 SPELL 3>
necessary that AIDS will be spread just by body contact or
sharing of utencils such as toilet or being with the person
          <4 SPELL>
who has the symptom of AIDS virus.   I think that catching
                                   <5 DIFFICULT
AIDS could have been prevented only if everyone have the
knowledge of what is AIDS and what causes AIDS and what is
the effect when you have an AIDS.   There is many ways of
                                  5>
catching AIDS but majorities of the people who have AIDS has
recieved AIDS is through unprotected sex, introvaineous drug
<6 SPELL>                                      <7 SPELL   7>
and infected woman passing AIDS during childs birth.
                                     <8 SPELL>


Aids is spread through unprotected sex such as, not using
condom or having sex with more than one person.   It means
<9 SPELL>
it will increase the chance of passing AIDS or recieving
                                                <10 SPELL>
AIDS.   AIDS is usually spread when opposite sex or same sex
                                          <11 TOO MANY MODS>
exchanges body fluid through any means of intercourse.   Also
         <11>                                            <12
 happens when there is a tare on the outer skin of the sex
<14 MISSING COMMA?>      <13 SPELL>
while doing sex.  It is very obvious that it is more likely
      FRAGMENT? 12>
to catch AIDS when a person does not use condom while having
                                                <15 SPELL>
sex with more than one person.   Another way of catching AIDS
      <16 MISSING COMMA>            <17 FRAGMENT?
through deep wet kissing with sore on the mouth.
                                             17>
Another way of catching Aids is through sharing of needle.
It usually occurs to those who use drug by injecting needle
into their vain and passing it to another drug user to use
the same needle.   While sharing needle, small amount of blood
is being carry to another drug user.   This small amount of
```

Appendix A continued

```
blood might hold AIDS virus which could be transmitted to
another drug user.  It is more likely to recieve AIDS because
                                              <18 SPELL>
needle is been injected directly into the vain.
        <19 MISSING COMMA?>

Another way of passing AIDS is when an infected mother gives
<20 UNCLEAR?>              <21 USAGE>
                              <21>
birth to a child.  It passed to a child as how gene is been
               20>
passed down to a child.  This AIDS is just as bad as catching
                   <22> <22 AID>
from another person through sex or sharing of needle with
another AIDS victims.  This is very unfair for the child
<23 23>        <23 victim>
because a child usually dies around after two years.  The
child dies because his or her immune system is taken over by
AIDS virus and can not fight of other foreign disease which
helps to speed up the death of a child.

In conclusion you will find that AIDS is a serious matter to
those already have AIDS virus.  To them it is a life and
death and fighting everyday of their life to vanish AIDS
              <24 USAGE?>
virus.  Scientists are studying and careful research to come
up with the cure but it is very difficult and unable to find
any cure for the AIDS victims.  My advice for other as well
as myself is to learn more about AIDS.

1. UNRECOGNIZED WORD
     attracts
     attacks
     attract
     attaches
2. POSSIBLE SENTENCE FRAGMENT
     This segment of text may not be a complete
     sentence. Make sure that it has a subject
     and verb, and that it is correctly worded.
3. UNRECOGNIZED WORD
     overwhelming
4. UNRECOGNIZED WORD
     utensils
5. SENTENCE TOO DIFFICULT TO PROCESS
     This sentence is too long or too complex for CRITIQUE
     to process. It should probably be simplified.
6. UNRECOGNIZED WORD
     received
     relieved
     receiver
     receives
7. UNRECOGNIZED WORD
     interpolating
     interrogating
```

Appendix A continued

```
     extraneous
     interleaving
     interlocking
     interplaying
 8. UNRECOGNIZED WORD
     chills
     child
     chides
     childish
     childly
     chilies
 9. UNRECOGNIZED WORD
     condor
     condemn
     condole
     condone
     condors
     conform
10. UNRECOGNIZED WORD
     receiving
     relieving
11. TOO MANY NOUNS AND ADJECTIVES PRECEDING THE HEAD NOUN
     Consider eliminating some of the underscored words
     or moving them to the right of the head noun.
12. POSSIBLE SENTENCE FRAGMENT
     This segment of text may not be a complete
     sentence. Make sure that it has a subject
     and verb, and that it is correctly worded.
13. UNRECOGNIZED WORD
     take
     tale
     tame
     tape
     tars
     tart
14. COMMA PROBABLY MISSING BEFORE SUBJUNCTIVE SUBORDINATE CLAUSE

     Insert a comma after the underscored word.
15. UNRECOGNIZED WORD
     condor
     condemn
     condole
     condone
     condors
     conform
16. MISSING COMMA AFTER SUBORDINATE CLAUSE
     Insert a comma after the underscored word (or
     before the new clause).
17. POSSIBLE SENTENCE FRAGMENT
     This segment of text may not be a complete
     sentence. Make sure that it has a subject
     and verb, and that it is correctly worded.
18. UNRECOGNIZED WORD
     receive
```

Appendix A continued

```
       received
       receiver
       receives
       relieve
19. COMMA PROBABLY MISSING AFTER SUBORDINATE CLAUSE
    Insert a comma after the underscored word (or
    before the new clause).
20. SENTENCE MAY BE UNCLEAR
    CRITIQUE has identified multiple structures for this
    sentence. You may want to rephrase it to make it clearer.
21. INCORRECT "IS WHEN" CONSTRUCTION
    Consider using "that" or a noun (such as "the
    case," "the time") instead of "when." It is also
    possible to use a different verb instead of "is."
22. NUMBER DISAGREEMENT BETWEEN PREMODIFIER AND NOUN
    AID
23. NUMBER DISAGREEMENT BETWEEN PREMODIFIER AND NOUN
    victim
24. PROBABLE CONFUSION OF "EVERYDAY" AND "EVERY DAY"
    Replace EVERYDAY with EVERY DAY

SUMMARY ANALYSIS
File:
   Flesch/Kincaid readability level 7.71
   Total number of paragraphs 5
   Total number of headings 0
   Total number of sentences 30
   Total number of words 540
   Total number of verbs 63
   Total number of passive verbs 5
   Average number of syllables per word 1.38

Paragraphs:
   Total number of paragraphs 5
   Average paragraph length in words 108
   Average paragraph length in sentences 6
   Shortest paragraph in words 76
   Shortest paragraph in sentences 4
   Longest paragraph in words 173
   Longest paragraph in sentences 10

Sentences:
   Total number of sentences 30
   5 Short  (10 words or fewer)
   7 Long   (25 words or more)
   17 Simple
   12 Complex
   0 Compound
   1 Compound-complex
   28 Active
   2 Passive
   28 Declarative
   0 Imperative
   2 Interrogative
```

Appendix A continued

```
0 Mixed
Average sentence length in words 18
Shortest sentence in words 4
Longest sentence in words 33

Percentages:
  7% of the verbs are passive verbs
 16% of the sentences are short
 23% of the sentences are long
 56% of the sentences are simple
 40% of the sentences are complex
  0% of the sentences are compound
  3% of the sentences are compound-complex
 93% of the sentences are active
  6% of the sentences are passive
 93% of the sentences are declarative
  0% of the sentences are imperative
  6% of the sentences are interrogative
  0% of the sentences are mixed
```

Appendix B

Questionnaire given to *Critique* subjects

1.	Did you find Critique easy or difficult to use?	EASY 5 4	DIFFICULT 3 2 1
2.	Were the suggestions given to you by the program easy or difficult to use?	EASY 5 4	DIFFICULT 3 2 1
3.	Was it easy or difficult to make changes in your composition when using Critique?	EASY 5 4	DIFFICULT 3 2 1
4.	In general, did you find the suggestions given to you by Critique to be helpful or not?	HELPFUL 5 4	NOT HELPFUL 3 2 1
5.	In general, how much do you think using Critique improved your compositions: a lot or none?	A LOT 5 4 3	NONE 2 1
6.	If you have the opportunity to use Critique in the future, do you think you will do so?	YES 5 4 3	NO 2 1
7.	Do you think other students at UH would find Critique helpful to their writing?	YES 5 4 3	NO 2 1
8.	Would you recommend Critique to other students?	YES 5 4 3	NO 2 1

Appendix C

Instructional protocol

For subjects using text analysis, the tutor:

Will	Will Not
Discuss suggestions offered by Critique (though not offering advice)	Discuss matters of content, organization, transitions, or coherence
Help the subject understand the analysis offered by *Critique* by explaining program metalanguage	Point out any problem area not flagged by *Critique*
Make sure the subject knows how to use the program thoroughly	Engage in pre-writing or other tutoring activities designed to aid the writer in clarifying his ideas
Help the subject input whatever changes he accepts from the *Critique* analysis	
* The emphasis is on *Critique* from beginning to end of the writing process, using the computer analysis for decisions concerning revision and clarification of drafts. When asked about issues of content, organisation, or any issue raised by a subject that has not been raised by *Critique*, the tutor will ask, 'What does *Critique* say?'	* The emphasis is on using the computer as the primary, if not the sole, writing tutor. The tutor's role is to facilitate the subjects' use of the computer and to observe the types of revisions that occur when *Critique* is used by an ESL writer.

For subjects using a process approach, the tutor:

Will	Will Not
Engage in pre-writing exploration of ideas, i.e. 'talking out' ideas	Correct punctuation, spelling, grammar
Encourage 'free writing'	Correct fragments or run-ons
Ask questions that help to generate and refine ideas	Require action verbs, delete *be* verbs, expunge passives
Ask about focus, audience and purpose	Require variety in sentence length

Ask students to 'nutshell' ideas and purpose Work on organisation of ideas	Correct case usage or subject–verb agreement Combine sentences
Ask students about logical progression of ideas	Cross out instances of wordiness or repetition
Ask questions about word choice (only) if meaning is unclear	Correct or suggest idioms
Discuss introductions and conclusions	Fix mixed metaphors or non-parallel constructions
Work on coherence of ideas and transition between ideas in a general way	Place misplaced modifiers Correct tense or person shift
* The key is to always encourage the subjects to use the computer to insert, delete, and move ideas. The focus is on using the computer to generate, organise, and refine ideas. The emphasis is thus on the process of writing used to generate, organise and refine ideas.	* Correct any matters of mechanics or style that do not obscure meaning. Sentence-level problems are not considered important unless they confuse or obstruct meaning. When asked about these kinds of problems, the tutor will ask, 'What do you think is best?'

Appendix D

Composition topic given to subjects

WORLD PROBLEMS AND SOLUTIONS

This semester we will work on three compositions. Each should deal with a world problem and with a solution to that problem that you or others have suggested. Some suggested areas from which you might choose a topic include: problems in a particular country, state or city; problems in politics, science, government, industry, agriculture, education, etc.; problems faced by a particular groups of people; other problems that you wish to write about. Think about a problem that concerns or interests you. Some questions that might help you think about what to write include: Why and how is this a problem? Who is affected by this problem? How are they affected? Is this a problem that can be solved easily or will it take a long time for a solution to be found? Who could solve this problem? How? What benefits would come from solving this problem? Why has a solution not been found? Can you offer a solution?

References

BROCK, M. N. (1988) *The computer as writing tutor: Is there a place in the process for computer-based text analysis?* Unpublished manuscript, Department of English as a Second Language. Honolulu, HI: University of Hawaii at Manoa.

CARNICELLI, T. (1980) The writing conference: A one-to-one conversation. In T. R. Donovan & B. W. McClelland (eds), *Eight Approaches to Teaching Composition.* Urbana, IL: National Council of Teachers of English.

CHERRY, L., FOX, M., FRASE, L., GINGRICH, P., KEENAN, S. & MACDONALD, N. (1983) Computer aids for text analysis, *Bell Laboratories Record*, May/June, 10–16.

COLLIER, R. (1983) The word processor and revision strategies, *College Composition and Communication*, 35: 2, 134–55.

CREED, W., & J. KAU (1988) *A Project to Implement IBM's Experimental Writing Program, Critique, in English 100 Classes.* Proposal to the Educational Improvement Fund. Honolulu, HI: University of Hawaii at Manoa.

DAIUTE, C. (1984) Performance limits on writers. In R. BEACH & L. BRIDWELL (eds), *New Directions in Composition Research.* New York: Gildford.

DAIUTE, C. (1986) Physical and cognitive factors in revising: Insights from studies with computers, *Research in the Teaching of English*, 20: 1, 141–59.

GINGRICH, P., *et al.* (1981) Writer's Workbench trials: Final report. Cited in Kiefer & Smith (1983).

HARRIS, J. (1985) Student writers and word processing: A preliminary evaluation, *College Composition and Commmunication*, 36: 3, 323–30.

HAWISHER, G. (1987) The effects of word processing on the revision strategies of college freshmen, *Research in the Teaching of English*, 21: 1, 145–60.

HOOT, J. L. & S. B. SILVERN (1989) *Writing with Computers in the Early Grades.* New York: Teachers College Press.

KIEFER, K. (1987) Revising on a word processor: What's happened, what's ahead, *ADE Bulletin*, 87: 1, 24–27.

KIEFER, K. & C. SMITH (1983) Textual analysis with computers: Tests of Bell Laboratories' computer software, *Research in the Teaching of English*, 17: 3, 201–14.

LUTZ, J. (1987) A study of professional and experienced writers revising and editing at the computer with pen and paper, *Research in the Teaching of English*, 21: 3, 398–421.

MCDANIEL, E. (1987) Bibliography of text-analysis and writing-instruction software, *Journal of Advanced Composition*, 7: 1, 139–169.

MURRAY, D. (1980) Writing as a process: How writing finds its own meaning. In T. R. DONOVAN & B. W. MCCLELLAND (eds), *Eight Approaches to Teaching Composition.* Urbana, IL: National Council of Teachers of English.

PEYTON, J. K. & T. BATSON (1986) Computer networking: Making connections between speech and writing, *ERIC/CLL News Bulletin*, 10: 1, 1–3.

PFS: Write. Mountain View, CA: Software Publishing Corporation.

PHINNEY, M. (1989) Computers, composition, and second language teaching. In M. C. Pennington (ed.), *Teaching Languages with Computers: The State of the Art.* La Jolla, CA: Athelstan.

PIPER, A. (1987) Helping learners to write: A role for the word processor, *ELT Journal*, 41: 1, 122–24.

RAIMES, A. (1983) Anguish as a second language? Remedies for composition teachers. In A. FREEMAN, I. PRINGLE & J. YALDEN (eds), *Learning to Write: First Language/Second Language.* New York: Longman.

— (1985) What unskilled ESL students do as they write: A classroom study of composing, *TESOL Quarterly*, 19: 2, 229–258.

REID, J. (1986) Using the Writer's Workbench in composition teaching and testing. In C.

W. STANSFIELD (ed.), *Technology and Language Testing*. Washington, DC: Teachers of English to Speakers of Other Languages.

REID, J., M. LINDSTROM & D. LARSON (1983) Computer-assisted text for ESL students, *CALICO Journal*, 1: 1, 40–46.

SOMMERS, N. (1982) Responding to student writing, *College Composition and Communication*, 33: 2, 148–156.

TAYLOR, B. (1981) Content and written form: A two-way street, *TESOL Quarterly*, 15: 1, 5–13.

WRESCH, W. (1987) *A Practical Guide to Computer Uses in the English/language Arts Classroom*. Englewood Cliffs, NJ: Prentice-Hall.

ZAMEL, V. (1982) Writing: The process of discovering meaning, *TESOL Quarterly*, 16: 2, 195–209.

6 Models of the Role of the Computer in Second Language Development

BERNARD MOHAN
University of British Columbia, Canada

Introduction

Early work on computers and language learning was highly concentrated on the production and evaluation of software designed to teach language. Naturally, the underlying assumption was that the computer would act as a language teacher. More recent work on computer and language learning has adopted a different stance, and different assumptions, and has researched language interaction between students during computer use. Often two or more students work together at the computer, and talk as they do so. Such interaction has begun to attract the attention of first and second language researchers as something which may have more than incidental value. For instance, in the field of first language learning there has been special interest in student–student collaboration while using word processing programs during the writing process (Dickinson, 1986). From here it is a short step to an exploration of the possible role of the computer in cognitive and academic language development. With this expansion in research focus, it has become clear there are a wide range of issues that the newer work needs to explore.

Some of the immediate research questions that face the second language researcher are:

— Is interaction around the computer valuable for second language learners? Will it help them develop their ability in the target language?
— If so, in what ways will it help and for what kind of language development is it likely to be useful?
— What are appropriate methods to analyse interaction around the computer?

— What part does the computer play in this interaction?
— Should the research focus be language development alone, or language development in the context of subject matter learning?

To begin to answer these questions, it is helpful to specify models of the role of the computer. This paper will discuss three models of the role of the computer in second language learning: the computer as language teacher; the computer as a stimulus for talk; and the computer as context for cognitive language development.

Leech (1981: 87) has noted a general tendency in the human sciences for talking about models rather than theories:

> [W]hereas theories claim to tell us what reality is like, models claim to tell us what reality can and could be like — given certain speculative assumptions. We can, for example, construct a model of the mind as a computer, or of society as a market, knowing that this is not true, or only partially true, but seeking in this way to provide a detailed but perhaps idealised understanding of some domain ...

Similarly, the models outlined here are intended to bring 'certain speculative assumptions' into the foreground, not only to sharpen analysis of the data, but also to stimulate constructive thought about future computer use. Furthermore, a variety of models allows a variety of perspectives from which to analyse data.

While there are a number of considerations by which these models of computer use can be assessed and evaluated, three criteria are obvious. The first criterion is whether the model is testable, so that its predictions can be checked against data. The second criterion is whether the model is consistent with research in language development and language education. And the third criterion is whether the model is consistent with research in computer science and makes appropriate use of computer resources.

The Computer as Language Teacher

The model of the computer as language teacher has drawn strong criticism. While it is clearly testable in a general sense, there is doubt whether it is consistent with current language research and whether it makes appropriate use of computer resources. Yet it would appear that these criticisms are attached to particular programs rather than to the model itself.

As with many technological innovations in education, the development of computer hardware has often not been matched by the development of educationally appropriate uses of the computer. Obtaining the hardware and software is one thing; using it well is quite another. This is particularly obvious in the field of computer-assisted language learning (CALL). Various writers have pointed out that those who produce computer software for language learners have frequently taken the easy but unrewarding route of using the computer to present traditional language workbook material. The computer becomes, in effect, an expensive page-turner. When the computer is used in this way, it is questionable whether any advantage is gained to compensate for the resulting cost and possible inconvenience, not to speak of doubts about the educational value of the traditional workbook material in the first place. Such use is poor employment of the computer resource.

Such programs for CALL implement the more mechanical grammar and vocabulary drills, or present information about the grammar of the language and test the students' ability to select grammatically correct sentences. These programs assume that the computer is to be a language teacher in the behaviourist tradition. As Underwood (1984: 45) describes it, the programs work on a 'Wrong—Try Again' model; they do not aim at encouraging the student to communicate, but instead focus on the form of the language, evaluating student responses in terms of correctness. As is well known, Krashen (1982; 1983) has argued that language teaching in grammar-based approaches which emphasise explanations of rules and correction of errors does not facilitate the acquisition of language. Thus these programs can be attacked as being in conflict with a body of current research on language development.

It is unfortunate that some of the work within this conception of the role of the computer has been of a low standard, but one should distinguish sharply between the specific examples of such programs and the general model of computer use. When the computer is seen as language teacher, the assumption is that the intentional teaching of language is appropriate. There is, however, no reason to suppose that the concept of teaching necessarily implies explicit statements of rules followed by correction. In an authoritative statement, Hirst & Peters (1970: 81) define teaching as an intentional activity which exposes the learner to what is to be learned in a way which takes into account the learners' state of knowledge. The reader will note that this definition will accommodate the mother's role in language acquisition by the young child: the mother wants the child to learn language, exposes the child to language input, and adjusts the language input to the child's understanding. The work of Krashen and others has challenged the belief that teaching (in the sense of explicit, metalinguistic teaching) is always appropriate but has not proved that it is never appropriate. An interesting example of an argument for appropriacy is provided by the work of Kress (1982), Martin (1985), Christie (1985), and other systemic linguists who have made a case for the formal teaching of genres of writing to school-age students who are native speakers of English (Hammond, 1987).

To criticise this model as a poor use of computing resources is again to fail to distinguish between specific programs and the general model. A number of CALL programs have been based on authoring systems such as *PILOT*, which provide a generic format for transferring workbook material in any subject area to the computer and which encourage the uninitiated to look no further. The reliance on authoring systems is symptomatic of the failure to take sufficient advantage of the powerful and elegant computer techniques for working with non-numeric symbolic data, particularly high-level programming languages such as BASIC, LOGO, or PASCAL.

More broadly, there is a failure to recognise that the computer has long been functioning as a language teacher in a great variety of circumstances, but as a teacher of 'artificial' rather than natural languages, and as a support for the use of programming languages and other means of communicating with the machine. In this sense, the computer as language teacher is a perfectly viable — and indeed a necessary — use of computer resources.

When a computer user enters statements in a high-level programming language, the statements are usually processed syntactically and semantically by a compiler or interpreter program. There is provision for error detection and diagnostic comment and there may even be help in the form of explicit statement of the rules. In some cases the compiler or interpreter may itself be based on a program which provides generic resources for the necessary syntactic and semantic processing, such as *MINT* (Godfrey, Hendry, Hermans & Hessenberg, 1982). Programs such as *MINT* provide a rich resource for work not only with programming languages but also with natural languages. For an application of an early version of *MINT* to the processing of the analysis of children's speech, see Turner & Mohan (1970).

The model of the computer as language teacher, despite a number of attacks, is certainly a defensible one. Interpreted with a sophisticated concept of teaching and a definition of language which includes both natural and artificial varieties, it opens up important avenues of research, not the least of which is the application of second language research techniques to the study of the acquisition of programming languages at the computer.

The Computer as a Stimulus for Talk

There is wide agreement that CALL should change its focus from providing formal language teaching to promoting communicative language use.

Higgins & Johns (1984), for instance, discuss examples of CALL programs which are intended for group use and group talk, such as *Invent a Monster*, in which the user has to answer a series of questions about an imagined creature, resulting in a screen layout that describes the monster.

But are such programs necessary? What if students already *do* communicate while using the computer? A very different approach is to explore the way talk arises naturally in the process of using the computer. This opens up a very broad field, a line of invesitgation that applies to any kind of program — not just to those aimed at language learning — and, ultimately, to all kinds of communication within groups using the computer. We are only at the beginning of exploring this area, though it has not been totally overlooked. For instance, noting that programs are often used by pairs or groups of students rather than by one student alone, Underwood (1984: 54) claims that 'the students get involved in much healthy discussion centering on how you get the thing to work, or the best way to solve the problem.' He suggests that this discussion is an important resource for language learning according to Krashen's theory of second language acquisition. There are four points about this theory and more recent related work which are particularly relevant to interaction at the computer: *comprehensible input, negotiation of input, the role of group work*, and *the effect of communicative tasks*. In what follows, each of these notions is briefly reviewed in the context of CALL.

Comprehensible Input

In Krashen's (1983: 60) view, 'people acquire second languages when they obtain comprehensible input...; comprehensible input is the true and only causative variable in second language acquisition.' Instruction in the second language 'helps second language acquisition only when it provides comprehensible input.' This means, for instance, that what is important about a computer program is not whether it aims to teach language, but whether it leads to comprehensible input.

Negotiation of Input

The *quantity* of comprehensible input available to second language learners is therefore vital; however, more recent research by Long (1980; 1981; 1983) has added to this requirement a concern for the *quality* of comprehensible input. 'Learners must be put in a position of being able to *negotiate* [emphasis in original] the input thereby ensuring that the level of language which is heard is modified to exactly the level of comprehensibility they can manage' (Long & Porter, 1985: 214). That is, a learner who does not understand what is being said should be in a position to help 'repair' the conversation so as to reach understanding.

This means that the learner must be engaged in some form of dialogue which allows for feedback and adjustment. Quality is affected where such feedback is not possible, as is generally the case when the learner is exposed to the mass media such as television, radio and books.

There is a general sense in which a computer negotiates with its user; this 'negotiation' depends on the degree to which the program is adaptive to the user. But what is at issue here is the specific sense of language negotiation as a linguistic process that occurs between interacting participants in a conversation. Research has only recently begun to describe the ways in which speakers negotiate comprehensible input (see, for example, Varonis & Gass, 1985); it remains to be proven that any existing computer program can simulate this linguistic process, performing as well as a human partner.

The Role of Group Work

How can learners best be provided with the opportunity for quantity and quality of comprehensible input? It has long been argued that students can interact more with each other than with the teacher, and that peer work can increase students' target language practice time. To assess evidence for the claim that peer interaction promotes the use of the target language, Long & Porter (1985) surveyed research studies of interactions between non-native speakers (NNSs). Compared with teacher-fronted lessons and interactions between native speakers and non-native speakers (NS/NNS interactions), NNS/NNS interactions provided more language practice opportunities and resulted in greater negotiation. That is, NNS/NNS interactions provided both greater quantity and greater quality of comprehensible input. NNS/NNS interactions at the computer may therefore be a favourable environment for talk, and a prime source of input and negotiation.

The Effect of Communicative Tasks

Is NNS/NNS interaction affected by the type of communicative task learners are engaged in? Crookes (1986: 7–18) reviewed the small but growing number of studies which examine the effect of task characteristics on NNS language use and, presumably, language learning, and found that communicative task does affect NNS/NNS interaction. Following Long's (1980) work on negotiation in tasks where the exchange of information was either optional or required, Doughty & Pica (1986) discovered that more negotiation was produced when the exchange of information was required. Further evidence of the effect of task on negotiation is provided by Duff (1986), who concluded that problem-solving tasks resulted in more negotiation than discussion tasks. With regard to interaction at the computer, these findings suggest that different kinds of tasks at the computer should be compared with each other. The research cited above also implies that communicative tasks performed with the computer should be compared to communicative tasks without the computer.

It is very important to note that spontaneous talk around the computer is a *natural* communication task occurring as part of a larger interaction that the participants engage in. Such spontaneous talk is part of an activity of computer use. It is purposeful rather than contrived or artificial. In this respect it is not to be confused with tasks which have been set by others (e.g. language teachers) simply for the purpose of getting students to talk.

Taken all together, these points build another model of the role of the computer in second language learning: the computer as stimulus for talk. According to this model, educators can ignore direct language instruction by the computer and instead focus on use of the computer for group work because peer interaction at the computer offers learners natural communication tasks. Doing so will promote language development, for in peer interaction learners will provide each other with comprehensible input and negotiated interaction, the prime conditions for second language growth. An attractive feature of this model is that it can be tested in a straightforward way, viz. by recording peer interaction between second language learners at the computer and then checking the quantity and negotiated quality of the talk. Thus, this model is testable, it embodies recent second language research, and it relies on a natural side-effect of computer use.

Analysing second language talk at the computer

The language data to be discussed below was collected in the following way. Subjects were eight pairs of intermediate proficiency, adult non-native speakers of English as a second language (ESL). There were four female pairs and four male pairs. No pair shared the same first language. There were three computer tasks: use of a grammar teaching program, use of a word processor, and use of a business simulation program. Subjects were asked to work together to use the programs co-operatively. In addition, there was a free conversation task, where each pair of subjects was asked to make conversation with each other away from the computer, talking about whatever topic they wished. Conversation was selected because it has been claimed that conversation is the basic or fundamental form of communicative language use, and that other forms of talk exchange are specialisations of conversation (see Levinson, 1983). However that may be, it does suggest that conversation is a viable baseline for comparison. Order of presentation of the tasks was counterbalanced and interactions were videotaped and transcribed.

In the texts which follow, Irid, a woman from Indonesia, and Marta, a woman from Mexico, both intermediate speakers of English, talk as they cooperate to use the different types of computer program. It is easy to see how the process of using the computer supplies many things to talk about, and how these texts seem fairly typical of the kind of interaction one might expect when two people jointly use a program. All three are about choice: choosing to borrow money, choosing which key to press, or choosing which sentence is correct. Notice how, paradoxically, the program intended to *teach* the language sparks off a discussion where the learners *use* the language.

Text 1. Business Simulation

Irid: Take out loan?
Marta: We borrow money from the bank for whatsits.
Irid: But maybe they charge some money.
Marta: No. You want to borrow money?
Irid: From the bank? No.
Marta: Okay, no.
Irid: Open for business.
Marta: We already did open it.

Text 2. Word Processing

[Irid is getting ready to type.]
Irid: With this machine. With this machine. Was it this one?
Marta: No. This is for capital letters.
Irid: Oh yeah. This one is for Return?
Marta: Uh huh. First learn how to type upper-case letters. Try typing in it.

Text 3. Grammar Program

[They are choosing between two different answers, two sentences, labelled B and C.]
Irid: B.
Marta: Or C?
Irid: C? This is past tense, eh?
Marta: Past. Past with past. B. Try B. [She quotes] 'I guess if the store was open she got it.'…'She got it'?…'She'll get it'?…'She will get it'? Which one do you think?

The fourth text is a sample of conversation:

Text 4. Conversation

Irid: Do you work here?
Marta: Here? Work? No. No I'm just student. It's really difficult to get work in another country.
Irid: In your visa, does it allow you to work?
Marta: No. I mean they say you can work in nothing. And I went to immigration office for to ask how to be resident in Canada and they say no, forget it… You don't go out from Canada for five years, and after you get job and after job you can get residence.

Text 4 suggests that the speakers talk more in conversation than at the computer. Listening to the tape recording shows that they talk continuously and that there are few if any gaps in conversation. This is in contrast with computer use, where periods of silence are frequent when speakers are watching the screen.

The question arises as to which of the types of program illustrated in Texts 1-3 results in the most speech, i.e. in the greatest quantity of input. In order to answer this question, the first ten minutes of each computer use task (grammar, simulation, and word processing) were analysed for three measures of quantity: words per minute, utterances per minute, and words per utterance, where utterance was defined as the spoken equivalent of the written sentence (simple, compound, or complex).[1] There were no clear differences among the three computer tasks according to these measures, although there was a trend for each pair to produce more words per minute when using the grammar program. Apparently, language instructional tasks may produce a large amount of language use. However, as can be seen from Text 3, some of the language use in this case may be due to speakers quoting sentences rather than creating them.

Another question arises as to which of these types of program results in the most negotiated speech, and so in the greatest quality of input. Drawing on previous research (Long, 1983), four features of negotiated or modified interaction were counted as measures of the quality of the input which speakers negotiated during the interaction: self-repetitions, other-repetitions, clarification requests, and confirmation checks. The following examples are from Marta and Irid. *Self-repetitions* occur when speakers repeat their own utterances, partly or completely, as in the example below:

Irid: With this machine. With this machine .

In *other-repetitions*, a speaker repeats the other speaker's utterance, partly or completely:

Marta: Or C?
Irid: C?

A *clarification* request is intended to elicit clarification of what the other speaker has just said:

Marta: If you buy just 99 it's more.
Irid: What do you mean?

A speaker utters a *confirmation check* to confirm understanding of what the other speaker has just said:

Marta: If you buy in the middle, for example 500, it's much cheaper than to pay just 99.
Irid: Oh, I see, 500.

Which of these programs showed the greatest amount of negotiated speech and so the highest quality of input? When all of these programs were compared on the features of negotiation, no clear difference in quality of input emerged, though there were some differences with respect to the individual measures, particularly for the grammar program as against the other two types of program (see Table 6.1 below).

Comparing one type of program with another does not, however, reveal how interaction at the computer compares with other kinds of communication tasks. In order to address this issue in the present study, a comparison was made of the talk that occurred within the student pairs during the computer tasks and during conversation. Table 6.1 reports the group data for the three computer tasks (grammar, simulation, and word processing) and the conversation task, giving means and standard deviations for the first ten minutes of each task according to the measures of quantity and quality described above.

When conversation was compared with computer use for all eight pairs of speakers, the difference was striking: there was a significantly higher quantity of talk in conversation. This result also held true for each individual speaker. Compared to conversation, all three computer tasks produced less than half the number of utterances per minute, about a quarter of the number of words per minute, and somewhat over half the number of words per utterance. Given this difference in quantity, was there a difference in quality? Again, Table 6.1 shows that compared to conversation, all three computer tasks were significantly lower in measures of negotiation or modification.

The main result that emerges from these comparisons is that interaction at the computer was significantly lower in quantity and qua'ty than interaction in conversation. If we hold to the assumptions of the input and negotiation perspective, this means that tasks like conversation are more likely to aid second language acquisition than the computer-based tasks studied here. This result also implies that there are shortcomings in the model of the computer as stimulus for

TABLE 6.1 *The effect of task type on language interaction of individuals (n of individuals = 16; n of dyads = 8)*

	Computer use			Conversation
Variable	Grammar Mean s.d.	Simulation Mean s.d.	Word process Mean s.d.	Mean s.d.
Utterances per minute	3.07 1.12	2.89 1.05	2.18 0.64	6.56 1.60
Words per minute	11.72 7.45	9.73 6.02	9.20 4.39	39.21 13.06
Words per Utterance	3.50 1.21	3.06 0.99	3.58 0.93	5.87 1.37
Confirmation Checks#	0.50 0.63	0.66 0.54	0.63 0.50	3.88 2.02
Clarification Requests#	0.13 0.22	0.44 0.54	0.44 0.79	2.19 1.83
Repetitions (Self)#	2.63 2.66	1.94 1.33	1.94 1.77	5.75 2.67
Repetitions (Other)#	1.44 0.96	1.03 0.71	0.59 0.49	1.91 1.84

\# Means are given per 10 minutes of dyadic interaction.
Note: For each variable, conversation was compared with each of the other tasks (planned, pair-wise comparisons). Conversation was significantly different from all other tasks for each of the variables ($p < 0.05$, univariate F-tests, repeated measures SPSS MANOVA). The same result was found with the nonparametric Wilcoxon matched pairs signed ranks test ($p < 0.05$), though only 1 contrast was significant for Other Repetitions.

talk since participants produced less talk at the computer than in conversation. Of course, one cannot generalise from one study to other speakers and computer tasks, but there do not appear to be any other studies which contradict this result. Moreover, this result can be tested in other circumstances without great difficulty, by comparing the quantity of interaction between conversation and computer use.

The Computer as Context for Cognitive Language Development

Computer interaction may appear differently when we look at it from another perspective, one which places more importance on the context of communication. Cummins has explored the relationship between bilingualism and educational success. Cummins (1984) stresses the importance of distinguishing between conversational or surface fluency in English and the cognitive/academic competence in English which is required for academic success. Cummins found that many immigrant ESL learners can develop conversational fluency in one to two years' exposure to English-speaking peers, television, and schooling, but that it took immigrant students on average between five and seven years to approach grade norms in English verbal-academic skills.

To explain this phenomenon and throw light on the contrast between casual conversation and the communication demands of academic tasks, Cummins proposes a bipartite model of language proficiency. He suggests that the type of language proficiency needed to carry out a communicative task depends on two features of tasks: cognitive demands and contextual support. *Cognitively undemanding* tasks require little active cognitive involvement; *cognitively demanding* tasks, on the other hand, require active cognitive involvement. With regard to contextual support, a *context-embedded* task allows participants to negotiate meaning and to provide each other with feedback, and their discourse is supported by a wide range of situational cues; a *context-reduced* task relies mainly on linguistic cues to meaning, and successful interpretation of the message depends heavily on knowledge of the language itself. Since school language demands may be difficult for many types of students, an interesting feature of this model is that it can be applied to both first and second language learners.

Cummins believes that a second language learner may fail in school when faced with tasks which are both cognitively demanding and context-reduced and therefore difficult to understand. He holds that the more instruction can initially be context-embedded, the more successful it is ultimately likely to be in developing cognitive-academic language proficiency. The principle is to provide the learner with cognitively demanding tasks which have adequate contextual support.

From this standpoint, another model of the role of the computer emerges: the computer as context for cognitive language development. It may be that the computer is more appropriate for the development of cognitive-academic language proficiency rather than conversational fluency. And it may be that the computer can be an important source of contextual support to aid language learners. Can the computer provide communication tasks which are both context-embedded and cognitively demanding? An important research problem here is that it is not possible to test this model until language measures of context-embeddedness and cognitive demand are developed.

Consider, first, the question of contextual support. Text 5 shows Yukio, a Japanese speaker, and Heinz, a German speaker, using the business simulation program.

Text 5. Business Simulation

[They are both looking at the computer screen.]
Yukio: That's right. Standard? Yes, standard.
Heinz: [He points at the screen.] This?
Yukio: Ah, no.
Heinz: [He points at the screen] This?
Yukio: Yes. [He presses the return key.] And return.

Text 6 shows the same speakers in conversation.

Text 6. Conversation

Yukio: We Japanese don't know about apartheid.
Heinz: You don't know what this means?
Yukio: Because South Africa is very far to Japan... Anyway, I'm interested in nuclear war.
Heinz: Nuclear war? What's this?
Yukio: I.C.B.M. Oh, nuclear war, atomic bomb.

In the conversation, the topics of apartheid and nuclear war are constructed through talk. Because of this, the conversation is much easier for the reader to interpret. Much of the relevant information is conveyed through the spoken text. By contrast, the interaction at the computer is much harder for the outsider to interpret. We know that the students are talking about something but need the videotape to find out what it is. The computer interaction is more context-embedded than the conversation. One clue is the use of pronouns like *this*. In the computer interaction (Text 5), *this* is used to refer to the screen., i.e. it refers to the situational context. In the conversation (Text 6), *this* is used to refer to the previous discourse, i.e. it refers to the text, not the context (see Halliday & Hasan, 1976). To sum up, it seems likely that the computer can provide contextual support for the dialogue between its users, as the focus of their attention and the target of their actions.

Now consider the question of cognitive demands. There is a pattern noticeable in many examples of computer-assisted learning and in much computer use generally: the program poses a series of choices or problems for the user, and the user makes a series of corresponding decisions or solutions. In other words, the computer makes a series of cognitive tasks available to the user. (How demanding and difficult these tasks are will depend on the match between the program and the user, among other things.)

When two people interact to use a program cooperatively, the series of choices or decisions appears as a series of discourse episodes of choice, decision-making or problem-solving: they comment on what is on the screen, they propose and discuss what to do, and they come to agree on an action and type in their choice. The central discourse units appear to be *Proposal* and *Agreement*, with Reasons appearing if the choice is discussed in more depth. Text 7 shows a simple form of this episode pattern between Koji, a Japanese speaker, and Ali, an Arabic speaker.

Text 7. Grammar Program

Ali: [PROPOSAL] Perhaps C. Yeah, that's it.
Koji: [AGREEMENT] C. Yes.

In Text 8, the same pattern occurs with reasons.

Text 8. Grammar Program

Koji: [PROPOSAL] 'I would have.'
[GIVES REASONS] If *if* clause is 'if I needed an answer quickly,' we can use a main clause 'I would have.' But in this case, [He points to another possible choice of sentence.] the *if* clause is past perfect, so we can't use, we have to use *have*. And we have to use present perfect in the main clause, I think. Yes, *have*. So I think... so 'I would have telephoned.'
Ali: [AGREEMENT] Yes, that looks right, okay.

Similar reasoning appears during the business simulation program.

Text 9. Business Simulation

Ali: [REASON] Bank's rate is high.
Koji: [PROPOSAL] So maybe pay principal on loan. So we have to pay interest on loan.
[REASON] So now we have taken loan but the market situation is poor ... so we can't make a profit now, so now we have to cut the cost. Inventory ... order more goods. But in poor market situation we can't do it, so maybe ... no, no, it's the cost.
[REPEATS PROPOSAL] So maybe just number 5, that means reduce cost of loan.

Ali: [AGREEMENT] Pay principal on loan.

To summarise, these examples show computer users engaging in the cognitive discourse of problem-solving discussion. Sometimes the reasoning involved is implicit, but sometimes it is explicit and discussed in considerable detail. It looks likely, then, that the computer can offer communication tasks with high cognitive demands and high contextual support. To say this is to begin to see computer use as an activity that relates action, knowledge and discourse.

Conclusion

To explore alternative models of the role of the computer is to see further possibilities for research and development and to reflect on the assumptions of research in language learning in general. Each of the above models of the computer's role is theoretically defensible; each can be investigated empirically with known techniques and measures. Each one of the models raises different and additional questions.

The model of the computer as language teacher raises the issue of when formal teaching of language is appropriate. It also raises questions about how computer resources can be used for this purpose with elegance and power.

The model of the computer as a stimulus for talk encourages researchers to examine verbal interaction during computer use and to relate it to the wider literature on the influence of task on discourse. The findings described here suggest that this role for the computer may not be an entirely appropriate one. Computer use does not seem to be especially valuable for the development of conversational fluency — at least not with the types of programs used in the present study.[2] Yet from the standpoint of research directions in the future, the careful examination of interaction at the computer on a principled basis is a major step.

The model of the computer as a context for cognitive language development aims at a different goal, viz. the development of cognitive-academic language proficiency. From this perspective, verbal interaction at the computer has to be conceived of and assessed in a different way, using measures of context-dependence and cognitive complexity.

There is a further, wider significance to this contrast of models. The deepest contrast is between the vision of the computer as a language teacher and the vision of language interaction at the computer as a medium of communication and learning. The latter view broadens the area of research and the research audience. It looks beyond programs intended to teach language specifically and considers all types of programs. It looks beyond the results of language learning and considers the process of language use. This paper has argued that such a view can be a basis for productive research.

Acknowledgement

This study was funded by the Social Sciences and Humanities Research Council of Canada.

Notes to Chapter 6

1. Sentences not completed by the speaker as a result of false starts, interruptions, or changes of plan were not counted as utterances. For an early discussion of these based on the examination of a large body of data, see Turner & Mohan (1970: 143–53).
2. This is not to disallow the possibility that special programs to address fluency at the computer could be developed.

References

CHRISTIE, F. (1985) *Language Education*. Geelong, Australia: Deakin University Press.
CROOKES, G. (1986) *Task Classification*. Technical Report, No. 4. Center for Second Language Classroom Research. Honolulu, HI: University of Hawaii at Manoa.
CUMMINS, J. (1984) *Bilingualism and Special Education*. San Diego: College Hill.
DICKINSON, D. K. (1986) Cooperation, collaboration and a computer, *Research in the Teaching of English*, 20: 4, 357–378.
DOUGHTY, C. & and T. PICA (1986) Information gap tasks: Do they facilitate second language acquisition?, *TESOL Quarterly*, 20: 2, 305–25.
DUFF, P. (1986) Taking task to task. In R. DAY (ed.) *Talking to Learn*. Rowley, MA: Newbury House.
GODFREY, M., D. HENDRY, H. HERMANS & R. HESSENBERG (1982) *Machine Independent Organic Software Tools (MINT)*, 2nd edn New York, NY: Academic Press.
HALLIDAY, M.A.K. & R. HASAN (1976) *Cohesion in English*. London, UK: Longman.
HAMMOND, J. (1987) An overview of the genre-based approach to the teaching of writing in Australia, *Australian Review of Applied Linguistics*, 10: 2, 163–81.
HIGGINS, J. & T. JOHNS (1984) *Computers in Language Learning*. Reading, MA: Addison-Wesley.
HIRST, P. & PETERS, R. (1970) *The Logic of Education*. London: Routledge & Kegan Paul.
KRASHEN, S. (1982) *Principles and Practice in Second Language Acquisition*. Oxford, UK: Pergamon Press.
— (1983) Applications of psycholinguistic research to the classroom. In C. JAMES (ed.),

Practical Applications of Research in Foreign Language Teaching. Lincolnwood, IL: National Textbook Company.
KRESS, G. (1982) *Learning to Write*. London, UK: Routledge & Kegan Paul.
LEECH, G. (1981) *Semantics*. 2nd edn Harmondsworth, UK: Penguin Books.
LEVINSON, S. (1983) *Pragmatics*. Cambridge, UK: Cambridge University Press.
LONG, M. (1980) Input, interaction and second language acquisition. Unpublished Ph.D. dissertation. Los Angeles, CA: University of California at Los Angeles.
— (1981) Questions in foreigner talk discourse, *Language Learning*, 31: 2, 135–158.
— (1983) Native speaker/non-native speaker conversation in the second language classroom. In M. CLARKE & J. HANDSCOMBE (eds), *On TESOL '82*. Washington D.C.: TESOL.
LONG, M. & P. PORTER (1985) Group work, interlanguage talk, and second language acquisition, *TESOL Quarterly*, 19: 2, 207–228.
MARTIN, J. R. (1985) *Factual Writing*. Geelong, Australia: Deakin University Press.
MOHAN, B. (1986) *Language and Content*. Reading, MA: Addison-Wesley.
TURNER, G. & B. MOHAN (1970) *A Linguistic Description and Computer Program for Children's Speech*. London, UK: Routledge & Kegan Paul.
UNDERWOOD, J. (1984) *Linguistics, Computers and the Language Teacher*. Rowley, MA: Newbury House.
VARONIS, E. & S. GASS (1985) Non-native/non-native conversations: A model for negotiation of meaning, *Applied Linguistics*, 6: 1, 71–90

7 Computer Applications in Second Language Acquisition Research: Design, Description, and Discovery

CATHERINE DOUGHTY
University of Sydney, Australia

Introduction

This article illustrates several IBM XT- and AT-level computer applications developed for a second language acquisition research project at the University of Pennsylvania. These applications were facilatory to the completion of an empirical study of the instructed acquisition of relativizsation by English as a Second Language (ESL) students (Doughty, 1988). Computer applications were integral to three phases of the research: the instructional and experimental design phase, the data description phase, and the discovery, or data analysis, phase. Examples of such computer applications for data collection, storage, handling, and analysis are provided as the methodology and findings of the second language acquisition experiment are summarised.

The Relativisation Study

The ESL relativisation study reported here was primarily motivated by Long's (1983) general question, 'Does second language instruction make a difference?' and by experimental studies that have provided cumulative evidence that second language instruction may be beneficial (as reviewed in Long, 1983;

1985). Unfortunately, past learning outcomes were not consistently and directly attributable to the second language instruction in those studies, as frequently the instruction investigated was defined too broadly (e.g. simply as attendance in second language classes). Consequently, Long urged researchers to concentrate on narrowly focused experiments and to consider precisely the nature of instruction employed in the research. In the relativisation study, it was hoped that the computer medium of delivery for the second language instruction would enable appropriate experimental controls and would make possible a detailed, post-experimental analysis of the instructional materials.

In order to avoid any ambiguity in the interpretation of the experimental findings, one grammatical system, English relativisation, was the target of the experimental instruction. The purpose of the experiment was to determine the effect of instruction on interlanguage development in the relativisation system of ESL subjects.

In light of the known difficulty in interpretation of results obtained after a period of instruction that is not observed by the researcher, the relativisation experiment was designed to incorporate computer-mediated instructional materials that were developed specifically for the research. An essential component of the study was the computer's built-in capability to preserve and subsequently replay the instruction that had been administered during the experimental treatment under precisely the same conditions as prevailed when the instruction was originally presented to subjects. Re-examination of the instruction in light of the learning outcomes provided an opportunity to arrive at an understanding of the nature of the effect of instruction on acquisition of the target system.

It is important to note that the study did not involve a comparison of computer-assisted instruction to non-technical classroom instruction. Rather, the computer provided the instructional context for all groups tested; thus, the computer medium facilitated the data collection phase of the research as well as the storage and eventual analysis of empirical findings. Empirical, theoretical and practical considerations favour a departure from the outdated methodology of comparing humans to computers, or, indeed, from any global comparisons among methods of second language instruction. Comparative research on methods has proven to be incapable of providing generalisable results, and previous attempts to demonstrate the superiority of one method over another have repeatedly failed (Smith, 1970; Richards & Rodgers, 1986). The lack of differentiation among methods can be traced to the influence of extraneous and conflated variables and to the lack of precision in description of methods (see review of Levin, 1972, and Scherer & Wertheimer, 1964, in Chaudron, 1988).

Inconclusive results on the effects of instruction have obtained whether or not any of the methods were technologically oriented; thus, comparisons of classroom vs. computer-assisted instruction have also not escaped this methodological limitation. The absence of significant findings in studies resulting from comparisons of technologically-mediated instruction to traditional classroom instruction has also been attributed to the difficulty in comparing the two modes of instruction (Barrutia, 1970; Mellgren, 1983; Morrison & Adams, 1968). Findings from studies comparing teachers with technology have also not been replicable due to a lack of discussion of the software/implementation/hardware involved, and of the counterpart classroom materials and instructional techniques.

In sum, there is no justification for further comparisons of human language instruction vs. computer-assisted language instruction. Rather, it is more appropriate to initiate research on those aspects of language learning that can be implemented efficiently using technological resources. Research designs should address issues relevant to understanding the process of second language acquisition. The experiment to be discussed below incorporated a theoretically-motivated instructional design, and though not the object of investigation, computer applications nevertheless were significant in all phases of the research: *design* and development of the experimental instrument, *description* of the data gathered, and *discovery* of the significance of the findings.

The Instructional Design

The lack of consistency in earlier findings, which have suggested, but have not confirmed, a positive effect of instruction on second language acquisition is potentially explained by hypothesising that subjects who have been studied to date did not receive the right kind of instruction. Therefore, in this experiment, careful consideration was given to the design of the relativisation instructional materials. The most important design decision was that of how best to sequence the presentation of the relative clause instruction in order to provide the greatest opportunity for subjects to incorporate the rules of the English relativisation system into their interlanguage. Recent research that has examined putative stages of interlanguage development has provided convincing evidence that acquisitional sequences do exist and that they must be taken into account in instructional design, although not necessarily in the manner that might have been expected (see studies by Ellis, 1984; Lightbown, 1981; and Pienemann, 1982). In light of the potential significance of acquisitional sequences for second language pedagogy, three hypotheses that predict an order of acquisition of relative clauses according to a scale of difficulty were considered during the instructional design phase of the relativisation study: (1) the *Parallel Function Hypothesis*, (2) the

Perceptual Difficulty Hypothesis, and (3) the *Accessibility Hierarchy Hypothesis*.

The Parallel Function Hypothesis, formulated originally to account for development of relativization in first language acquisition, proposes a cognitive-processing interpretation of the syntactic relationship between the function of the head noun in the matrix sentence (i.e. the sentence into which the relative clause is embedded) and the function of the co-referential relative pronoun in the embedded relative clause. The Parallel Function Hypothesis assumes that the grammatical functions (e.g. the subject or object of the clause) of the coreferential noun phrases (e.g. head noun and relative pronoun) play a significant role in ease of comprehension and, thus, specifically predicts 'a strategy of interpreting the grammatical function of the relative pronoun as being the same as its antecedent [the head noun]' (Sheldon, 1974: 274). In other words, the Parallel Function Hypothesis predicts that sentences in which the noun phrases in the matrix and relative clauses have the same function are easier to comprehend than are sentences in which the identical noun phrases have different syntactic functions in their respective clauses. Consequently, the Parallel Function Hypothesis predicts that relative clauses with different functions would be more difficult to acquire than those with functions parallel to the noun in the matrix clause (see Figure 7.1 below for examples).

Another prediction of a natural order of difficulty of relative clauses may be derived by taking universal constraints on the process of embedding as a basis for prediction. Kuno (1974) proposed that, due to the limitations of human short-term memory, centre-embedding — in which the processing of the matrix sentence is interrupted by the relative clause — is perceptually the most difficult type of embedding, as compared with relativisation involving right- and left-embedding — in which the processing of each clause, matrix and relative, is uninterrupted. In terms of predicting an acquisition order, Kuno's observations may be formulated as the Perceptual Difficulty Hypothesis, which states that centre-embedded relative clauses will be acquired later than branching relative clauses (see Figure 7.1 for examples).

The third hypothesis that was applied to predict an order of difficulty for relativisation in English is also based upon a proposed universal constraint. Keenan & Comrie (1977; 1979) noted that there is a universal hierarchy of grammatical relations for relative clause formation across languages. Specifically, although the details of the relativisation process differ from language to language with respect to frequency and number of possible syntactic functions of the relative pronoun in its clause (i.e. subject or object), it is possible to describe a particular, hierarchical ordering of the ease of accessibility to relativisation for these functions. If a language has one type of relativisation in

The Parallel Function Hypothesis: proposes a cognitive-processing interpretation of the relationship between the functions of the HN and RP in the matrix and embedded clauses, respectively. The PFH suggests a cognitive strategy of interpreting the grammatical function of the RP as being the same as that of the antecedent HN and suggests that this interpretation facilitates comprehension.

SS   OO   >   OS   SO

The Perceptual Difficulty Hypothesis: proposes that there are universal constraints on the process of embedding. In particular, the PDH proposes that, due to the limitations in STM, center-embedding, where the RC interrupts the matrix, is perceptually the most difficult as compared with right- and left-branching clauses, where there is no interruption.

OS   OO   >   SS   SO

The Accessibility Hierarchy Hypothesis: considers only the function of the RP in the RC and takes into account a proposed universal implicational ordering of the six possible grammatical functions of the RP with respect to ease of accessibility in the relativization process.

Subject > Direct Object > Indirect Object > Oblique Object > Genitive > Object of Comparison

SS   OS   >   OO   SO   [i.e., S > O]

Data Set #1 (relevant to PFH and PDH)

The *people* (*who* live in LA) are busy.	SS
I know some *people* (*who* live in LA).	OS
I know the *people* (*who* you know).	OO
The *people* (*who* we know) live in LA.	SO

Data Set #2 (relevant also to AHH)

The *people* (*who* live in LA) are busy.	SS
I know some *people* (*who* live in LA).	OS
The *people* (*who* I know) live in LA.	S(D)O
I know the *people* (*who* you know).	O(D)O
The *people* (*who* I gave the tickets to) live in LA.	S(I)O
You saw the *people* (*who* I gave the tickets to).	O(I)O
The *people* (*who* you talked with) live in LA.	SO(P)
I know the *people* (*who* you talked with).	OO(P)
The *people* (*whose* name is Taylor) live in LA.	S -
I know the *people* (*whose* name is Taylor).	O -
?The only *person* (*who* I am taller than) lives in LA.	SO(C)
?I know the only *person* (*who* you are taller than).	OO(C)

FIGURE 7.1 *Relativisation — Predictors of order of difficulty.*

the hierarchy, it also has been shown to have all of the types before it on the hierarchy (i.e. the easier ones). Through this typological comparison of fifty languages, Keenan & Comrie have concluded that those relative clause types which exist in all languages are easiest and that the less frequently occurring relative clauses are more difficult to produce. The typological relationship which obtains among the relativisable syntactic functions of noun phrases, known as the *Noun Phrase Accessibility Hierarchy*, defines an implicational ordering of the six possible types of relative clauses, from easiest to most difficult (Keenan & Comrie, 1977). The Accessibility Hierarchy Hypothesis, therefore, predicts such an implicational ordering in the acquisition of the six types of relativisation. The implicational ordering according to the function of the relative pronoun, from easiest to most difficult is: subject, direct object, indirect object, object-of-preposition, possessive, object of a comparison (see Figure 7.1 for examples).

Figure 7.1 provides examples of sentences containing relative clauses in the order of difficulty predicted by each hypothesis. As can be seen in the figure, different difficulty orders for English relativisation are derived from the predictor hypotheses. Because empirical studies have failed to support the predictive powers of the Parallel Function Hypothesis and the Perceptual Difficulty Hypothesis and because there is some support for the Noun Phrase Accessibility Hierarchy Hypothesis as a reasonable predictor of difficulty in relative clause acquisition (Gass, 1982; Hyltenstam, 1984; and Pavesi, 1986), the implicational ordering evident in that hierarchy was taken as the basis for sequencing materials in the instructional design (see Doughty, 1988, for a review of this research).

Though there is some evidence that difficulty orderings are relevant to second language acquisition, a 'lockstep' progression from simplest to most complex is not automatically implied. An important aspect of the Noun Phrase Accessibility Hierarchy is that the implicational scale comprises a marked relationship (i.e. the less accessible end of the hierarchy is the more marked). Some recent studies have revealed that marked relationships may be exploited for the purposes of instruction. Zobl (1985) has shown that learners who are given instruction on the more marked member of an implicational pair can project the generalisation learned during instruction onto the unmarked member of the pair, but the reverse is not true. Thus, while processing considerations would suggest beginning instruction at the most accessible end of the Noun Phrase Accessibility Hierarchy, marking conditions indicate that instruction should start at the less accessible, or more marked, end of the hierarchy.

The dilemma for materials designers is to determine which sequence is best in instructional application. For the purposes of this experiment, it was hypothesised that, if markedness relationships are relevant in the instructed interlanguage development of relativisation, then structures which are organised according to implicational relations can be efficiently taught by exploiting the learners' ability to generalise the instruction. Consequently, subjects were to be provided with relative clause data from a marked position in the Noun Phrase Accessibility Hierarchy, viz. the object-of-preposition type of relativisation.

The second instructional design decision involved choosing the lesson containing the relative clause material. Ideally, the design of instructional materials should be based upon a combination of theoretical perspectives (such as the above markedness relations), relevant empirical findings (e.g. the need to specify the nature of the lesson), and practical considerations of the instructional context (e.g. the computer medium). In fact, as Richards & Rodgers (1986) suggest, materials development begins at the level of philosophy of language teaching which, in turn, is based upon theory and principles of language learning. From a theoretically-based philosophy, an approach to language teaching may be motivated. Once an approach to language teaching is established, a method and the techniques for the implementation of the method can then be developed. The language teaching method is an overall plan for the presentation of material and is procedural in nature. At the most specific level of the instructional design, the techniques are the actual mechanisms of instruction. The principles for materials design that Richards & Rodgers propose and which have been elaborated by Hubbard (this volume, Chapter 3) provide a good foundation for the design of computer-assisted instruction, which too often in the past has been based solely on computer capabilities.

Approach, Lesson, and Techniques

A comprehension-based approach to language teaching was adopted for the experiment. The comprehension-based approach states that language acquisition cannot proceed in the absence of comprehension and has been motivated by evidence that the learner's exposure to a target language is not, in itself, a sufficient condition for second language acquisition. What is essential is not merely that target language input be present, but also that the learner comprehend the message (Krashen, 1982; Long, 1980; Pica et al., 1987). Considerable effort in second language research has been devoted to determining precisely what makes input comprehensible to learners (see Day, 1986, or Gass & Madden, 1985, for collections of such studies).

Because the comprehension-based approach to language teaching emphasises facilitating the comprehension of linguistic input, the stated goal for learners in the experimental lessons of this study was the comprehension of the material in which the relative clauses and the relativisation instruction were embodied. To this end, the relative clause instruction was incorporated into computer reading lessons that culminated with comprehension measures. The reading lessons were designed according to current models of effective reading and, thus, emphasised the use of skills such as skimming for overall meaning, reading carefully for deeper comprehension, and scanning for specific details. Such text presentation features were easily implemented within the computer reading lesson format. The topics of the texts in the reading lessons were selected so as to reflect the kinds of activities in which students frequently are asked to participate in an ESL classroom. The content included an unresolved situation, as well as a certain amount of information useful for arriving at a logical solution.

The comprehension-based acquisition research informed the development of the techniques that were incorporated into the design of the relative clause instructional treatment. However, since SLA researchers and classroom instructors remain uncertain as to how best to encourage linguistic competence in the classroom — and this is particularly evident for methods within a comprehension-based approach to language instruction — decisions regarding which instructional techniques to employ were difficult. In order to gain insight into the kind of instruction which best facilitates the acquisition of relativisation, two different sets of instructional techniques were developed within the computer-assisted reading lessons to function as the kinds of aids to comprehension that have been identified as potentially crucial to acquisition. *Meaning-oriented* and *rule-oriented* instructional techniques were investigated in experimental groups, and each was compared to a control group that received no instruction. Both sets of instructional techniques were intended, in various ways, to focus the attention of the subjects who participated in the experiment on the components of the target of instruction (i.e. on the elements of relativisation).

Each computer lesson contained a paragraph of reading material that appeared on the screen sequentially in three reading-skill formats: skimming, reading-for-understanding, and scanning. Figure 7.2 depicts the overall design of the lessons. The stated goal of the lesson was to encourage better reading skills as well as to provide specific instruction in English grammar. Vital to experimental control was the computer-directed timing element that was under the control of the main program. Any portion of the overall lesson which was a part of the experimental treatment was presented to subjects for uniform periods of time. Subjects controlled the amount of time they had for understanding the screens that presented directions for the tasks. The experimental treatment was contained entirely within the reading-for-understanding portion of the lesson design.

A total of three complete stories were used in the course of the experiment. Each text was divided into several parts, resulting in a total of ten days of

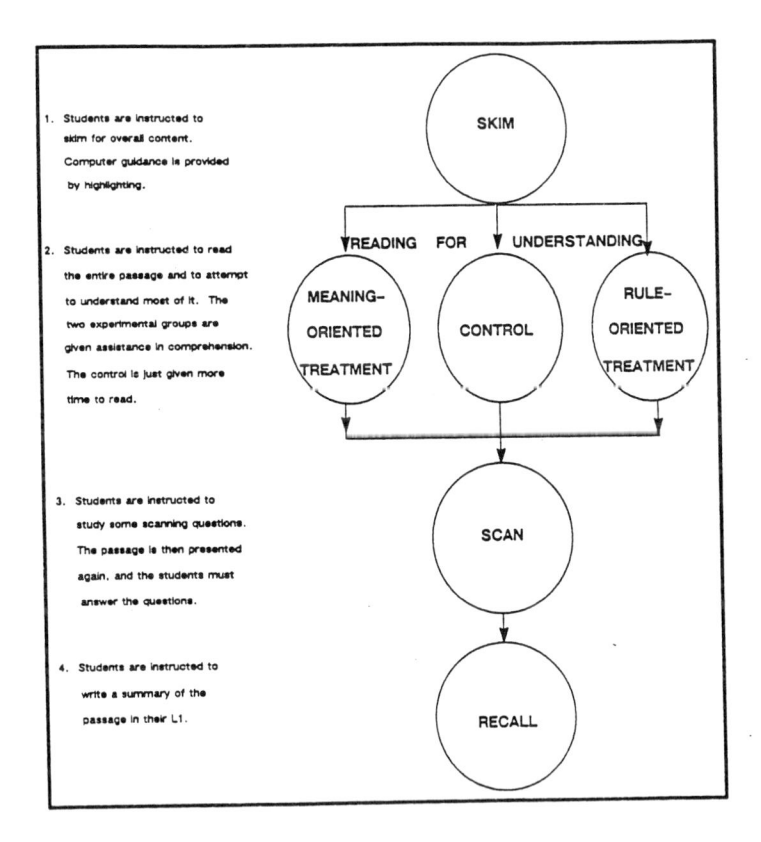

FIGURE 7.2 *Design of the experiment.*

instruction. Each lesson text was one paragraph long and was composed entirely of complex sentences containing relative clauses in which the relative pronoun functioned as object-of-preposition in the clause. The topics of the reading material, typical of those used in ESL classroom activities, were: (1) a dilemma over whether or not to disconnect the life support system of a loved one; (2) the decision about whether and whom to marry made by a successful lawyer; and (3) the awarding of a population growth permit to one of a number of applicants, each of whom has both positive and negative qualifications.

Two programming utility packages were used to build the C language applications necessary for the experimental instrument. The *Vitamin C* programming package was used to build the windowing functions necessary for displaying the screens in the main Microsoft C program. *VCScreen*, another C utility allowed the on-screen creation of the instruction to be displayed in lessons and the automatic generation of the C code that is subsequently incorporated into the main program. Some of the authoring capabilities of VCScreen include screen location of characters, selection of colours, highlighting features, and overall window design (i.e. borders, etc.).

The Lesson Design

In the first portion of the lesson (see Figure 7.2), all three groups of subjects (meaning-oriented, rule-oriented, and control) were instructed to skim the highlighted sentences in the paragraph for the purpose of obtaining a rapid understanding of the main focus of the reading material. Highlighted material included the title of the story and the first and last sentence of the paragraph. While subjects were permitted to read the skimming directions for as long as necessary, the skimming activity was timed and under the control of the computer program. Subsequently, the program moved on automatically to the reading-for-understanding portion of the lesson. Each group completed the skimming, reading-for-understanding, and scanning portions of the overall reading lesson. The experimental treatment resided in the reading-for-understanding format; hence, this portion of the overall lesson differed across groups (see Figure 7.2). Again, students in all three groups were permitted to control the amount of time necessary to read the directions on how to proceed through this part of the lesson, but once into the reading-for-understanding presentation of the paragraph (i.e. the experimental instructional treatment), the computer timer was in control and screens changed automatically.

During reading-for-understanding, all subjects were instructed to read the material for the purpose of understanding as much of the information as possible, were encouraged to use the instruction provided to aid their comprehension, and were notified in advance through the task directions that the next section of the lesson would include questions about the content of the reading. The sentences of the paragraph were presented one at a time in a window in the top third of the computer screen. Another window containing the experimentally manipulated instruction appeared in the remaining screen space, except in the case of the control group subjects, who saw the text sentence only. Following are descriptions and some sample screens from the three possible experimental portions of the lesson (i.e. meaning-oriented instruction, rule-oriented instruction, and the control treatment).

The meaning-oriented experimental instruction was developed at the University of Pennsylvania Language Analysis Project (Dr. John G. Fought, director) to be incorporated into the overall reading program (also developed in that project). The experimental, instructional technique was derived from an interactional view of how input becomes comprehensible to learners. From this perspective,

> language [is] a vehicle for the realization of interpersonal relations and for the performance of social transactions between individuals.... Interactional theories [of second language acquisition] focus on the patterns of moves, acts, negotiation, and interaction found in conversational exchanges. (Richards & Rodgers, 1986: 17).

For interactionists, a necessary condition for the acquisition of a language is the comprehension of input through *negotiated interaction* involving either linguistic or conversational modification or both (see Mohan, this volume, Chapter 6, for further discussion).

The meaning-oriented relative clause instructional technique thus sought to focus the attention of the subjects on the inter-relationship between meaning and the function of elements in the matrix and relative clauses, using techniques derived from research on spontaneous interactional modifications which arise in the course of the negotiation of meaning. The aim was to increase the salience of the components of relativisation and to clarify the semantics of the matrix and relative clauses. Some evidence for the benefits of pre-modified input has been shown in the work of Long (1985) and Chaudron (1985), who demonstrated that lecturettes which had built-in modifications such as repetitions and paraphrases were more easily comprehended than unmodified lecturettes. Pica *et al.* (1986, 1987) additionally have shown that comprehension is even greater as a consequence of the negotiation of meaning between interlocutors than when input to a listener is modified *a priori*. The meaning-oriented instructional techniques were consequently based upon interactional features, such as emphasis, semantic repetitions of words (i.e. definitions or paraphrases) and/or clarifications (such as of reference), all of which have been observed in interactionist research to serve to repair communication breakdowns in conversation and, hence, to facilitate comprehension.

Two screens of meaning-oriented instruction appeared on the screen during the reading-for-understanding portion of the lesson for the meaning-oriented group (MOG) of subjects: dictionary help and explanation. Dictionary help provided lexical clarification of the majority of the words in the sentence which appeared at the top of the screen. Words from the sentence were listed either singly or in phrasal combination and were graphically highlighted. Each listed word or words was presented in conjunction with (a) referent clarification (an example is anaphoric clarification for a personal pronoun), (b) semantic rephrasing, and/or (c) an equivalent, but more frequently occurring, vocabulary item.

Reading for Understanding

Obviously, the woman who he was very concerned about filled his thoughts.

Dictionary Help

Obviously: Clearly

the woman: Mrs. Peters

he: Mrs. Peters

was concerned about: was worried about

filled his thoughts: was ALL he thought about

FIGURE 7.3 *The dictionary help (vocabulary assistance).*

Dictionary help remained on the screen for two minutes and was always presented in conjunction with the original sentence at the top of the screen. No dictionary help, however, was provided for the relative pronouns in the sentences. Figure 7.3 gives an example of the vocabulary assistance provided to MOG subjects in the dictionary help type of aid to overall comprehension.

The second screen of comprehension assistance presented in the meaning-oriented instruction was explanation. Explanation consisted of expansion and/or rephrasing of the content of the original sentence, using redundant and salient visual cues to draw the attention of learners to the connection between the meaning of the sentence and its grammatical construction. Redundancy was accom-

COMPUTER APPLICATIONS IN LS ACQUISITION 139

Reading for Understanding

Obviously, the woman who he was very concerned about filled his thoughts.

Explanation

Now the story tells about how Mr. Peters felt. He was very worried about THE WOMAN (his wife). He could think only of THE WOMAN. So, obviously, THE WOMAN WHO he was very concerned about was THE ONLY WOMAN WHO he could think about.

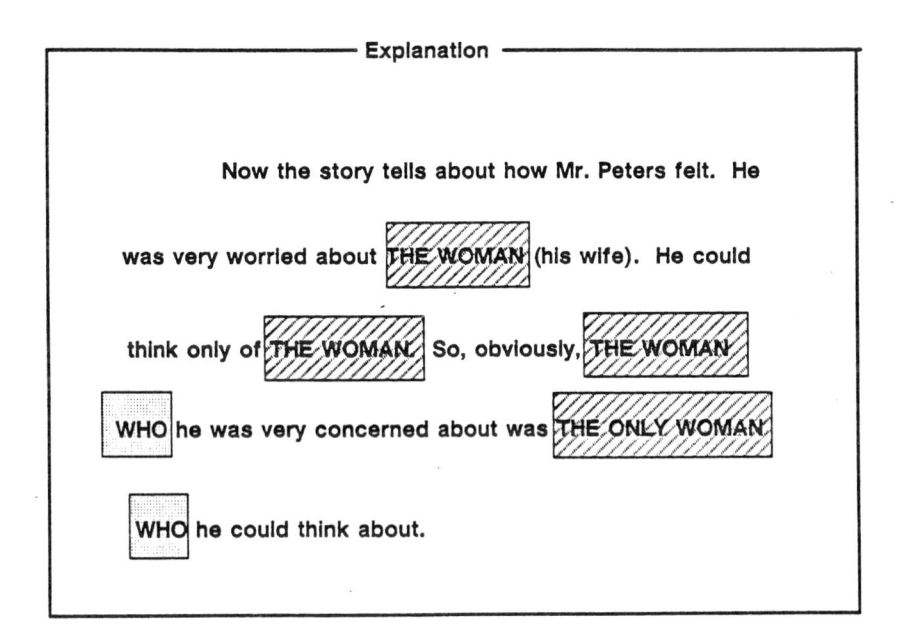

FIGURE 7.4 *The explanation (paraphrase).*

plished through rephrasing of the propositional content of the original sentence still visible at the top of the screen. Saliency was achieved with differential highlighting (i.e. one colour for relative pronouns and a different colour for the head nouns) and by positioning these nouns in initial and final position in the explanatory sentences. All of these techniques were aimed at clarifying meaning while at the same time making the structure of the relative clause apparent through visual isolation of its major elements. Highlighting and capitalisation were considered to be the visual equivalents of the verbal stress and emphasis features noted in interactionist research. The explanation portion of the meaning-oriented instruction also remained on screen for two minutes. Figure 7.4 shows a sample screen of meaning-oriented explanation.

The rule-oriented instructional techniques were derived from a structural view of how the English relativisation system is to be taught. According to the structural view, 'language is a system of structurally related elements for the coding of meaning' (Richards & Rodgers, 1986: 17). The goal of language learning, from a structural perspective, is mastery of the rules of the system. This goal of providing a focus on form during instruction is not necessarily in conflict with a comprehension-based approach to language learning. Rather, within a comprehension-based approach, rule-oriented instructional techniques may reasonably be hypothesised to be effective in making input comprehensible to the learners. In fact, recent research has indicated 'that during implicit and incidental learning of structural elements attention to form at input encoding is a sufficient condition' (Hulstijn, in press). There have also been some informal observations to the effect that noticing the structure of the elements contained within the input may be a necessary condition for internalising them (Schmidt & Frota, 1986). A focus on form in second language instruction makes the target of the instruction perceptually salient to the learner by directly and explicitly drawing his/her attention to the relevant formal properties of the language.

The rule-oriented relative clause instruction of the present study was developed to be similar to a program called *ANIMATED GRAMMAR* created at Ohio University (Soermarmo, 1986). The source code for the original program, written in Pascal, was given to the author for use in this experiment. As the grammar program had to be integrated into the main reading lesson program, it was re-coded in C, keeping many features of the original program intact. Some editing of the screen display was necessary, as the language of the relativisation rules was considered to be too complex for the proficiency level of the subjects. Essentially, the grammar instruction provided subjects with rules about relativisation through simultaneous statement of a rule and animated demonstration of the formation of the relative clause.

After a general description of the process of relativisation, subjects in the rule-oriented group (ROG) were taken step-by-step through the decomposition of a complex sentence containing a matrix clause and a relative clause into two simple sentences with co-referential nouns. The steps of the decomposition process were:

(1) a direction to study the complex sentence containing a relative clause;
(2) the identification and labelling of the relative pronoun;
(3) the identification and labelling of the head noun in the matrix;
(4) information on where the relative pronoun came from and its replacement by that duplicate noun;
(5) information about the position of the duplicate noun with respect to the verb phrase and its movement when necessary;

(6) the identification of the original main clause and relative clause;
(7) the separation of the two clauses into simple sentences.

Next, ROG subjects were shown the recombination of these two simple sentences into the original sentence containing a relative clause. The steps of the recombination process were essentially the reverse of the steps listed above for the decomposition of the original sentence. The total time required for the decomposition and recombination processes was four minutes per sentence. Figures 7.5 and 7.6 and provide two sample screens from the animated sentence decomposition, corresponding to steps 2 and 3 above.

The control treatment involved no instructional techniques at all and consisted only of exposure to the same text sentences as were present in the two types of instructional treatment (see upper portion of screens shown in Figures 7.4–7.6). The control group (COG) was given task directions emphasising comprehension of the text and was shown each sentence in turn with no additional information provided.

For all three groups, the computer program automatically moved on to the scanning portion of the overall reading lesson at the completion of the reading-for-understanding section (see Figure 7.2). The scanning activity was exactly the same for all three groups. Subjects were directed to scan through the entire paragraph for specific kinds of information needed to answer the two scanning questions that were presented both before and after the timed presentation of the text. Scanning time was restricted to sixty seconds, after which subjects recorded their answers to the scanning questions. In the final section of the overall reading lesson, all subjects were required to complete a reading recall exercise to demonstrate their comprehension of the information in the text.

The Experimental Design

To summarise, in the overall design of the experiment, the main question of interest was whether or not instruction would have an effect on the acquisition of relativisation in English. Two groups of subjects who received exposure to relative clause data plus an instructional treatment (one meaning-oriented and one rule-oriented) were compared with a control group which was provided only with the relative clause sentences. While keeping the language teaching approach and lesson design for the treatment groups constant, two experimental instructional techniques were compared to the exposure-only control group in an effort to determine whether a differential effect for the meaning-oriented vs the rule-oriented instruction would obtain.

```
┌─────────────── Reading for Understanding ───────────────┐
│                                                         │
│  Obviously, the woman who he was very concerned about filled │
│  his thoughts.                                          │
│                                                         │
└─────────────────────────────────────────────────────────┘


┌─────────────────────────────────────────────────────────┐
│ The noun-phrase before the relative pronoun is THE WOMAN. │
│ ──────────────────────────────────────────────────────  │
│                                                         │
│                                                         │
│    THE WOMAN WHO HE WAS VERY CONCERNED ABOUT FILLED     │
│              ───                                        │
│              └── Relative pronoun                       │
│                                                         │
│    HIS THOUGHTS.                                        │
│                                                         │
└─────────────────────────────────────────────────────────┘
```

FIGURE 7.5 *Identification of the relative pronoun.*

A consideration of previous research on second language acquisition in general and of the evidence from previous investigations of the effects of instruction on language acquisition motivated the following four hypotheses of the study (see Doughty, 1988, for a detailed discussion of the theoretical motivation for each hypothesis):

Hypothesis 1: Instruction has a positive effect on the acquisition of relativisation.
Hypothesis 2: Instruction which affects relativisation at one position in the Noun Phrase Accessibility Hierarchy will also affect all positions below it in the hierarchy.

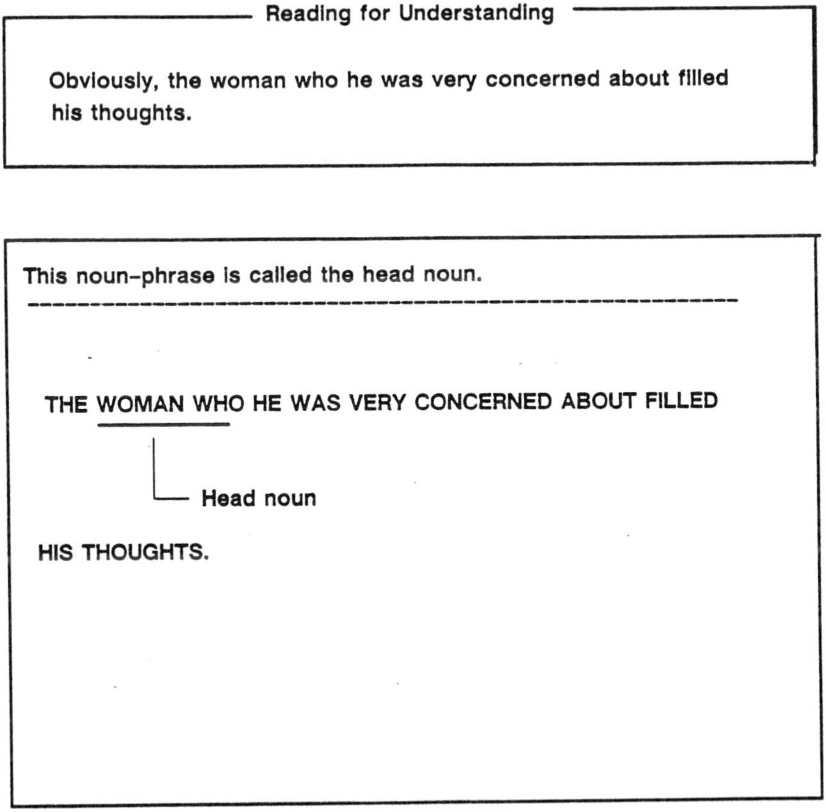

```
┌─────────────── Reading for Understanding ───────────────┐
│                                                         │
│   Obviously, the woman who he was very concerned about  │
│   filled his thoughts.                                  │
│                                                         │
└─────────────────────────────────────────────────────────┘
```

```
┌─────────────────────────────────────────────────────────┐
│  This noun-phrase is called the head noun.              │
│  ─────────────────────────────────────────────────────  │
│                                                         │
│                                                         │
│     THE WOMAN WHO HE WAS VERY CONCERNED ABOUT FILLED    │
│         ─────                                           │
│              └── Head noun                              │
│                                                         │
│     HIS THOUGHTS.                                       │
│                                                         │
│                                                         │
└─────────────────────────────────────────────────────────┘
```

FIGURE 7.6 *Identification of the head noun.*

Hypothesis 3: Instruction that is semantically and interactionally based (the meaning-oriented treatment) has a greater effect on the acquisition of relativisation than does no instruction.

Hypothesis 4: Instruction that is structurally based (the rule-oriented treatment) has a greater effect on the acquisition of relativisation than does no instruction.

A pretest-posttest, controlled experimental design was used to compare relativisation ability among the three groups in the experiment. Thus, the independent variable in the study was the instructional treatment, and the dependent variable was the change in relativisation ability from the pretest to the posttest. Written and oral pretests were given just prior to the treatment period.

Subsequent to the pretesting and random assignment of subjects, the experiment was conducted over ten working days, with subjects completing a one and one half hour lesson each day. Subjects were permitted to ask questions about how to operate the computer or how do the computer lessons. However, any questions pertaining to the general content of the reading material, the meaning of lexical items, the significance of a particular rule, or other information germane to relativisation or to the comprehension of the reading lessons were not allowed.

From the above description of the experimental computer lessons, it is clear that the role of the learner in the instructional design was necessarily limited by the need to monitor the presentation of material in the instructional treatment. Whereas in a non-experimental situation, control over the path taken through the lesson would ideally be in the hands of the learner, in the experiment, the capacity for computer-controlled presentation of materials was utilised. The amount of time and the order in which subjects viewed the linguistic material in the lessons was determined entirely by the computer program. Additionally, the role of the teacher, who might ordinarily be available in a computer lab for assistance with the lesson material, was limited to assistance with the operation of the computer.

During the experimental treatment period, subjects were tested daily on their comprehension of the reading material. These comprehension tests were built into the overall reading lesson of each instructional day and added to the lesson-like nature of the experimental treatment. After completing the skimming and reading-for-understanding portions of the computer lesson, subjects completed the scanning section of the lesson, which incorporated questions aimed at ascertaining the comprehension of specific pieces of information in the reading text. At the conclusion of the scanning portion of the lesson, students were directed to write a reading recall summary in their native language so that second language production constraints would not interfere with the assessment of comprehension. At the completion of the experiment, oral and written posttests were given to all three groups of subjects.

Data Description

All data gathered under pre- and posttesting conditions were entered into computer files on an Apollo DN300 system for the purposes of data description and analysis. Data from the written pre- and posttests were keyboarded into several files. Each file included a test item number, subject number, and test response. Oral pre- and posttests were transcribed directly into computer files using the Apollo *Aegis* editor and a Sanyo *Memoscriber* to facilitate the transcription process. Oral data were also labelled according to subject number, relativisation category, and elicitation technique.

Data gathered during the written and oral elicitations were scored and then coded for error categories. Raw data were then manipulated with the AWK programming language, a pattern matching language which allows the creation of data handling tools consisting of just one- or two-line programs. AWK searches files on a line-by-line basis for any specified pattern within a field. When the pattern is found, one or several actions are executed. Typically, data may be searched for a code, and only those lines containing the code may be redirected to a new file. For example, by searching on the 'subject number' field, all responses by any one subject may be printed out together. Alternatively, all subjects' answers to one particular question may be compiled into a separate file. AWK was also used to facilitate some simple calculations such as numerical summation and divisions. Though very simple to accomplish with AWK, considerable time was saved by arranging the data in various configurations that were conducive to the calculations. Through the use of these simple programs, an overall sense of the data was easily gained within a very short period of time.

Data Discovery

Data Analysis

All statistical analyses were carried out on a Texas Instruments AT-compatible computer linked to an IOMEGA Bernoulli Box mass storage device. Data files resulting from the AWK programs were transferred from the Apollo environment to the AT via DomainPC interface software, and both files and statistical software simultaneously resided on a 20 Mg Bernoulli Cartridge. The statistical software employed was *SYSTAT* (version 3; Wilkinson, 1986), and the predetermined alpha level of significance for all statistical analyses was set at 0.05.

A one-way ANOVA, using SYSTAT's MGLH module (a true least squares program), was calculated to compare the relativisation ability of all subjects in the three groups at the outset of the experiment. Results of the ANOVA indicated that there was no significant difference among the groups on the variable of pre-treatment knowledge of relativisation ($p < 0.30$). Percent changes in scores on tests taken before and after instructional treatment were then calculated for each group to determine the change in relativisation ability of the subjects after completion of the experimental treatment (percent change = mean posttest score minus mean pretest score divided by mean pretest score). The percent change in relativisation that obtained was in a positive direction for all three groups (MOG = 49.30%; ROG = 55.25%; COG = 12.00%). Thus, the percent change scores indicated that subjects were affected by the treatment and that this effect was particularly large in the two experimental groups.

To test the first hypothesis of the study (that instruction would positively affect the acquisition of relativiation), a paired samples (or dependent) t-test (using SYSTAT's STATS module) was performed comparing posttest to pretest scores for each group. Results of the paired samples t-tests indicated that all three groups, MOG, ROG, and COG, improved significantly in relativisation ability ($p < 0.0001$, $p < 0.005$, $p < 0.002$, respectively). As indicated by the result of the paired-samples t-test, the change in the two experimental groups appeared to be larger than that which obtained for the control group, suggesting that a differential effect from the treatment had obtained among the three groups.

To compare the amount of improvement in relativisation ability after the instructional treatments among the three groups, gain scores representing each subject's change in relativisation ability were calculated with the STATs module (gain = posttest score minus pretest score). Results indicated that the mean gain scores of the two experimental groups (MOG = 26.49; ROG = 25.31) were similar, and both were more than double the mean gain score that was observed for the control group (12.02). The mean gain scores were compared across groups using the one-way ANOVA procedure in SYSTAT's MGLH module. The results of the comparison across MOG, ROG, and COG of the group mean gain scores indicated a differential treatment effect among the groups ($F = 4.386$; $p < 0.029$).

In order to determine exactly where the treatment effects obtained, a comparison of groups was carried out using SYSTAT's HYPOTHESIS and CONTRAST programs. First the two experimental group means were compared, and then each experimental group mean was compared, in turn, with the control group mean. The results of the multiple mean comparisons on the groups MOG, ROG, and COG showed that while there was no difference between the two experimental groups ($F = 0.47$, $p < 0.831$), the difference between each of the experimental groups and the control group was significant (for MOG vs. COG: $F = 7.626$, $p < 0.013$; for ROG vs. COG: $F = 5.668$, $p < 0.029$). Hence, both experimental treatment groups were shown to have improved significantly more than did the control group.

To examine the effects of the instruction across relativisation categories, a two-way ANOVA comparing the group mean gain scores on the factors of treatment by relative clause type was calculated using the MGLH two-way analysis of variance sub-program. Results confirmed a significant effect for treatment ($F = 7.752$, $p < 0.001$) and no significant effect for relativisation type ($F = 1.970$, $p < 0.89$). No interaction effect for treatment by relative clause type was evident

($F = 0.619$, $p < 0.795$). Therefore, it was determined that, although only instruction in the object-of-preposition type of relativisation was incorporated into the treatment, the amount of improvement was consistent across all categories of relativisation.

In summary, the results of the paired samples t-tests showed that all subjects who participated in the study improved on the posttest over the pretest evaluation of their relativisation ability. However, the calculated percentage changes as well as the varying significance levels of the three paired t-tests suggested that there was a difference among the three groups regarding the amount of improvement. This possibility was in fact confirmed by an ANOVA comparing the mean gain scores of the three groups. Analysis of the data revealed that subjects in the two experimental groups (MOG and ROG), who were exposed to marked cases of the target structure and who received meaning- and rule-oriented instruction, respectively, achieved significantly higher gain scores than did the control group subjects, who received only exposure to the marked target structure. Thus, the instructional treatment given to the two experimental groups enabled those subjects to improve significantly more in relativisation ability than did the control group subjects.

Session replay analysis

In order to explain two major findings of the study — (1) that the two experimental groups improved significantly more than the control group and (2) that the two experimental groups performed equally well — it was useful to examine the specific elements of each treatment, MOG, ROG, and COG. Such a detailed analysis was possible via the computer's capability to re-play the instructional sessions. The three treatments varied across groups and differed according to the manner in which the components of the relativisation process were presented. In particular, the instruction vs. control treatments differed greatly with respect to the degree of explicitness with which subjects' attention was drawn to the constituents of a relative clause and its host matrix sentence. Figure 7.7 depicts the elements of both types of instruction and of the control treatment along a continuum ranging from the explicit presentation of the features of relativisation to an implicit focusing of the user's attention. Due to limitations of space, a detailed discussion of the nature of the experimental treatments is not possible here (for such a detailed discussion, see Doughty, 1988). However, a summary of observations made during the computer session replays is provided below.

Both experimental treatments provided in this study were similar in that the major elements of relativisation were brought into prominence via

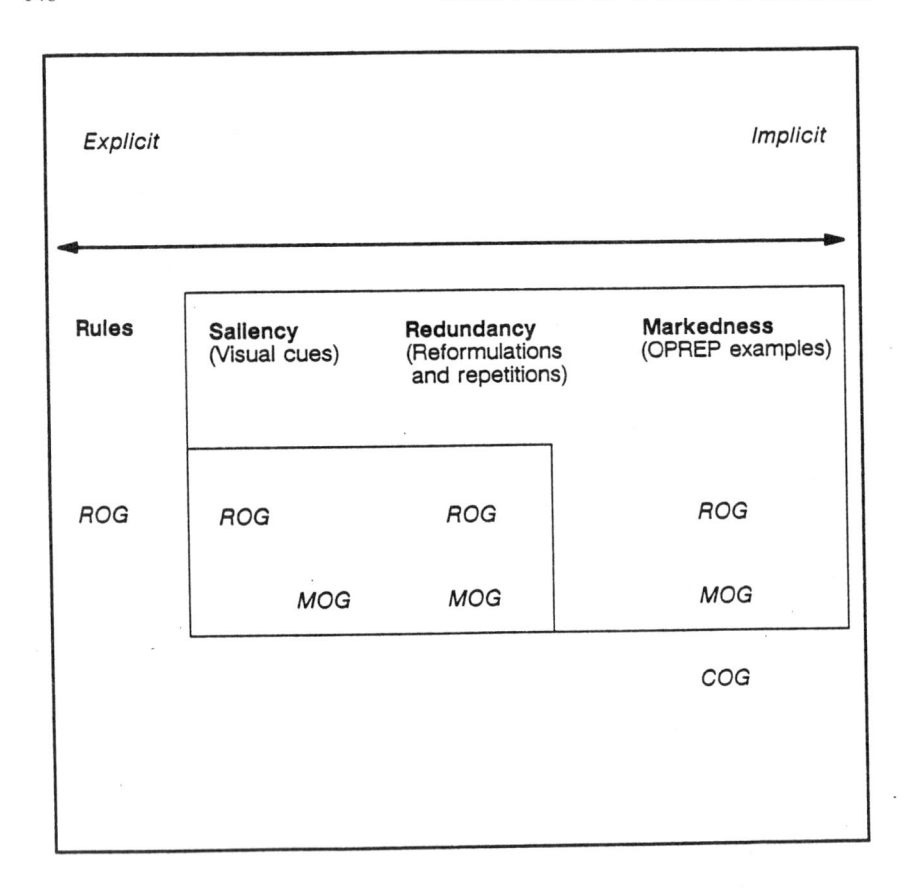

```
                  Explicit                              Implicit

        ◄─────────────────────────────────────────────────────►

   Rules    Saliency         Redundancy          Markedness
            (Visual cues)    (Reformulations     (OPREP examples)
                             and repetitions)

   ROG      ROG              ROG                 ROG

                     MOG            MOG                 MOG

                                                        COG
```

FIGURE 7.7 *Features of the instructional and control treatments.*

perceptual saliency, redundancy features, and the frequent presentation of marked examples of the target structure. Only the marked relative clauses and, to a limited degree, the redundancy features were available to control subjects. Only ROG subjects' attention was explicitly drawn to the formal properties of relativisation via metalinguistic description. Such information was available implicitly to the MOG group through highlighting and capitalisation of head nouns and relative pronouns. Control subjects were not assisted with any components of relativisation, and their attention was drawn to relative clauses only to the extent that they were exposed to an artificially high frequency of marked relative clauses in the reading text. Extensive redundancy features and saliency, the features common to the instructional treatment groups and excluded from the control treatment, appear to have contributed to the greater success of the MOG and ROG subjects.

Saliency

Several elements of both the rule- and meaning-oriented instructional treatments contained computer-generated perceptual cues which served to focus subjects' visual attention on the major components of relativisation. In the case of ROG instruction, visual cues included labelling, disappearance and replacement of elements, and animated movement across the computer screen. These visual cues were consistently and directly associated with the explicit articulation of relativisation rules through synchronised screen presentation. For example, during the sentence-combination process in which one sentence became the relative clause that was then embedded into the other sentence, subjects could watch one co-referential noun change into the appropriate relative pronoun on the computer screen: they saw the relative pronoun move to the correct position, and finally, the relative clause itself moved to the target position adjacent to the head noun. Each step was explained to ROG subjects with an explicit statement of the relevant rule at the top of the computer screen.

In the meaning-oriented instruction, the visual attention of subjects was captured via computer highlighting as well as typographical capitalisation of the head noun and relative pronoun. However, the relativisation rules underlying the emphasis of the highlighted and capitalised components were not expressly stated. Rather, the discovery of the functional and semantic connections between the head noun and the relative pronoun was left to the subjects' powers of inference. No explicit techniques were applied to draw control group subjects' attention to the components of relativisation.

Redundancy

The two instructed groups also received treatments with a much higher level of redundancy than was the case in the control group treatment. The explanation portion of the meaning-oriented treatment and the animated sentence combinations/decompositions of the rule-oriented treatment provided additional redundancy via reformulations of the original text sentences, with the former aimed at clarifying the story line and the latter at demonstrating visually the metalinguistic description of the process of relativisation. The feature of redundancy was available to COG subjects only to the extent that they were able to read and re-read the same original sentences, but only for as much time as was allowed by the computer. Such freedom to re-read the text sentences was also a component of the ROG and the MOG instructional treatments. Although all three groups could freely and repeatedly read the sentences containing relative clauses, only the instructed groups could apply the instructional reformulations of the original text sentences toward comprehending the new instances of relativisation, as well as toward internalising the rules of the English relativisation system.

Finally, it should be noted that the sentences which comprised the reading texts were specially formulated to contain only one type of relative clause. All were of the object-of-preposition relative clause type, a low, inaccessible, and, therefore, marked position on the Noun Phrase Accessibility Hierarchy. Furthermore, every sentence in the paragraph to be read during the computer lesson contained such a marked relative clause. The finding that indicated a certain amount of improvement in all groups could be attributed to the marked nature of the sentences in the reading passages and to the frequent exposure of subjects to such pre-selected data. Thus, all subjects could have benefited from exposure to marked data and may have been able to project a degree of understanding of these marked sentences to the less marked domains of relativisation (see Doughty, 1988, for a full discussion of the markedness issue). Subjects who received instruction in addition to marked exposure gained substantially more in relativisation ability, however.

That both instructed groups in the present study made equivalent gains in relativisation demonstrates that there are many different ways of encouraging learners to notice forms other than traditional methods of metalinguistic presentation (Rutherford & Sharwood Smith, 1988). Though the attention of all instructed subjects was drawn to the features of relativisation, one major difference between the two groups was that only ROG subjects also received the explicit metalinguistic presentation of the rules underlying the labels and movements visible on the screen. Such techniques fall into positions from the centre toward the implicit end of the continuum shown in Figure 7.7. While the instruction provided to the MOG subects contained none of the explicit rule articulation available to ROG subjects, the MOG subjects' attention was deliberately drawn to those components of relativised sentences which form the connection between the relative and matrix clauses, namely, the relative pronoun and the head noun, respectively.

In terms of the observed gains in relativisation ability, a focus on meaning and a focus on rules were equally successful techniques within the comprehension-based approach, provided that subjects were directed to notice the elements of relativisation in the input. Furthermore, whereas both instructed groups viewed the major elements of relativisation as they were brought into prominence through perceptual saliency and the control group did not, and since both instructed groups outperformed the control group, it is apparent that the visual direction of the learners' attention to the elements of the relative clause construction influenced their learning of the relativisation system. However, because the MOG subjects benefited from the instruction to the same degree as the ROG subjects, it is also evident that the explicit metalinguistic presentation was not necessary to facilitate improvement in relativisation.

Another primary difference among groups in this experiment was that the MOG group received considerable assistance with comprehension of the texts, whereas the ROG and COG groups did not. Vocabulary clarification (or confirmation, depending upon individual subjects' prior knowledge) was presented to MOG subjects together with every sentence during the reading-for-understanding portion of the computer reading lesson. Further elaboration of the content of the texts was also provided to MOG subjects via the explanation aid to comprehension, which followed the dictionary assistance. The explanation assistance was also always presented in conjunction with the original text sentence. Because comprehensible input alone may not be a sufficient condition for second language acquisition, or more specifically, since attending only to comprehensible input does not ensure grammatical accuracy in the target language, comprehensibility of the input was fostered in the MOG group in combination with the bringing to prominence of the structural elements of relativisation. Consequently, sentences could be comprehended while simultaneously allowing subjects to notice the targeted structure.

An examination of the results comparing comprehension scores across the three groups — MOG, ROG, and COG — revealed an apparent advantage for MOG with respect to comprehension of the reading lesson texts. As judged by native speakers/teachers, MOG subjects understood and were able to recall, on average, approximately 70% of the material, whereas the average comprehension and recall of the texts by the ROG and COG subjects was only approximately 40%. This result is not surprising, given the amount of vocabulary assistance provided to the MOG group and the difficulty level of the texts. The differences among the group means determined on the basis of the native speakers'/teachers' evaluations of the recall summaries was statistically significant (F = 9.648, $p < 0.002$). The difference among groups is evident in comparing the MOG subjects to the COG subjects (F = 15.217, $p < 0.001$) and in comparing the MOG subjects to the ROG subjects (F = 12.228, $p < 0.003$). No difference was found when the ROG and the COG subjects were compared (F = 0.143, $p < 0.710$).

The overall comprehension of the texts by the MOG subjects was largely and significantly greater than that of either the ROG subjects or the COG subjects. Furthermore, while both instructed groups improved equally in relativisation ability, the MOG subjects demonstrated an advantage for comprehension of the content of the material presented in the reading lessons. Thus, a focus on meaning, while not at all detrimental to the development of linguistic competence, additionally facilitated greater comprehension of the propositional content of text (Larsen-Freeman, 1982).

Conclusion

Throughout the development of the computer-assisted relativisation instruction, which was central to this study demonstrating the effectiveness of second language instruction, empirical findings and design considerations from previous research, interrelated principles of instructional design, and the exploitation of computer coding elements for lessons as well as for the research applications were important and interdependent elements. In-depth analysis of the experimental instruction was facilitated by computer storage and replay of all treatment materials. The cohesive development of the project, the in-depth post-experimental analysis of the treatment, and the experimental findings of the investigation each contribute to a fuller understanding of the nature of successful instructional materials for language learning and to the conclusion that computer-assisted language instruction is beneficial for second language acquisition.

References

BARRUTIA, R. (1970) Two approaches to self-instructional foreign language study: Computerized foreign language instruction, *Hispania*, 53, 361–71.
CHAUDRON, C. (1985) A method for examining the input/intake distinction. In S. GASS & C. MADDEN (eds), *Input in Second Language Acquisition*. Rowley, MA: Newbury House.
— (1988) *Second Language Classrooms: Research on Teaching and Learning*. New York: Cambridge University Press.
DAY, R. (1986) *Talking to Learn: Conversation in Second Language Acquisition*. Rowley, MA: Newbury House.
DOUGHTY, C. (1988) The effect of instruction on the acquisition of relativization in English as a second language. Unpublished Ph.D. dissertation. Philadelphia, PA: University of Pennsylvania.
ELLIS, R. (1984) Can syntax be taught? A study of the effects of formal instruction on acquisition of iwhi questions by children, *Applied Linguistics*, 5: 2, 138–155.
GASS, S. (1982) From theory to practice. In M. HONES & W. RUTHERFORD (eds), *On TESOL '81*. Washington, DC: Teachers of English to Speakers of Other Languages.
GASS, S & C. MADDEN (1985) *Input in Second Language Acquisition*. Rowley, MA: Newbury House.

HULSTIJN, J. (In press) Implicit and incidental second language learning: Experiments in the processing of natural and partially artificial input. In H. DECHERT (ed.), *Interlingual Processing*. Tubingen: Gunter Narr.

HYLTENSTAM, K. (1984) The use of typological markedness conditions as predictors in second language acquisition: The case of pronominal copies in relative clauses. In R. ANDERSEN (ed.), *Second Languages: A Cross-linguistic Perspective*. Rowley, MA: Newbury House.

KEENAN, E. & B. COMRIE (1977) Noun phrase accessibility and universal grammar, *Linguistic Inquiry*, 8: 1, 63–99.

— (1979) Data on the noun phrase accessibility hierarchy, *Language*, 55: 2, 333-51.

KRASHEN, S. (1982) *Principles and Practice in Second Language Acquisition*. Oxford: Pergammon Press.

KUNO, S. (1974) The position of relative clauses and conjunctions, *Linguistic Inquiry*, 5: 1, 117–36.

LARSEN-FREEMAN, D. (1982) The WHAT of second language acquisition. In M. HONES & W RUTHERFORD (eds), *On TESOL '81*. Washington, DC. Teachers of English to Speakers of Other Languages.

LEVIN, L. (1972) *Comparative Studies in Foreign Language Teaching*. Stockholm: Almqvist and Wiksell.

LIGHTBOWN, P. (1981) Acquiring English in Quebec classrooms. In H. WODE & S. FELIX (eds), *Language Development at the Crossroads*. Tubingen: Gunter Narr.

LONG, M. H. (1980) Input, interaction and second language acquisition. Unpublished Ph.D. dissertation. Los Angeles, CA: University of California at Los Angeles.

— (1983) Does second language instruction make a difference?, *TESOL Quarterly*, 17: 3, 359–82.

— (1985) Input and second language acquisition theory. In S. GASS & C. MADDEN (eds), *Input in Second Language Acquisition*. Rowley, MA: Newbury House.

MELLGREN, M. (1983) Applying micro-computers in the foreign language classroom: challenges and opportunities. In A. GARFINKEL (ed), *The Foreign Language Classroom: New Techniques*. Lincolnwood, IL: National Textbook Company.

MORRISON, H. & E. ADAMS (1968) Pilot study of a CAI laboratory in German, *The Modern Language Journal*, 52: 279-87.

PAVESI, M. (1986) Markedness, discoursal modes, and relative clause formation in formal and informal settings, *Studies in Second Language Acquisition*, 8: 1, 38–55.

PICA, T., C. DOUGHTY & R. YOUNG (1986) Making input comprehensible: Do interactional modifications help?, *ITL Review of Applied Linguistics*, 72, 1–25.

PICA, T., R. YOUNG & C. DOUGHTY (1987) The impact of interaction on comprehension, *TESOL Quarterly* 21: 4, 737–58.

PIENEMANN, M. (1982) Psychological constraints on the teachability of languages, *Studies in Second Language Acquisition*, 6: 2, 186–214.

RICHARDS, J. & T. RODGERS (1986) *Approaches and Methods in Language Teaching*. Cambridge, UK: Cambridge University Press.

RUTHERFORD, W. & M. SHARWOOD SMITH (1988) *Grammar and Second Language Teaching*. Rowley, MA: Newbury House.

SCHERER, G. & M. WERTHEIMER (1964) *Psycholinguistic Experiment in Foreign Language Teaching*. New York: McGraw Hill.

SCHMIDT, R. & S. FROTA (1986) Developing basic conversational ability in a second language: A case study of an adult learner of Portuguese. In R. DAY (ed.), *Talking to Learn: Conversation in Second Language Acquisition*. Rowley, MA: Newbury House.

SHELDON, A. (1974) The role of parallel function in the acquisition of relative clauses in English, *Journal of Verbal Learning and Verbal Behavior*, 13, 272–81.

SMITH, P. (1970) *A Comparison of the Cognitive and Audiolingual Approaches to Foreign Language Instruction.* Philadelphia, PA: Center for Curriculum Development.

SOERMARMO, M. (1986) ANIMATED GRAMMAR. Athens, OH: The Ohio University.

WILKINSON, G. (1986) SYSTAT. Kansas City, KS: Kansas State University.

ZOBL, H. (1985) Grammars in search of input and intake. In S. GASS & C. MADDEN (eds), *Input in Second Language Acquisition.* Rowley, MA: Newbury House.

8 Microcomputer Adventure Games and Second Language Acquisition: A Study of Hong Kong Tertiary Students

ANTHONY CHEUNG
University of New South Wales, Kensington, Australia
and
COLIN HARRISON
University of Nottingham, England

Introduction

The employment of computers in education and research has become a widespread phenomenon, and Hong Kong is no exception. In the past few years, an increasing number of secondary and tertiary educational institutions have acquired microcomputers and are now using them in various academic disciplines across the curriculum, including English language teaching. Computer-assisted language learning (CALL) is still a relatively new area in education, and research literature on CALL methodology and software evaluation is scarce, especially anything with particular reference to Hong Kong.

The need for research on CALL methodology and software evaluation was spelled out during a course on Computers in Language Education and Research organised by the British Council at Lancaster University, U.K., in September, 1984. The editors of the course papers, Leech & Candlin (1986), advocate an urgent need for a critical examination of the educational potential of CALL. The study reported here is one such examination. It begins with a discussion of the type of software employed in the research, deriving three experimental hypotheses based on the nature of that software. The next three sections describe the design of the experiment, the results, and the interpretation of results in relation to the three experimental hypotheses. The concluding section summarises the major findings and identifies further questions that may be addressed by future researchers.

Background and Hypotheses

A primary question about CALL software is how much students actually gain linguistically from working on it. Although various writers have suggested that CALL evaluation is needed, the amount of published research is still meager. (For an overview and analysis of CALL research, see Chapelle & Jamieson, 1989.) The present study empirically examines the phenomenon of CALL application in a Hong Kong tertiary educational setting.

The software employed for the study is entitled *COLOSSAL ADVENTURE*, an interactive text-only adventure game, referred to by Higgins & Johns (1984: 64) as a variety of move-based simulation (MBS). For Higgins & Johns, there are two types of microcomputer simulations, namely, real-time simulations (RTSs) and move-based simulations. In RTSs the action is continuous. The player can fail by simply doing nothing or reacting too slowly. In MBSs the computer holds the display constant and waits for a decision. Higgins & Johns are in favour of exploiting MBSs in the language learning context. Comparing MBSs with RTSs, they assert that 'there is usually even richer use of language in move-based simulations'. Furthermore, Coupland (1983: 104), in his overview of CALL software development, draws attention to the place of MBSs in ESL: 'This overview of the development of software suitable for use by teachers of English would be incomplete without a description of ADVENTURE.' Reporting on the attitudes of the participants who attended a summer seminar at the University of Delaware on *MYSTERY HOUSE*, a text adventure game, Culley *et al.* (1986: 69) comment that 'no one could deny how much sheer fascination it [MYSTERY HOUSE] provided'. Many other authors are also in favour of using MBSs in language learning. They include McLeod (1984), Miller & Burnett (1986), and Goulding (1986).

Higgins & Johns (1984) suggest that MBSs often arouse motivation and interest. They assert that 'there is room for both real and simulated or narrated experience. Both are food for learning and communication' (p.63). Malone (1980) also agrees there is a highly motivating factor in MBSs. He sees MBSs as being able to engage the player in a simulation of a 'real' situation, in which a goal must be achieved through a process of active decision-making, involving the element of risk. Harrison (1983: 37) comments, 'With adventure games there is a real spirit of discovery and exploration....The excitement and interest that the decision making process arouses in a small group is quite considerable.'

COLOSSAL ADVENTURE includes a collection of rather unfamiliar words. In an English for Specific Purpose (ESP) context such as that of the subjects in this study, coming across new lexical items specific to a given register and having to learn them is not uncommon. Hence, the extent to which subject-specific, i.e. program-specific, lexical items was acquired was examined.

Prepositions of place were one of the elements which the students came across frequently while they were working on the game. There was at least one occurrence in every text string which appeared on the screen. The question was. Did this frequent exposure to prepositions lead to acquisition? Higgins & Johns (1984) also suggest that while students work on MBSs, 'there is a real need for ... IF clauses'. Conditionals, therefore, qualify as a good candidate for investigation. The first hypothesis of the study is formulated as follows:

> Working intensively on move-based simulations enables students to improve in areas of the target language which include prepositions of place, program-specific lexical items, and conditionals.

In addition, the attitudes of students towards *COLOSSAL ADVENTURE* was examined by means of the second hypothesis as follows:

> Students will have a favourable attitude towards move-based simulations as a language learning exercise.

Questions asked included aspects such as whether or not the game was easy, enjoyable, interesting, and enlightening. Students' opinions relating to time spent on the game were also sought.

Miller & Burnett (1986: 162) state that MBSs provide opportunities for 'actively engaging the student in using a language in a problem solving context'. *COLOSSAL ADVENTURE* is essentially a piece of computer software which incorporates a number of complex problems. While students work on the game in pairs, they are expected to communicate with one another in the target language, i.e. English. The problems presented in the game are essential to trigger this communication.

Kahney (1986: 20) distinguishes between well-defined and ill-defined problems. He points out that in a well-defined problem, the solver is provided with four different types of information. This is information on the initial state of the problem; the goal states; the legal operators, i.e. the legal moves to solve the problem; and operator restrictions which constrain the application of operators. An ill-defined problem, on the other hand, lacks some or all of the information described above.

Following Kahney's paradigm, the initial state of *COLOSSAL ADVENTURE* is the background information of the game. The goal states are the game objectives and various treasures to be discovered and collected by the user. The legal operators are the clues, the directions, and the definitions of difficult program-specific lexical items. The operator restrictions are the impossible or disastrous moves. At the outset of the experiment, almost none of the above information was readily available to the subjects who were all MBS novices.

During the experiment, information relating to the goal states and legal operators of the task was released at different stages. The information was offered at the request of the subjects and generally consisted of hints concerning the treasures available and pitfalls to avoid. However, since the problem is so ill-defined, it was hypothesised that the students would like to have more information provided to them while they were playing the game. This leads to the third hypothesis of the study.

In solving ill-defined problems, such as the type represented by *COLOSSAL ADVENTURE*, the provision of information about the problem is desirable; such information should include the problem's initial state, goal state, legal operators, and operator restrictions.

It was hoped that the result of this experiment would provide some useful input for the implementation of the type of MBS represented by *COLOSSAL ADVENTURE* in an ESP learning context. Indeed, we believe that the findings of this study, as described below, have relevance for future training in CALL and for future research in CALL that seeks to evaluate student performance and attitudes using this type of program.

Design of the Experiment

Experimental treatment

In the experiment, there were 84 subjects and they were all first-year students of the Hong Kong Polytechnic who spoke Cantonese (a variety of Chinese) as their mother tongue. They were drawn from five first-year classes of the Hong Kong Polytechnic. They were evenly and randomly divided into two groups which are referred to as Groups A and B. As will be discussed in greater detail later, their second language proficiency at the outset of the study, as reflected in their GRADE scores, was very much alike. Language attainment tests were administered after they had worked intensively on the game. The tests aimed at investigating students' performance in three areas of the target language: prepositions of place, program-specific lexical items, and conditionals.

The experiment consisted of two phases. In Phase One, Group A was the experimental group. The subjects worked in pairs on *COLOSSAL ADVENTURE* for eight separate hours over a two-week span. As the subjects were all novices to MBSs, a pre-work preparation session was conducted. To enable the subjects to have an easier start in using the game, each pair was given a clue sheet which included. (a) the two objectives of the game; (b) all of the possible directions; (c) all of the verbs the computer recognised; and (d) all of the special instructions, e.g. CATALOGUE, DESCRIBE, SAVE, etc. However, the nouns that the computer understood were not listed. This was mainly to retain the mystery of the game and to stimulate the curiosity of the subjects. During the preparation session, it was suggested that a good strategy would be to make a record of specific locations and paths taken.

The role of the researcher (Cheung) was just to load the program at the beginning of each session and to inform the students when time was up. He stayed away from the subjects for the rest of the time during the experiment so as to cause the least disturbance or interference. As a result, a relatively free and relaxed experimental environment was provided. While the subjects were working on the game, a dictionary was also provided. After each session, subjects had the opportunity of asking for one or two clues if they so wished. At the end of the fourth hour, a treasure list consisting of all the treasures in *COLOSSAL ADVENTURE* was given out to the students so that they would know more about the goal states of the game.

Group B was the control group. The subjects did not have a pre-work preparation session, and they learned word processing for four hours during the same two-week period. At the end of this time, an attainment test was administered to both groups. The test was designed to measure three specific areas of the target language which students were hypothesised to show gains in after working with the MBS, namely, prepositions of place, conditionals, and program-specific lexical items. An attitude test in the form of a questionnaire (see Appendix A) was also administered.

In Phase Two, Group A became the control group and Group B became the experimental group. Again, after the experimental group had completed their eight hours on the MBS and the control group their four hours of word processing training, the same attainment test and questionnaire were administered to both groups.

Evaluation Instruments

The language attainment test consisted of three parts. Part 1 related to prepositions of place, Part 2 to program-specific lexical items, and Part 3 to conditionals. Using public examination scores, i.e. English attainment grades on entry to the course, as a predictor, multiple regression analyses were conducted, using Youngman's (1979) SMLR multiple regression program, to produce residual scores in order to compare attainment with expectations on the Phase One and Phase Two tests.

An individual's residual score is the difference between that person's actual score on a test and that predicted by the regression model. In the present study, the residual scores generated are all based on a mean of zero and a standard deviation of one. The residual scores provide a useful and rapid check on how well a person has performed on a test: a positive residual score indicates a better-than-expected score, and a negative residual score suggests that the person has done worse than would have been expected on the basis of whatever predictor score was used. In this experiment, GRADE was employed to predict the Phase One scores, and the Phase One scores were in turn employed to predict the Phase Two scores.

The questionnaire comprised three parts. Part 1 aimed at eliciting information on students' attitudes towards using English generally. Part 2 inquired about students' attitudes towards *COLOSSAL ADVENTURE*. Part 3 asked students about their opinions on the information provided about *COLOSSAL ADVENTURE*.

At the end of Phase One, the full questionnaire was administered to Group A. As Group B was not exposed to the experimental treatment, and as Parts 2–3 of the questionnaire were specifically related to *COLOSSAL ADVENTURE*, only Part 1 was administered to Group B. However, at the end of Phase Two, the full questionnaire was administered to both groups. For the parts that were administered a second time, the aim was to check if attitudes had firmed up, polarised or reverted.

Measurement Technique

Grade

GRADE is a variable which accounts for a subject's English language attainment in public examinations. Currently in Hong Kong, at the upper-secondary level, there are two major public examinations of this sort. The first one is the Hong Kong Certificate of Education Examination (HKCEE), which is mainly attempted by Form Five students. The second is the Advanced Level Examination (ALE), mainly attempted by Upper Form Six students who intend to secure a place at the University of Hong Kong. Subjects in the experiment were given a GRADE score in the range 0–10 based on their level of attainment in English as measured by their performance on one or both of these tests.

The language attainment test

Each of the three parts of the language attainment test was administered to the students in turn. Part 1 consisted of 15 items. It was presented to the subjects in the form of a modified cloze test, in which deleted words were not randomly chosen but focused on prepositions. The text presented was similar to that of *COLOSSAL ADVENTURE*. Part 2 consisted of 30 items which were presented in a multiple choice format. For each item, a key and three distractors were provided. Half of the items had direct relevance to *COLOSSAL ADVENTURE*, while the other half were taken from other contexts. As this part of the test did not require as much 'production' from the subjects as the other two parts would have, the latter group of items was included to provide distraction so as to minimise the effect of learning from the Phase One test. Part 3 consisted of 30 items in which verb stems were presented in sentence contexts and subjects were required to provide the correct verb forms.

For each correct answer, a score of '1' was awarded. No marks were given for incorrect attempts. Hence, the highest possible score for Part 1 was 15. In Part 2, only the program-specific lexical items were processed, and the highest possible score was also 15. The highest possible score for Part 3 was 30. Therefore, the highest possible total score for the whole test was 60. Altogether, there were two sets of test scores. There were the Phase One scores (PO), which were obtained following Group A's exposure to the adventure game, and the Phase Two scores (PT), which were obtained following Group B's exposure to the game. As explained above, each group functioned as a control group on one occasion, when they received word processing training on microcomputer.

The questionnaire

Part 1 of the questionnaire related to the way subjects felt when they talked to another person in English. They were labelled as 'GQs', i.e. general questions. There were three of these questions. Parts 2–3 related to *COLOSSAL ADVENTURE* and they were labelled 'Qs'. There were twenty of these.

The questionnaire comprised three types of question. First, there were two yes/no questions. Second, there were ten items which required responses to be made on six-point scales. Last, there were eleven items which constituted three checklists.

For each yes/no question, there was an additional 'not sure' option. A 'yes' response was coded as '3', a 'not sure' response was coded as '2' and a 'no' response as '1'. For questions which required subjects to provide responses on six-point scales, polarities of a particular phenomenon were given at the ends of the scales. For instance, to elicit student opinions on the game, scales with polarities such as 'very interesting' vs. 'not interesting at all', and 'very easy' vs. 'very difficult' were given. For these questions, responses were coded with the same value as those provided to the students. In other words, a response of '1' was coded as '1', a response of '2' was coded as '2', and so on. For questions which constituted the checklists, a ticked response was coded as '1' and a blank was coded as '0'. Moreover, this type of question did not always require answering. For instance, whether or not responses were required for items Q06 to Q16 depended on how a subject answered Q05. A 'yes' response given in Q05 would require the subject to answer these questions. A 'no' or a 'not sure' response would require a jump to Q17. Throughout, blanks and non-responses were treated as 'missing cases' and were all coded as '9'.

Results

In this section, a summary of the results of the experiment is presented. First, the means, standard deviations, and t-values of the following variables/test scores of Groups A and B are given:

(1) GRADE;
(2) Phase One test (PO): The test consists of three sub-parts, namely, prepositions of place (POP), program-specific lexical items (POV), and conditionals (POC); the total of the test scores (POT) was also calculated;
(3) Residuals of PO: GRADE is used as a predictor to predict the four PO scores;
(4) Phase Two test (PT): The three sub-parts are referred to as PTP, PTV, and PTC; the total is referred to as PTT;
(5) Residual scores on PT using PO as predictor.

Second, the correlation coefficients of the four pairs of PO and PT scores of Group A are listed, i.e. POP and PTT, POV and PTV, POC and PTC, POT and PTT. Finally, the means, standard deviations, and t-values of the questionnaire responses of the two groups are provided.

Results and residuals of language attainment tests

Table 8.1 presents the GRADE scores of Groups A and B. The details include the means, standard deviations, and the t-value of a two-tailed t-test of the means. In the tables, t-values significant at the 0.01 level are double-asterisked and those significant at the 0.05 level are single-asterisked. Those with no asterisks are non-significant.

Details of the results and residuals of PO of the two groups are given in Tables 8.2 and 8.3, respectively. The means and standard deviations of POP, POV, POC, and POT are listed in Table 8.2. A 2-tailed t-test was applied to the means of the four pairs of scores and the t-values are also provided. Table 8.3 presents the means and standard deviations of the residuals scores. The t-values derived from a 2-tailed t-test of the means of the residuals of the four pairs of scores are also listed. In this instance, GRADE was used to predict POP, POV, POC, and POT.

Details of the results of PT of Groups A and B are given in Table 8.4. Details of the residuals of PT of the two groups are given in Table 8.5. Again, the means, standard deviations, and t-values of all the scores in question are presented. In Table 8.5, residuals of PO scores predicting PT scores are provided.

Details of the correlation coefficients of the four pairs of PO and PT scores of Group A are listed in Table 8.6.

Questionnaire responses

The means, standard deviations, and t-values of the questionnaire responses of Groups A and B are presented in Table 8.7. Both groups have GQ scores for Phases One and Two. However, Group B only has Phase Two Q scores because Parts 2–4 of the questionnaire were not administered to Group B until the conclusion of Phase Two of the experiment. 2-tailed independent t-tests were applied to the means of (a) Phase One Group A scores and Phase Two Group B scores and (b) Phase Two Group A scores and Phase Two Group B scores. A dependent t-test was applied to the means of the Phase One and Phase Two Group A scores.

TABLE 8.1 *GRADE scores: Groups A and B*

Variable	Group A Mean	S.D.	Group B Mean	S.D.	t
GRADE	4.09	2.8	3.83	2.62	0.43

TABLE 8.2 *Results of Phase One language attainment test (PO): Groups A and B*

Variable	Group A Mean	S.D.	Group B Mean	S.D.	t
POP(prep)	8.85	2.41	7.97	2.56	1.60
POV(vocab)	9.33	2.03	6.09	2.30	6.74**
POC(cond)	13.14	4.46	12.42	5.23	0.66
POT(total)	31.33	7.12	26.50	8.15	2.86**

TABLE 8.3 *Residual scores of Phase One language attainment test with GRADE as predictor: Groups A and B*

Criterion	Group A Grade (Predictor) Mean	S.D.	Group B Grade (Predictor) Mean	S.D.	t
POP(prep)	0.38	2.10	−0.38	2.16	−1.61
POV(vocab)	1.55	1.70	−1.55	1.65	−8.32**
POC(cond)	0.22	3.84	−0.22	3.90	−0.50
POT(total)	2.14	5.47	−2.14	4.93	−3.73**

TABLE 8.4 *Results of Phase Two language attainment test (PT): Groups A and B*

Variable	Group A Mean	S.D.	Group B Mean	S.D.	t
PTP(prep)	9.04	2.41	8.50	2.47	1.01
PTV(vocab)	9.52	2.38	8.59	2.48	1.73
PTC(cond)	13.76	5.03	13.33	5.54	0.37
PTT(total)	32.33	7.57	30.42	8.50	1.07

TABLE 8.5 Residual scores of Phase Two language attainment test with Phase One scores as predictors: Groups A and B

Criterion	Group A Mean	S.D.	Group B Mean	S.D.	t
PTP(prep)	POP (Predictor) −0.04	1.38	POP (Predictor) 0.05	1.87	0.25
PTV(vocab)	POV (Predictor) −0.42	1.78	POV (Predictor) 0.42	2.09	1.98*
PTC(cond)	POC (Predictor) −0.12	2.33	POC (Predictor) 0.12	2.72	0.44
PTT(total)	POT (Predictor) −1.12	3.35	POT (Predictor) 1.12	4.82	2.44*

TABLE 8.6 Correlation coefficients of the four pairs of PO and PT scores: Group A (N = 42)

Variables	Correlation Coefficient
POP × PTP	0.82**
POV × PTV	0.71**
POC × PTC	0.88**
POT × PTT	0.90**

In order to assist the reader in interpreting Table 8.7, it may be mentioned at this point that for Q05 and Q18, the range is 1 to 3 with a mean of 2; for Q06 to Q16, the range is 0 to 1 with a mean of 0.5, while the rest of the questions have a range of 1 to 6 with a mean of 3.5.

Discussion and Interpretation of Results

The reliability of the language attainment test

To establish the reliability of the language attainment test used in the experiment, the test-retest method was employed. Towards the end of Phase One, after Group A (N = 42) had received the experimental treatment, the test was

TABLE 8.7 *Means, standard deviations and t-values of student self-appraisal questionnaire responses: Groups A and B*

		Group A Phase 1 Mean	Group A Phase 1 S.D.	Group A Phase 2 Mean	Group A Phase 2 S.D.	Group B Phase 1 Mean	Group B Phase 1 S.D.	Group B Phase 2 Mean	Group B Phase 2 S.D.	t A1–B (Independent)	t A2–B	t A1–A2 (dep.)
GQ1	Talk Eng to Another Person — Easy	3.67	1.04	3.64	0.97	3.98	0.78	3.60	0.82	0.35	−0.24	−0.24
GQ2	Talk in English — Enjoyable	3.60	0.95	3.57	0.73	3.81	1.06	3.55	1.00	−0.22	−0.12	−0.18
GQ3	Talk in English — Confident	3.83	1.02	3.81	1.01	4.14	1.03	3.86	1.01	0.11	−0.21	−0.19
Q01	Game Interesting	2.64	1.13	3.02	1.10			2.38	0.95	−1.14	−2.83**	3.23**
Q02	Game Easy	4.14	0.94	4.00	0.85			3.88	0.96	−1.25	−0.60	−0.88
Q03	Game Enlightening	3.29	1.03	3.31	0.80			3.19	0.85	0.46	−0.65	0.15
Q04	Game Enjoyable	3.00	1.11	3.19	0.98			2.74	0.93	−1.16	−2.14*	1.31
Q05	Want Help to Play Game	1.10	0.37	1.10	0.37			1.33	0.68	1.98*	1.98*	0.00
Q06	Need Game Objectives	0.67	0.47	0.64	0.48			0.55	0.50	−1.04	−0.82	0.25
Q07	Need Game Background Info	0.54	0.50	0.64	0.48			0.73	0.45	1.66	0.77	1.00
Q08	Need Treasure List	0.79	0.40	0.77	0.42			0.67	0.47	−1.23	−0.96	−0.44
Q09	Need Direction List	0.51	0.50	0.49	0.50			0.33	0.47	−1.54	−1.32	−0.33
Q10	Need Discsn Techniques in Eng	0.23	0.43	0.21	0.40			0.18	0.39	−0.50	−0.25	0.00
Q11	Need (Others — Pre-work Prep)	0.05	0.22	0.03	0.16			0.00	0.00	−1.32	−0.92	−1.00
Q12	Need Clues Whenever Required	0.26	0.44	0.23	0.42			0.18	0.39	−0.75	−0.50	−0.33
Q13	Need Clues When Badly Required	0.56	0.50	0.67	0.47			0.55	0.50	−0.16	−1.04	1.40
Q14	Need Dictionary	0.87	0.33	0.90	0.30			0.91	0.29	−0.50	−0.16	1.43
Q15	Need Teacher to Explain Diff Terms	0.28	0.45	0.33	0.47			0.15	0.36	−1.33	−1.79	0.90
Q16	Need (Others — While Working)	0.03	0.16	0.00	0.00			0.03	0.17	0.12	1.09	−1.00
Q17	Time spent on game worthwhile	3.14	1.28	3.31	0.96			2.79	0.83	−1.50	−2.64**	1.19
Q18	More Time on Game	1.62	0.82	1.86	0.77			1.67	0.75	0.28	−1.14	−2.68**
Q19	Used Eng Very Often in Game	2.43	0.90	2.57	0.98			2.98	0.91	2.73**	1.94	0.95
Q20	Eng Better after Playing Game	3.00	0.76	3.24	0.68			3.05	0.49	0.34	−1.45	1.88

administered the first time. Two weeks afterwards, at the conclusion of Phase Two, the same test was administered. Group A then took the test the second time.

It will be recalled that the test consists of three sub-parts: prepositions of place, program-specific lexical items, and conditionals. Phase One scores of Group A were compared to those of Phase Two, as shown in Table 8.6. The correlation coefficients obtained are reasonably high. The coefficient obtained by the method is 0.82 between POP and PTP; 0.71 between POV and PTV; 0.88 between POC and PTC; and 0.90 between POT and PTT. Hence, the stability and the reliability of the test is established.

Hypothesis one

Working intensively on move-based simulations enables students to improve on areas of the target language which include prepositions of place, program-specific lexical items, and conditionals.

The difference in the means of GRADE between the two groups is only 0.16, out of a possible 10. This difference is minimal. The insignificant t-value of 0.43 obtained after applying a 2-tailed t-test to the scores, as shown in Table 8.1, provides further evidence for the parity in the GRADE score of the groups.

This minimal difference of the GRADE scores indicates that the level of English of the two groups at the outset of the study was close. Such parity is crucial, as it provides a valid basis for making comparisons of scores of the language attainment tests at the conclusion of Phases One and Two of the experiment. Differences in test scores may then be attributable to the experimental treatment.

The scores were compared in two ways. The first involved an examination of the results in terms of means and standard deviations of each group, followed by the application of 2-tailed t-tests. Secondly, following a multiple regression analysis, the residual scores were examined. In the first instance, GRADE was employed as a predictor of the Phase One scores, which included POP, POV, POC, and POT. Then, the four Phase One scores were employed as predictors of their Phase Two counterparts. Finally, GRADE was employed as a predictor of the four Phase Two scores.

The t-values of the Phase One scores (Table 8.2) indicate that there are significant differences in vocabulary (POV) and the total language score (POT) between the two groups. On the other hand, the differences of POP and POC between the groups are insignificant. No further discussion of POT is necessary, as the difference is mainly contributed by POV. For POV, Group A scored a mean of 9.33 and Group B scored 6.09.

These results show that of the three areas of English tested at the conclusion of Phase One, there was little difference between the groups on prepositions and conditionals. However, for program-specific lexical items, the performance of Group A, i.e. the experimental group, was significantly superior to that of Group B, the control group for this phase of the experiment.

As seen in Table 8.3, the residual scores of the Phase One language attainment test involved employing GRADE as a predictor of POP, POV, POC, and POT. Again, it is POV and POT which have significant t-values: -8.32 and -3.73 respectively. On the other hand, POP and POC have non-significant t-values. An examination of the means of POV residuals reveals that Group A has a positive mean of 1.55, while Group B has a negative mean of -1.55. This implies that Group A has done better than predicted, while Group B has done worse than predicted. This difference is attributable to the experimental treatment which Group A received in Phase One. In other words, the superior performance of Group A with the program-specific lexical items would appear to be a result of their having played the adventure game.

The t-values of Phase Two scores, shown in Table 8.4, indicate that the differences of all the scores — i.e., PTP, PTV, PTC, and PTT — between the two groups are all non-significant. Part of the Phase Two results appear to be consistent with those of Phase One. There was little difference in PTP and PTC between the two groups. However, compared to Phase One, the means of PTV and PTT of the groups in Phase Two are much closer to each other. A comparison of the means of POV and PTV reveals that Group B has now improved on the program-specific lexical items: from a mean of 6.09 to one of 8.59, an increase of 2.50.

These results show that both groups, towards the end of Phase Two, had improved on all the three areas, i.e. prepositions, program-specific lexical items, and conditionals. Whether or not these improvements are significant will be examined below.

As shown in Table 8.5, the residual analysis of the Phase Two language attainment test used Phase One scores as predictors of their Phase Two counterparts. POP, POV, POC, and POT are predictors of PTP, PTV, PTC, and PTT respectively. Again, it is POV-PTV and POT-PTT which have significant t-values. An examination of the means of POV-PTV residuals scores reveals that Group A has a negative mean of -0.42, while Group B has a positive mean of 0.42. This implies that Group A has done worse than predicted while Group B has done better. This difference is attributable to the experimental treatment which Group B had in Phase Two.

The employment of Phase One vocabulary scores to predict those of Phase Two is based on the assumption that Group B will not be good at program-specific lexical items, and therefore the prediction is that Group B subjects would not do well. However, the results indicate that they did a lot better. The reason seems obvious: while they were working on the adventure game in Phase Two, learning of the lexical items had taken place. On the other hand, although Group A had a negative PTV mean, it is not necessarily the case that Group A subjects had forgotten everything they learned in Phase One. It is only that in Phase Two, they had not been working intensively on the adventure game and learning new vocabulary. A comparison of the POV and PTV means of Group A reveals a small gain of 0.19 towards the end of Phase Two in spite of the fact that the group did not have any experimental treatment in the second phase. This indicates that they had actually improved slightly, yet not enough for their residual scores to be as good as those of Group B.

Hence, the first hypothesis can only be partially supported. Based on the results of this study, it could be reformulated as:

> Working intensively on move-based simulations enables students to improve on program-specific lexical items of the target language.

Of the three areas of the target language investigated, perhaps the only area that subjects were processing actively was program-specific lexical items. That is, in the event of the occurrence of an unfamiliar lexical item, it was likely that a student would strive to discover the definition of the item, either from his partner or from a dictionary. Chances of the student acquiring the item thus became greater. On the other hand, subjects appeared not to be paying as much attention to prepositions of place and conditionals as to lexical items. Perhaps mastery of the definitions of lexical items, including program-specific lexical items, was a crucial vehicle for progressing in the game, while knowing prepositions and conditionals was not.

Hypothesis two

> Students will have a favorable attitude towards move-based simulations as a language learning exercise.

In the questionnaire, there were four questions which had direct relevance to *COLOSSAL ADVENTURE*. They were Q01, Q02, Q03, and Q04. All four questions required responses on six-point scales. Q01 asked subjects if they found the game interesting. In Phase One, the mean of Group A (A1) was 2.64. In Phase Two, the mean of Group A (A2) was 3.02 and the mean of Group B (B) was 2.38. Means below 3.50 would indicate that subjects found the game interesting. Therefore, it would appear that both groups found the game interesting. The result of a dependent t-test suggests that there is significant difference between A1 and A2. The mean of A2 was higher than that of A1, which suggests that in Phase Two, Group A found the game less interesting than they had in Phase One. On the whole, however, they still found it interesting. During Phase Two of the experiment, for obvious reasons, Group A subjects were not given access to *COLOSSAL ADVENTURE*. Perhaps interest waned as a result of not having a chance to work on the game. Moreover, the significant t-value of a 2-tailed independent test between the means of A2 and B suggests that the difference between Groups A and B in Phase Two was significant. An examination of the means reveals that the B group found the game very interesting, while the A group in Phase Two found it only interesting.

Q02 asked subjects if they found the game easy or difficult. Means smaller than 3.50 signify that subjects judged the game easy and those greater than 3.50 signify that they judged the game difficult. For this item, A1 had a mean of 4.14, A2 had one of 4.00, while B had 3.88. These scores imply that both groups found the game rather difficult. The values of the t-tests indicate that the differences in attitude of the groups were not significantly different.

Q03 asked subjects whether they found the game enlightening. The means of A1, A2, and B were 3.39, 3.31, and 3.13, respectively, indicating that both groups found the game somewhat enlightening.

Q04 asked subjects if they found the game enjoyable. A1 had a mean of 3.00, A2 had a mean of 3.19, and B had a mean of 2.74. Therefore, it can be inferred that both groups enjoyed playing the game. The t-value between A2 and B is -2.14 and is significant at the 0.05 level. A comparison of the means reveals that B found the game more enjoyable than A2. The 'no play' effect discussed in connection with Q01 might be at work here as well. The attitude of Group A subjects seems to have drifted towards a more neutral stance.

The three general questions (GQs) assessed the general attitude of the subjects towards talking to another person in English. These questions were presented on six-point scales. Their means range from 3.55 to 4.14. The values reflect that while subjects talked to another person in English, they were generally unsure of themselves and found the experience difficult and unpleasant. Conversely, the means of Q19, also a question presented on a six-point scale, range from 2.43 to 2.98. This range of values indicates that students thought that they used English quite frequently while they were working on the game. If this self-reported measure is reliable, then the game can be regarded as a good stimulator of target language use.

There were two questions which related to time spent on the game. Q17 asked subjects if they thought time spent on the game was worthwhile. Q18 asked them if they wanted to spend more time on the game.

Again, Q17 was presented on a six-point scale. The means of A1, A2, and B were 3.14, 3.31, and 2.79, respectively. In general, both groups thought the time they had spent on the game was worthwhile. However, B had a much lower mean. This indicates that subjects felt even more strongly that the time they had spent was worthwhile. It was not surprising, therefore, to find the t-value between A2 and B of -2.64 to be significant.

Q18 was a yes/no question. For all the yes/no questions, there is an additional 'not sure' option. For Q18, a mean lower than 2.0 would indicate that subjects would have liked to spend more time on the game, and a mean higher than that would indicate otherwise. A1 had a mean of 1.62, A2 had one of 1.86, while B had one of 1.67. The values indicate that both groups wanted to spend more time on the game. However, the t-value of -2.68 between A1 and A2 was signficant. This suggests that although Group A subjects still wanted to spend more time on the game towards the end of Phase Two, there was a significant shift of attitude: they did not want to spend as much time on the game as they had first thought in Phase One. Here, a lessening of enthusiasm in Group A is again evident, perhaps attributable once more to the 'no play' effect.

Hence, it can be seen that subjects found the game interesting, difficult, enlightening, and enjoyable. They thought they used the target language quite frequently while they were working on the game. They even considered time spent on the game, i.e. the eight hours in the experiment, worthwhile. Moreover, they were willing to spend more time on it. These findings support the second hypothesis.

The shift in attitudes of Group A subjects from Phase One to Phase Two appears to carry a pedagogical implication. If one wishes to keep students continuously interested and enthusiastic about MBSs, ones that are similar to *COLOSSASL ADVENTURE*, an important rule to follow is that such games ought to be presented in a continuous manner. If not, some of the original interest and enthusiasm might gradually fade away.

Hypotheses three

> In solving ill-defined problems, such as the type represented by *COLOSSAL ADVENTURE*, the provision of information about the problem is desirable; such information should include the problem's initial state, goal state, legal operators, and operator restrictions.

In the questionnaire, there was a set of questions designed specifically to elicit student opinions relating to the above hypothesis, Q05–Q16. Q05 was the leading question. It asked subjects if they wanted help in playing the game, with answer choices yes/no. Only those who chose 'yes' were required to answer Q06–Q16, the checklist questions. The means of A1, A2, and B were 1.10, 1.10, and 1.33, respectively. 39 subjects out of 42 in A1 and A2, and 33 out of 42 in B selected 'yes'. This response shows that the majority of subjects thought they needed help in playing the game, though the t-values between A1–B and A2–B are both 1.98 and significant at the 0.05 level. Group A had the greatest majority of subjects who thought that help was needed. The specific areas of help that subjects regarded as necessary are discussed below.

Q06–Q16 were checklist questions. Means higher than 0.50 would indicate that a particular item was considered to be required, while those lower than 0.50 would indicate otherwise. Q06, Q07, Q08, Q13, and Q14 had means higher than 0.50 for A1, A2, and B. This result indicates that subjects wished to be provided with game objectives (Q06), background information (Q07), a treasure list (Q08), clues when such were badly needed (Q13), and a dictionary (Q14). Among these, it was Q14 (requiring a dictionary) which had the highest means: 0.78, 0.90, and 0.91, for A1, A2, and B, respectively.

On the other hand, Q10, Q11, Q12, Q15, and Q16 had means lower than 0.50 for A1, A2, and B. Thus, subjects thought that they did not require training in discussion techniques in English (Q10), clues whenever they wanted them (Q12), and their teacher to explain difficult terms to them (Q15). Q11 and Q16 invited subjects to suggest further help that they might need to play the game. Q11 related to the pre-work preparation and Q16 related to help while the subjects were working with the game. As their means were very low, ranging from 0.00 to 0.05, the responses to these items were not considered important.

Q09 had a mean of 0.51 for A1, 0.49 for A2, and 0.33 for B. This result indicates that the stance of Group A on the provision of a list of directions for the game was quite neutral. On the other hand, many Group B subjects thought that they could have done without such a list.

All of the t-values of the above checklist questions are non-significant. It appears that on these issues subjects of both groups were thinking quite alike. The attitudes of Group A members also remained consistent in both phases of the experiment.

One can conclude from the above discussion that while solving ill-defined problems, i.e. working with the game, subjects found the provision of the following information valuable:

(1) the problem's initial state — background information about the game;
(2) the goal states — the game objectives and the treasure list;
(3) the legal operators — a dictionary containing definitions of difficult words; and
(4) operator restrictions — clues.

Hence, the third hypothesis is supported. From this finding, it appears that a preferred mode of administering *COLOSSAL ADVENTURE* and other similar MBSs in an ESP learning context is to have the above information relating to the game readily available for use by the students whenever they need it.

Q14 had exceedingly high mean values, which ranged from 0.87 to 0.91 Q15 had rather low means, which ranged from 0.15 to 0.33. Both questions were related to the provision of definitions of difficult words. The means indicate that subjects preferred to consult the dictionary themselves instead of getting quick answers from their teacher. This finding suggests another preference with regard to administration of this type of MBS: teacher intervention, in the form of providing definitions of lexical items, should be restricted.

Conclusion

The aim of the present study was to investigate the language learning effect of MBSs on Hong Kong tertiary students. In the language attainment tests, three areas of the target language were examined. They were prepositions of place, program-specific lexical items, and conditionals. In the questionnaires, two further aspects were explored. These were students' attitudes towards *COLOSSAL ADVENTURE* and their opinions on the provision of information for ill-defined problems of the sort present in many types of adventure games. The major findings are summarised below.

First, subjects made significant improvement on program-specific lexical items as a result of working on the game. In the other two areas, there was only marginal improvement. One possible reason for this was that learning the lexical items was a key to making progress in the game. During the experiment, subjects were actively processing the lexical items. This processing led to subsequent acquisition. On the other hand, the correct use of prepositions of place and conditionals was not so essential for making progress in the game.

Second, subjects were found to hold favourable attitudes towards *COLOSSAL ADVENTURE* as an ESP exercise. For them, although the game was difficult, it was interesting, enlightening, and enjoyable. They reported that they used

English quite frequently while they were working on the game and regarded the time spent on the game as being worthwhile. Many were even prepared to spend more time on it.

Third, the shift of attitude of Group A subjects from Phase One to Phase Two carries a pedagogical implications. Teaching materials such as the *COLOSSAL ADVENTURE* type of MBS ought to be presented in a continuous manner if one wishes to hold students' interest and enthusiasm for a substantial span of time.

Fourth, while solving this particular type of ill-defined problem, students were in favour of having access to more information. Such information should include the initial state, the goal states, the logical operators, and the operator restrictions of the problem. Hence, when this type of MBS is administered in a CALL context, the above information should be readily available to users whenever necessary.

Last, subjects preferred to consult the dictionary themselves instead of getting quick answers from the teacher. This finding suggests another preferred mode of administering the *COLOSSAL ADVENTURE* type of MBS, that is, restricted teacher intervention in providing definitions of lexical items.

On the basis of the findings of the present study, a number of further questions may be identified. First, while the subjects were working on the game, what actually occurred that led to (a) the acquisition of program-specific lexical items and (b) the non-acquisition of prepositions of place and conditionals? Second, were the subjects enjoying the game? Third, were they really using the target language frequently? Fourth, how did they manage to arrive at solutions to the various problems? What mental processes were involved in their problem-solving and how were these realised in the discourse between pairs of students?

With respect to the questions above, one further wonders if there is any difference in the linguistic performance between subjects who are strong in the target language and those who are not. Moreover, should there be a difference, it would be interesting to examine whether this difference would affect the game-playing ability of the subjects. These and other questions, some of which have been addressed elsewhere (see, e.g. Cheung, 1987, 1988), provide important insights for courseware developers, curriculum planners, and teachers in making decisions about how best to implement CALL in a variety of educational contexts. Only through continued research on how students use and prefer to use CALL can we begin to develop a foundation for rational decision-making, not only at tertiary level, but at all levels of education, about how best to apply computers in the language classroom.

Appendix A

The questionnaire

G. In general, when you are talking to another person in English, how do you feel?

very easy	1	2	3	4	5	6	very difficult	G01
very enjoyable	1	2	3	4	5	6	not enjoyable at all	G02
very confident	1	2	3	4	5	6	not confident at all	G03

1. How do you find the adventure game?

very interesting	1	2	3	4	5	6	not interesting at all	01
very easy	1	2	3	4	5	6	very difficult	02
very enlightening	1	2	3	4	5	6	not enlightening at all	03
very enjoyable	1	2	3	4	5	6	not enjoyable at all	04

2.1 While you were playing the game, did you want to have any help?   05

	YES
	NO
	NOT SURE

If YES, please answer Question 2.2.

2.2 What sort of help would you like to have?
Please 'tick' as many items as you think fit below.

In a pre-work preparation, the following should be provided:

	game objectives	06
	background information of the game	07
	a list of the treasures	08
	a list of all possible directions	09
	some discussion techniques in English	10
	others (please specify)	11

Appendix A continued

While working on the program,

	clues should be given whenever required	12
	clues should ONLY be given when badly required	13
	a dictionary should be provided	14
	difficult terms should be explained by the teacher	15
	others (please specify)	16

3.1 What do you think of time spent on adventure games?

very worthwhile | 1 | 2 | 3 | 4 | 5 | 6 | not worthwhile at all   17

3.2 Would you like to spend more time on the same adventure game again?   18

	YES
	NO
	NOT SURE

4.1 How often do you think you used English while you were playing the adventure game?

very often | 1 | 2 | 3 | 4 | 5 | 6 | never   19

4.2 How much better or worse do you think your English is after playing the adventure game?

a lot better | 1 | 2 | 3 | 4 | 5 | 6 | a lot worse   20

4.3 After you have played the adventure game, can you now identify areas of English that you are weak in?

	YES
	NO
	NOT SURE

If YES, please answer Questions 4.3.1 and 4.3.2.

Appendix A continued

4.3.1 Which areas of weakness in English can you identify?

	understanding difficult words	22
	comprehending reading passages	23
	convincing your partner	24
	giving instructions	25
	giving explanations	26
	providing clarification	27
	formulating hypotheses	28
	others (please specify)	29

4.3.2 Would you like your teacher to help you improve on the areas that you have identified?   30

	YES
	NO
	NOT SURE

References

CHAPELLE, C. & JAMIESON, J. (1989) Research trends in computer-assisted language learning. In M. C. PENNINGTON (ed.), *Teaching Languages with Computers: The State of the Art*. La Jolla CA: Athelstan.

CHEUNG, A. C. M. (1987) The 'common sense' approach in artificial intelligence. Paper presented at the 20th Annual British Association of Applied Linguistics, Nottingham, UK, June.

— (1988) Microcomputer moved-based simulations: An investigation of the English language performance of Hong Kong tertiary students. Unpublished Ph.D. dissertation. Nottingham, UK: University of Nottingham.

COUPLAND, J. (1983) Software: An historical overview. In D. CHANDLER (ed.), *Exploring English with Microcomputers*. Newcastle on Tyne, UK: Centre for Educational Technology.

CULLEY, G., G. MULFORD & J. MILBURY-STEEN (1986) Foreign-language adventure game: Progress report on an application of AI to language instruction, *CALICO Journal*, 4: 2, 69–87.
GOULDING, S. (1986) Problem-solving: Slow learning using a microcomputer adventure game. Unpublished M. Phil. thesis. Nottingham, UK: University of Nottingham.
HARRISON, C. (1983) English teaching and computer assisted simulations. In D. CHANDLER (ed.), *Exploring English with Microcomputers*. Newcastle on Tyne, UK: Center for Educational Technology.
HIGGINS, J. & T. JOHNS (1984) *Computers in Language Learning*. London, UK: Hazell, Watson and Viney Ltd.
KAHNEY, H. (1986) *Problem Solving: A Cognitive Approach*. London, UK: Open University Press.
LEECH, G. & C. N. CANDLIN (1986) *Computers in English Language Teaching and Research*. London: Longman.
MALONE, T. W. (1980) *What Makes Things Fun to Learn?: A Study of Intrinsically Motivating Computer Games*. Palo Alto, CA: Xerox.
MAYER, R. E. (1983) *Thinking, Problem-solving, Cognition*. New York: Freeman and Company.
MCLEOD, R. (1984) *Learning with Adventure Programs*. Hertfordshire, UK: Melbourne House.
MILLER, L. & J. D. BURNETT (1986) Theoretical considerations in selecting language arts software. In P. R. SMITH *et al.* (eds), *Computers and Education*, 10: 1. Toronto, Canada: Pergamon Press.
YOUNGMAN, M. B. (1979) *Analysing Social and Educational Research Data*. London, UK: McGraw-Hill.

Part III:
Analysis Tools for a New Generation of Language Applications

9 Analysed Corpora of English: A Consumer Guide

GEOFFREY SAMPSON
University of Leeds, England

Introduction

This article surveys the range of machine-readable analysed corpora of English that now exist as publicly available research resources. Since corpus linguistics is not yet a universally familiar branch of computational linguistics, I begin by defining some terminology.

A *corpus*, in the context of computational linguistics, is simply a sizeable machine-readable sample of a language, which will commonly be constructed using random-sampling techniques in such a fashion as to form a 'fair cross-section' of authentic usage for the language as a whole or for some particular genre. Several large standard corpora of English have been available for many years: the best-known are the Brown University Corpus (one million words of written — more specifically, published — American English), the Lancaster–Oslo/Bergen (LOB) Corpus (a British English 'twin' to Brown), and the London–Lund Corpus (almost half a million words of spoken British English). (Appendix A gives information about how to obtain these and other corpora mentioned below.) By now there exists a large and growing body of research publications which exploit these resources in order to make advances in many different branches of linguistics; the one feature uniting the diverse findings of corpus linguistics is that they depend on access to quantities of authentic language data, and could not meaningfully be established on the basis of the invented example sentences which play a central role in some areas of linguistics. The ICAME on-line bibliography of publications which exploit these corpora, while inevitably incomplete, contained 362 items in October 1988 (see Appendix A for ICAME).

A corpus becomes a more valuable research tool if coding is added to the raw texts to identify features of their linguistic structure. The simplest step in this direction is to produce a *tagged corpus*, in which each word has a code showing its grammatical category. This is particularly useful for a near-isolating language like English, where words contain few morphological cues to their grammatical status, and many words are capable of playing a variety of grammatical roles in different contexts (e.g. *saw* can be a singular noun, a base form of a verb, or a past-tense form of another verb). A tagged version of the complete LOB Corpus has been available since 1986 (Garside *et al.*, 1987, describe the partly-automatic, partly-manual techniques that were used to do the tagging); for spoken British English the Lancaster Spoken English Corpus (52,000 words transcribed from radio broadcasts) is now available in tagged form. A tagged version of the Brown Corpus of American English is also available.

The term *analysed corpus* refers to a corpus equipped with fuller grammatical information than merely categories of individual words. An analysed corpus encodes the grammatical structures of the sentences, normally via some notation formally equivalent to labelled tree diagrams, though the precise nature of the analysis will naturally depend on the grammatical theory to which the analyst subscribes, and the practicalities of computational information processing usually mean that the relationship between the tree structure that a linguist ascribes to a sentence and the representation of that structure in machine-readable form is rather indirect. One could envisage an analysed corpus including semantic information of various sorts in addition to grammatical information, and moves in this direction are now starting to take place.

In the present state of computational-linguistic technology, analysed corpora normally have to be created wholly or mainly by hand, though one example, described below, has recently been produced by automatic techniques [see also Pienemann & Jansen, this volume, Chapter 10, for an example of a partially automated technique — MCP/VS]. This work is both highly skilled and extremely time-consuming, so it is not easy to create an analysed corpus of worthwhile size. Nevertheless, there do now exist a number of analysed corpora which each have their own advantages and drawbacks.

Before describing these, let me briefly refer to some of the current and potential uses for such resources.

The Use of Analysed Corpora

Probably the most important motive for the creation of analysed corpora relates to the development of probabilistic techniques in automatic natural language processing; this has led to the production of at least one large non-public analysed corpus in a commercial context, as well as several of the public corpora listed below. Almost any useful natural language processing application, from machine translation through intelligent data-retrieval systems to voice-driven typewriters, crucially requires automatic language-analysis (parsing) ability. After many years during which computational linguists approached the problem of parsing natural language using logic-based techniques resembling those used for compiling artificial, rigorously-defined programming languages, it is increasingly coming to be accepted nowadays that real-life natural language is too 'messy' for such techniques to be applicable — so that successful, robust parsing systems should seek analyses which maximise a continuous variable representing some measure of statistical similarity to the configurations observed to occur in the language, rather than seeking a 'perfectly legal' analysis for an input string. Garside *et al.* (1987, ch. 6) and Sampson *et al.* (1989) describe two variants of this approach, each of which has achieved a degree of success: namely, the system developed for the Science and Engineering Research Council by the Lancaster Unit for Computer Research on English Language (UCREL) under Geoffrey Leech and Roger Garside, and the *APRIL* system of parsing by stochastic optimisation being developed with Royal Signals and Radar Establishment sponsorship at the Leeds Centre for Computer Analysis of Language and Speech (CCALAS) under my direction. Any statistics-based automatic parsing technique depends on the availability of a body of manually-parsed material from which relevant statistics can be extracted.

There are also various applications unrelated to automatic natural-language processing for which parsed corpora offer potential benefits. Many debates in theoretical linguistics turn on the grammatical status of particular constructions which one theorist is inclined to star as ungrammatical while another theorist claims them to be acceptable. While a corpus cannot settle abstract questions about the relationship between grammaticality and acceptability, nevertheless if it can easily be shown by searching an analysed corpus that examples of some debatable construction occur repeatedly in authentic usage, this will surely cast doubt on any theory which requires the construction to be classified as ungrammatical. With a large enough analysed corpus, absence of a particular construction may become a phenomenon from which inferences can be drawn. And at a more general level, analyzed corpora offer a healthy corrective to the tendency to focus attention on a few constructions which happen to have become prominent in theoretical debate: working with a corpus offers constant reminders that there is a massive range of grammatical phenomena which rarely or never crop up in the theoretical literature. I have quoted elsewhere (Garside *et al.*, 1987: 90) a trivial but nevertheless interesting example: exposure to textbooks of linguistic theory can lead one to see the two 'core' sentence-types of English as being the subject-transitive verb-object type, as in *John hit Mary*, and the subject-intransitive verb type, as in *Mary wept*. Research using the Lancaster-Leeds Treebank (see below), however, shows that while the transitive pattern is indeed the commonest single sentence type, the *Mary wept* pattern is strikingly rare — an intransitive verb will usually be followed by a complement of some sort; on the other hand, the second-commonest sentence type consists of a single noun-phrase with no verb, a pattern not often mentioned in textbooks but which is frequently used in headings, captions, and so forth.

Findings on the relative salience in real-life usage of different grammatical constructions should have relevance for syllabus design in language teaching. So too should the findings that are emerging on inter-genre grammatical differences (or lack of differences). In this connection I should explain that the LOB and Brown Corpora, and hence also those analysed corpora which are based on subsets of LOB or Brown, are organised in a way that facilitates comparisons between genres. Both of the 'raw' (unanalysed) corpora consist of 500 text-extracts each of about 2000 words, grouped into fifteen genre categories intended to cover the gamut of published (British and American) written English and to reflect the broad relative importance of the respective genres in the language as a whole: thus there are 44 text-extracts in Category A (press reportage), 80 in Category J (learned and scientific writing), 29 in Category P (romance and love stories), and so on. Ellegård (1978) and Sampson & Haigh (1988) are two examples of the use of analysed corpora derived from Brown and LOB respectively to examine the nature of grammatical differences between genres; both sets of findings tend to suggest that genres as diverse as scientific writing and fiction differ grammatically less than one might suppose.

The Analysed Corpora

I know of five publicly-available analysed corpora for English: the Gothenburg Corpus, the Nijmegen Corpus, the Lancaster–Leeds Treebank, the Parsed LOB Corpus, and the Polytechnic of Wales (PoW) Corpus. We have copies of each of these at CCALAS, except for the Parsed LOB Corpus, of which at the time of writing I have seen only extracts. Intellectual property rights (ipr) in the corpora are owned by CCALAS only in the case of the Lancaster–Leeds Treebank, and permissible uses of the various corpora are subject to various ipr and copyright restrictions. CCALAS is currently constructing a further analysed corpus, the SUSANNE Corpus, which when complete will also be made publicly available.

Five of these six corpora are (in the case of SUSANNE, will be) based wholly or mainly on written language; the PoW Corpus is based on spoken English. The Gothenburg and future SUSANNE Corpora are based on American English, the other four on British English. The Parsed LOB Corpus was produced using automatic parsing techniques; in the other five cases the analyses were done wholly by hand. Appendix B provides sample extracts from these corpora.

The Gothenburg Corpus

The Gothenburg Corpus is described in Ellegård (1978). It contains analyses of material totalling about 128,000 words, comprising 64 of the 500 text extracts in the Brown Corpus. The 64 extracts include 16 from each of four Brown genre categories, namely A (press reportage), G (belles lettres, biography), J (learned and scientific), and N (adventure and Western fiction). It thus contains material from each of the four broad genre divisions established by Hofland & Johansson (1982: 22–32) on the basis of word-frequency statistics.

The scheme of analysis in the Gothenburg Corpus is a form of dependency-tree analysis. Unlike in phrase-structure grammar where the words of a sentence occur only at the 'leaf' nodes of a tree, and higher nodes bear symbols for phrase or clause categories, in dependency grammar words are associated with nonterminal as well as terminal nodes. A 'mother' node is labelled with the head word of a constituent, and its daughter nodes are labelled with the words that modify the head, or with the head words of multi-word modifying elements. The Gothenburg Corpus uses dependency analysis everywhere except for the relationship between clauses and their immediate constituents (ICs): a clause has a node of its own, with all its ICs including the verb being treated as daughters of the clause node.

Unlike some of the other analysed corpora to be discussed, the Gothenburg Corpus codes functional as well as formal properties (e.g. it represents the fact that a constituent is the direct object of its clause as well as the fact that it is a noun phrase); and it includes some limited indications of logical or 'underlying' structure where this differs from surface grammatical structure.

Balancing these strong points, the Gothenburg Corpus has several disadvantages. Much orthographic detail of the original texts (which is preserved in the original Brown Corpus) has been thrown away: words appear in upper-case only, without punctuation. The notation by which grammatical parse-trees are encoded linearly is cumbersome, so that it is quite difficult to recover the tree structures from the coding even when this can be done unambiguously (we have a program which takes about 350 lines of code to achieve this less than perfectly); and furthermore the notation includes systematic ambiguities, so that in some cases trees can only be reconstructed manually. The scheme of functional and formal categorisation of grammatical constituents is rather rich, but the published description of this scheme gives little detail on the definitions of these categories and the boundaries between them, so that it is difficult to know how consistently they have been applied. (My own experience suggests that making decisions about the analysis of debatable constructions, and ensuring that such decisions are consistently adhered to, is a problem whose significance for the construction of analysed corpora is difficult to overstate.) The Gothenburg analyses were produced by students, and Ellegård himself points out that there is a certain incidence of errors. Also, in contrast to the richness of the scheme of higher-level categories, the set of word-class categories used is relatively crude by the standards of some other analysed corpora (see Appendix B of Garside *et al.*, 1987, for a comparative table of word-classes used in various corpora).

Figure 9.1 (Appendix 2) shows an extract from the Gothenburg Corpus (part of Brown text G17, taken from an article in *The Georgia Review*). The analysis is in a one-word-per-line format. In the first field of each line a reference number is immediately followed by the text word. The second field contains a seven-character cross-reference, beginning 'G17', to a line of the Brown Corpus, immediately followed by a code identifying and characterising the clause to which the word belongs: for instance, the code 'ZDF12' for the direct quotation *we in New England have long since segregated our children* shows that this is a finite declarative non-subordinate clause (ZDF) and is the second clause IC of the main clause (clause 1, A Yale *historian ... said*) of its sentence. The third field codes the functional roles of the ICs of the clause: *we* is subject (S); *in New England* functions as an adverb of place, A, within which *in* is a prepositional modifier, P (the plus and minus signs show that *New England* is a multi-word phrase which as a whole acts as a proper noun); *have* is the primary predicate verb (V) and *segregated* modifies it (V1); and so on. The fourth field contains a wordtag. Note that the clause ZDF12 is preceded by a line containing this clause-code in place of a text word: the role field in this line shows that the clause as a whole is the direct object of its superordinate ZDF1 clause.

The Nijmegen Corpus

The Nijmegen Corpus is described in de Haan (1984). It contains analyses of about 130,000 words, made up of a small number of relatively long texts: namely, 20,000-word extracts from two detective novels, one book each on literary criticism, biology, and popular sociology, and the written text of a play (more exactly, the whole of one play and part of a second play by the same playwright), together with 10,000 words of transcribed sports commentary. The total number of authors represented in the written material is five, since one of the detective novels was written by the same man as wrote the literary criticism.

The analytic scheme is of phrase-structure rather than dependency type, and the corpus is coded in a relatively straightforward fashion. As in the Gothenburg case, the scheme encodes functional as well as formal properties of constituents. Again, only limited detail is available on the definitions of the various grammatical categories used in the scheme; and a significant fraction (say, between 5% and 10%) of the sentences in the Nijmegen Corpus have not had their constituents categorised — that is, tree structures have been drawn, but no labels have been added to the nodes. (These unlabelled analyses frequently, but by no means always, are ones which involve some unusual grammatical problem.)

The Nijmegen Corpus is designed to be used in conjunction with a sophisticated database system for grammatical research, the *LDB* (Linguist's Database), also developed at Nijmegen; the LDB allows a user to explore parse-trees represented in graphic form on screen, and to search for configurations of interest via simple commands. The extract from the Nijmegen Corpus shown in Figure 9.2 represents the tree structure assigned to a sentence in two formats: above, the tree is drawn out graphically, and below, the node-labels are set out in a self-explanatory fashion, with functional and formal indications separated by colons.

The Lancaster–Leeds Treebank

The Lancaster–Leeds Treebank is described in Chapter 7 of Garside *et al.* (1987). It is much smaller than the two preceding corpora, containing analyses of about 45,000 words. These are made up of short runs usually of two or three sentences from many parts of the LOB Corpus; all fifteen genre categories of LOB are represented, broadly in proportion to their representation in LOB (category J, learned and scientific writings, is over-represented).

The scheme of analysis is of phrase-structure type, and is purely formal and 'surfacy': the role of a constituent within its superordinate unit is not indicated unless it is implied by the formal category of the constituent (as in the case of the category 'relative clause', for instance), and there is no indication of 'underlying structure' — notably, the logical unity of discontinuous constituents is not shown. On the other hand, within its own terms the scheme of grammatical categories is rather rich (the permissible combinations of category and subcategory symbols would in principle allow on the order of 60,000 distinct labels for parse-tree nodes); and two chief advantages of the Lancaster–Leeds Treebank are that the categories and the boundaries between them are defined in considerable detail, and that considerable efforts have been devoted to the goal of ensuring that the analyses in the Treebank are consistent and error-free. The analytic scheme used is laid down in a manual of over 100,000 words, which aims to specify an unambiguous analysis for any phenomenon occurring in authentic written English, including not just discursive text but items such as addresses, sums of money, bibliographical citations, and purely orthographic phenomena such as punctuation. (The Lancaster–Leeds Treebank, and the closely related Parsed LOB Corpus — see below — are the only two of the analysed corpora listed to treat punctuation marks as parsable items on a par with words.)

Figure 9.3 shows an extract from the Lancaster-Leeds Treebank, comprising analyses of two sentences from LOB text E01 (from a book on lace crafts). Rows of hyphens mark sentence boundaries, and between such rows the text is in a one-word-per-line format. The first field is a reference number. The second, one-character field marks cases where a contraction such as *wasn't* has been split by the analysis into two words. The third field contains a wordtag, using the 'Leeds' variant of the LOB tagset (Garside *et al.*, 1987, Appendix B) — the current version of the Treebank incorporates a few further modifications of this tagset, making all tags purely alphanumeric for the sake of computational tractability (thus comma and full stop are now tagged 'YC', 'YF', rather than acting as their own tags as previously, and possessive personal pronouns, such as *its*, are tagged 'PPG' rather than earlier 'PPS'). The text word occurs in the fourth field.

The grammatical analyses themselves are coded in the rightmost field. The text word is represented by a vertical bar, preceded by labelled opening brackets for any constituents begun by the word, and followed by labelled closing brackets for any constituents terminated by the word (thus a one-word phrase will have symbols on either side of the vertical character). The first sentence displayed has a tree structure in which the root node (O) immediately dominates a 'sentence' node (S) whose first IC is the one-word noun phrase *it* (N means 'noun phrase', and noun phrases consisting of just the word *it* are subcategorised as 'Ni' to reflect the fact that this particular word can play a special grammatical role as epenthetic pronoun, as it does in the example shown); the second IC of the sentence node is the two-word verb phrase *wasn't*, which is marked as third person singular and negative and has a form of be as its main verb ('Vzeb' — note that in our terminology a 'verb phrase' is a sequence which may include auxiliary and main verbs but does not cover objects, complements, etc.); subsequent ICs of the 'S' include two one-word adverb phrases ('R') and two commas, followed by an adverbial clause ('Fa') with a complex internal structure of its own. The closing full stop is treated as a sister to the 'S' node as an IC of the root. Our parsing scheme includes detailed rules about the placement of punctuation marks in parse trees, which specify, for instance, that the commas surrounding *however*, since they balance one another logically, must be daughters of the same mother node — the second comma is not to be analysed as cohering more closely with the intervening word, as it does orthographically.

The Parsed LOB Corpus

The UCREL automatic parsing system has used statistics drawn from the Lancaster–Leeds Treebank to analyse a larger subset of the LOB Corpus, and the output of this is referred to here as the Parsed LOB Corpus. (The UCREL group plan eventually to parse the entire LOB Corpus in a similar style.) The automatic parser was run over ten texts from each of the fifteen LOB genre categories (over all the texts in categories containing fewer than ten texts). This amounted to 145 texts, but many sentences in these texts were rejected by the system as too long to process, since the UCREL automatic parsing technique currently encounters combinatorial-explosion problems with longer inputs — the set of sentences which were parsed comprises about 65,000 words. The output parsing scheme is essentially similar to that of the Lancaster–Leeds Treebank, though it has been simplified by eliminating some subcategory symbols: for instance, noun phrases are not coded as singular vs. plural, verb phrases are not coded for third-person singular morphology.

Figure 9.4 shows an extract from the automatic parsing of LOB text A01, a news story from the *Daily Herald*. The file is in a 'horizontal' format in which the text words and the labelled brackets of the parsing are interspersed on a single line; each text word is followed after an underline character by its tag, and as this corpus uses the original LOB wordtags, each punctuation mark has a tag identical to itself.

The PoW Corpus

The analysed Polytechnic of Wales Corpus is based on transcriptions of children's speech, published as Fawcett & Perkins (1980) and described briefly in Fawcett (1980). The speakers are about 120 children aged between six and twelve from the Pontypridd area (excluding children whose English is significantly influenced by Welsh or other languages), who for analytical purposes are classified into four age-ranges, four socio-economic classes, and by sex. Each passage in the PoW Corpus comprises either a ten-minute segment of the speech of one child in a play session with two other children, or a six-minute segment of the speech of a child being interviewed by a friendly adult about a child-oriented topic; the segments begin at the point when the child appeared to forget about the microphone, so that they should represent informal speech. The parsed corpus contains 11,396 parse-trees (sentences, or sentence-fragments treated as independently parsable sequences) comprising some 100,000 words. The unanalysed version of the PoW Corpus contains indications of intonation contours as well as words, but the intonation markings are not preserved in the analysed version.

The analytic scheme used is a variety of Michael Halliday's 'systemic-functional' grammar (on which see, e.g. Butler, 1985); the scheme includes coding for functional as well as formal properties of constituents, and it permits discontinuous constituents to be recognised. In this and other ways the scheme goes some distance towards representing logical as well as surface grammatical form, and the set of grammatical categories is reasonably rich.

The extract shown in Figure 9.5 is the beginning of text 12AGIAH, whose code-name indicates that the speaker is a 12-year-old class A girl in an interview situation: 'AH' are her individual initials. Parse-trees 1a and 1b are analyses of an utterance which in ordinary orthography might be transcribed *Oh we just put down anything ... made the base and then mm ...* The items *Oh* and *mm* have been excluded from the parse-trees as 'nonverbal' ('NV'). The remainder of the coding, while somewhat confusing at first sight, does succeed in unambiguously representing in linear form hierarchical structural analyses which can contain discontinous constituents (trees with crossing branches). The root of any tree is denoted by 'Z'. The left-to-right sequence of non-numerical symbols represents progression down a branch of a tree, but the item following a number will be the daughter of the item preceding the number only at the first occurrence of that number; when a number recurs, what follows it is a daughter of the item preceding the first occurrence of the number.

In tree 1b, for instance, the root dominates two IC nodes, labelled 'CL' (clause) and 'CLUN' (unfinished clause), the CLUN consisting only of the 'linker' ('&') *and-then*, treated in the PoW system as a single word. Within the full clause, there are function slots for subject (elided as recoverable from context, represented by 'S' in round brackets — elisions due to rapid speech are indicated by angle brackets), main verb ('M'), and complement ('C'), the latter realised as a noun group ('NGP') consisting of deictic determiner ('DD') *the* and head ('H') *base*.

The PoW files code each tree as a single record no matter how long, and in order to fit them onto the paper long records have been split into two or more lines at arbitrary points in printing out the extract shown in Figure 9.5:

note that the text word *anything* in tree 1a is not divided into two words in the electronic file.

Project SUSANNE

While each of the five analysed corpora described above has its virtues, none is ideal. Potentially the most valuable of them for many general purposes, I believe, is the Gothenburg Corpus, which includes a broad coverage of written English (as opposed to the small number of mainly literary texts in the Nijmegen Corpus), uses a relatively sophisticated analytic scheme, and is large enough to yield statistical findings that should be much sounder than those derivable from the small Lancaster–Leeds Treebank. However, the complexities and inadequacies of the Gothenburg Corpus coding scheme have led it to be wholly neglected; I know of no research in which it has figured since its public availability was announced in Ellegård (1978).

Accordingly, I am now directing a project (SUSANNE — Surface and Underlying Structural Analyses of Naturalistic English) whose aim is to turn the Gothenburg Corpus into a more accessible and useful research resource, by replacing its existing coding with a more transparent and unambiguous notation, eliminating inconsistencies and errors, and incorporating various categories of additional information. The SUSANNE Corpus will restore full orthographic details of the original texts by running Gothenburg against corresponding sections of Brown, integrating punctuation marks appropriately into the parse-trees, and will replace the crude Gothenburg wordtags with a scheme at least as detailed as the most detailed tagset discussed in Appendix B of Garside *et al.* (1987). We plan to include more complete information about underlying grammatical structure than Gothenburg now has, and to add codes showing whether referring expressions have the same or different referents (thus enabling the Corpus to be used for research on anaphora), ascribing simple semantic categories (e.g. human/nonhuman, animate/inanimate, concrete/abstract) to referring expressions, and perhaps identifying relevant senses of semantically ambiguous words by linking them to appropriate subentries in a standard machine-readable English dictionary.

Project SUSANNE, sponsored by the Economic and Social Research Council, is due to be completed not later than March 1992, and we hope by that time to have created and documented a publicly available resource that will be more useful (at least for work on written English) than any analysed corpus now extant. The fact that it is based on American English may also be seen as a positive consideration, since this is an internationally significant variety of the language which seems to date to have received less than its fair share of attention from corpus linguists. But it must be stressed that these are hopes for the future rather than existing achievements, since Project SUSANNE is at the time of writing still young.

Conclusion

A machine-readable language corpus (of any type) is a general-purpose resource, capable of being put to uses that were never envisaged by its creators. The central concern of the present volume is language teaching, and it is plain that analysed corpora have potential applications in that domain among others; I made some brief suggestions earlier in this article, and the topic has been discussed at rather greater length by Geoffrey Leech, the creator of the LOB Corpus (Leech, 1986). But both Leech's and my comments are necessarily programmatic. Most of us who are involved in producing corpora have limited expertise in the special problems of language teaching (I have none). We can only make known the availability of these resources, which we are putting to other uses, and invite teaching specialists to exploit them in their fields. I hope this article may help to promote such exploitation.

Appendix A

Sources of materials

The 'raw' LOB and Brown Corpora (in various formats), the Tagged LOB Corpus, the Lancaster Spoken English Corpus, various other corpora of English, and related research resources are distributed by the Norway-based International Computer Archive of Modern English (ICAME), who also publish *ICAME Journal*, the international journal of English corpus linguistics. Contact:

Knut Hofland
Norwegian Computing Centre for the Humanities
PO Box 53 Universitetet
N-5027 Bergen, Norway.

Knut Hofland's earn/bitnet address is fafkh@nobergen.

A convenient brief account of the LOB and Brown Corpora is provided in Chapter 1 of Garside *et al.* (1987). Each Corpus distributed by ICAME comes with a manual giving details of coding and references to the sources of the text extracts.

The Tagged Brown Corpus is available from:

W. Nelson Francis & Henry Kuçera
Box E
Brown University
Providence, RI 02912, USA.

The contact who supplied CCALAS with a copy of the Gothenburg Corpus was:

Gudrun Magnusdottir
SPRÅKDATA (Institutionen för språkvetenskaplig databehandling)
Göteborgs Universitet
S-412 98 Göteborg, Sweden.

The Nijmegen Corpus is distributed as part of a package including the Nijmegen LDB software by:

The TOSCA Working Group
Department of English
University of Nijmegen
PO Box 9103
NL-6500 HD Nijmegen, The Netherlands.

The Lancaster–Leeds Treebank has not to date been distributed outside those institutions, but there is no bar to doing so; anyone interested may contact:

Carol Lockhart (CCALAS Secretary)
Department of Linguistics and Phonetics
University of Leeds
Leeds LS2 9JT, England.

Carol Lockhart could also be approached for information about the progress of Project SUSANNE.

The Parsed LOB Corpus is available to the public from:

The UCREL Secretary
Department of Linguistics and Modern English Language
University of Lancaster
Lancaster LA1 4YT, England.

The PoW Corpus, in the version discussed above, is obtainable from:

Robin Fawcett
Department of Behavioural and Communication Studies
Polytechnic of Wales
Treforest
Mid Glamorgan CF37 1DL, Wales.

The PoW Corpus is currently being used as a database in the *COMMUNAL* automatic language understanding project, sponsored by the Royal Signals and Radar Establishment, International Computers Ltd, and a major publishing firm, and directed by Robin Fawcett and my CCALAS colleague Eric Atwell; in connection with this, the Corpus is being translated into a computationally more tractable format at Leeds. Those interested in using this version should contact:

Eric Atwell
Division of Artificial Intelligence
School of Computing
University of Leeds
Leeds LS2 9JT, England.

Appendix B

Corpus excerps

```
000609002162A            *G171780ZDF1       2 S1      F
000609002163YALE          G171780ZDF1       2 S2      C
000609002164HISTORIAN     G171780ZDF1       2 S       N
000609002165/RDG11        G171780ZDF1       2 S3/
000609002166WRITING      *G171780RDG11        V       VG
000609002167A             G171780RDG11        C1      F
000609002168FEW           G171780RDG11        C2      Q
000609002169YEARS         G171780RDG11        C       NS
000609002170AGO           G171780RDG11        CP      P
000609002171IN            G171780RDG11        AP      P
000609002172THE           G171780RDG11        A1      T
000609002173YALE          G171780RDG11        A2      C
000609002174REVIEW        G171790RDG11        A       N
000609002175SAID         *G171790ZDF1       3 V       VD
000609002176/ZDF12        G171790ZDF1       3 O/
000609002177WE           *G171790ZDF12        S       RS
000609002178IN            G171790ZDF12        AP      P
000609002179NEW           G171790ZDF12        A1+     J+
000609002180ENGLAND       G171790ZDF12        A+      C+
000609002181              G171790ZDF12        A-      C-
000609002182HAVE          G171790ZDF12        V       H
000609002183LONG          G171790ZDF12        C       A
000609002184SINCE         G171790ZDF12        CP      P
000609002185SEGREGATED    G171790ZDF12        V1      VD
000609002186OUR           G171790ZDF12        O1      RSX
000609002187CHILDREN      G171800ZDF12        4O      NS
000610002188HE           *G171800ZDF1         S       R
000610002189WAS           G171800ZDF1         V       BD
000610002190REFERRING     G171800ZDF1         V1      VG
000610002191NOT           G171800ZDF1         M       G
000610002192ONLY          G171800ZDF1         E       A
000610002193TO            G171800ZDF1         KP      P
000610002194THE           G171800ZDF1         K1      T
000610002195GENERAL       G171800ZDF1         K2      J
000610002196COLLEGE       G171800ZDF1         K3      N
000610002197SITUATION     G171810ZDF1         K       N
000610002198BUT           G171810ZDF1         AY      Y
000610002199MORE          G171810ZDF1         D1      QR
000610002200ESPECIALLY    G171810ZDF1         D       A
000610002201TO            G171810ZDF1         KP      P
000610002202THE           G171810ZDF1         K1      T
000610002203PREPARATORY   G171810ZDF1         K2      J
000610002204SCHOOLS       G171810ZDF1         4K      NS
```

FIGURE 9.1 *Extract from the Gothenburg Corpus.*

Appendix B continued

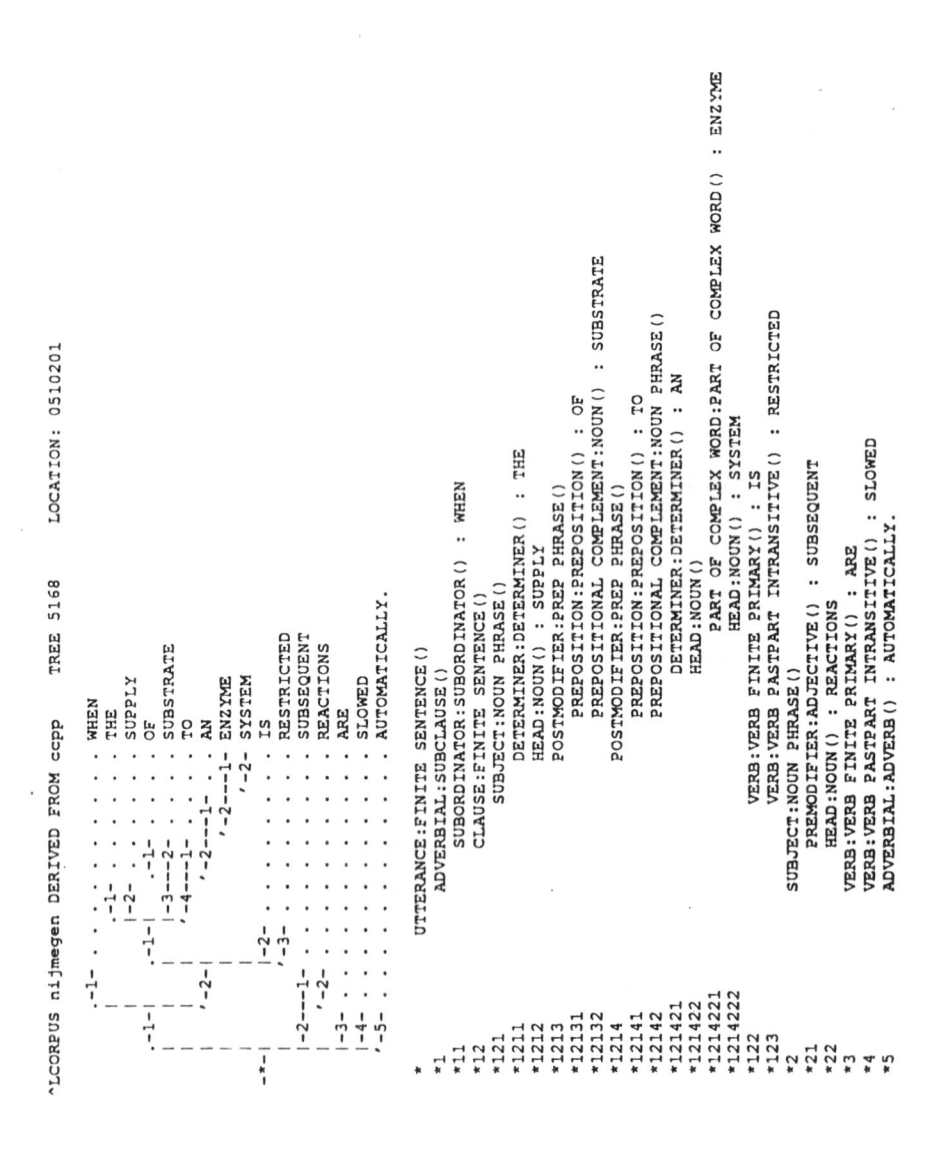

```
^LCORPUS nijmegen DERIVED FROM GCPP    TREE 5168    LOCATION: 0510201

  -*-|   -1-  .   .   .   .   .   .   .   . WHEN
          |   -1- .   .   .   .   .   .   . THE
          |    |  -2- .   .   .   .   .   . SUPPLY
          |    |   |  -1- .   .   .   .   . OF
          |    |   |   |  -2- .   .   .   . SUBSTRATE
          |    |   |  -3---2- .   .   .   . TO
          |    |   |  -4---1- .   .   .   . AN
          |    |   |       |  -2- .   .   . ENZYME
          |   -2---1- .    |   |  -2- .   . SYSTEM
          |        |  -2---1- .   .   .   . IS
          |        |       |  -2- .   .   . RESTRICTED
          |       -2- .    |   |  -2- .   . SUBSEQUENT
          |       -3- .    |   |       .   . REACTIONS
         -2- .    .   .   .   .   .   .   . ARE
         -3- .    .   .   .   .   .   .   . SLOWED
         -4- .    .   .   .   .   .   .   . 
         -5- .    .   .   .   .   .   .   . AUTOMATICALLY.

*        UTTERANCE:FINITE SENTENCE()
*1       ADVERBIAL:SUBCLAUSE()
*11         SUBORDINATOR:SUBORDINATOR() : WHEN
*12         CLAUSE:FINITE SENTENCE()
*121           SUBJECT:NOUN PHRASE()
*1211             DETERMINER:DETERMINER() : THE
*1212             HEAD:NOUN() : SUPPLY
*1213             POSTMODIFIER:PREP PHRASE()
*12131               PREPOSITION:PREPOSITION() : OF
*12132               PREPOSITIONAL COMPLEMENT:NOUN() : SUBSTRATE
*1214             POSTMODIFIER:PREP PHRASE()
*12141               PREPOSITION:PREPOSITION() : TO
*12142               PREPOSITIONAL COMPLEMENT:NOUN PHRASE()
*121421                 DETERMINER:DETERMINER() : AN
*121422                 HEAD:NOUN()
                          PART OF COMPLEX WORD:PART OF COMPLEX WORD() : ENZYME
*1214221                  HEAD:NOUN() : SYSTEM
*1214222        VERB:VERB FINITE PRIMARY() : IS
*122            VERB:VERB PASTPART INTRANSITIVE() : RESTRICTED
*123         SUBJECT:NOUN PHRASE()
*2              PREMODIFIER:ADJECTIVE() : SUBSEQUENT
*21             HEAD:NOUN() : REACTIONS
*22         VERB:VERB FINITE PRIMARY() : ARE
*3          VERB:VERB PASTPART INTRANSITIVE() : SLOWED
*4          ADVERBIAL:ADVERB() : AUTOMATICALLY.
*5
```

FIGURE 9.2 *Extract from the Nijmegen Corpus.*

Appendix B continued

```
^E01021001      -----   --X--    -----        -----
E01021010         -      PP3     it           [O[S[Ni|Ni]
E01021020         >      BEDZ    was          [Vzeb|
E01021021         <      XNOT    n't          |Vzeb]
E01021030         -      RBX     long         [R|R]
E01021031         -      YC      ,            |
E01021040         -      RB      however      [R|R]
E01021041         -      YC      ,            |
E01021050         -      CS      before       [H|
E01021060         -      QLR     less         [Np[Jn|
E01021070         -      JJ      pious        |Jn]
E01021080         -      NNS     hands        |Np]
E01021090         -      VBD     took         [V|V|
E01021100         -      RP      up           [R|R]
E01021110         -      ATI     the          [Ns|
E01022010         -      JJ      lovely       |
E01022020         -      NN      craft        |
E01022030         -      INO     of           [Po|
E01022040         -      NN      lace-making  |Po]Ns]H]S]
E01022041         -      YF      .            |O]
^E01022042      -----   -----    -----        -----
E01022050         -      NN      lace         [O[S&[S&[Ns|Ns]
E01022060         -      VBD     became       [V|V]
E01022070         -      ATI     the          [Ns|
E01022080         -      NN      servant      |
E01022090         -      INO     of           [Po|
E01022100         -      NN      vanity       |Po]Ns]
E01022110         -      CC      and          [S+|
E01023010         -      VBD     lent         [V|V]
E01023020         -      PPG     its          [Ns|
E01023030         -      JJ      rich         |
E01023040         -      NN      decoration   |Ns]
E01023050         -      INT     to           [P|
E01023060         -      NNS     robes        [NNS&|
E01023070         -      CC      and          [NNS+|
E01023080         -      NNS     dresses      |NNS+]NNS&]P]S+]S&]
E01023090         -      CC      and          [S+|
E01023100         -      CD1     one          [Nlcs|Nlcs]
E01023110         -      VBZ     thinks       [Vz|Vz]
E01024010         -      RB      particularly [R|R]
E01024020         -      INO     of           [Po|
E01024030         -      ATI     the          [N&|
E01024040         -      JJ      extravagant  |
E01024050         -      JNP     Elizabethan  |
E01024060         -      NNS     ruffs        |
E01024070         -      CC      and          [Np+|
E01024080         -      JNP     Carolean     |
E01025010         -      NNS     collars      |Np+]N&]Po]S+]S&]
E01025011         -      YF      .            |O]
```

FIGURE 9.3 *Extract from Lancaster–Leeds Treebank.*

Appendix B continued

```
A01  2  ^ *' *' [S[V stop_VB V][Tg[Vg electing_VBG Vg][N life_NN
A01  2  peers_NNS N]Tg] **' **' ._. S]
A01  3  ^ [S[P by_IN [N Trevor_NP Williams_NP N]P] ._. S]
A01  4  ^ [S[N a_AT move_NN [Ti[Vi to_TO stop_VB Vi][N \0Mr_NPT
A01  4  Gaitskell_NP [P from_IN [Tg[Vg nominating_VBG Vg][N any_DTI
A01  4  more_AP labour_NN
A01  5  life_NN peers_NNS N]Tg]P]N]Ti]N][V is_BEZ V][Ti[Vi to_TO be_BE
A01  5  made_VBN Vi][P at_IN [N a_AT meeting_NN [Po of_INO [N
A01  5  labour_NN \0MPs_NPTS N]Po]N]P]Ti][N tomorrow_NR N] ._. S]
A01  6  ^ [S&[N \0Mr_NPT Michael_NP Foot_NP N][V has_HVZ put_VBN V][R
A01  6  down_RP R][N a_AT resolution_NN [P on_IN [N the_ATI subject_NN
A01  6  N]P]N][S+ and_CC
A01  7  [Na he_PP3A Na][V is_BEZ V][Ti[Vi to_TO be_BE backed_VBN Vi]
A01  7  [P by_IN [N \0Mr_NPT Will_NP Griffiths_NP ,_, [N \0MP_NPT [P
A01  7  for_IN [N Manchester_NP
A01  8  Exchange_NP N]P]N]N]P]Ti]S+] ._. S&]
```

FIGURE 9.4 *Extract from the Parsed LOB Corpus.*

Appendix B continued

```
**** 49    2    0    2    3   .51
12AGIAH
1a [NV:CH] Z CL 1 S NGP HP WE 1 AI JUST 1 M PUT 1 CM QQGP AX DOWN 1 C NGP HP ANYTHING
1b Z 1 CL 2 (S) 2 M MADE 2 C NGP 3 DD THE 3 H BASE 1 CLUN & AND-THEN [NV:MM]
2 Z CL NO
3 Z CL 1 (S) 1 (OM) 1 (X) 1 (M) 1 C 2 NGP 3 DQ A 3 MO QQGP AXT BIGGER 3 H HOUSE 2 NGP 4 DQ A 4 MO QQGP AX TA
LLER 4 HP ONE
4 Z CL 1 (S) 1 ON DUN 1 M NO
5 Z 1 CL F YEAH 1 CL 2 S NGP HP SHE 2 OX WAS 2 X GONNA 2 M MAKE 2 C NGP 3 DQ A 3 H CAR
6 Z CL 1 S NGP HN BETHAN 1 (O) 1 (X) 1 (M) 1 (C)
7 Z CL 1 (S) 1 (M) 1 (C) 1 A CL 2 B WHEN 2 S NGP HP I 2 OM WAS 2 C NGP DQ QQGP 3 T ABOUT 3 AX MINE
8 [NV:UM] Z CL 1 (S) 1 (M) 1 C NGP HN MONOPOLY
10 Z CL F YEAH
11 Z CL 1 S NGP HP I 1 ON DON'T 1 M KNOW 1 (C) [NV:UM]
12 [HZ:WELL] Z 1 CL 2 S NGP HP YOU 2 XM HAVE-TO 2 M GIVE 2 C NGP H PEOPLE 2 C NGP H MONEY 1 CL 3 & AND [NV:U
H] 3 S NGP HP YOU 3 M COLLECT 3 C NGP 4 DD YOUR 4 MO OWN 4 H MONEY 1 CL 5 & AND 5 S NGP HP YOU 5 M BUY 5 C N
GP H PROPERTIES
13 [HZ:WELL] Z CL 1 S NGP 2 DD THE 2 HP ONE 2 Q PGP 3 P WITH 3 CV NGP 4 DS QQGP 5 DD THE 5 AXT MOST 4 H MONE
Y 1 (M) 1 AM CL 6 S NGP HP I 6 M THINK
14 Z 1 CL 2 S NGP DD THAT 2 OM 'S 2 C NGP 3 DD THE 3 H WAY 3 Q CL 4 S NGP HP WE 4 M PLAY 1 CL 5 & OR 5 S NGP
6 (DD) 6 (HP) 6 Q PGP 7 P WITH 7 CV NGP 8 DS QQGP 9 DD THE 9 AX MOST 8 H PROPERTIES 5 (M)
15 Z CL 1 (S) 1 M PLAY 1 C NGP H CARDS
16 Z 1 CL F YEAH 1 CL 2 (S) 2 (M) 2 C PGP 3 P WITH 3 CV NGP 4 DD MY 4 H SISTER
17 Z CL F NO
```

FIGURE 9.5 *Extract from the Polytechnic of Wales Corpus.* —

References

BUTLER, C. S. (1985) *Systemic Linguistics: Theory and Applications.* London, UK: Batsford.
ELLEGÅRD, A. (1978) *The Syntactic Structure of English Texts.* Gothenburg Studies in English, 43. Stockholm, Sweden: Almqvist and Wiksell.
FAWCETT, R. P. (1980) Language development in children 6-12: interim report, *Linguistics*, 18, 953–58.
FAWCETT, R. P. & M. R. PERKINS (1980) *Child Language Transcripts 6-12* (4 vols.). Treforest, Wales: Polytechnic of Wales.
GARSIDE, R. G., G. N. LEECH & G. R. SAMPSON (eds) (1987) *The Computational Analysis of English: A Corpus-based Approach.* London, UK: Longman.
DE HAAN, P. (1984) Problem-oriented tagging of English corpus data. In J. AARTS & W. MEIJS (eds), *Corpus Linguistics.* Amsterdam, Netherlands: Rodopi.
HOFLAND, K. & S. JOHANSSON (1982) *Word Frequencies in British and American English.* Bergen, Norway: Norwegian Computing Centre for the Humanities.
LEECH, G. N. (1986) Automatic grammatical analysis and its educational applications. In G. N. LEECH & C. N. CANDLIN (eds), *Computers in English Language Teaching and Research.* London: Longman.
SAMPSON, G. R. & R. HAIGH (1988) Why are long sentences longer than short ones? In M. KYTÖ, O. IHALAINEN, & M. RISSANEN (eds), *Corpus Linguistics, Hard and Soft.* Amsterdam, Netherlands: Rodopi.
SAMPSON, G. R., R. HAIGH & E. S. ATWELL (1989) Natural language analysis by stochastic optimization: A progress report on Project APRIL. *Journal of Experimental and Theoretical Artificial Intelligence*, 1, 271–287.

10 Computational Analysis of Language Acquisition Data[1]

MANFRED PIENEMANN
University of Sydney, Australia
and
LOUISE JANSEN
Australian National University, Canberra, Australia

Background

Working with large sets of data in linguistic analysis is very time-consuming, particularly if the data are analysed by hand. Many empirical researchers share the frustrating experience of having analysed a large set of data to test one particular hypothesis, only to discover that the same data have to be analysed again for the same features as in the first round to test a modified hypothesis.

Bearing this experience in mind, we have developed an approach to computer-aided linguistic analysis which leaves much of the counting of defined linguistic structures and functions to the machine. In our approach, the manual preparation of the data for the automatic analysis is restricted to the insertion of a limited amount of structural and functional information which enables the automatic components of the system to utilise the coded information for a wide range of structural/functional analyses.

For our own empirical work, presently involving a morphosyntactic analysis of German interlanguage — i.e. that variety of German spoken by classroom learners of German as a foreign language — we have designed an integrated system for these tasks which is powerful, yet only requires the power of a microcomputer. Devising such a system is a painstaking and very time-consuming undertaking. We would therefore like to share our system with fellow researchers.

To this end we have left the system as open and flexible as possible and enlarged its scope, originally confined to morphosyntax, to allow also for the analysis of semantic and discourse phenomena. Furthermore, we are currently adding a corresponding version for English interlanguage (IL) data — i.e. the English spoken by non-native speakers — to our package. The system can be similarly adapted for IL studies of other languages.

Before we describe the system in detail, we address some fundamental questions concerning computational analysis of non-native varieties and briefly review related approaches. This background will hopefully illuminate the linguistic motivation for the design of our system.

A parser for language acquisition data?

The COALA system has been designed particularly for the analysis of language acquisition data, i.e. of varieties of a developing language which vary to different degrees from the structure of the target language. One crucial feature of all interlanguage varieties of a given target language is that they share a lexicon, an as yet undetermined subset of the rule system of that target language and a set of rules which are neither part of the source language nor of the target language. Thus, many formal features of these developing linguistic systems are unknown to the researcher.

It appeared inappropiate to us to attempt to write a single parser for the analysis of such data, as can be done for the analysis of a native language (Kay, 1982; Grosz et al., 1985; van Halteren & Oostdijk, 1986; Charniak & McDermott, 1985), because the construction of a parser presupposes the knowledge of the rule system of the language to be parsed.

A parser for non-native — and structurally unknown — varieties would have to be fundamentally different in its architecture from parsers for native languages. The 'parser' for unknown varieties would primarily have to *discover* the rule system expressing the form-function relationships in a given set of data in a way similar to a language learner, rather than recognise the instantiations of a given rule system.

Such automated learning procedures have been successfully developed for very restricted and narrowly defined domains, such as learning to read aloud (see Sejnowski & Rosenberg, 1986) or learning to mark verbs for past tense without programming the underlying rule system (Rumelhart & McClelland, 1986). An automated learning procedure, however, that would be capable of analysing the form-function relationships of an unanalysed linguistic variety would be exponentially more complex than such limited procedures and is, to our knowledge, far out of reach.

Let us take the following utterance of a learner of English as an example to illustrate the different prerequisites for a parser designed for a readily analysed native language and the one designed for basically unknown varieties of a non-native language:

(1) *Germany plenty work.*

In a given context a competent speaker of English can assign a particular meaning to this utterance even though its structure may be highly ambiguous. The parser, however, has to rely on a set of structural properties of the given language in order to analyse the constituent structure and to assign the correct grammatical functions to the constituents. In example (1) the parser would get stuck very easily, because it would first find a proper noun (*Germany*) and then a type of determiner which ought to be followed by a noun (= *plenty*). If *work* were classified as a noun, the result of the analysis of the constituent structure would be:

$[[N]_{NP1} + [det + N]_{NP2}]_S$

Alternatively, the parser could classify *plenty* as an adverb and *work* as a verb and analyse (1) as follows:

$[[N]_{NP1} + [[adv]_{PP} + V]_{VP}]_S$

The real problem, however, is not the fact that different constituent structures can be assigned to (1) but that a parser based on English grammar would simply not allow a transition from a proper noun in sentence initial position to a determiner (leaving appositions aside for the moment). Consequently, it would fail on this type of structure.

This could, of course, be avoided if the parser was less constrained than a parser for English and would allow more transitions from one constituent to another than are permissible in the target language. This solution, however, would raise two serious problems. First, constituent boundaries would not be defined unambiguously. For instance, the phrase:

(2) *the leaves on the house*

could be analysed as either of the following:

(2a) $[det + N]_{NP} + [prep + [det + N]_{NP}]_{PP}$
(2b) $[\ [det + N]_{NP} + [prep + [det + N]_{NP}]_{PP}]_{NP}$

Such a difference would be essential for such things as the analysis of subject–verb agreement, because the grammatical number of NPs and PPs would be stored with the corresponding phrase. In (2a) there are two phrases, one of which would be marked as 'plural' (*the leaves*) and one as 'singular' (*on the house*), while in (2b) the whole phrase would be marked as 'singular'.

Hence, the different analysis in (2a) and (2b) would create different inputs for the analysis of subject–verb agreement.

As we said above, the problem lies in the delimitation of the phrase boundaries. In (3) *the leaves* and *on the roof* fulfil two different grammatical functions, while in (4) the whole constituent *the leaves on the roof* fulfils only one function.

(3) *The wind blew the leaves on the roof.*
(4) *The leaves on the roof may block the gutter.*

Hence, a prerequisite for the correct delimitation of constituent boundaries is the correct assignment of grammatical functions. This leads to the second problem of an 'under-constrained' parser: without the constraints of the target language, the parser would not have sufficient clues for the assignment of grammatical functions to constituents. The parser must rely on those markers for grammatical functions which are used in the target language, particularly free and bound morphemes and word order. If the rules underlying the usage of these markers are not included in the parser, an analysis of the data will not be possible.

In the analysis of non-native data, the latter problem is a principled one, even if the parser is not 'under-constrained': access to the constraints of the target language does not guarantee a correct analysis, since the data may not display some of the target-language constraints or may contain a set of different constraints. Such structural properties of the data are due to the fact that they reflect the gradual *acquisition* of markers of grammatical functions by the language learner.

An English-based parser, for instance, would probably assign the function 'subject' to the constituent *Germany* in example (1) making use of the property of English that in most cases the first NP (dominated by S) is the subject of the sentence. This analysis may, however, be wrong. Example (1) may be part of the following text:

(5) S1: *What did you do in Germany?*
    S2: *Germany plenty work.*

In this case the constituent *Germany* would have been used in an adverbial function (= *in Germany*). Hence, a correct analysis of such structures can only be carried out on the basis of the context in which they appear.

A fully automatic system for the analysis of non-native varieties would therefore have to incorporate the semantic and discourse rules operational in the understanding of stretches of discourse such as (5), so that it would be able to discover/recognise the predicate-argument relationships underlying them and base any structural analyses on the semantic and discourse structure. Presently there are systems available which can handle small sub-sections of this analytical task, such as the analysis of pronominal reference (Hobbs, 1978). However, a semantic and discourse system with features similar to a human interlocutor, which would be sufficiently accurate in the present context, does not exist (see the work in Grosz et al., 1985).

Obviously, such an undertaking would be far more complex than developing a structural parser for data from a mature language, as, for instance, in the Dutch Computer Corpus Pilot Project (van Halteren & Oostdijk, 1986; Aarts & van den Heuvel, 1985).

Why semi-automatic analysis?

Ruling out a fully automatic analyis device for language acquisition data, the other extreme would be a computational system in which all coding of structural/functional information about the data had to be carried out by hand. Such systems have been developed, for instance, by MacWhinney (1987) and Clahsen (1986b). These systems are certainly far superior to the pencil and paper-style manual analysis, because information can be more easily retrieved, sorted, calculated, and displayed.

However, hand-coding every token occurring in the data is time-consuming, repetitive and — especially where complex coding conventions are used — subject to typographical errors. One factor which can make manual coding labour-intensive is that one item can occur many times in the data, e.g. a verb requiring a dative. If this item occurs, say, twenty times in the data, then in systems like that of MacWhinney its syntactic features have to be coded each time it occurs. Such multiple coding is clearly inefficient.

A second factor which increases the amount of work involved in manual coding is that the coded information is often not exploited economically: as a result, information has to be entered repeatedly in different places, though it would be sufficient to code it once. An example of uneconomical coding would be a system in which information about number and person marking of grammatical subjects, the position of the subject in the sentence, its constituent structure, and other information about the subject would all be coded separately, while some of this information was in fact contained in related parts or could be derived from other parts. Also, such a procedure would require the human analyst to go over the same consituents again and again for the data entry.

We think it is more efficient to steer a way between the two extremes of fully automatic and fully manual coding by using automatic components in the linguistic analysis for operations which are predictable and repetitive, and by carrying out those aspects by hand which would require an unduly complex and expensive computational tool. One such example of a compromise between manual and automatic analysis is COALA's parser. Since the main problem in the automatic structural analysis of language acquisition data is the identification of grammatical functions of constituents and the identification of their boundaries, we designed a parser which takes the analysis from the point where the above pieces of information have been coded manually.

We believe the amount of repetitive hand-coding required can be further reduced substantially by the following means:

(a) *Automatic devices* can be used where tasks are essentially repetitive and predictive in nature. A second example, besides the parser, is the insertion of markers for morpheme boundaries which can simply be added to the data by comparing the words in the data with the lexicon where the morpheme boundaries have been added by hand. Again, time and effort is saved for any new set of data which will contain many items already present in the lexicon.

(b) The data can be connected with an annotated *lexical grammar* which only requires an annotation for each type rather than each token of a lexical item. A further advantage of a linked lexico-grammar is that the amount of coding decreases with every new set of data, and it can be exchanged between researchers, thus further reducing the amount of manual coding.

(c) The *information* gathered for any one step of coding should be recorded and *fully exploited* for all aspects of the analysis. For instance, the identification of the grammatical subject can be linked to the annotation of pronouns in the lexical grammar component, thus providing information about person marking in subject NPs without any additional coding.

(d) *Inferring information* from existing information is a further important time-saving principle. To illustrate this, let us return to the example of the coding of the grammatical subject. When information about the grammatical subject is coded, naturally, the person analysing the data will have to identify the following features:

— the boundaries of the constituent
— its grammatical function
— its position in the sentence
— its relation to the phrase structure of the sentence.

A carefully worked out coding convention will make it possible to code only two of the four kinds of information by hand, namely, 'constituent boundary' and 'grammatical function', which in our system can be done in one move. The other two pieces of information can be inferred from the first two, e.g.:

— The position of constituents in the sentence is retrievable from the constituent boundary markings, provided these are placed in accordance with their occurrence in the data. Hence word order analyses can be carried out without any additional coding.
— The relation to the sentence's phrase structure (NP dominated by S) can be inferred from the grammatical coding of the subject.

To implement our proposals for a semi-automatic analysis, different interacting components are needed, as described below. At this point we want to mention the most central of these components, namely, the one in which the data will be stored and partly prepared for the automatic analysis. This core component is a relational database,[2] which will store the annotated lexical grammar and the actual interlanguage data. In contrast to databases which consist of a single file or a set of unrelated files, a relational database consists of a set of interconnected files. Information stored in one file can be linked to information stored in other files.

A simple example of a relational database is a system with two files, one containing pronouns which are annotated for a number of linguistically relevant grammatical features (such as person, number, etc.) and the other containing interlanguage data. In such a set-up it is sufficient to place the pronoun(s) of a given sentence into a predefined field of the data file to access the annotation of that particular pronoun. This allows the database system to run an analysis on the data making use of the features stored in the lexical grammar.

It should be noted that many aspects of the target language can be stored in the lexical grammar and that such a system allows an easy access to features of target language items occuring in the interlanguage data. Hence, such a system is a useful basis for a comparison between a distributional analysis of a set of data and the structure of the same items in the target language.

Some related work

It is not possible to give a fair account of all the related work presently being done in the area of computational linguistic tools, such as the one we are presenting in this paper, even if we restricted ourselves to the (semi-) automatic analysis of interlanguage data. This is because computational linguistic tools, which are becoming more and more common in empirical linguistic studies, are often not discussed as a separate issue in any well-defined forum. [For additional discussion, see Sampson, this volume, Chapter 9 — MP/VS.]

Where the disciplines of linguistics and computer science intersect, one finds great diversity. Computational tools for linguistics represents one area in this intersection zone, which in turn is related to many diverse disciplines. In Artificial Intelligence research, language parsing is, in addition to vision, one of the two best researched areas (Charniak & McDermott, 1985), and it is at the core of many computational tools. Research into natural language parsing is a crucial prerequisite for enterprises such as machine translation (Wilks, 1982) or natural language interfaces (Hendrix *et al.*, 1978; Martin *et al.*, 1983).

Approaches to natural language parsing are as diverse as the linguistic theories from which they are derived (Grosz *et al.*, 1985), partly based on specific linguistic theories and stressing to different degrees the role of syntax, semantics and discourse. They are related to aspects of speech processing (Schank, 1980; Wanner & Maratsos, 1978) and models of learning (Rumelhart, 1986), which are manifestations of the links of language parsing to psychology and epistemology.

The design and output of available computational tools vary greatly in their level of sophistication. They range from simple but effective features in word processing (like a 'search' feature) to complex parsing algorithms. Volume 23 of the journal *Linguistics* (1985) focuses on computational linguistics and contains a number of reports on various computational tools.

Concordance programs and word counting programs have been used for a long time to simplify linguistic research (Lenders & Willée, 1986). With the arrival of the microcomputer and the wide range of commercially available software, such programs were superceded by standard features of ready-made software packages. No one needs to write a program for word counts these days, since a word count can conveniently be done in a standard spelling program. Similarly, the function of a concordance program is included in standard database systems, which contain many additional features. This means that computational tools do not necessarily have to be developed anew for each analytical project. In many cases it will be sufficient to exploit available software, or the functions required may be contained in the operating system of the computer (Atwell, 1986).

Furthermore, the development of computational tools does not necessarily require the expertise of a programming whiz, because many software packages allow the user to define his/her own functions in a fairly straightforward way. One example which has been used extensively in the COALA system is a versatile text editor (*ME*dit), which can compare the contents of different files and make predefined changes to one of the files on the basis of the comparison.

Computer-aided language learning (CALL) is a relatively new branch of applied linguistics, quite different in its aims and objectives from any of the above-mentioned domains in the intersection of language and computer. Its main objective is computer-assisted language learning. One branch of CALL, however, is concerned with language assessment and linguistic analysis. This is evidenced, for example, in a volume on CALL edited by Leech & Candlin (1986) which contains a collection of articles on both computer-aided learning and computational linguistic analysis.

Some of the existing projects on the computational linguistic analysis of *native varieties* such as British English contain features which are similar to some aspects of the design of COALA. For instance, in the TOSCA system (Aarts & van den Heuvel, 1985), the raw data, the lexicon, and the parser are treated as separate components, and the parser is linked to the lexicon. The linking of the parsing component to an annotated lexicon is a feature of lexically driven parsers, particularly of augmented transition networks. The basic difference between TOSCA and COALA is that the latter is designed for *non-target varieties* of a language, and because of this it is based on an 'over-constrained' partial parser and a particular interaction of manual and automatic steps in the analysis of the data.

Leech (1986), in his description of work carried out at the Unit for Computer Research on the English Language (UCREL) at the University of Lancaster, discusses a number of principles for automatic grammmatical analysis which are similar to some of our points on semi-automatic analysis of non-native varieties in the preceding section: (1) What Leech calls the 'recycling' of information corresponds to our principle of 'economical exploitation' of information obtained in earlier steps of the analysis. (2) The UCREL group, too, has taken a lexical approach to parsing and opted for a *partial* parser. However, their object of analysis is a native variety of a language, which requires a different design for the parser and for the interaction of analytical tools to non-native varieties.

In the remainder of this section we discuss two systems which were designed for the same purpose as COALA, namely, the computer-aided analysis of non-native language samples.

Clahsen's approach (1986b) to computer-aided analysis of non-native speech is based on his profile analysis of German child language (Clahsen, 1986a). It is a single-file database system with a number of very useful customised reports. The database consists of eighteen different fields into which information about the functional and formal structure of the learner's language can be entered. The entries must be made according to a formal coding system which refers to the categories of Clahsen's profile analysis. For instance, there is provision for five different types of grammatical subjects which are coded as:

'C.1,4'
'C.1,5'
etc.

Clahsen's system allows effective searches and fast counts once the data have been analysed by hand. It can produce a quantified profile of the analysed data — similar to the computerised version of LARSP (Crystal et al., 1976) written by Bishop (1985) — and contains sub-programs for more detailed quantitative analyses. Its major disadvantage is that information entered into the system cannot be 'recycled', which limits the effectiveness of the system for analyses beyond the range of the manual coding in the way described in the preceding section.

We would like to add, however, that Clahsen's approach is very straightforward and well-suited for the purpose for which it is designed, namely, computer-based profile analysis. For this type of pre-defined analytical task and for a comparatively small set of data it may be preferable to have a less flexible system than COALA because the work necessary for preparation of the data for the automatic analysis might outweigh the manual work necessary for a profile analysis of a comparatively small set of data. In the context of linguistic research with large sets of data and with varying hypotheses about structural/functional features of the data, however, we believe that a system with more flexibility and automatic components is more effective. Ultimately, the efficiency of the systems can only be evaluated in practical tests.

The basic way in which data are coded in MacWhinney's (1987a) CHAT system (Codes for the Human Analysis of Transcripts) for a later computer-aided analysis with the CLAN (Child Language ANalysis) computer programs is the following. There are provisions for 20 lines underneath the transcript which can be used to annotate the transcript according to different grammatical features. One way of annotating the data is to provide information about grammatical forms and functions, e.g.:

*MAR: I want-ed a toy
%mor: 1SGPRO|I V|want-PAST|ed ART|a N|toy
(MacWhinney, 1987a: 23)

In the above example, the second line is an annotation of the morphological structure of the data in the first line. '1SGPRO' is an identification of the function of the pronoun. 'PAST' marks the tense denoted by the morpheme -ed, and 'V', 'ART,' and 'N' identify the grammatical classes of the words after the symbol '|'.

As in Clahsen's approach, grammatical annotations have to be made for every token, e.g. for every occurrence of the pronoun *I*. In contrast to Clahsen's approach, however, the data can be tagged in such a way that all coded information can be related to other coded information and is always retrievable. The disadvantage of the morpho-syntactic part of the annotation system in CHAT is that the necessary coding conventions are very complex (with 185 different categories, many of which are represented only by slightly different sequences of characters). Annotation with such a system is repetitive, time-consuming and not guarded against typing errors. The CLAN analyses are still very limited and could, at the present stage, equally well be carried out using either a versatile operating system (Atwell, 1986) or commercially available software.

Both approaches, Clahsen's and MacWhinney's, have been developed in the context of *primary language acquisition* (PLA). It has often been pointed out by researchers dealing with first *and* second language acquisition data that SLA data are structurally more regular and closer to adult language than PLA data (Felix, 1978). This observation may be quite important when comparing different approaches to the analysis of developing linguistic systems, because the structure of early PLA data might not allow the sort of automatic analysis which can be carried out on SLA data. To find a satisfactory answer to this question the different types of approaches need to be trialed with different types of data.

Overview of COALA

Basically, the COALA system is a relational database[2] which stores linguistic data at different structural levels and which is linked to a lexical grammar of the target language, to a device which can automatically insert markers for morpheme boundaries, and to an ATN parser for noun phrases, prepositional phrases, and copula complements. The database management system incorporates a complex query language which makes it possible to retrieve data from any part of the database and to make quantifiable comparisons between the lexical grammar of the target language and the structure of the interlanguage data.

Figure 10.1 gives an overview of the structure of COALA. It also illustrates some of the main steps of the manual and automatic parts of the analysis. The speech samples are transcribed according to conventions specified in the COALA manual (Jansen & Pienemann, 1988).

The database system

As shown in Figure 10.1 the core of the COALA system consists of two database components: an interlanguage (IL) component which stores informa-

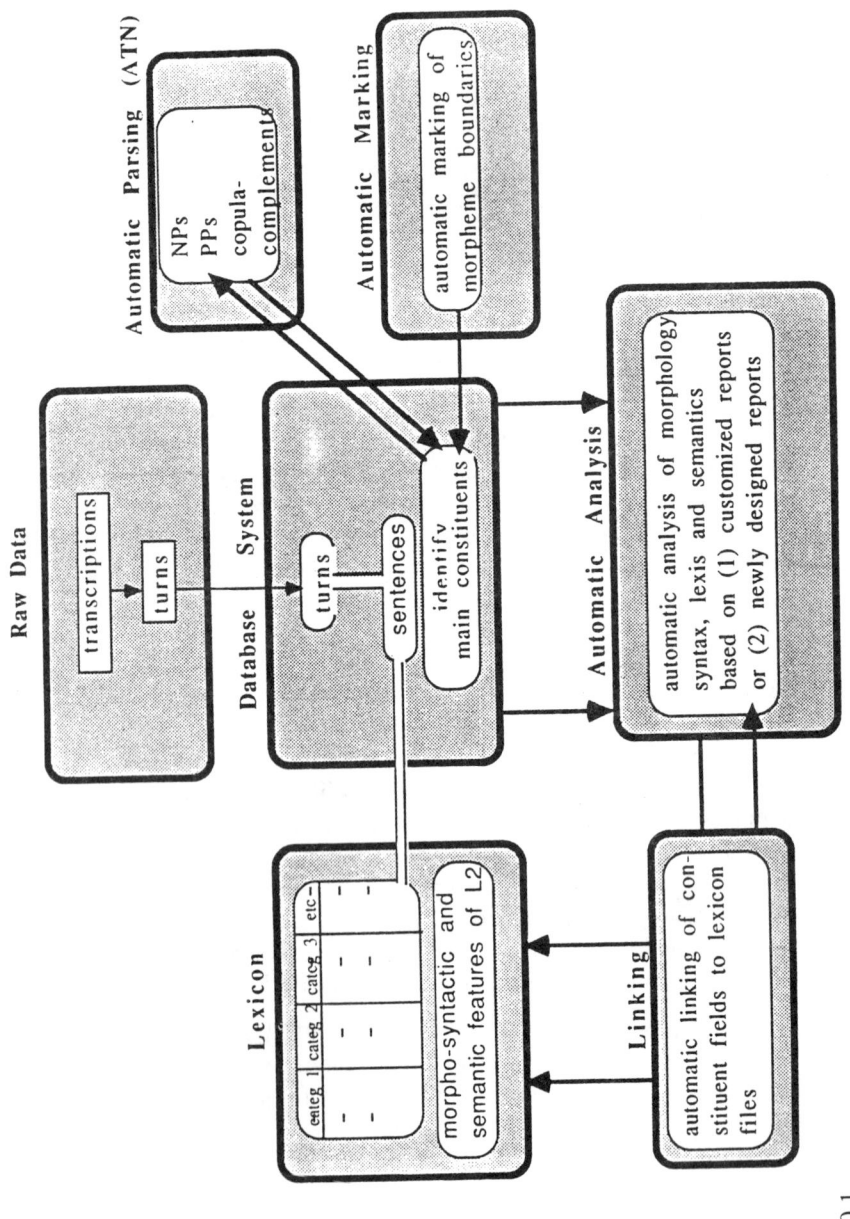

FIGURE 10.1

tion on the data, and a target language (TL) component which stores a lexico-grammar of the target language.

The Interlanguage (IL) Component

The IL component, represented in the centre of Figure 10.1, is a database system which stores the data essentially at two different levels: the level of turns and the level of sentences. In the turn database (at the top of Figure 10.1), the data are stored turn by turn. This makes it possible to extend the COALA system to the analysis of discourse phenomena. The sentence database stores the sentences contained in the data and information about them, such as speech-act type, time reference, syntactic structure, and lexical categories.

The turn and sentence databases are linked (symbolised by the open line connecting them). Thus, it is possible to access any information about the turns from within the sentence database and vice versa. At present, the main function of the linking of these databases is to provide, within the database system, the necessary discourse context for sentence analysis. In practical terms, this is achieved by displaying the linked records of the two files simultaneously in two separate 'windows', so that for each sentence the corresponding stretch of discourse is displayed automatically even when browsing through the sentence file.

The IL component can be used as a stand-alone database and handles the distributional analyses of the data. However, it is designed to be used in connection with the TL lexicon and is more powerful when used in this way.

The Target Language (TL) Component

The TL component, represented to the left in Figure 10.1, is a database containing information on the structure of the target language. Essentially it contains a data-specific, target language lexico-grammar. It is data-specific in the sense that it is based exclusively on the lexicon of the interlanguage data to be analysed.

The lexicon, compiled from the IL data, forms the skeleton for the TL grammar. The IL grammar is derived from the distributional analysis of the data stored in the data files. We elaborate on the importance of this principle below.

The TL component consists of fourteen lexicon files (one for each subcategorisation class), nine of which are annotated for syntactic and morphological features of the target language. Each of the annotated files is linked to a corresponding field in the IL component. In Figure 10.1 these links are represented in a simplified form by the open line connecting the two databases.

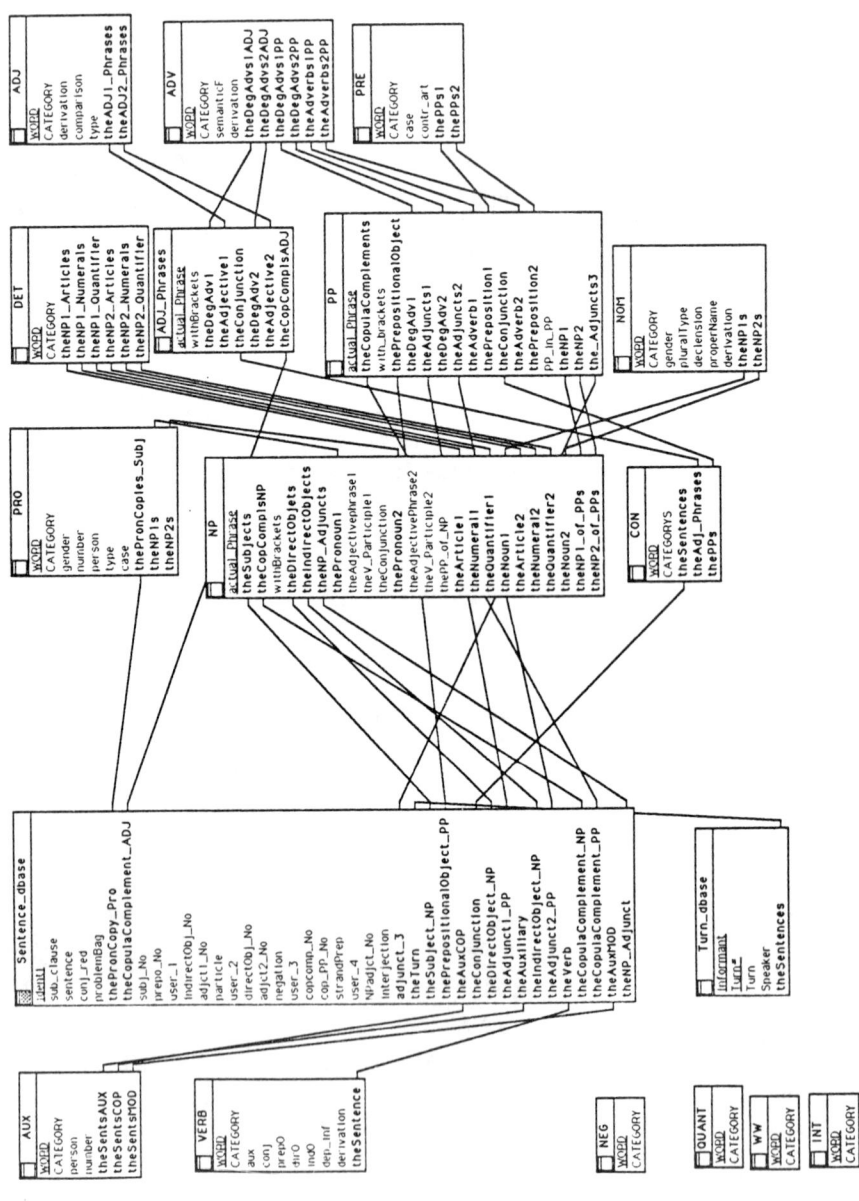

FIGURE 10.2

Structure of the database

The structure of the system of linked files is displayed in more detail in Figure 10.2. It is this relational file structure which allows the system to retrieve information contained in any of these files and to link it with any other information stored in the data.

As shown in Figure 10.2, the sentence file — which stores the sentence constituents and further information about each sentence — is the core of the database system. The sentence database file is linked to three auxiliary files: NP, ADJ, and PP, the records of which are analysed by the parser. The lexicon files (containing annotated lexical items) are linked to those fields of the above four files in which the corresponding lexical items are placed in the course of the (manual and automatic) analysis of the data. There are three links to lexicon files at the sentence level (manual analysis) and nine at the constituent level (automatic analysis). All lexical items contained in the sentence database subsystem are merely represented as a link to the TL lexico-grammar. Because of the relational power of the database, the TL lexicon can serve as a stand-in for the actual occurrences of the lexical items in the data. The constituent files (NP, PP, ADJ) are linked in three ways: (1) to the level of the sentence, (2) to the lexical level, and (3) to each other. The latter type of link accounts for the fact that NPs can be embedded in PPs, and vice versa, and that ADJ can be embedded in NPs and PPs.

The database is designed in such a way that the actual phrases and lexical items are the *key fields* of the corresponding files. This ensures that all lexical items and phrases can be pulled out of their context at any time to be processed in isolation and then placed back into their original context. This set-up also reduces the amount of work involved in the actual processing of the data because some phrases and words will be repeated many times in the data.

Because of the architecture of the database design, the system can access information about every lexical item contained in the data, e.g. its grammatical form, its position in sentences, its grammatical function, the distribution of categories in the data, and its subcategorisation in the target language. All of these different pieces of information can be related and retrieved in any conceivable combination. The retrieval process is greatly facilitated by the sophisticated query language which is part of the database management system.

The automatic parts

As shown in Figure 10.1, COALA provides the database core with four main tools: (1) a facility for the automatic insertion of indexed brackets in a sentence (for details see below), (2) the morpheme boundary marker, (3) the parser, and (4) the report library. These four devices automatically perform some otherwise tedious and time-consuming manual tasks involved in data preparation and analysis.

The Morpheme-Boundary Marker

The lexical component of COALA makes possible the automatic handling of the insertion of morpheme boundaries into the data. Derivational and inflectional morpheme boundaries need to be marked manually only once per lexical item. This marking is done within the lexicon. The lexicon then serves as input for the morpheme boundary marker, which automatically inserts the morpheme boundaries into the data.

The Parser

The lexical component of COALA is further utilised by the lexically driven ATN parser, which automatically annotates the internal structure of noun phrases, prepositional phrases and copula complements. As pointed out above, the structure of the parser has been restricted to these constituents because the structure of interlanguages does not, with the means presently available, permit the automatic assignment of grammatical functions to constituents.

Another feature of the parser is that it is over-constrained in the sense that it will not accept some structures which are possible in the TL. The desired side-effect of this is that it will also reject most structures which are not acceptable in the TL. Such items will be written to a separate file for further manual analysis. We think that it is simpler to sort suspect cases out rather than check the whole annotation of the parser for all records as the UCREL group does (Leech, 1986).

The Report Library

COALA contains a library of customised reports, which can be used once the manual and automatic preparation of the data has been completed. The reports make it possible to obtain specific subsets of the data and to perform automatic analyses for a wide range of linguistic features. Any further reports can be designed by future users of the system. We hope to add such newly designed reports to the existing library so that they can be shared by all other users.

In the following sections we look in greater detail at the major components that make up the present structure and functioning of COALA.

Manual Analysis

Basic principles

Our primary goal in the construction of COALA was to perform an unbiased distributional analysis of the data. If, to give one example, we classified the word *worked* as a verb in the lexicon because of its verbal ending, then we would exclude the possibility that it might function as a noun in the data. For the same reason, we also decided to mark as few grammatical functions of the data as possible. If, for instance, we find an s on the end of verbs, we do not mark it for subject verb agreement, but leave it to the distributional analysis to decide which function those suffixes serve in the data.

Another principle is to carry out the analysis as closely to the original transcription as possible. The reason for this is that much of the information about the functional structure of the sentence can only be obtained from the discourse context. A further principle is to code as little information as possible (manually or automatically). There are two reasons for this principle. One is just a simple economy consideration: coding is very time-consuming. The second is that we try to avoid imposing target language categories on the interlanguage.

We prefer to obtain as much information as possible about structural properties of the sample through the distributional analysis. With the present structure of COALA, it is possible to draw many inferences about the structure of the sample by analysing the limited amount of coded information and comparing it with structural properties of the target language. This reduces the need for manual coding.

One example of inferred information involves the omission of prepositions. Prepositions occur in the following grammatical functions: prepositional objects, prepositional phrases, and adverbials. However, there are also nominal adverbials such as *every day* or *last year* which do not require prepositions. We simply separate this grammatical function (nominal adverbials) from the rest of the adverbial like phrases in the manual analysis and do not code missing elements in any of these phrases.

The parser can, then, in a separate step, analyse the constituent structure in all of these phrases. We can now define conditions under which prepositions are obligatory in the above-mentioned phrases, and it will be possible to separate those cases in the data where the lack of a preposition is in accordance with the structure of the target language and cases of preposition ommision. Other so-called 'missing elements' can be analysed in a similar fashion.

A further principle is that we do not code any mistakes in the database because what is a mistake in the data can always be retrieved as such, by comparing the structure of the data with the structure of the target language which is encoded in the grammatical component of COALA. We can simply assume some of the features of the target languages to be known to the analyser. Examples are word order or a list of inflectional and derivational morphemes. Therefore, such things as 'wrong' stem forms of the verb, non-targetlike inflectional morphemes or 'deviant' subcategorisations of nouns or verbs, are picked up by COALA automatically through a specification of the linguistic context in the 'reports' on the data.

Sentence analysis

There are three major steps in the analysis of sentences in COALA. The first is concerned with the identification of sentences in the data and is carried out manually. The second step — also manual — involves the analysis of the sentence into main constituents. The third step, which is carried out automatically, involves the analysis of the constituents.

The first step of the sentence analysis is carried out within the full transcriptions. It comprises two actions: (A) delimiting the boundaries of the sentences to be analysed and (B) providing functional information about the sentence. The latter action involves information about speech acts, time reference and aspect. This information is coded manually and in normal characters as illustrated in Figure 10.3.

Upon completion of these functional codings, the system will automatically number the turns and import them into the database system where the sentences with the added information are automatically extracted and stored in a separate file in such a way that each sentence is linked with the turn in which it occurs. (Note that the turns are stored in the order of their occurrence.)

The second step is the identification of sentence constituents and their grammatical function. Figure 10.4 provides the reader with an overview of different sentence constituents and their functions. The basic activity involved in this second step of manual analysis is 'selecting' the relevant constituent of the sentence and 'copying' it into the appropriate field. This activity of selecting and copying, which in practical terms is much simpler than entering code for the data, provides the system with two essential types of information about the sentence: (1) the constituent boundaries and (2) their grammatical function. In the example provided in Figure 10.4, the constituent *they*, for instance, has been copied from the sentence-field and pasted into the field 'subject'.

ANALYSIS OF LANGUAGE ACQUISITION DATA

Turn#	Speaker	Turn
35	GB	That's alright...okay...um...did you read some books about Australia when you were in Poland?...did you see any films or books about Australia?
36	I	Books...boo...zooks mm, hm...read...mm...um...1[I came here with my familia..husband and son..&p]1 and is next son.2[..second son ...gee has...mm...familia...wife and two children.]2
37	GB	Mm, hm...is he in Australia?
38	I	Yes, yes.
39	GB	So all the family...
40	I	1[Oh...we came here...mm...togezer.&p]1
41	GB	I see...mm, hm...is it very difficult now to go out of Poland?
42	I	1[Yes...yes..,yes ..er...we...um...we have passpor.&p]1 2[...mm...first I...wiz my husband &p]2 3[...and two months past...came in Austria...son...my son with familia.&p]3
43	GB	Oh I see...mm hm...um...so how long does it take now to come from Poland to Australia?
44	I	How long?...from Poland to Australia?
45	GB	Mm...if you want to come to live in Australia...what do you have to do?...if you want to...if you're living in Poland and you say right I want to go to Australia...what must you do?
46	I	Mm...mm...worket und...und and, er...mm, good leef
47	GB	No I don't think you understand...um...you...were in Poland, OK, you lived in Poland and you said:...
48	I	Uh huh!
49	GB	"I want to go to Australia"...okay...one day you said: "Right I'm going to Australia now..."
50	I	Uh huh...uh huh...
51	GB	What do you do?
52	I	1[My husband...uh...uh, has...has, er conflict...conflict, &p]1 2[er... I...I wasn't in Partia in Poland.&p]2 my husband too 3[...und, um...we must...er...mm, leave Poland.&p]3
53	GB	Oh...you had to leave.
54	I	Mm.
55	GB	Uh...because you weren't in the Communist Party?... you weren't...
56	I	Huh...huh...yes, yes, yes.
57	GB	You weren't...a member...uh huh I see...um...
58	I	1[Um,.I was...in Poland...er...manager shops &p]1 2[,,,mm...on zer..boss...come...mm...wiz me and er, speak &p]2 3[you must,..you must in de Partia]3
59	GB	And you said...
60	I	No.
61	GB	No...ah...and what happened after that?
62	I	1[That...that...das is...that's, mm...very, very, very problem.&p]1

FIGURE 10.3

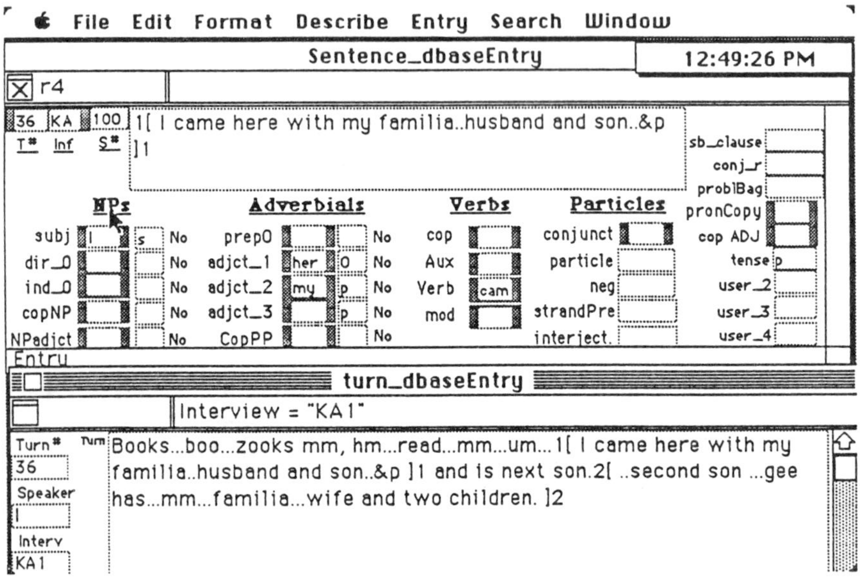

FIGURE 10.4

In this context, it is important to note that although the individual sentences are lifted out of the discourse context for the sentence analysis, the whole transcription always remains visible in the turn file as illustrated in Figure 10.4 because the records of the turn file are always displayed on the screen together with the linked record of the sentence file as illustrated in Figure 10.4. This makes it possible to analyse each sentence in its proper context.

As can be seen from Figure 10.4, the basic assumption is that, with the exception of prepositional phrases, there is always only one constituent to fulfil one grammatical function, such as subject, verb, etc. Looking at the actual data, however, this assumption turns out to be an idealisation, because the data contain a lot of repetitions, self-corrections, and false starts. However, these cases can be singled out and identified by placing them in special fields of the sentence file in the database. Embedded and co-ordinated constituents are treated as fulfilling one grammatical function, e.g. *the fool on the hill* ([NP+PP]$_{NP}$) or *Mary and Jim* ([NP+conj+NP]$_{NP}$). Cases of 'conjunction reduction' are placed in a separate field of the same database file and analysed separately. In (6), for instance, the constituent *and had dinner* would be copied into a separate field and analysed separately.

(6) *He went home and had dinner.*

Together with the identification of major constituents, another type of information needs to be coded manually, namely, the grammatical number of noun phrases. This will be coded in separate fields for the different constituents containing noun phrases. This information, in connection with other pieces of information already stored in COALA, makes it possible to analyse such things as plural marking, subject–verb agreement, adjectival morphology, gender marking, and other morphological phenomena.

The grammar component

The grammar component consists of the set of files for the lexical categories listed below:

no. category	*annotated*
1 adjective	+
2 adverb	+
3 auxiliary (incl. copula, modal)	+
4 conjunction	+
5 determiner (incl. article, numeral, quantifier)	+
6 interjection	−
7 negator	−
8 noun	+
9 particle	−
10 preposition	+
11 pronoun (with various sub-classes)	+
12 question word	−
13 verb	+
14 word fragments	−

The entries to the different lexical files have been annotated for their subcategorisation. In some cases, some components of COALA will be based partly on subclasses of the above-mentioned lexical categories. One example is the class of degree adverbs, which behave syntactically differently from other types of adverbs and which are treated as a different class by the parser. For German, a lexicon has been annotated for a substantial set of data from Pienemann's (1987) longitudinal study, and this set of data will be complemented by a larger set of data from Jansen's (1987) cross-sectional study. A lexicon for English is currently being annotated.

The annotation of lexical entries is based on their stem form, not on the fully inflected form in which the lexical entry occurs in the data. All variations of the same stem are listed in the lexicon. As we pointed out above, this is an important aspect of COALA, because our primary goal in the construction of COALA was to be able to obtain an unbiased distributional analysis of the data.

For both target languages, English and German, the verb file contains the greatest number of grammatical features. The following examples illustrate the structure of the verb file for two records:

antwort
aux   h
stem present
3.pers pres
stem past
stem perfect
participle   gexantwortxet
sep pref
reflexive
passive   +
subcat   [_]/[_(NPdt),(auf POak),(_da S)]
deriv

anxfang'en
aux   h
stem present   fang
3.pers pres   fäng
stem past   fing
stem perfect   fang
participle   anxgexfang'en
sep pref   an
reflexive
passive   +
subcat   [_]/[_(mit POak)]/[(NPak)]/[(_daß S)]/[(S_inf)]
deriv

Note: 'S_inf' stands for sentences such as *him to go home* in *She wants him to go home*.

Information is given on: the type of auxiliary the verb takes (*h* or *s* for *haben* and *sein*), the different stem forms of strong verbs, the form of the participle, and identification of separable prefixes if such exist, whether the verb is reflexive, whether it can be passivised, a list of its syntactic subcategorisations, and an identification of derivational morphemes. Further features such as semantic features can easily be added to the record.

In the case of German verbs, most of this information can be obtained from Helbig-Schenkel (1973). The subcategorisation frames contain information about prepositional objects, accusative and dative objects, dependent infinitives, dependent clauses, etc. Optional complements are put in parentheses and alternative subcategorisation frames are separated by slashes. All NPs contained in the syntactic frame are marked for case. We use 'ak' for accusative, 'dt' for dative, 'gn' for genitive. NPs in prepositional objects are labelled 'PO' in order to distinguish them formally from case NPs. The entry '[_]' is used to indicate that all complements are optional.

The following English examples further illustrate the conventions for subcategorisation:

introduce
V, [_NP2 (to NP)]

demand
V, [_NP2 (from-NP3)]/[_that S]/[_to V]

like
V, [_NP2]/[_V-ing(x)]/[_to V (x)]

wish
V, [_NP2]/[_to-V(NP2)]/[_S]

The noun file contains the following grammatical features: gender, derivational morphemes, syntactic subcategorisation. The other lexical categories are listed in Figure 10.5.

A careful classification of the lexical items into the different categories is essential for the reliable operation of the parser and a reliable automatic analysis of data. Note that it is not mandatory to annotate the lexical grammar for all the grammatical features mentioned above. Particularly, the subcategorisation frames create a lot of manual work, though it is still possible to perform a great number of interesting analyses with COALA without this grammatical feature being annotated.

The last major manual component of the preparation of the data is the updating of the lexicon for those items of the new set of data which are not contained in the lexicon. COALA will produce a list of 'new lexical items' which have to be grouped into the appropriate grammatical category so that these new entries can be annotated in the lexicon files. Also, morpheme boundaries have to

Adjective	attributive vs. predicative, type of comparison, syntactic subcategorization, derivational morph.;
Adverb	semantic features, derivational morph.;
Article	definite vs indefinite, gender, number, case
Auxiliary	number, person, tense;
Conjunction	subordination vs. co-ordinating;
Copula	number, person, tense;
Interjection	
Modal	number, person, tense;
Negator	
Noun	gender, syntactic subcategorization, derivational morph.;
Numeral	
Particle	
Preposition	case, contracted 'prep+art';
Pronoun	
personal	case, gender, number, person;
possessive	case, pro vs. _NP, person;
demonstrative	case, pro vs. _NP, number;
interrogative	case, syntactic subcategorization;
relative	case;
indefinite	case; pro vs. _NP;
Verb	type of AUX, present stem, 3rd pers pres., perfect stem participle, separable prefix, reflexive, passive, syntactic subcategorization, derivational morpheme
Word fragments	

FIGURE 10.5 *List of lexical categories and of the parameters for their annotation.*

be marked in the new items. For German data we use an extensive morpheme dictionary (Augst, 1975) to verify the correctness of our morphological analyses and to check for possible homographs. COALA will transfer these markers to all instances of the given item in the data.

Automatic Analysis

Apart from the *customised reports*, which are treated in the following section, there are three main components of the automatic part of COALA. One is responsible for the insertion of indexed brackets in the sentence file, the second for the insertion of markers at morpheme boundaries, and the third one for automatically parsing the constituent structure of the main constituents.

The latter three automatic parts of COALA do not really produce the final analysis of the data which the linguistic researcher might initially expect of the COALA package. Instead, they prepare the raw data in such a way that the computer can, through the report programs, perform those calculations on the data which are described in the section below.

Insertion of indexed brackets

After the manual analysis has been carried out, COALA will automatically place indexed brackets around the appropriate constituents of the sentence file which contains the actual sentence. The brackets will delimit the boundaries of the constituents and the indices will make it possible to retrieve the position of the constituent in the sentence. The only reason for the insertion of indexed brackets is to be able to locate the position of specified constituents in the sentence. All other information about the constituents has already been stored in the different constituent fields.

The following example illustrates the format of the sentence with annotated brackets:

$_1[_{sbj}[\text{der student}]_{sbj}\ _{vb}[\text{geht}]_{vb}\ _{neg}[\text{nicht}]_{neg}\ _{pa}[\text{nach hause}]_{pa}]_1$

The basic principles behind the syntax of the bracketing operation are the following: the indices for different categories must be varied in such a way that there will be no ambiguity in automatic analyses. Both constituent boundaries must be marked because this information will be needed later. The complete format of the bracketing system is described in the COALA manual (Jansen & Pienemann, 1988).

Thus, COALA retrieves the information coded in the database in two different ways: (1) The grammatical function of the constituent is retrieved by knowing which field it has been entered into (e.g. 'subject'); (2) the position of the constituent is retrieved from the position of the inserted indexed bracket.

The insertion of indexed brackets is also an option in the CHAT system (MacWinney, 1987a), where it has to be carried out by hand. In further contrast to the CHAT system, the annotated brackets in our system refer not only to the constituent structure, but also — according to the units of the manual analysis — to the grammatical function of the constituents.

The morpheme marker

Once the morpheme boundaries have been inserted into the entries in the lexicon, they are copied automatically onto the data. This is done according to a very simple principle. A file is created from the lexicon which contains each lexical item in two versions: one with and one without the morpheme boundaries inserted. A macro-defined sequence of operations then carries out a series of 'change all' commands to the data textfile, whereby each lexical item without the markings is changed to the corresponding word form containing the markings.

We use the following convention for the marking of morpheme boundaries: first, the letters x and y are removed from the data, i.e. they are replaced by i and ks. An x is inserted between the different parts of compounds as well as between the root form and the derivational morpheme. An apostrophe is inserted between the root form and any inflectional morpheme. A y is added to the beginning and the end of all words which contain more than just the root form. In this way, the beginning and end of words as well as the different type of morpheme boundaries can be accessed by the system. It should be added that derivational morphemes are also coded in the lexicon so that it is possible to differentiate between compositional and derivational morpheme boundaries.

We are currently creating basic English and German lexicons with several thousand entries containing the information about morphological structure described in this section and the annotations described in the next section. Future users of the COALA package will have to update the lexicon for their particular new entries. COALA's morpheme marker will then automatically insert the correct markers for morpheme boundaries in the whole set of data.

COALA can also pick up homographs in the data, provided they have been assigned a different morphological structure. An example is the German word *lehre*. In the lexicon, this word is spelled as follows: *lehrxe* or *lehr'e*. In the first case, the suffix *e* has been identified as a derivational morpheme and has thus been separated by an *x*. The word *lehrxe* is a deverbal noun based on the root form of the verb and the derivational morpheme *e*. In the second case, the word *lehr'e* is a verb, inflected for first person, singular, present tense. COALA will make a list of the homographs occurring in the data and identify their location so that — depending on the given context — the correct marking can be inserted manually.

The parser

A further automatic component of COALA is the parser, capable of analysing the constituent structure of noun phrases, prepositional phrases, and the different types of copula complements. These constituents form the input to the parser which inserts indexed brackets to the constituents to represent their phrase structure. In the case of main constituents, the use of indexed brackets is primarily a convenient form of storing information about their internal structure, since the position of elements does not have the primary interest that it has in the analysis of sentence structure. The parser also copies the lexical item(s) contained in the corresponding phrase in a format which allows the output to be read into the linked database. This ensures that all parts of the database are properly linked to the lexicon component.

Output of the Parser

Here we describe the features of the system of annotated brackets for the internal constituent structure of main constituents.

(A) The following indexed brackets are placed around parsed phrases:

NP[ ]NP noun phrases
PP[ ]PP prepositional phrases
PA[ ]PA participial phrases

(B) The following indexed brackets are placed around parsed words:

adj[ ]adj	adjective	N[ ]N	noun
adv[ ]adv	adverb	num[ ]num	numeral
art[ ]art	article	pre[ ]pre	preposition
aux[ ]aux	auxiliary verb	pro[ ]pro	pronoun (arc1)
con[ ]con	conjunction	pon[ ]pon	pronoun (arc2)
cop[ ]cop	copula	qua[ ]qua	quantifier
int[ ]int	interjection	V[ ]V	verb
neg[ ]neg	negator	wh[ ]wh	wh-word

(C) The brackets reflect the hierarchical structure of phrases, e.g.:

NP[art[the]art N[fly]N PP[pre[on]pre NP[art[the]art
   N[wall]N]NP]PP]NP
NP[art[the]art N[flying]N gen[of]gen NP[N[kids]N]NP]NP

Design of the Parser

The parser is based on augmented transition networks (ATN) (Woods, 1970, Wanner & Maratsos, 1978) and consists of five sub-networks. The parsers for English and German are identical in structure, although the two languages are obviously different (particularly, the richer morphological system of the German language). The reason for this is that the parser is

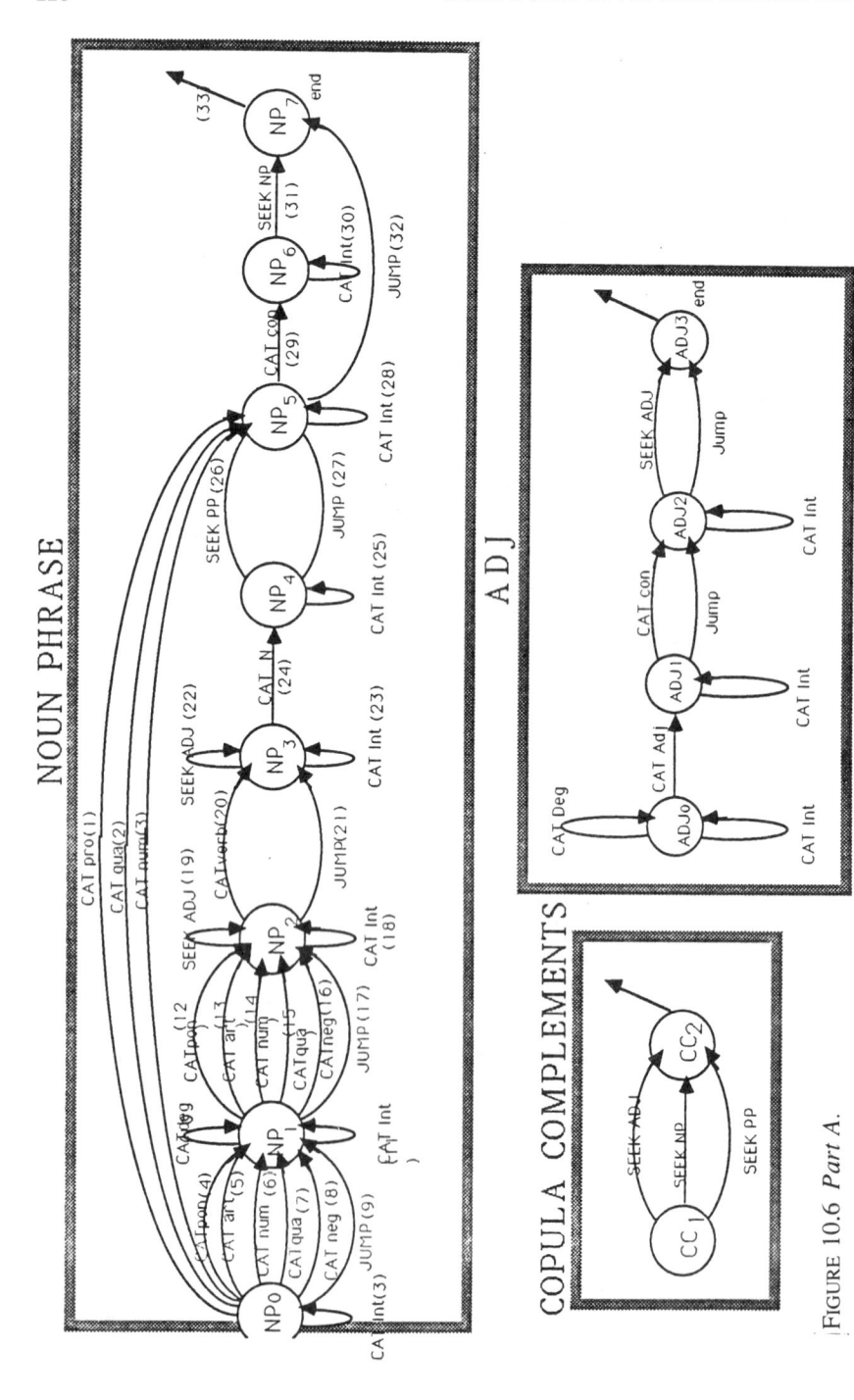

FIGURE 10.6 *Part A*.

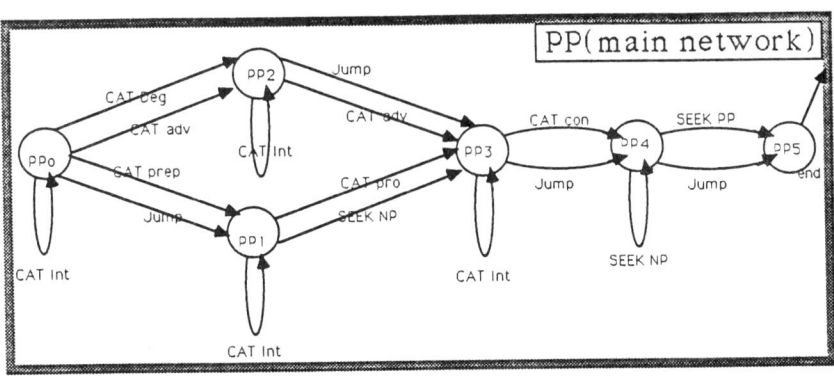

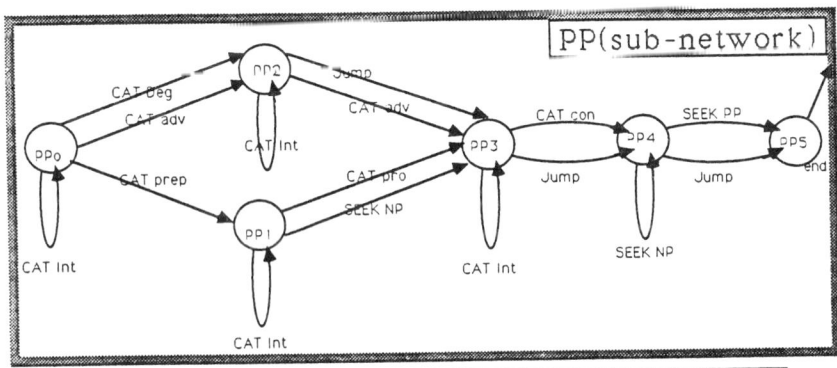

ANALYSIS OF LANGUAGE ACQUISITION DATA

FIGURE 10.6 *Part B.*

intended for interlanguages and accepts only a subset of the structures possible in both target languages.

We constrained the parser as much as possible because an overly general parser might process structures incorrectly, and it would be very time-consuming to check its output manually. Therefore, we designed the parser to reject certain types of structures. Such structures are written to a special file which can then be analysed manually.

Figure 10.6 displays the ATNs for NPs, copula complements and adjectival phrases. The NP network has provisions for co-ordination of NPs, as in (7); for multiple embeddings of PPs, as in (8); and for embedded participial phrases, as in (9). It has provisions for the multiple insertion of adjectives, as in (10), and is sensitive to the use of interjections at all conceivable points within the noun phrase, as in (11).

(7) *the farmer and me*
     der Bauer und ich
(8) *the cat on the house on the hill*
     die Katze auf dem Haus auf dem Hügel
(9) *der verlorene Sohn*
     the lost son
(10) *the beautiful and expensive blue car*
     das schöne und teure blaue Auto
(11) **eh** *der* **ehm** *kleine* **hm** *Kerl*
(12) *der den Vertag unterzeichnende Vorsitzende*
     literally: * the the treaty signing chairperson, meaning: the chairperson who is signing the treaty.

There is no provision in the parser for participial phrases containing embedded NPs or PPs. Hence, noun phrases such as (12) cannot be parsed because this would involve analysing a grammatical relation between the embedded NP *man* and the verb of the participial phrase, *eat*. First of all, the parser is not capable of identifying grammatical relations, and it should not be because for this purpose, it would have to analyse — and so rely on — morphological structures. Since, however, the morphology of interlanguages is irregular, the parser would be 'misled' and would either fail or — even worse — produce incorrect results.

Hence, the parser will only accept verbs in the position of participial phrases. Arc 20 in the NP network, which was designed to account for participles, also makes it possible to parse phrases like *the singing* and *das Singen* in which cases the NPs do not contain any nouns (normally to be parsed in arc 24). Such cases can be parsed because a special condition ensures that a transition from NP3 to NP4 is possible if arc 20 is taken as the transition from NP2 to NP3.

There are two networks for PPs, one for main constituents (main network) and one for embedded PPs (sub-network). The only difference between the two is that the main network allows PPs with missing prepositions, while the sub-network does not. In combination with the rest of the system this ensures that missing prepositions in main constituents will be picked up by the parser. Allowing missing prepositions in embedded PPs, however, would mean that the parser would not be able to distinguish between embedded NPs and embedded PPs. Hence, it might parse the phrase *my mother's house* as follows:

P[NP[pro[my] **N**[mother's] **PP[prep**[Ø] **NP[N**[house]]]

Obviously, such an incorrect analysis, which would be very hard to detect in a large amount of data once it had been carried out automatically, would ruin the whole analysis.

In summary, the parser is more rigidly constrained than the target language so that 'suspect' structures can be singled out automatically and processed by hand. One exception to this principle, apart from missing prepositions, is the structure of the determiner. Here the parser allows ungrammatical structures such as (13):

(13) * *three which boys*

The reason for this 'under-constrained' aspect of the parser is that selection restrictions underlying the (German) determiner system are mostly not purely grammatical in nature. However, we do not think that this exception to our general policy of keeping the parser over-constrained will affect its analytical task, namely, the delimitation of constituent boundaries and the identification of embedded and co-ordinated phrases.

The COALA system also contains a number of routines which can be used as linguistic tools independently of the normal analytical steps. Examples of these are the line-numbering facility, various routines for changing characters and the text, and the possibility of creating a lexicon of the data, including frequency counts.

Linguistic 'Calculations'

Once data have been prepared in the manual and automatic steps completed as described above, the query language of the database system makes it possible to perform a wide range of analyses on the data.

Simple query generation

Simple searches can be performed on the data with the help of the dialogue box reproduced in Figure 10.7. When the user selects the appropriate field and one of the operators or functions listed on the righthand side of Figure 10.7, the database system automatically creates a query formula and can access all the records in the specified file which satisfy the definition made in the query formula. In this way, it is possible to produce lists of particular words or sentences contained in the data. If the search is performed on the sentence file, then it is possible, for instance, to produce a list of all the sentences containing one particular grammatical subject by setting the value of the subject field in the sentence file equal to the specified word. In a similar way, searches can be performed using other files, other fields in the files and other operators. Of

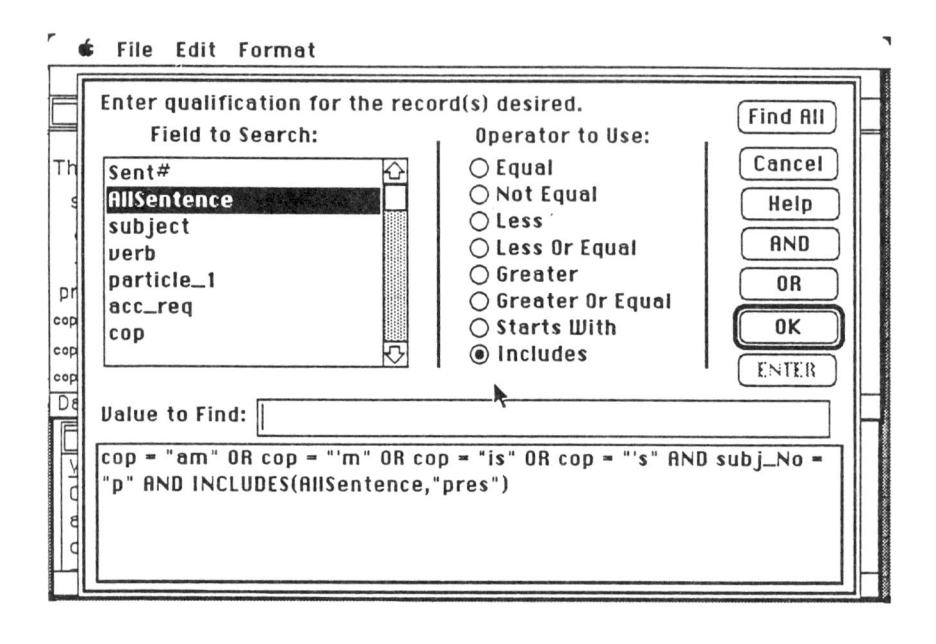

```
 ▲  File  Edit  Format

┌──────────────────────────────────────────────────────────┐
│ Enter qualification for the record(s) desired.           │
│      Field to Search:        Operator to Use:  [Find All]│
│   ┌─────────────┬─┐          ○ Equal           [ Cancel ]│
│   │ Sent#       │▲│          ○ Not Equal                 │
│   │ AllSentence │ │          ○ Less                [Help]│
│   │ subject     │ │          ○ Less Or Equal      [ AND ]│
│   │ verb        │ │          ○ Greater                   │
│   │ particle_1  │ │          ○ Greater Or Equal  [  OR  ]│
│   │ acc_req     │ │          ○ Starts With       [  OK  ]│
│   │ cop         │▼│          ● Includes                  │
│   └─────────────┴─┘                            [ ENTER  ]│
│ Value to Find: │                                         │
│ ─────────────────────────────────────────────────────    │
│ cop = "am" OR cop = "'m" OR cop = "is" OR cop = "'s" AND subj_No = │
│ "p" AND INCLUDES(AllSentence,"pres")                     │
└──────────────────────────────────────────────────────────┘
```

FIGURE 10.7

particular interest are the operators 'EQUAL', 'NOT EQUAL', and 'INCLUDES'. The operator 'INCLUDES' can be used for searches on parts of words or particular phrases in sentences.

Editing query formulae

A more sophisticated way of making use of the potential of the query language is to edit the search formula oneself. The structure of the query language is well-suited to linguistic analysis. It contains five types of functions, two of which are of particular interest to linguistic analysis: text functions and logical functions. The other three function categories are: arithmetic, date and time functions.

Among the text functions, there are the following very powerful ones: The 'INCLUDES' function searches for a specified text string and returns 'true' if the exact target text pattern is found in any given text string. Otherwise, it will return 'false'. The 'LENGTH' function calculates the length of any text value (in terms of characters) and returns an integer value. The 'LOCATE' function locates the starting position of target text patterns in text strings. The 'STARTS' function searches for a defined text string in the beginning of text records. It returns 'true' if the target string starts with the target text pattern. Otherwise, it returns 'false'.

Of the arithmetic functions 'COUNT' is of special interest. It counts lists, including lists which have been created with text functions. For instance, the formula:

COUNT (verb STARTS ('gex'))

will return an integer which is equal to the number verbs of containing the *ge* prefix in a given set of data. An arithmetic function can also be used to calculate percentages or more sophisticated arithmetic formulae which are based on lists created by the database system.

Of the logical functions, the following are of special interest: 'IF', 'EXISTS', and 'NO'. They can be used to modify terms or functions or to create special search conditions.

Example 1: Missing elements

Figure 10.8 illustrates the use of a fairly simple but effective formula which reads:

COUNT (sentence FROM Guy WHERE subject EQUALS '0' and INCLUDES identi,'g03')

Figure 10.8 is a count of missing subjects in eight consecutive interviews with one informant. It displays the absolute numbers of missing subjects and sentences, and in the third column, the resulting percentage of the omission of subjects. The percentage is calculated by entering $f1/f2$ into the formula panel for the formula for the first field from the top in the right hand column, where f1 is the formula for the first field from the top in the lefthand column and f2 is the formula for the first field from the top in the middle column.

Figure 10.8 shows a report on a single file which involves only two fields of this file, namely, the one called 'subject' and the one called 'identi'. In this case, the qualification of the field 'subject' is that its contents equals '0'. We noted above that we do not code missing subjects in the manual part of our analysis. However, COALA is capable of detecting fields without entries and entering specified values there, so that the '0' does not need to be entered by hand. If nothing had been entered into the field 'subject', the query would have simply included:

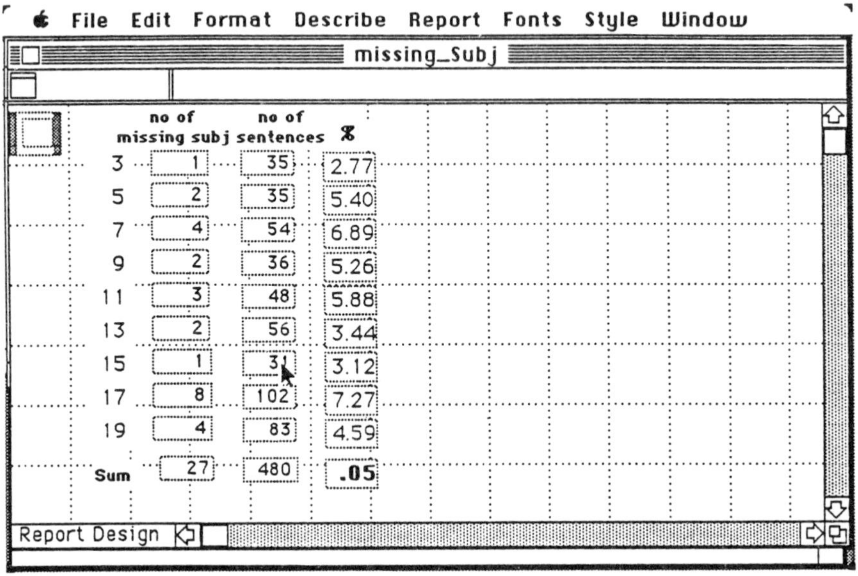

missing_Subj

no of missing subj	no of sentences	%
3	1	35	2.77
5	2	35	5.40
7	4	54	6.89
9	2	36	5.26
11	3	48	5.88
13	2	56	3.44
15	1	31	3.12
17	8	102	7.27
19	4	83	4.59
Sum	27	480	.05

FIGURE 10.8

NOT EXISTS (subject)

as a specification of the field subject.

It is also possible now to include more specifications of different fields in the query formula. It would be possible, for instance, to count missing subjects in particular linguistic environments. We could specify the person marking of the verb and obtain different counts for missing subjects with particular verb markings. We could also specify the number and type of further constituents contained in the sentence or any other information coded either in the lexicon or in the data files.

Example 2: Subject–verb agreement

Figure 10.9 reproduces a slightly more sophisticated analysis. It reports on subject–verb agreement and third person singular with pronominal subjects, NP subjects, and main verbs in present tense on the same set of data as used in Figure 10.8. This report also demonstrates the limits of a single-file analysis. To

ANALYSIS OF LANGUAGE ACQUISITION DATA 235

```
🍎  File  Edit  Format  Describe  Report  Fonts  Style  Window
```

	SUagree_3rdP
f8	COUNT(sentence FROM SATZGuy WHERE INCLUDES(verb,"xt") AND NOT INCLUDES(verb,"gex") AND NOT EXISTS(mod) AND NOT EXISTS(aux) AND subj = "sie" OR subj = "es" OR subj = "er" AND INCLUDES(identi,"GO3"))

Subject-verb agreement in third person singular with pronominal and NP-subjects and main verbs in present

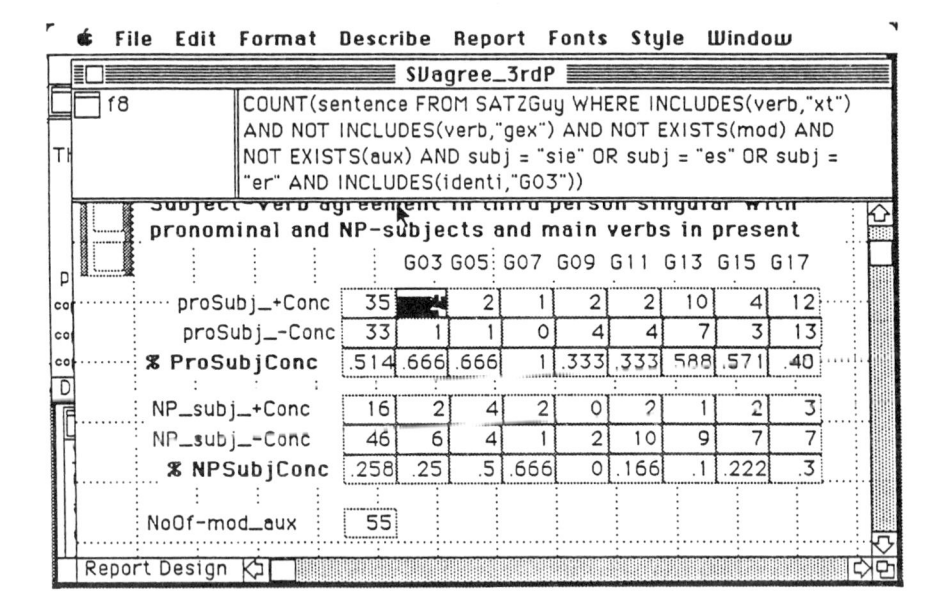

	G03	G05	G07	G09	G11	G13	G15	G17
proSubj_+Conc	35		2	1	2	2	10	4	12
proSubj_-Conc	33	1	1	0	4	4	7	3	13
% ProSubjConc	.514	.666	.666	1	.333	.333	.588	.571	.40
NP_subj_+Conc	16	2	4	2	0	2	1	2	3
NP_subj_-Conc	46	6	4	1	2	10	9	7	7
% NPSubjConc	.258	.25	.5	.666	0	.166	.1	.222	.3
NoOf-mod_aux	55

FIGURE 10.9

be able to fully appreciate this, one must note that the verbal marker for the third person singular present tense in German is *t*. But *t* also occurs as an inflectional morpheme at the end of participles with weak verbs; thus, the third person singular pronouns German are *er*, *sie*, and *es*. Now, in order to exclude participles like *ge-sag-t* from being counted as a correct marking of third person, we added to the formula:

AND NOT INCLUDES (verb, 'gex')

This ensures that the participles containing the prefix *ge-* are excluded from the analysis. Since the verb appears in the infinitive form, if a modal is used in the sentence, modals must also be explicitly excluded from the analysis. This is done by including:

AND NOT EXISTS (mod)

In a similar way, auxiliaries that appear in the list under analysis also have to be excluded. Non-pronominal subjects are simply defined by the specification:

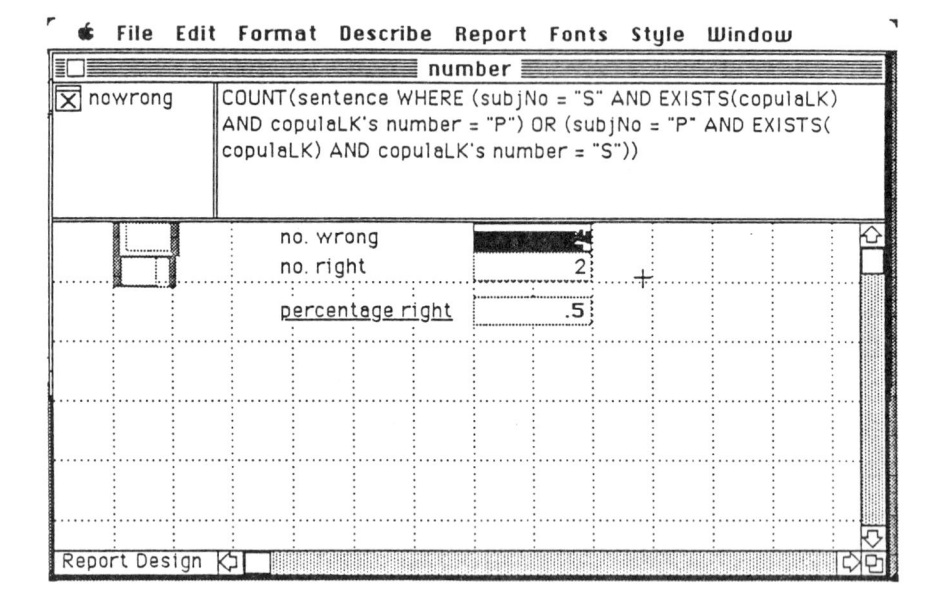

```
┌──────────────────────────────────────────────────────────────────┐
│  ▤ File  Edit  Format  Describe  Report  Fonts  Style  Window   │
├──────────────────────────────────────────────────────────────────┤
│                           number                                 │
│ ☒ nowrong  │ COUNT(sentence WHERE (subjNo = "S" AND EXISTS(copulaLK)│
│            │ AND copulaLK's number = "P") OR (subjNo = "P" AND EXISTS(│
│            │ copulaLK) AND copulaLK's number = "S"))              │
│                                                                  │
│                   no. wrong        [ ▮▮▮ 4 ]                    │
│                   no. right        [     2 ]    +               │
│                   percentage right [    .5 ]                    │
│                                                                  │
│ Report Design                                                    │
└──────────────────────────────────────────────────────────────────┘
```

FIGURE 10.10

    INCLUDES (subject, 'N[')

Note that the characters 'N[' have been added by the parser to the appropriate records in the 'subject' field. If we also wanted to add a specification of the subcategorisation of the verb, we would have to retrieve information from a different file because this type of information is stored not in the data file, but in one of the lexicon files.

Reports on linked files

    Figure 10.10 gives an example of a simple report on linked files. It analyses number agreement in equational sentences. Remember that the grammatical number of noun phrases is recorded in the data file and the number marking of copulae, auxiliaries, and modals are coded in the corresponding lexicon files. Thus, this report retrieves information from the file labelled 'sentence' and a file labelled 'copula lk'.

ANALYSIS OF LANGUAGE ACQUISITION DATA

These principles can be used to define linguistic environments for the automatic analysis. For instance, it is possible to study the different morphological forms of the determiner in connection with the grammatical function in which the corresponding noun phrase appeared and in connection with the subcategorisation of the verb. A query could, for instance, analyse the agreement in gender, number, and case between the verb and its accusative object. In such a case, information would be retrieved from the data file, an auxiliary file ('NP') and two lexicon files ('determiner' and 'noun').

We are presently building up a library of reports which can also be used by others. It may have become clearer now in which way information can be accessed that has been stored at different places in the database system during different stages of the manual and automatic preparation of the data for the automatic analysis. In addition, it is always possible to add further grammatical features to the lexicon files, for instance, semantic features, and retrieve this information in later automatic analyses.

Word order

As we indicated above, the range of possible analyses also includes sequential phenomena, i.e. word order. The basic principles of the word order analysis in the COALA system are the following. We use the 'locate' function of the query language to identify the position of specified constituents. One component of the COALA system then transforms the absolute positions of specified constituents into relative positions in such a way that it is possible to make frequency counts for specified terminal strings, such as the following:

V + NP 1 + X
PP + AUX + NP 1 + X + V

That is, particular word order rules can be analysed in the data by counting the occurrence of specified terminal strings. This is illustrated in Figure 10.11, which displays the idealised results of the analysis of verb-second placement in German main clauses (excluding sentences with AUX or MOD) for the two interlanguages I_1 and I_2. The two interlanguages may either represent speech samples collected from two different informants or from the same informant at different points in time.

The first column on the left in Figure 10.11 refers to the terminal strings which are analysed in the data. Note that 'NP1' always refers to the grammatical subject of the sentence. Constituents may be precisely defined or defined as a variable (X, Y, Z). For the report in the database, the terminal strings would, of course, be defined in the query language. For reasons of convenience we are

environments	11	12
wh + V + NP1 + X	0.11	0.78
PP + V + NP1 + X	0.08	0.56
NP2 + V + NP1 + X	ERROR	(0.50)
Z + V + NP1 + X	0.08	0.64
X + V + NP1 + Y	0.09	0.68

X, Y = 0   Z = WH, PP, NP2   NP1 = subject

FIGURE 10.11 *Report on word order (German) Verb-second (main clauses without AUX and MOD)*.

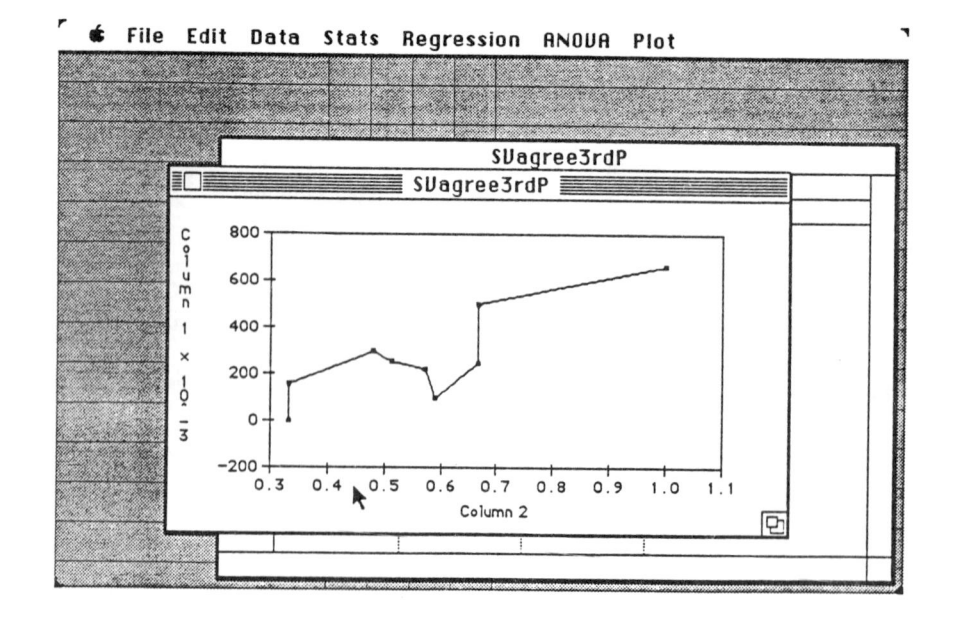

FIGURE 10.12

ANALYSIS OF LANGUAGE ACQUISITION DATA

now referring to a linguistic notation which is more easily readable than formulae of the query language.

In Figure 10.11 the percentage of rule application (of 'verb-second') is based on the number of obligatory contexts in each sample. Figures based on less than five tokens are put in brackets. The system outputs 'ERROR' if a number is divided by zero. Thus 'ERROR' indicates that there are no obligatory contexts in the given sample for the rule in the environment specified by the terminal string. In addition, this analytical procedure can also be linked to other types of information contained at any point of the database system, including a specification of the particular lexical items or their semantic features. Also, any numerical results of the analyses can be entered into statistics and graphics programs to create charts, tables and other types of figures. One simple example of this is given in Figure 10.12.

Figure 10.12 illustates the display of fequency counts for SV-agreement for a series of interviews on two axes (0–800 = correctness; 0.3–1.1 = points in time).

Behind the Scenes

This brief section provides some information about the software used for the COALA system in order to give some indication of the ways in which they can be modified by other users.

COALA was developed on an Apple MacIntosh. The hardware requirements are a McPlus system with at least one megabyte of RAM and two double-sided 800k disk drives — or preferably one floppy disk drive and a twenty megabyte hard disk. The following list describes the chronology of the different steps which are involved in setting up COALA for the automatic analysis of a given set of data:

1.	Transcription of data	MS Word
2.	Turn numbering	MEdit
3.	Format checking	MEdit
4.	Identify sentence boundaries and analyse tense and question type	MS Word
5.	Import transcription into turn database	REFLEX
6.	Import sentences into database file	REFLEX, Tempo
7.	Create text file of imported sentences	REFLEX
8.	Data formatting	MEdit
9.	Data-specific lexicon	Hayden Speller, Tempo

10.	x-update in lexicon	MS Word
11.	x-insertion into data	MEdit
12.	y-insertion in lexicon and data	MS Word
13.	Annotate lexicon (new entries)	REFLEX
14.	Link database files	REFLEX, Tempo
15.	Sentence analysis	REFLEX, Tempo
16.	Analysis of subordinate clauses	REFLEX, Tempo
17.	Analysis of conjunction reductions	REFLEX, Tempo
18.	Bracket insertion	REFLEX, MEdit
19.	Parser	Prolog
20.	Import parser output	REFLEX, Tempo
21.	Reports	REFLEX, (Tempo)

Not all of these steps have been mentioned in the preceding sections, because the ones not mentioned are mostly carried out automatically and are of primarily technical interest.

As can be seen from the above list, we are using six different applications, namely, *Microsoft Word*, *MEdit*, *Reflex*, *Tempo*, *Hayden Speller*, and *Prolog*. Most of the complex steps in the analysis are tied together with macros written in either MEdit or Tempo. It would have been much more elegant, of course, to have had a single 'double-clickable' application because moving files from one application to another can often be very tedious. Things are simplified greatly if the Multitasking Finder[3] is used. It should be noted, however, that there should be at least two megabytes of RAM available for the Multitasking Finder to operate efficiently with the given set of applications.

However, it was not our intention to develop a commercial product, but rather a convenient research tool which we are prepared to share with other researchers. The present prototype version of the COALA system only makes use of a fraction of the features available in the different applications. On the one hand, this might appear to be a waste of software and hardware. On the other hand, it has the definite advantage for researchers that they can make use of more of the available features and change the system according to their particular needs. In the future, we will try to restructure the system in such a way that fewer applications are needed in order to run it.

Notes to Chapter 10

1. This paper describes the structure of COALA in its 1988 version. Since then COALA has been totally rewritten in another environment, 4th Dimension. Although it was not intended as a commercial product, it has in fact become one in this new format. COALA Version 1 was launched at the Second Language Research

Forum in Los Angeles in March 1991, and Version 2 is already in preparation. Part of this research was supported by a grant from the Australian Research Grant Scheme (ARGS) to Manfred Pienemann and a Special Research Grant to Louise Jansen from the Australian National University. We would like to thank the following people for their support, advice and encouragement in the development of COALA: Harald Clahsen, John Clifton-Everest, Michael Chu, Konrad Ehlich, Malcolm Johnston, Conrad McKenzie, Frank O'Carrol, Nick Oppen, Peter Petersen, Ulrich Schmitz, Mark Simblist, Lydia White. A thankyou also goes to Martha Pennington for her most valuable editorial comments on this manuscript.

2. The following excerpt from the COALA manual (Jansen & Pienemann, 1988, 1f.) gives a brief explanation of databases:

Structure of Databases

A database is a system for storing and retrieving information in a principled, quick and efficient way. Databases are useful when we have a large number of items for which the same categories of information are to be stored and retrieved.

A database basically consists of a large number of so-called RECORDS. For every different category of information a separate space is reserved. Such spaces are called FIELDS. All records in the same database have the same structure, that is the same number and sequence of fields. The record structure must be determined before data can be entered. However, it can always be modified later.

In our case our data are conversations which consist — in the first instance — of a large number of turns. Thus we have designed a Turn-database the basic units of which are so-called turn-RECORDS. (COALA also has a Sentence-database, which stores information on sentence-records, and a complex of lexical databases).

For each turn we wish to store information on at least:
— the position of each turn relevant to the other turns;
— the identity of the speaker; and
— the actual text of the turn.

For each of these we have reserved a field. Thus each record of our turn-database consists of three fields:
— a *Turn#* field to store a number indicating the consecutive position of each turn;
— a *Speaker* field to store an abbreviation for the respective interlocutor; and
— a *Turn* field to store the text of each turn.

Although this is only a minimal database any number of additional fields to store further information on each turn can be added. All information stored in the turn-database is LINKED to information stored in our sentence-database and to other COALA databases.

Once stored in a database the information can be retrieved very quickly and very selectively. Moreover, automatic calculations can be performed on such information (e.g. through the stroke of a key we can identify which sentences in our sentence database contain no explicit subject and the percentage of such subjectless sentences in relation to all sentences).

Compatibility between Textfiles and Database Files

The structure of a database is automatically marked as follows:

- *records* are separated by a *carriage return* character which marks the end of each record;
- *fields* are separated by a *tab* character marking the end of one field and the beginning of another. The beginning of the first field and the end of the last field of a record are marked by the carriage return character separating the database records.

Thus, the structure of a three-field database such as our turn-database is marked as follows:

FIELD >> FIELD >> FIELD <R>
FIELD >> FIELD >> FIELD <R>
FIELD >> FIELD >> FIELD <R>
(where >> = a tab and <R> = a carriage return).

It is possible to get a copy of the contents of a database in a text-file format (this is called EXPORTING the data). Conversely it is possible to IMPORT data from a properly formatted text file. (Jansen & Pienemann, 1988: 1ff.).

3. [The 'multitasking finder' is the]... 'multitasking version of the Macintosh operating system. It allows users to switch easily between applications, share data or run two applications simultaneously. Spooling, hard disk backup, recalculation or sorting operations can all run in the background mode. To take full advantage of MultiFinder, at least two megabytes of RAM is required and a large screen is preferable when working with several applications or open documents. An interesting aspect of MultiFinder is that it allows cutting, copying and pasting between MS-Dos, UNIX and Macintosh applications on Macs with the appropriate hardware.' (Richetti, A. & Menegol, E., 1987 software guide, *Australian MACWORLD*, December 1987/January 1988, p. 28)

References

AARTS, J. & T. VAN DEN HEUVEL (1985) Computational tools for the syntactic analysis of corpora, *Linguistics*, 23, 303–335.
ATWELL, E. (1986) Beyond the micro: Advanced software for research and teaching from computer science and artificial intelligence. In G. LEECH & C. N. CANDLIN, *Computers in English Language Teaching and Research*. London: Longman, 168–183.
AUGST, G. (1975) *Untersuchungen zum Morpheminventar der deutschen Gegenwartssprache*. Tübingen, Germany: Gunter Narr.
BISHOP, D. (1985) *Language Assessment, Remediation and Screening Procedure (LARSP) by Crystal, Fletcher & Garman. Computerized Version for Apple I and IIe*. Department of Speech, University of Newcastle-upon-Tyne.
CHARNIAK, E. & D. MCDERMOTT (1985) *Introduction to Artificial Intelligence*. Reading, MA: Addison-Wesley.
CLAHSEN, H. (1986a) *Die Profilanalyse*. Berlin, Germany: Marhold-Verlag.
— (1986b) Computergestützte Profilanalyse (COPROF) — Benutzeranleitung. Unpublished ms. Düsseldorf, Germany: University of Düsseldorf.
CRYSTAL, D., P. FLETCHER & M. GARMAN (1976) *The Grammatical Analysis of Language Disability*. London, England: Longman.
FELIX, S. W. (1978) Some differences between first and second language acquisition. In

C. Snow & N. Waterson (eds), *The Development of Communication*. London, England: Longman. 469–479.
Grosz, B. J., K. S. Jones & B. L. Webber (eds) (1985) *Readings in Natural Language Processing*. Los Altos, CA: Morgan Kaufmann.
Helbig, G. & W. Schenkel (1973) *Wörterbuch zur Valenz und Distribution deutscher Verben*. Leipzig, Germany: VEB Verlag Enzyklopädie.
Hobbs, J. (1978) Resolving pronoun reference, *Lingua*, 44, 311–338.
Jansen, L. (1987) The development of word order in formal German language acquisition. Paper presented at the International Workshop on Explaining Interlanguage Development, La Trobe University, Melbourne, Australia, August.
Jansen, L. & M. Pienemann (1988) *COALA manual*. Unpublished ms. Australia: Australian National University and University of Sydney.
Kay, M. (1982) Parsing in functional unification grammar. In D. R Dowty, L. Kartunnen & A. Zwicky (eds), *Natural Language Parsing*. Cambridge, England: Cambridge University Press, 251–278.
Keulen, F. (1985) The Dutch computer corpus pilot project: Some experiences with a semi-automatic analysis of contemporary English. In J. Aarts & W. Meijs, *Corpus Linguistics II: New Studies in the Analysis and Exploitation of Computer Corpora*.
Leech, G. (1986) Automatic grammatical analysis and its educational applications. In G. Leech & C. N. Candlin (eds), *Computers in English Language Teaching and Research*. London, England: Longman, 205–214.
Leech, G. & C. N. Candlin (1986) *Computers in English Language Teaching and Research*. London, England: Longman.
Lenders, W. & G. Willée (1986) *Linguistische Datenverarbeitung: Ein Lehrbuch*. Opladen, Germany: Westdeutscher Verlag.
MacWhinney, B. (ed) (1987a) *Transcript Analysis*, Vol 4, Nos 1 & 2. Pittsburgh, PA: Department of Psychology, Carnegie-Mellon University.
— (ed) (1987b) *CLAN: Child Language ANalysis. Manual for the CLAN Programs of the Child Language Data Exchange System*. Pittsburgh, PA: Department of Psychology, Carnegie-Mellon University.
Pienemann, M. (1987) Determining the influence of instruction on L2 speech processing, *Australian Review of Applied Linguistics*, 10: 2, 83–113.
Rumelhart, D. E. & J. L. McClelland (1986) On learning the past tense of English verbs. In D. E. Rumelhart & J. L. McClelland (eds), *Parallel Distributed Processing: Explorations in the Microstructure of Cognition*. Cambridge, MA: MIT Press.
Schank, R. (1980) Language and memory, *Cognitive Science*, 4: 3, 243–284.
Sejnowski, T. J. & C. R. Rosenberg (1986) *NETtalk: A Parallel Network that Learns to Read Aloud*. Baltimore, MD: The Johns Hopkins University, Electrical Engineering and Computer Science, Technical Report JHU/EECS-86/01.
van Halteren, B. J. M., & N. H. J. Oostdijk (1986) Using an analyzed corpus as a linguistic database. In *Proceedings of the XIXth ALLC Conference*, Norwich, England.
Wanner, E. & M. Maratsos, M. (1978) An ATN approach to comprehension. In M. Halle, J. Bresnan & G. A. Miller (eds), *Linguistic Theory and Psychological Reality*. Cambridge MA: MIT Press, 119–161.
Wilks, Y. (1983) Machine translation and the artificial intelligence paradigm of language processes. In W. A. Sedelow, Jr. & S. Y. Sedelow (eds), *Computers in Language Research*, 2. Berlin, Germany: Mouton, 61–111.
Woods, W. A. (1970) Transition network grammars for natural language analysis. *CACM*, 3: 10, 591–606. Reprinted in Grosz, Jones, & Webber (eds) (1985), 71–88.

11 Speech Technology Systems in Applied Linguistics Instruction

JOHN H. ESLING
University of Victoria, B.C., Canada

Introduction

Phonetics is said to be 'the indispensable foundation of all study of language' (Sweet, 1877, in Henderson, 1971: 30), and the importance of the aural medium of language (Abercrombie, 1967: 2) is apparent in the teaching of applied linguistics. Not only is the spoken language the essential initial vehicle by which language is normally perceived, acquired or taught (Brown, 1977), but natural speech is also the most appealing means of presenting beginning language-learning material using technological means, whether by tape recorder — as in audiovisual methodology (Renard, 1965; 1976) — or by computer. Examples of speech-oriented computer applications are the *VISIBLE SPEECH AID* (VSA) intonation displays for the hearing-impaired (Dickson & Ingram, 1982), the Kay Elemetrics *VISI-PITCH* system (Molholt, 1988; Pennington, 1989) and the development of computerised tutorials in EFL using synthetic speech (Esling, Warbey & Scholefield, 1984; PES, 1985).

It is primarily because of the role of phonetics in language study that speech technology — including the development of computerised devices for measuring, analysing or synthesising aspects of spoken language — occupies a place in the training of students of linguistics. Preparation programs for students in applied linguistics and teachers of second languages, for example, also generally include a phonetics component, which can be delivered efficiently through the assistance of computer encoding, storage and replay of language sounds. In this sense, computer systems operate as tools to access spoken language in the same way that tape recorders offered a technological means of handling data in previous decades. In the case of students who intend to work in applied fields such as speech and language pathology, computerised systems offer valuable training in terms of exposure to speech patterns as well as to the equipment likely to be found in the workplace. In more general terms, research-based uses of computerised systems of speech analysis offer results that carry a direct impact on the quality of teaching in applied linguistics programs (cf. Esling, 1991).

It is necessary to teach applied linguistics students: (1) the essential nature of variation in language; (2) the nature of 'focusing', (acquisition of language by progressive approximations and from the global to the specific); (3) the role of collection and manipulation of language items in the beginning stages of language learning; (4) the role of subject-matter teaching in the later stages (Esling, in press b); and (5) the effect of a collaborative learning environment. All of these principles can be incorporated into the presentation of the subject of phonetics in the applied linguistics degree program itself, as a model for subsequent practice by students in their role of language-specialist professionals. Along with material from other disciplines, applied linguistics content offers a suitable focus for fluent but nonnative speakers to refine language skills in a university or professional environment (see Edwards *et al.*, 1984; Burger *et al.*, 1984). Computers can be adapted to enhance the learning experience of all applied linguistics students according to the above principles, while at the same time providing an indication of the potential uses of CALL in a wide range of professional activities.

Computer-assisted phonetics laboratory procedures range from the computerised adaptation of phonetic label-to-symbol matching exercises to digital storage, graphic representation and acoustic analysis available in increasing sophistication through the decreasing size and cost of micro-processing hardware. One essential application of computers is to provide a facility where students can have quick and easy access to a database of voices, sounds and phrases that represent a wide sampling of the languages of the world. This capability provides students with aural as well as visually displayed input more quickly than through a linear audiotape library. The next step is the related capability of adding written input to the visual display by providing a phonetic transcription system. The possibility of transcribing speech on computer is analogous to the function of word processing, but where the subject matter content is general phonetics rather than composition. As the sophistication of speech analysis and synthesis increases, computerised laboratory systems become more directly appropriate in the training programs and professional experience of students of speech science or speech and language pathology. These specialised applications notwithstanding, all of the procedures described in this paper are designed to accommodate advanced (upperclass or postgraduate) students while following recommendations derived from the research literature on second-language acquisition and from effective methodologies of second-language instruction.

The Role of Speech Technology in Teacher Training

Academic programs in linguistics generally incorporate a phonetics component. The necessity of this was implied by Sweet a hundred years ago:

> All study of language must be based on phonetics...Without it, we can neither observe nor record the simplest phenomena of language. It is equally necessary in the theoretical and in the practical study of language (in Henderson, 1971: 28).

These assumptions underlie early descriptive linguistics, as in Sapir's view that 'language is primarily a system of phonetic symbols for the expression of communicable thought and feeling' (Mandelbaum, 1962: 1), and continue to be considered important by those who view phonetics as key in the context of artificial intelligence (Ladefoged, 1987).

The phonetics component of linguistics instruction is increasingly influenced by the growth of speech technology as a viable academic as well as commercial enterprise, brought about largely as a result of the steady growth of the computer industry (Fujimura, 1984). Because phonetics is an area strongly affected by developments in speech hardware and software, students of linguistics are likely to be exposed to computer systems in their phonetics course, if anywhere at all. In some universities, a result of these developments is that the distinction between theoretical linguistics and applied linguistics has decreased, and academic programs now concentrate on preparing 'language specialists'.

In applied linguistics programs in particular, computers also form a part of professional preparation, giving students an idea of the range of computer-assisted language learning (CALL) methodology and an idea of the ways in which this type of methodology is likely to be effective (or not). The principles presented in the training program and detailed in the next section can therefore serve as a guide to the process of analysing and evaluating the quality of CALL materials in general. It is essential that these principles be reflected in the procedures followed in the training programs themselves, as an example of responsible pedagogical practice in the education of people who are aiming to become teachers. Thus the presentation of phonetics materials to prospective teachers ultimately has a direct impact on the presentation of pronunciation materials to language students.

Computers are integrated as tools into applied linguistics programs to help demonstrate the principles that have evolved in the field over the decades (Dulay et al., 1982; Savignon, 1983; Terrell, 1986). These include training language teachers: (a) to present a range of diverse input in meaningful situations rather than concentrating prematurely on units at the segmental, phonemic level; (b) to allow receptive cognitive processes to operate before requiring production, rather than assuming articulatory production by imitation and memorisation; (c) to allow students to set their own pace and establish concrete referents rather than restricting presentation of examples to a predetermined order of assumed ease of acquisition; and (d) to recognise that learners will reflect their peers' interlanguage rather than trying to impose a fully-formed model of the target phonology.

A final area of impact of computers on applied linguistics instruction is the relationship of research to teaching. The vast majority of experimental phonetic and sociophonetic research — not to mention psycholinguistic and educational research — now involves computer processing of data (Esling, in press a; Lieberman & Blumstein, 1988: 77–89). The results of this research form the substance presented in courses on second-language acquisition and a basis for structuring theory. In addition, when students prepare research reports, they are likely to do their writing on a word processor and to perform specialised analysis using computer software. Not only are students being influenced through these procedures to view information processing as an inherent component of education, they are also learning technical research skills central to a range of academic disciplines and likely to be of use when teaching language students with professional backgrounds. For some language specialists, it is possible for computing to become a secondary area of expertise which serves as an other-than-language-content vehicle for language instruction (Barlow, 1987; Hooper, 1984; Mohan, 1986). As the undergraduate or graduate student of applied linguistics relates knowledge of second-language acquisition processes to problems of application in specific teaching situations, innovations are likely to occur. Graduate research to design CALL systems in the content areas of expertise of ESL academic professionals with high-level language skills, for instance, has a direct influence on improving the quality of teaching programs in the institution at large.

Some Basic Principles for Applied Linguistics Instruction

Variation in language

Before showing in the next section how these principles can be implemented in instructional procedures, it will be useful to discuss them in more detail. The first is that language varies. This essential linguistic fact is perhaps best demonstrated through observation and analysis by computer, as initiated in a number of key sociolinguistic applications (Cedergren & Sankoff, 1974; Guy,

1975; Labov, 1969). More recent development in this area is summarised in Sankoff (1978) and Labov (1980), and in the documentation accompanying the *VARBRUL* program on microcomputer (Fasold, 1986). Hands-on computer experience with desk-top speech analysis can also provide users with a demonstration that utterances differ intra-individually and that phonological patterns differ across socioeconomic groups. Perception exercises set up on a microcomputer illustrate that aural perception, like production, also depends on neurological, psychomotor, cognitive, affective and linguistic variables. Examples of such exercises are explored in the next section. In applied linguistics, it is crucial to describe language acquisition and language change as the products of a variable and dynamic system rather than in terms of static sets of features. Phonetics offers a particularly salient context for making this point, and computers allow students to learn by doing.

Focusing

Another important principle in applied linguistics is that a process involving correction to a standard model of speech is less valuable than exposure to the collected variants which linguists observe and which language teachers present as input for their students to observe and experience (Esling, 1987a). This has been called the principle of 'focusing' or 'targeting', analogous to the process of focusing a lens. In that process, a sharp target image cannot be attained or even recognised before first sampling a range of possible images by moving in and out of focus to define the periphery of the visual field — crossing at least once the boundary between obscurity and clarity — into a fuzzy picture and back again to clear definition (Esling, in press b). The metaphor relates to the process of acquiring an accent by implying that the fuzzy images of 'hearing it wrong' are necessary to the cognitive process of eventually 'getting it right', and that items are difficult to locate in cognitive space except in relation to the background or field against which they appear. These ideas are not new in the description of human behaviour (Pike, 1959; 1967). They correspond closely to the requirements in the sequence of second-language acquisition identified by Dulay *et al.* (1982) of: input, available referents, a silent observational phase, and personally relevant models. This philosophy is also central to European 'structuro-global audio-visual' language teaching methodology (Renard, 1981), and is supported by experimental research suggesting that a process of approximation is necessary to gradually define the learner's developing phonological system (Flege, 1980; 1981). The use of computers in applied linguistics should incorporate these characteristics of language learning, both because the subject matter involves spoken language and because they can serve as an example for teaching or clinical applications.

Collection and manipulation

Computer technology in phonetics instruction illustrates the value of an indirect methodology in second-language teaching. Language material can be collected, divided, reassembled, reorganised, transcribed, and manipulated in digital form in ways that are impossible with linear recordings of speech. Attention can easily be directed towards other-than-language tasks rather than overtly at language performance, whether of general phonetic sounds or in a specific second language. CALL presentations of phonetics also offer a means of approaching pronunciation at an advanced level of language proficiency by presenting speech and accent as academic subject matter rather than concentrating on a single static target-language model for pronunciation practice. The major difference between an earlier Direct Method formulation (cf. Lado & Fries, 1954) and a CALL approach is that the former presents the selection of examples, transcription and analysis as completed activities prepared by the authors of a text or tape series, whereas the latter provides access to organisational, transcriptional and analytical tasks for students to perform. Once basic material has been encountered in this way, students are ready to continue on to more complex intellectual activities in the discipline. Inherent within this cognitive view of learning are the principles of teaching language through subject-matter content and of collaboration in learning, both of which will be discussed in more detail in later sections.

One manipulation-oriented adaptation of a pencil-and-paper task is my own *IPALABEL* exercise, in which a set of phonetic symbols and list of their corresponding descriptive labels must be matched and then ordered according to place, or manner, of articulation. This activity has been developed on the Apple Macintosh using *LaserIPA* (1986), a commercial character set of International Phonetic Alphabet (IPA) symbols. Early examples of such tasks and their solutions are illustrated in Tables 11.1 and 11.2. The most recent version of this activity resides in a *HyperCard* stack. A database of movable symbols and their labels serve as a pool for searching, selection and matching, as in a corresponding phonetic chart task (proposed below) where the IPA chart in spreadsheet format is to be filled in. These activities satisfy the 'range of variation' criterion by presenting holistic tasks to be completed instead of discrete items to be memorised linearly. The static illustrations in Table 11.1 and 11.2 are necessarily limited in this respect compared to the dynamics of choice in the CALL program.

The principle of manipulation is based on a philosophy of providing a tool rather than a tutor, which implies that the criteria applied to evaluate a program should be essentially the same for student users as for general consumers of the product. This is as true of phonetic applications of computer tasks as it is of computers used as writing tools. In the same way that CALL is used to teach

250 COMPUTERS IN APPLIED LINGUISTICS

TABLE 11.1 *IPALABEL task: Identification of nasals*

Order the following nasals according to place of articulation,
and select the corresponding phonetic symbol for each:

List:		Solution:	
	palatal	bilabial	m
	velar	dental	n̪
	dental	alveolar	n
voiced	bilabial (nasals)	retroflex	ɳ
	alveolar	palatal	ɲ
	uvular	velar	ŋ
	retroflex	uvular	ɴ

Set: [ŋ ɴ n̪ m n̬ ŋ̊ ɴ ɲ
ɲ̊ m̥ ɱ n̥ ɳ n ɱ̊ ɳ̊]

composition skills (Neu & Scarcella, 1991), speech and language tasks can be designed to take advantage of the character input, graphics access, recovery/display, and grouping/organising facilities of computers. One program of relevance to applied linguistics which is phonemically based and which provides a service designed to some extent with learner-users in mind is the *TianMa* (1986) Chinese-character word processor with roman-letter 'pinyin' input. Chinese words are entered in pinyin transliteration and converted automatically to their Chinese character counterparts. TianMa is intended for the general Chinese-writing population, but it is also ideally suited to the learner of Chinese because of its value as a reference tool and as a device for associating and manipulating characters according to their pronunciation. For students in applied linguistics, the use of the TianMa system illustrates the philosophy of employing technology for a specific purpose, such as letter writing, while at the same time assisting the user to learn language.

Computer-Assisted Phonetics Laboratory Procedures

Computer-assisted phonetics laboratory procedures can be performed with a number of available hardware/software packages, many of which are enumerated and described by Parkinson & Bladon (1987). In interpreting any of these systems for applied linguistics purposes, the emphasis should be on their use as tools (a) to economise on time and to process effective amounts of input, (b) to focus the attention of users on perceptual and manipulative

TABLE 11.2 *IPALABEL task: Identification of fricatives*

Order the following set of fricatives according to place of articulation, and select the corresponding IPA symbol for each:

Set: [h ʁ ç χ ɸ z ʂ x ð ʒ β v ʐ ɦ f ɕ ş s θ ʐ h ʕ j ʑ ɣ ʃ]

		20-Label Solution:	
	(fricatives)	voiceless bilabial fricative	ɸ
		voiced bilabial fricative	β
		voiceless labio-dental fricative	f
	velar	voiced labio-dental fricative	v
	palatal	voiceless interdental fricative	θ
voiceless	retroflex	voiced interdental fricative	ð
	uvular	voiceless alveolar fricative	s
and	labio-dental	voiced alveolar fricative	z
	pharyngeal	voiceless retroflex fricative	ʂ
voiced	alveolar	voiced retroflex fricative	ʐ
	palato-alveolar	voiceless palato-alveolar fricative	ʃ
	interdental	voiced palato-alveolar fricative	ʒ
	bilabial	voiceless palatal fricative	ç
		voiced palatal fricative	j
		voiceless velar fricative	x
		voiced velar fricative	ɣ
		voiceless uvular fricative	χ
26-Symbol Solution:		voiced uvular fricative	ʁ
		voiceless pharyngeal fricative	h
[ɸ β f v θ ð ʂ ʐ s z ş ʐ		voiced pharyngeal fricative	ʕ
ç ʑ ʃ ʒ ɕ j x ɣ ʁ h ʕ ɦ fi]			

activities in dealing with introductory material, and (c) to cultivate an awareness that studying the academic content of a specific discipline (phonetics, in this case) is a valuable way of approaching new language material, whether in a first language or at an advanced level of learning another language (Hauptman *et al.*, 1988).

Computer recording and storage of speech

One example of a speech analysis system is the *MICRO SPEECH LAB* (MSL), developed by the Centre for Speech Technology Research in co-operation with the Department of Linguistics at the University of Victoria. MSL is a random-access speech recording, storage, playback, editing and analysis system that operates on IBM-PC/XT/AT microcomputers (Dickson, 1985), intended for use by linguists or speech scientists in analysing acoustic phonetic information. To adapt its use to the needs of the applied linguist or language teacher in a manner consistent with the principles cited above, it is necessary to assemble a body of language material as 'input' for students of introductory phonetics.

The Phonetic Data Base (PDB) project (Esling, 1987b; 1987c) is an effort to obtain speech sounds of languages of the world that are not usually encountered or available in ordinary phonetics classes. The languages in the PDB include, at present: Nyangumarta and Umpila (Australian); Miriam (Papuan); Rutooro, Runyoro, and Xhosa (Bantu); Yoruba (Kwa); Egyptian Arabic (Semitic); Turkish (Turkic), Japanese and Korean ('Altaic'); Cantonese and Modern Standard Chinese (Sinitic); Sinhala (Indic); Scots Gaelic (Celtic); Garifuna (Carib); Inuktitut (Eskimo); Skagit and Spokane (Salish); and Ditidaht (Wakashan). Files are organised according to phonemic inventory within each language, beginning with 30 to 70 words followed by several longer phrases and/or narrative texts. The length of text that can be captured or loaded depends on computer RAM and bit-rate (up to 23 seconds on an AT for 10-bit data). Word or text files are accessed from diskettes or hard disk for presentation in class, using MSL connected to an amplifier and speakers, or for listening by groups of up to four students in a work-station facility equipped with speakers or headphones and space to allow writing and consultation of references. File contents, documented by language in user-guide packets, are essential for cross-reference and in planning the listening task.

Perception-oriented activities are emphasised before articulatory production is required, and characteristics of prosody, including voice setting, are presented before identification of segmental length phonetic units is expected. The aim is to increase exposure to input from sources other than the instructor's own model, in order to prepare students more adequately for subsequent aural recognition of sounds as they occur naturally in the languages of the world. This goal resembles the approach to developing spoken language skills based on observation of discourse, auditory recognition, and task performance proposed by Brown *et al.* (1984). Directing attention to the segmental linguistic level of analysis is the task and objective of the phonologist but would be premature in the schedule recommended for the applied language specialist. When a listener first encounters a new language, that person pays attention to the interpretation of indexical (speaker-identifying) in addition to phonological properties of speech (Abercrombie, 1967). Indexical properties include indices of regional, social, affective and physical traits that are most salient in the longer-term strands of accent. A global approach focusing on long-term stretches of speech allows listeners time to formulate an impression of the general properties of a voice as a background mechanism for gradually discovering linguistically salient units. This approach parallels the activities of some second-language listening classes prior to focusing on phonemic discrimination, listening comprehension exercises or speaking activities.

Following this introductory global activity, phonetic items are presented aurally, with opportunities for recognition and categorisation before transcription is attempted. Items are collected from the PDB and organised auditorily according to categories of speech sounds, multiplying opportunities for students to become familiar with the matrix of possible articulations. Ultimately, students complete the IPA symbol chart, annotating symbols with examples drawn from the various source languages discovered during the listening phase.

The computer as a tool for listening

Speech editing, listening for voice setting, observation and manipulation, analysis as content, and collaboration are explored in detail in this section to illustrate how the basic principles for applied linguistics instruction are realised with phonetics as academic subject matter. These illustrations, accompanied by figures, include recommendations for the use of visual displays of speech patterns in the teaching and learning process.

Speech Editing

MSLEDIT is a supplementary program in the MSL system which allows up to five stored speech files to be loaded and displayed for observation of waveforms, division of the sampled files into pieces of varying length, and selective listening or saving of combinations of the five samples (Dickson, 1987). *MSLEDIT* is the most effective mode for listening, editing and splicing sections of speech from the PDB. Sounds or phrases can be played repeatedly and in varying order, with from 2 to 0 seconds between repetitions. Functions include listening at half speed (pitch-corrected) and in reverse, which are useful perceptual exercises to illustrate the nature of phonetic reduction and the aerodynamic properties of speech production.

The speed of random-access comparison makes it possible to display, hear and investigate a series of sounds represented with the same or similar symbols in broad phonetic transcription but which differ slightly from language to language. Another appropriate phonetic task is the collection of syllables from a language where one manner of articulation contrasts distinctively at several places of articulation, for example, nasal consonants in Australian languages. The most useful aspect of these procedures is the initial manipulative and creative power they give learners. It is a valuable pedagogical demonstration for prospective teachers that language students need to discover and collect target speech sounds in a format that allows easy reorganisation (Asher, 1982; Stevick, 1976; Smith, 1982). In this way, CALL techniques for phonetic purposes in applied linguistics parallel and serve as a model for the use of CALL in learning a second language.

It has been argued (Esling, 1987b) that the methodology expected of teachers in a second-language curriculum, particularly at lower proficiency levels, may differ considerably from methods that they once experienced themselves as students in phonetics classes. Innovative approaches to language teaching at the beginner or intermediate level (Oller & Richard-Amato, 1983; Richards & Rodgers, 1986) often lack innovative methodological equivalents in the academic program of linguistics courses presented to students with advanced or native fluency in the language of instruction. In addition, some second-language acquisition research implies that explicit classroom presentation of traditional pronunciation exercises at lower levels has little effect on the outcome of students' accents (Krashen & Terrell, 1983; Purcell & Suter, 1980). The resulting gap in the amount of overt attention given to the pronunciation component of language classes, pointed out by Wong (1986), and in the time allotted to pronunciation methodology in teacher preparation programs may leave many language teachers with no recent, recognisable image of how to present the speech sounds of the target language other than the recollection of how they themselves were taught phonetics.

Listening for Voice Setting

To address the issue of input, applied linguistics students can observe phonetic material in linguistic contexts that are as elaborate in variety and register as foreseen at the time of initial recording. Problem solving and manipulation can be introduced to these students, and phonetic substance presented from the 'outside in', or from the periphery towards the locus, by beginning with voice setting features and gradually arriving at the identification of consonant and vowel segments. This follows trends in pronunciation teaching where phrase- or word-level prosodic cues, rather than phoneme-level contrasts, form the basis for listening exercises (Dunkel & Pialorsi, 1982; Fox & Woods, 1980; Gilbert, 1984; Harmegnies, 1987; Kenworthy, 1987; Pennington & Richards, 1986; Wong, 1987; Woods, 1978).

Initial emphasis in accessing the PDB with *MSLEDIT* is on the voice setting strand of accent, or what is also known as voice quality (Abercrombie, 1967: 89–93). There are two reasons for this. One is due to the indexical properties of accent that convey information about regional, social and personal background characteristics (see Laver, 1974). The other reason is the phonological relationship of the long-term traits of voice quality to the shorter-term linguistically contrastive units of speech. Both of these functions, according to the focusing principle, provide background information necessary for eventually identifying traits that carry linguistic distinctiveness in a particular language. This process implies that the inductive experience of a range of examples from various coherent language systems gives a firmer basis for forming concepts of phonetic units than the deductive experience of hearing only isolated examples of phonetic sounds said to represent an ideal model of those cardinal units.

Useful associations of voice setting features with particular languages, as detailed in Laver's (1980) framework and outlined in Esling & Wong (1983) for one variety of North American English, are evident in the PDB. Nyangumarta, Miriam, and Umpila from Australia, for example, illustrate the auditory difference between lip spreading, retroflexion and nasal voice. Southern African Xhosa is a good example of breathy phonation, while the North American languages Skagit, Spokane, and Ditidaht illustrate the recognisable areal feature of faucal (upper pharynx) constriction. Manner and place of articulation are also globally evident in long-term listening: the clicks of Xhosa, the numerous fricatives and affricates of North American Pacific coast languages, which are also tongue retracted and frequently glottalised; while Scots Gaelic, Turkish, and Korean are fronted. Egyptian Arabic, on the other hand, is pharyngealised, and Inuktitut uvularised.

An illustration of a single-screen *MSLEDIT* display is given in Figure 11.1 — a Xhosa tongue twister which is one of the most popular items in the PDB. The display shows sequences of high-amplitude clicks interspersed with low-amplitude breathy vowels. It is not expected that students will imitate this sequence, or even that the visual cues observable here are necessarily the ones that will eventually produce insight into aspects of phonetic production. The intention of the display is to present real-time aspects of rhythm, relative consonant and vowel prominence, and timing in a natural language sample. Specifying the perceptual interaction between voice setting and individual segments is a difficult acoustic research question, precluding a prescriptive approach to using the auditory signal as a model. The value to students is seen in the basis which the signal provides for exploration (by teachers as well as students) of the acoustic representation of what is heard. Technical operation consists of turning on the computer equipped with MSL, specifying the desired language directory on the hard disk, selecting speech files to display, making menu choices, and listening through headphones or speakers. Figures 11.1–3 and 11.7–9 give an indication of menu items. Figure 11.1 also demonstrates the textual material available to users in the written documentation accompanying each set of language files.

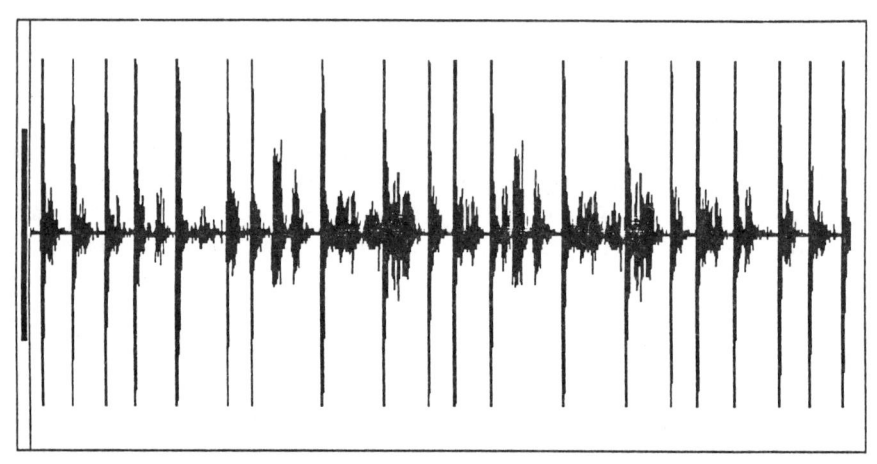

```
ACTIVE SCREEN   A   (PAUSE: 1000 msec)                              WIDTH: 5.454 sec
TIME:  0.0000 sec   VALUE: 3         OUTPUT SEQUENCE:  A            O/P TYPE:   3
[F1] DISPLAY MARKED (ACTIVE SCREEN)   [F2] DISPLAY ALL (ACTIVE SCREEN)   [PgDn]-)
```

Phonemic: / iCaCa beliziCikaCika kuCaCaCa kwat^{h}i g̃Ci C^{h}aji iCaba liC^{h}ij umCaji iCaCa laC^{h}awuk' uCoCoCo /

Orthographic: iqaqa beliziqikaqika kuqaqaqa kwathi gqi qhayi iqaba liqhiya umqayi iqaqa laqhawuk'a uqoqoqo

Gloss: ' a skunk was frolicking on the lawn, a man appeared swinging a stick and cut the skunk's throat '

FIGURE 11.1 *MSLEDIT single-screen display: Xhosa file XHS001x, tongue twister.*

Observation and Manipulation

To address perceptual skills, exercises are provided which give students a chance to manipulate the items and order of listening and viewing before being expected to practice orally. Interactive, task-oriented work-stations are an essential physical requirement for this kind of learning to occur. One task, analogous to the communicative (and language-experience) teaching technique of filling blank cards with new vocabulary items for reference in review activities and in story building (Heyer, 1984), consists of building sets of files that illustrate the inventory of the phonetic chart or of a particular language's phonology. Criteria for assessment include the conceptual range of the collection of items, the representative adequacy and quality of each example, and the coherence of organisation into phonetic categories. These criteria resemble those which language teachers need to apply in their own teaching experience.

One essential aspect of using computers is the simultaneous provision of written materials for reference. In the case of the PDB, reference materials consist of information folders for each language specifying all words and texts by filename. Lists include phonetic and phonemic transcriptions of each item, an orthographic representation in the native language if available, and an English gloss. Tasks can be set with reference to the written guides, but based on listening: 'Find all the words from the following group that have sound X, Y or Z in them', and 'Find the sounds that the following words have in common', or 'Group the following words together according to the sounds that they have in common.' These procedures delay premature production of new sounds from languages not previously heard, and instead allow learners to formulate and build concepts with only limited influence from literary strategies as in spelling pronunciations. Four similar but contrasting phonetic sounds from Skagit are aligned using *MSLEDIT* in Figure 11.2. Students learn to distinguish the timing of different phonetic events, and to recognise the distinctive characteristics of initial plosive bursts at the beginning of each waveform.

MSLSORT is a speech-editing program which elaborates on *MSLEDIT* by allowing portions of files to be copied into new files iteratively, for collection and subsequent analysis. This 'bucketing' technique is used to assemble tokens of a specified sound category into a single illustrative file. Designed as a tool for sociophonetic speech analysis and not explicitly for training applied linguists, *MSLSORT* is an example of the manipulation-oriented approach which computers bring to the listening tasks assigned to phonetics students.

Computer technology thus makes it possible to access many pertinent items of data that would otherwise be extremely difficult, or even impossible, to extract from an interfering matrix of irrelevant material. Tasks that concentrate on collecting elements of a phonetic series or on cross-linguistic comparisons of unfamiliar articulations illustrate the integration of the technology of access with the learning process. A manipulation-oriented analogy in the language classroom is a listening procedure where Language Master recordings of items with varying intonation contours are grouped into appropriate categories according to context or emotion (Oxtoby, 1981). A similar principle applies to the recent development of computer-controlled video materials which give students optimal access to audio as well as visual aspects of language and paralinguistics. Hypermedia language teaching techniques described by Underwood (1988) are an example of this approach and constitute, therefore, an integral part of teacher preparation. Use of group dynamics to assist in the learning process and of both auditory and visual referents are the recommended 'language laboratory' or 'media centre' procedures for assisting language learners as well as for training language teachers.

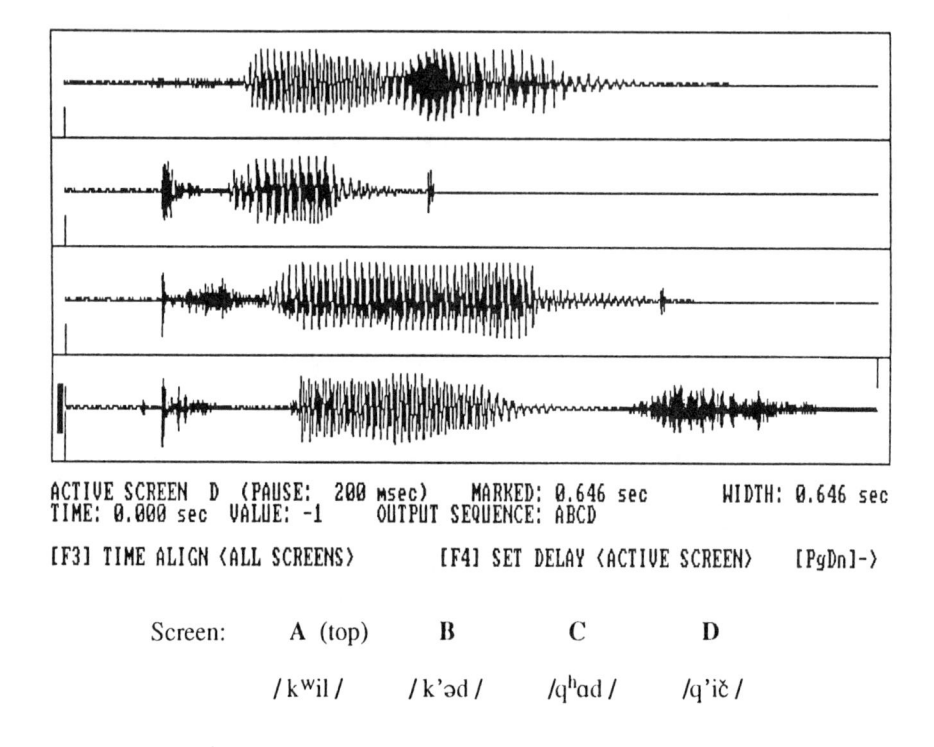

```
ACTIVE SCREEN  D   (PAUSE:  200 msec)      MARKED: 0.646 sec        WIDTH: 0.646 sec
TIME: 0.000 sec    VALUE: -1        OUTPUT SEQUENCE: ABCD
[F3] TIME ALIGN (ALL SCREENS)         [F4] SET DELAY (ACTIVE SCREEN)        [PgDn]-)
```

Screen: A (top)   B   C   D

/kʷil/   /k'əd/   /qʰad/   /q'ič/

FIGURE 11.2 *MSLEDIT: Four contrastive plosives in Skagit.*

Analysis as Content

The requirement for concrete referents in language teaching is basic to both context-based (Finocchiaro, 1974) and content-based (Mohan, 1986) approaches to language teaching, at beginning as well as advanced levels, and deserves to be explored more carefully in applied linguistics teaching. On the one hand, computerised access to phonetic data begins to solve the problem of how to increase the number of examples available to represent the diversity of speech sounds taught in phonetics courses. On the other, the items of study in phonetics — sounds and their analysis, symbols and their articulatory points of reference — represent valid academic subject-matter content for language teaching at the advanced level of language proficiency.

One technique of presenting phonetics for applied linguistic purposes, with associative images for the sounds, symbols, recognition and transcription tasks being studied, is to build up a set of visual images with pictures, maps of language families, and other concrete referents that can be linked linguistically and culturally with the individual languages used to illustrate the sounds. The theory behind this procedure is to fix images in memory that will assist in recall of specific sounds or sound systems (Stevick, 1986). It follows that visual correlates should also be available on a computer system as in the laserdisc format described by Underwood (1988). Although developing such a capability demands considerable effort, it would be a disservice to future teachers to suggest that computer programs can aid in learning without incorporating a visual component in some form to satisfy the imaging principle.

The MSL system itself presents images in the form of acoustic waveforms and spectral representations of speech. Experiments by de Bot (de Bot, 1983; de Bot & Mailfert, 1982) show a positive short-term effect of computer-generated visual displays on perception and production of intonation in a second language. Experience with visual output of speech may also have a positive long-term effect on students' production in the same way that physical presence in another culture has a global effect on success in language acquisition (Carroll, 1967). An MSL display of amplitude and pitch over time gives a memory-fixing visual image, as shown in Figure 11.3. The Xhosa word /úkúkʰaba/ ('to kick') illustrates the otherwise breathy features of the language (cf. Figure 11.1) as well as tonal characteristics. Without a visual image, students often have difficulty distinguishing whether pitch rises or falls.

Caution must still be advised in interpreting machine representations. The aperiodic noise of [h] in the middle of the word recurs in the vowel at the end of the word, indicating breathiness. In the pitch display, where pitch appears to fall then rise, the pitch-extraction routine has in fact simply lost the periodicity of voicing in the noise of breathy phonation. This demonstrates an important lesson about the value of machines in phonetics: that the signal is an imperfect reflection of what is perceived. Linguists have long remarked on the difficulty of establishing a bi-unique relationship between articulatory and acoustic events (Pike, 1967: 348). Although computer images of the acoustic signal can help phonetics students sharpen their skills for perception of co-occurring aspects of speech and can assist applied linguistics researchers in the analysis of speech data (e.g. Pennington, 1991), far from providing a constant model or automatic answers to confirm or disprove auditory judgements, the acoustic image supplies its own characteristics and problems for study and resolution.

More elaborate acoustic analysis is available through *MSLPITCH* and *MSLSPECT*. Graduate students can prepare thesis projects with these programs, or sets of figures that illustrate a contrast of particular formal interest to language students. Work with languages such as Japanese or Chinese, with pitch or tonal properties, is facilitated by *MSLPITCH*. The display of pitch is menu-driven, unlike the real-time display of VSA (Dickson *et al.*, 1984) produced for

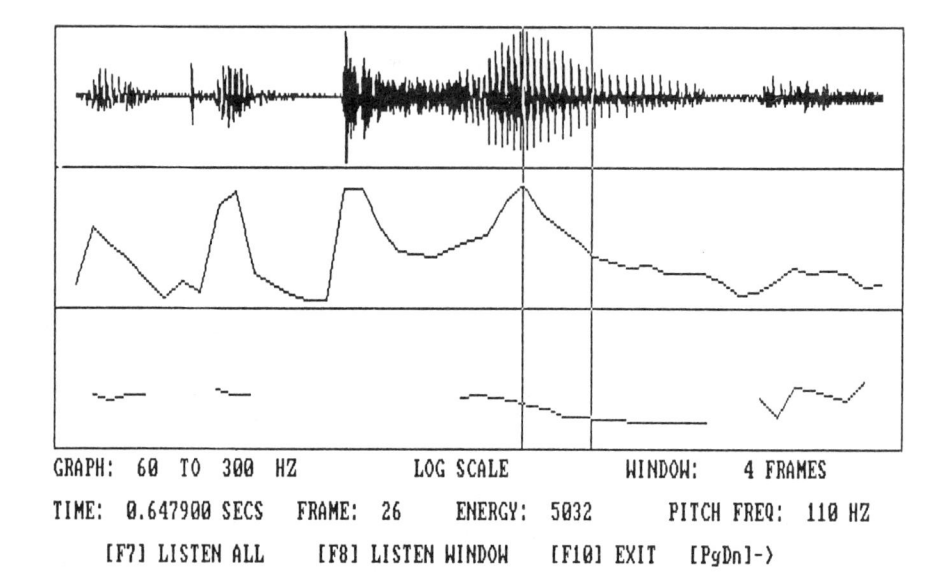

```
GRAPH:  60 TO 300 HZ          LOG SCALE           WINDOW:    4 FRAMES
TIME:   0.647900 SECS    FRAME: 26    ENERGY: 5032    PITCH FREQ:  110 HZ
        [F7] LISTEN ALL    [F8] LISTEN WINDOW    [F10] EXIT    [PgDn]-)
```

Acoustic waveform (screen A), amplitude (screen B), pitch (screen C).

FIGURE 11.3 *MSL display: Xhosa / úkúkʰaba / 'to kick'.*

Apple II hardware (see also programs developed by Loritz in Stevens *et al.*, 1986: 19). The explicit function of the *MSLPITCH* format of presentation is analysis and research, and it would therefore be useful only to second-language students who are already advanced enough to be taking phonetics in their L2. For an applied linguistics population (L1 or L2), the analysis and research components are fundamental, and a microcomputer-assisted format makes them more accessible. Pitch can be derived using MSL, as in Figure 11.3, but can be controlled and defined more accurately with *MSLPITCH* as shown in Figure 11.4. The display shows three of the possible contrasts in Yoruba register tone, a mid-high, mid-mid, and mid-low bisyllabic sequence.

Chinese contains numerous lessons about linguistic variability which are essential for applied linguistics students, especially with respect to the notion of 'standard'. Modern Standard Chinese — MSC (Kratochvíl, 1968: 19–22) as spoken by a Sìchuān native is included in the PDB. Variation in tone and segmental articulation is omnipresent in the word inventory and in the contrasting ('dialect' vs. 'standard') versions of the narrative text. The lesson is clear to PDB users that a single model for instruction is not linguistically realistic.

```
TIME: 1.76921 sec  VALUE:    9                                      [ C ]
```

[waveform display]

```
                                                         STATISTICS
                                                         -----------
                                                         LENGTH: 2.967s
                                                         FRAMES:    99
                                                         VOICED:    63

                                                         A.MEAN: 149 Hz
                                                         G.MEAN: 147 Hz
                                                         MEDIAN: 149 Hz
                                                         ST.DEV:  25 Hz
FRAME: 60 ( 1.768 - 1.798 sec)    PITCH: 157 Hz  LEVEL: 26 dB

[F1] ANALYSE ALL DATA       [F2] ANALYSE MARKED DATA        [PgUp][PgDn]
```

/ áwó / ' guinea fowl '   / āwó / ' mystery '   / āwò / ' fishing net '

Acoustic waveform (screen A), pitch (screen B).

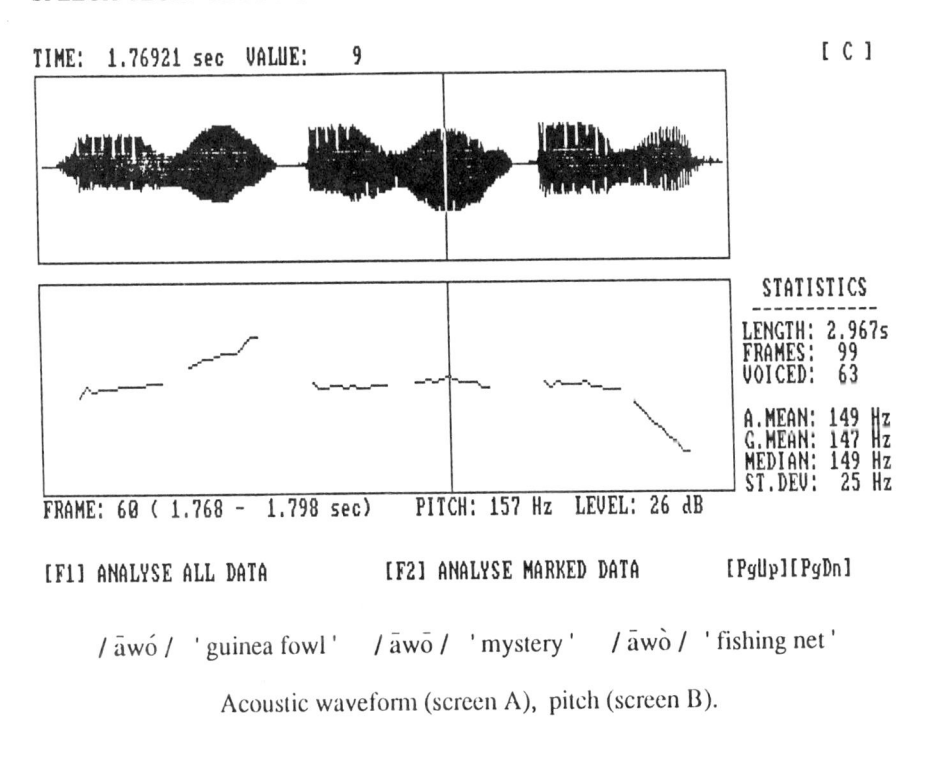

FIGURE 11.4 *MSLPITCH analysis of three Yoruba bisyllabic tonal contrasts.*

Most educated Chinese eliminate possible communicational barriers only by relatively minor adjustments of their speech behaviour in favour of the 'correct' language forms, while they prefer to consider the total of these forms, MSC, as a symbol of national language unity...rather than a practical language norm....Instead of a concrete norm there is a range of variants both in the written style and the standard language together with an abstract idea of unity based on past traditions and stimulated by modern needs (Kratochvíl, 1968: 20).

Therefore, it is not enough to illustrate the 'four tones of Mandarin' as if these were the norm even for foreign learners. This concept is demonstrated through all the MSC data, as in the pitch analysis of the four classic examples in Figure 11.5, where the slight rise of tone 1 and the high short fall of tone 4 suggest a variable system differing from the model usually presented to learners of Chinese.

Traditional analogue spectrograms are the most familiar way of visualising the spectral range of acoustic changes over time. This type of spectrographic

```
TIME: 1.43986 sec   VALUE: -12                              [ C ]
```

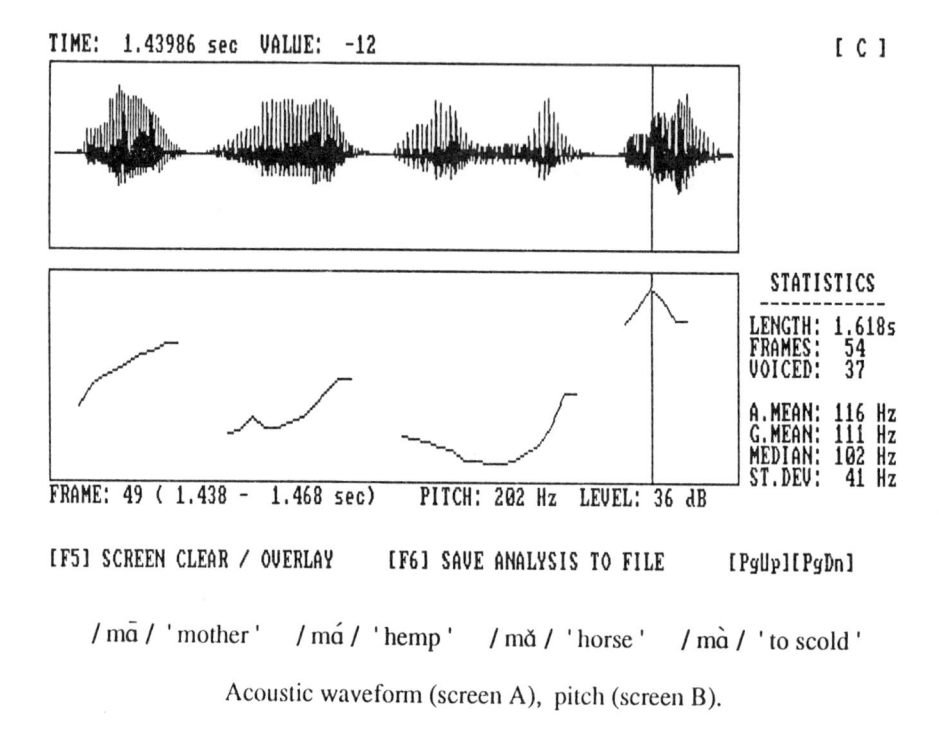

```
                                                    STATISTICS
                                                    ----------
                                                    LENGTH: 1.618s
                                                    FRAMES:   54
                                                    VOICED:   37

                                                    A.MEAN: 116 Hz
                                                    G.MEAN: 111 Hz
                                                    MEDIAN: 102 Hz
                                                    ST.DEV:  41 Hz
FRAME: 49 ( 1.438 - 1.468 sec)    PITCH: 202 Hz  LEVEL: 36 dB

[F5] SCREEN CLEAR / OVERLAY    [F6] SAVE ANALYSIS TO FILE    [PgUp][PgDn]
```

/ mā / 'mother'   / má / 'hemp'   / mǎ / 'horse'   / mà / 'to scold'

Acoustic waveform (screen A), pitch (screen B).

FIGURE 11.5 *MSLPITCH display of contour tones in Modern Standard Chinese.*

display can be produced by computer imaging, and has been used in ESL pronunciation training (Molholt, 1988). *MSLSPECT* (Wynrib, 1988) performs 3-D and long-term average spectral analysis and, like *MSLPITCH*, is intended to be used for analysis purposes, that is, in a course whose explicit content is phonetics. Such techniques are valuable tools in the application of linguistic theory in the clinical as well as teaching professions, e.g. for students in linguistics programs who are planning to enter speech pathology or audiology. A sample of the 3-D display produced with *MSLSPECT* is shown in Figure 11.6. Vowel quality, consonant transitions, the low-frequency noise of back fricatives and high-frequency noise of sibilants appear in detail in this display of a Ditidaht phrase.

Applied linguistics students are usually introduced to acoustic relationships in a phonetics class, but the capability of deriving spectra easily by computer brings the concept closer to home with less effort of explanation. In laboratory settings, it is also possible to derive spectral displays using synthesised speech and to change spectral parameters by means of mouse-driven software to alter

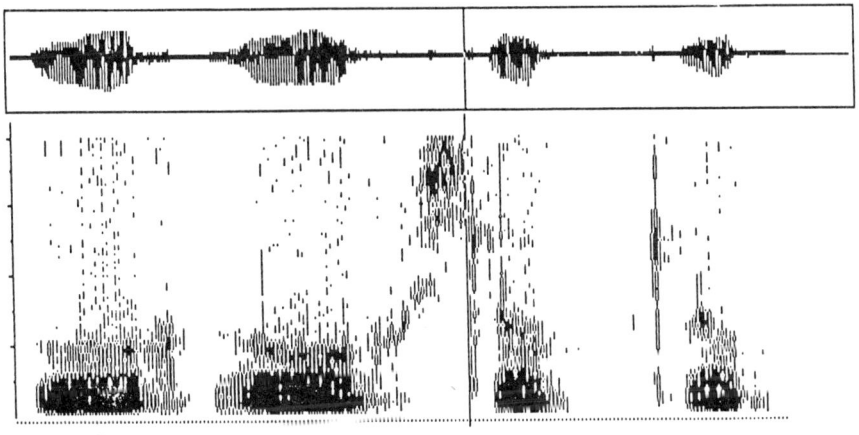

START: 0.000 sec   END: 1.843 sec
TIME: 1.08480 sec   VALUE: 1
COMPLETED FRAME 194 OF 194   [F1] PROCEED WITH ANALYSIS   [PgDn]->NEXT

/ ʔu·χʷ ʔu·χʷs tɬ'uχʷ tɬ'uχʷ /   'I am chewing oysters'

FIGURE 11.6 *MSLSPECT: 3-D spectrographic analysis of Ditidaht.*

the speech signal automatically. Such a procedure is also a potentially powerful device in the interactive, cooperative-learning atmosphere recommended here for phonetics in applied linguistics. Changing sound quality according to an acoustic 'recipe' is a useful tool in understanding how sounds are related. As computer-assisted speech synthesis procedures become technologically commonplace, the only constraints remaining to their implementation in applied and general linguistics phonetics courses are space — because of the increased demand on facilities for independent study — and time — because of the extra effort required to produce the expanded banks of materials and the additional personnel needed to supervise and maintain computer facilities.

As a final note on analysis procedures, the clinical applications of speech technology bear a direct relationship to the procedures introduced in applied training programs. B.Sc. candidates, for example, need to be familiar with speech and language aids for the handicapped such as the VSA system which gives hearing-impaired users up to 4-second pitch contours in real time with microphone input (Dickson *et al.*, 1984), text-to-speech products that give synthetic-voice renditions of words entered by keyboard, and analysis-by-synthesis routines for extracting and reconstructing detailed components of speech as a means of better understanding the articulatory process of speech production. The important element to stress in training, as opposed to clinical practice, is the recommended format for developing and implementing computer-assisted devices. Students in a graduate program can be expected to contribute directly to the development of new software or techniques for practical implementation.

Collaboration: Transcription Exercises

In addition to the lessons discovered about variation, using the PDB gives students a chance to study with peers, to share and discuss auditory judgements and transcription conventions. One natural component of learning phonetics is the need to *see* an instructor's or other speakers' vocal production (hence the desirability of video as well as audio, discussed above). However, the principal demand on time (and space) is the need to hear authentic illustrations of sounds within a format that promotes practice and feedback. The group format encouraged with CALL (Tyacke *et al.*, 1985) is an opportunity for students to access quickly large amounts of specific phonetic material, and to share feedback by observing each other's 'interlanguage vocal modelling' of various utterances in an interactive atmosphere. In addition to the PDB, material drawn from sociolinguistic surveys of English can also provide valuable insights into language variation (Esling, 1987d).

This collaborative approach is invoked when students perform transcription tasks. The facility to transcribe speech from the PDB or from other sources of data is contained in the program, *IPAEDIT*. In *MSLEDIT* mode, the alphabet and diacritic characters of the International Phonetic Association (IPA) are entered on the screen below the waveform display, characteristically in narrow transcription. Transcriptions can be saved in library fashion, i.e. to be recalled and added to speech files. The opportunity is present for either an instructor or students to enter and save transcriptions for sets of assignments. Using the capability of MSL to encode and store speech entered by microphone, students can produce their own illustrations of phonetic contrasts, transcribed in IPA, when phonetic production activities become relevant to the learning experience. Again, the approach to teaching phonetics is patterned after language teaching approaches. Figure 11.7 repeats the Ditidaht utterance analysed in Figure 11.6, with transcription added beneath the waveform. Two standards of characters are illustrated — North American and IPA. The first type is used to represent the voiceless (labialised) uvular fricative and voiceless (glottalised) lateral affricate in the first and third syllables of the utterance, while the corresponding IPA symbols are used in the second and fourth syllables. The Active Mode toggles between a main keyboard reassigned with phonetic characters and a keyboard of diacritics,

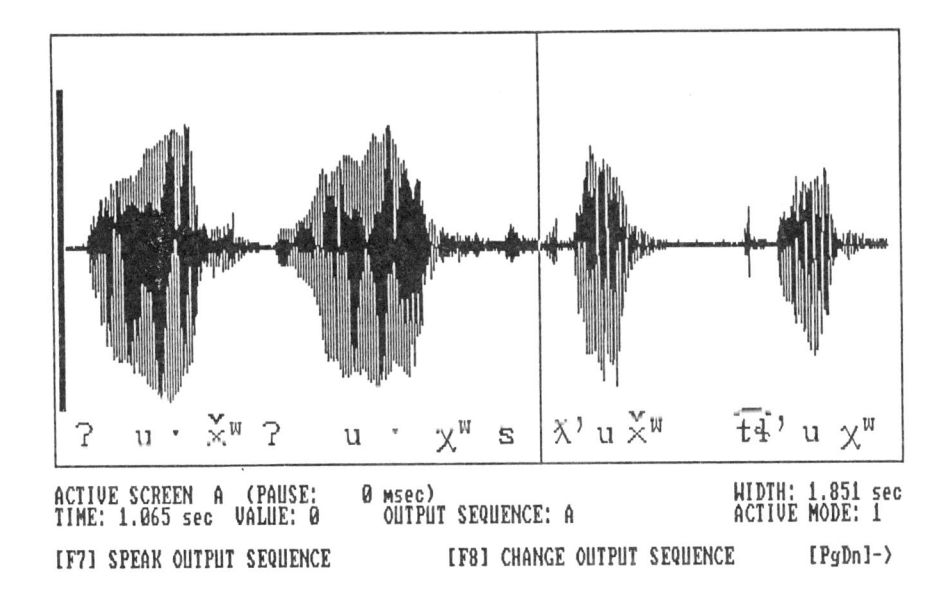

FIGURE 11.7 IPAEDIT: *Variable phonetic transcription of Ditidaht (as in Figure 11.6).*

adapted from Pullum & Ladusaw's (1986) reference guide. A third keyboard option inserts superscripted versions of the vowel and consonant symbols found in Mode 1.

Alphabetical organisational principles have a key role to play in learning to describe and annotate speech in phonetic transcription, just as orthography is a powerful concordance tool in learning languages. The views expressed in reading theory (Downing, 1979) emphasise these cognitive organisational aspects of writing systems, where each new reader discovers something of the original process of reducing speech to writing. Smith (1984) outlines the benefits of an alphabetic system, also stressing properties that facilitate manipulation rather than 'decoding' of discrete units. Phonetic symbols follow these same principles and, rather than trying to memorise them on the basis of mimicry and a single example, it is more practical to plan tasks that illustrate actual linguistic occurrences of series of sounds represented by similar symbols. During the transcription activity, students rely on each other's reactions and suggestions so that the level of consensus is reasonably high before the instructor is consulted to review completed work.

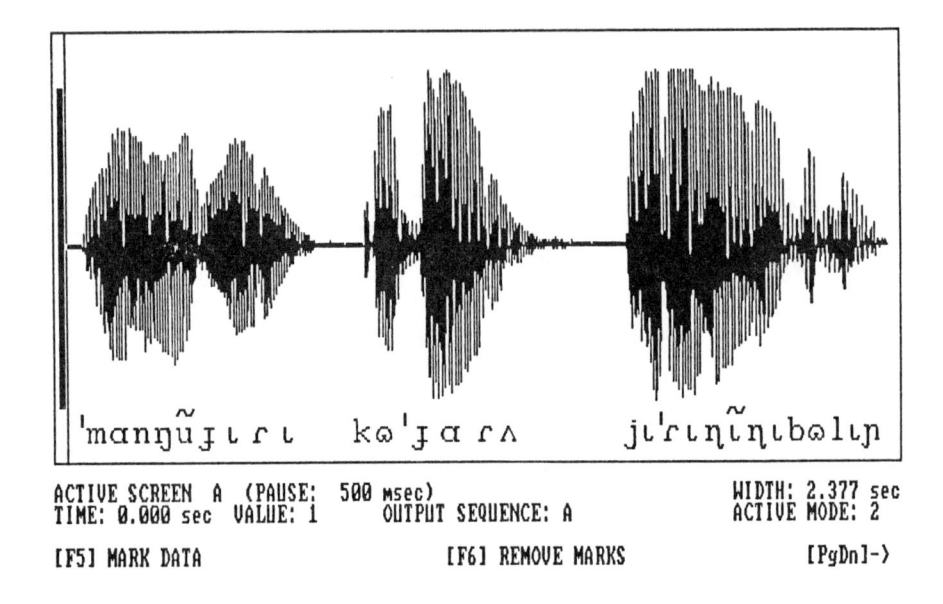

FIGURE 11.8 IPAEDIT: *Narrow phonetic transcription of Nyangumarta 'I see two men'*.

Figure 11.8 is an example of the linguistic detail in the nasal series in Nyangumarta. Bilabial, alveolar, velar, retroflex and palatal nasals contrast in the transcribed utterance. The use of taps, the tendency towards approximation in general, and rapid syllable succession are also apparent in listening to this example, and can be followed in the time domain of the display by marking a particular area and expanding it to fill the screen.

A final illustration of the use of transcription together with waveform analysis is a set of particularly clear consonantal contrasts of syllable-initial clicks from Xhosa. Figure 11.9 shows four single syllables beginning with a lateral click and contrasting aspirated, nasalised and velarised secondary manners of articulation. There are, in Xhosa, 12 distinct click consonants with the same four patterns also occurring at the dental and palatal places of articulation. The clicks appear as high energy bursts, while the [h], [n] and [g] components are realised in the time domain as friction, nasal resonance, and a secondary burst, respectively. Speech events can be picked out visually and matched with the corresponding IPA symbols listed in the reference guide, with sequences of narrow representations, or with their orthographic representations ('x, xh, nx, gx'), to help students

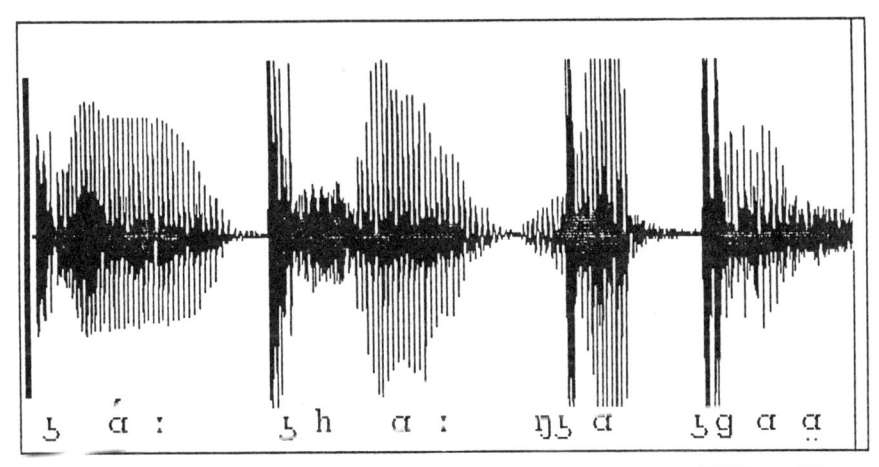

FIGURE 11.9 *IPAEDIT: Four contrastive Xhosa lateral clicks.*

understand speech processes and properties of the phonological system. It is of some interest that prosodic elements can also be recognised in the acoustic waveform. High tone on syllable 1 is realised as cycles that cross the baseline more frequently (more vertical lines), while the pitch of syllable 4 is lower (vertical lines further apart) and terminates in breathy voice (high amplitude vocal resonance gives way to increasing noise of glottal friction). Although users' roles are not formalised, a pattern usually develops in the use of MSL/PDB to practice material outside of class. Typically, one student takes charge of the keyboard while another takes on the role of organiser, co-ordinating tasks assigned in class with the written reference guides to the various languages. A third student serves as reporter, making notes of observations, and a fourth is free to contribute details of pronunciation or of visual acoustic correlates.

Conclusion

It is increasingly necessary to train language specialists in applied linguistics programs to become familiar with the use of technological systems for the recording, storage and delivery of speech sound information. The place to do this training is in the phonetics course, where content is introductory in terms of academic subject matter, but advanced with regard to language proficiency level. The characteristics of this situation invite applied linguistics students to draw the comparison between their phonetics course experience and advanced language courses that they are likely to teach. Hence, methods of instruction in the phonetics course are designed to be consistent with principles of second-language acquisition theory and with methodologies at the advanced level. It is admittedly difficult to emulate a situation where teachers in training can draw a direct parallel between their own coursework and the experience of the beginning-level language class, but some of the techniques proposed have been adapted indirectly from manipulative, task-based, organisational, holistic language learning activities that are appropriate at all levels.

The development of a Phonetic Data Base on microcomputer, supported by several types of speech processing, editing, analysis, synthesis and transcription software, makes it possible to revise the presentation of speech-sound material for phonetic study, to provide expedient access to a greater variety and amount of data, and to permit organisation and manipulation of speech items in an active learning format. The emphasis is on the use of the computer as a tool instead of a tutor, on input rather than on oral performance in phonetics, on cross-referencing several forms of written and auditory information in order to build associations between sound and symbol, on analysis in its holistic sense as a learning exercise as opposed to a point-by-point didactic style, on collaboration instead of memorisation, on the observation of language from the prosodic and indexical perspective before concentrating on segmental phonology, and on linguistic variation as a norm.

Similar approaches, focusing on variation and emphasising the instrumental aspects of phonetic observation, have been introduced for language specialists studying phonetics and principles of phonetic transcription for various applied purposes (Bailey, 1985). This brief description of speech technology systems in applied linguistics instruction represents a tentative model for integrating computer-assisted procedures into a phonetic approach to applied language study.

Acknowledgements

Appreciation is extended to Craig Dickson and Roy Snell and to the staff of Speech Technology Research Limited, Victoria, for making a broad range of speech analysis programs available for use by students in linguistics. The assistance of colleagues in the Department of Linguistics at the University of Victoria in providing language recordings for PDB archiving is also gratefully acknowledged.

References

ABERCROMBIE, D. (1967) *Elements of General Phonetics.* Edinburgh: Edinburgh University Press.
ASHER, J. J. (1982) *Learning Another Language Through Actions: The Complete Teacher's Guidebook* (2nd edn). Los Gatos, CA: Sky Oaks.
BAILEY, C-J. N. (1985) *English Phonetic Transcription.* Arlington, TX: Summer Institute of Linguistics.
BARLOW, M. (1987) *Working with Computers: Computer Orientation for Foreign Students.* La Jolla, CA: Athelstan.
BROWN, G. (1977) *Listening to Spoken English.* London: Longman.
BROWN, G., A. ANDERSON, R. SHILLCOCK & G. YULE (1984) *Teaching Talk: Strategies for Production and Assessment.* Cambridge: Cambridge University Press.
BURGER, S., M. CHRÉTIEN, M. GINGRAS, P. HAUPTMAN & M. MIGNERON (1984) Le rôle du professeur de langue dans un cours de matière académique en langue seconde, *The Canadian Modern Language Review/La Revue canadienne des langues vivantes*, 41, 397–402.
CARROLL, J. (1967) Foreign language proficiency levels attained by language majors near graduation from college, *Foreign Language Annals*, 1, 131–151.
CEDERGREN, H. & D. SANKOFF (1974) Variable rules: Performance as a statistical reflection of competence, *Language*, 50, 333-355.
DE BOT, K. (1983) Visual feedback of English intonation, I: Effectiveness and induced practice behavior, *Language and Speech*, 26, 331–350.
DE BOT, K. & K. MAILFERT (1982) The teaching of intonation: Fundamental research and classroom applications, *TESOL Quarterly*, 16, 71–77.
DICKSON, B. C. (1985) *User's Manual for Micro Speech Lab.* Victoria, BC: Software Research Corporation.
— (1987) *User's Manual for the MSL Comparison and Editing Program: MSLEDIT.* Victoria, BC: Centre for Speech Technology Research Society.
DICKSON, B. C. & J. C. INGRAM (1982) *A Teacher's Manual for the Visible Speech Aid for the Hearing-impaired Microcomputer Package.* Victoria, BC: Software Research Corp./CSTR.
DICKSON, B. C., J. C. INGRAM & R. C. SNELL (1984) Development of microcomputer-based Visible Speech Aids for the hearing-impaired. *Proceedings of the 2nd International Conference on Rehabilitation Engineering*, pp. 275–276. Ottawa, Canada.
DOWNING, J. (1979) *Reading and Reasoning.* New York: Springer-Verlag.
DULAY, H., M. BURT & S. D. KRASHEN (1982) *Language Two.* Oxford, England: Oxford University Press.
DUNKEL, P. A. & F. PIALORSI (1982) *Advanced Listening Comprehension: Developing Aural and Note-taking Skills.* Rowley, MA: Newbury House/Harper & Row.
EDWARDS, H., M. WESCHE, S. KRASHEN, R. CLÉMENT & B. KRUIDENIER (1984) Second-language acquisition through subject-matter learning: A study of sheltered psychology classes at the University of Ottawa, *The Canadian Modern Language Review/La Revue canadienne des langues vivantes*, 41, 268–282.
ESLING, J. H. (1987a) Methodology for voice setting awareness in language classes, *Revue de Phonétique Appliquée*, 85, 449–473.
— (1987b) Microcomputer-based phonetics instruction using the Phonetic Data Base, *Revue de Phonétique Appliquée*, 85, 425–448.

— (1987c) Teaching phonetics using the Phonetic Data Base on microcomputer, *Proceedings XIth International Congress of Phonetic Sciences*, vol. 5, pp. 298–301. Tallinn: Academy of Sciences of the Estonian SSR.
— (1987d) Vowel shift and long-term average spectra in the Survey of Vancouver English, *Proceedings XIth International Congress of Phonetic Sciences*, vol. 4, pp. 243–246. Tallinn: Academy of Sciences of the Estonian SSR.
— (1991) Researching the effects of networking: Evaluating the spoken and written discourse generated by working with CALL. In P. A. DUNKEL (ed.), *Computer-assisted Language Learning and Testing: Research Issues and Practice*. Cambridge, MA: Newbury House/Harper & Row.
— (in press a) Sociophonetic variation in Vancouver. In J. CHESHIRE (ed), *English Around the World*. Cambridge, England: Cambridge University Press.
— (in press b) La parole sur ordinateur dans l'enseignement de la phonétique et de la langue seconde: Matière académique au niveau avancé, *Revue de Phonétique Appliquée*, 95-96-97.
ESLING, J. H., M. WARBEY & J. R. SCHOLEFIELD (1984) ESL courseware: A developmental framework including discussions of university-level and elementary-level programs, *TEAL Occasional Papers*, 8, 41–51.
ESLING, J. H. & R. F. WONG (1983) Voice quality settings and the teaching of pronunciation, *TESOL Quarterly*, 17, 89–95.
FASOLD, R. W. (1986) *Microcomputer VARBRUL 2 system* (MS-DOS version). Department of Linguistics, Georgetown University, Washington, DC.
FINOCCHIARO, M. (1974) *English as a Second Language: From Theory to Practice*. New York: Regents.
FLEGE, J. E. (1980) Phonetic approximation in second language acquisition, *Language Learning*, 30, 117–134.
— (1981) The phonological basis of foreign accent: A hypothesis, *TESOL Quarterly*, 15, 443–455.
FOX, J. & H. B. WOODS, with C. DEEBLE (1980) *Telephone Gambits: A Module for Teaching English to Second Language Learners*. Hull, Québec: Canadian Government Publishing Centre.
FUJIMURA, O. (1984) The role of linguistics for future speech technology, *Linguistic Society of America Bulletin*, 104, 4–7.
GILBERT, J. (1984) *Clear Speech*. Cambridge, England: Cambridge University Press.
GUY, G. (1975) Use and application of the Cedergren–Sankoff Variable Rule Program. In R. FASOLD & R. SHUY (eds), *Analyzing Variation in Language*, pp. 59–69. Washington, DC: Georgetown University Press.
HARMEGNIES, B. (1987) SGAV, informatisation et recherche expérimentale, *Revue de Phonétique Appliquée*, 82-83-84, 149–160.
HAUPTMAN, P. C., M. B. WESCHE & D. READY (1988) Second-language acquisition through subject-matter learning: A follow-up study at the University of Ottawa, *Language Learning*, 38, 433–475.
HENDERSON, E. J. A. (ed.) (1971) *The Indispensable Foundation: A Selection from the Writings of Henry Sweet*. London: Oxford University Press.
HEYER, S. (1984) A technique for teaching vocabulary, *TESOL Newsletter*, 18 (2), 8–9.
HOOPER, H. (1984) Computer literacy and the public school ESL teacher, *TEAL Occasional Papers*, 8, 53–62.
JONES, C. & S. FORTESCUE (1987) *Using Computers in the Language Classroom*. London and New York: Longman.
KENWORTHY, J. (1987) *Teaching English Pronunciation*. London: Longman.

KRASHEN, S. D. & T. D. TERRELL, (1983) *The Natural Approach*. Oxford: Pergamon Press.
KRATOCHVÍL, P. (1968) *The Chinese Language Today*. London: Hutchinson & Co.
LABOV, W. (1969) Contraction, deletion, and inherent variability of the English copula, *Language*, 45, 715–762.
— (ed) (1980) *Locating Language in Time and Space*. New York: Academic Press.
LADEFOGED, P. (1987) The place of phonetics in American academia, *The Phonetician*, CL-44, 4-7.
LADO, R. & C. C. FRIES (1954) *English Pronunciation (An Intensive Course in English)*, vol. 3. Ann Arbor: University of Michigan Press.
LASERIPA (1986) Linguist's Software: Edmonds, WA.
LAVER, J. (1974) Labels for voices, *Journal of the International Phonetic Association*, 4 (2), 62–75.
— (1980) *The Phonetic Description of Voice Quality*. Cambridge, England: Cambridge University Press.
LIEBERMAN, P. & S. F. BLUMSTEIN (1988) *Speech Physiology, Speech Perception, and Acoustic Phonetics*. Cambridge, England: Cambridge University Press.
MANDELBAUM, D. G. (ed.) (1962) *Edward Sapir: Culture, Language and Personality*. Berkeley and Los Angeles, CA: University of California Press.
MOHAN, B. A. (1986) *Language and Content*. Reading, MA: Addison-Wesley.
MOLHOLT, G. (1988) Computer-assisted instruction in pronunciation for Chinese speakers of American English, *TESOL Quarterly*, 22, 91–111.
NEU, J. & SCARCELLA, R. (1991) Word processing in the ESL writing classroom: A survey of student attitudes. In P. A. DUNKEL (ed.), *Computer-assisted Language Learning and Testing: Research Issues and Practice*. Cambridge, MA: Newbury House/Harper & Row.
OLLER, J. W., Jr. & P. A. RICHARD-AMATO (eds) (1983) *Methods that Work: A Smorgasbord of Ideas for Language Teachers*. Rowley, MA: Newbury House.
OXTOBY, M. J. (1981) Unpublished classroom materials. Vancouver, BC: Vancouver Community College.
PARKINSON, S. & A. BLADON (1987) Microcomputer-assisted phonetics teaching and phonetics word-processing: A survey, *Journal of the International Phonetic Association*, 17 (2), 83–93.
PENNINGTON, M. C. (1989) Applications of computers in the development of speaking and listening proficiency. In M. C. PENNINGTON (ed.), *Teaching Languages with Computers: The State of the Art*, pp. 99–121. La Jolla, CA: Athelstan.
— (1991) Computer-assisted analysis of English dialect and interlanguage prosodics: Applications to research and training. In P. A. DUNKEL (ed.), *Computer-assisted Language Learning and Testing: Research Issues and Practice*. Cambridge, MA: Newbury House / Harper & Row.
PENNINGTON, M. C. & J. C. RICHARDS (1986) Pronunciation revisited, *TESOL Quarterly*, 20, 207–225.
PES (1985) *English in Japan Series*. Victoria, BC: Pacific Educational Systems.
PIKE, K. L. (1959) Language as particle, wave, and field, *The Texas Quarterly*, 2, 37–54.
— (1967) *Language in Relation to a Unified Theory of the Structure of Human Behavior*. Mouton: The Hague.
PULLUM, G. K. & W. A. LADUSAW (1986) *Phonetic Symbol Guide*. Chicago, IL: University of Chicago Press.
PURCELL, E. T. & R. W. SUTER (1980) Predictors of pronunciation accuracy: A reexamination, *Language Learning*, 30, 271–287.

RENARD, R. (1965) *L'enseignement des langues vivantes par la méthode audio-visuelle et structuro-globale de Saint-Cloud — Zagreb.* Paris: Didier.
— (1976) *La méthodologie SGAV d'enseignement des langues: Une problématique de l'apprentissage de la parole.* Paris: Didier.
— (1981) La notion de structuro-global et l'approche communicative, *Revue de Phonétique Appliquée,* 59–60, 223–238.
RICHARDS, J. C. & T. S. RODGERS (1986) *Approaches and Methods in Language Teaching.* Cambridge, England: Cambridge University Press.
SANKOFF, D. (ed) (1978) *Linguistic Variation: Models and Methods.* New York: Academic Press.
SAVIGNON, S. J. (1983) *Communicative Competence: Theory and Classroom Practice.* Reading, MA: Addison-Wesley.
SMITH, F. (1982) *Understanding Reading* (3rd edn). New York: Holt Rinehart & Winston.
— (1984) *What's the Use of the Alphabet?* Victoria, BC: Abel Press.
STEVENS, V., S. SPURLING, D. LORITZ, R. KENNER, J. ESLING & M. BRENNAN (1986) New ideas in software development for linguistics and language learning, *CALICO Journal,* 4 (1), 15–26.
STEVICK, E. W. (1976) *Memory, Meaning and Method: Some Psychological Perspectives on Language Learning.* Rowley, MA: Newbury House.
— (1986) *Images and Options in the Language Classroom.* Cambridge, England: Cambridge University Press.
SWEET, H. (1877) *A Handbook of Phonetics.* Oxford: Clarendon Press.
TERRELL, T. D. (1986) Acquisition in the natural approach: The binding/access framework, *The Modern Language Journal,* 70, 213–227.
TIANMA (1986) Victoria, BC: Asia Communications Inc.
TYACKE, M., J. BEYERS & J. HUNTER (1985) Interacting with and around a computer. Paper presented at TESL Canada '85, Toronto.
UNDERWOOD, J. (1988) Language learning and 'hypermedia', *Association of Departments of Foreign Languages Bulletin,* 19(3), 13–17.
WONG, R. F. (1986) Does pronunciation teaching have a place in the communicative language classroom? In D. TANNEN & J. ALATIS (eds), *Georgetown University Round Table '85, Languages and Linguistics: The Interdependence of Theory, Data, and Application.* Washington, DC: Georgetown University Press.
— (1987) *Teaching Pronunciation: Focus on English Rhythm and Intonation.* Englewood Cliffs, NJ: Prentice-Hall, Inc.
WOODS, H. B. (1978) *Syllable Stress and Unstress.* Hull, Québec: Canadian Government Publishing Centre.
WYNRIB, A. (1988) *Preliminary User's Manual for the Spectral Analysis Program: MSLSPECT.* Victoria, BC: Centre for Speech Technology Research Society.

12 The Use of PC-Generated Speech Technology in the Development of an L2 Listening Comprehension Proficiency Test: A Prototype Design Effort

PATRICIA DUNKEL
Pennsylvania State University, U.S.A.

Introduction

The need to develop valid and efficient methods of assessing proficiency in a second/foreign language (L2) is viewed by many educators and administrators to be a critical educational issue in the United States today. Standardised metrics of L2 proficiency are needed because of the burgeoning numbers of non-native listeners in the nation's elementary, high schools, colleges, and universities,[1] and because of the increasing numbers of American students now taking foreign language courses in our high schools and universities.[2] The demands for measures of proficiency in L2 language abound even as professionals in the field of L2 learning and testing are debating the diverse perspectives and theories concerning the nature of language and its measurement (Rivera, 1984), and as they are attempting to define and operationalise the construct of L2 proficiency and relate it to classroom activities (see Bachman & Savignon, 1986; Kramsch, 1986; Lowe, 1986; Schulz, 1986).

L2 Proficiency has been defined as the global rating of general language ability over a wide range of functions and topics at any given level (Lowe, 1986). Proficiency tests are used to measure an individual's general competence in a second language, independent of any particular curriculum or course of study (Omaggio, 1986). While acknowleding the difficulties involved in developing valid proficiency measures, Bachman & Savignon (1986: 380) recognise, nevertheless, that some degree of standardisation of assessment is desirable and achievable, highlighting the advantages of proficiency tests as the following:

(1) They would provide a standard for defining and measuring language proficiency that would be independent of specific languages, contexts, and domains of discourse;
(2) Scores from these tests would be comparable across different languages and contexts.

L2 educators and administrators are today in need of valid, efficient, non-institution-specific tests of L2 proficiency in all of the component skill areas of the language curriculum, especially listening comprehension. Proficiency tests of L2 listening comprehension are needed because comprehension skills are involved in three-fifths of all communicative interactions; approximately 15% of these interactions involve reading comprehension, whereas 50% involve listening comprehension (Rivers, cited in Omaggio, 1986). The need for measures of L2 listening fluency also stems from the fact that listening comprehension has been identified as a — possibly *the* — critical component in L2 acquisition. The key role listening comprehension plays in the L2 acquisition process has been suggested by research into child language acquisition (Bloom, 1970; Brown, 1973; Lahey & Bloom, 1977; Miller, 1978) and the writings of the comprehension approach methodologists such as Belasco (1981), Winitz (1981), and theorists such as Krashen (1982). The importance of extensive listening comprehension practice is listed by Morley (1982) as 'one of the "convergences on common focal points" concerning second language learning/teaching shared among L2 researchers and materials developers' (cited in Dunkel, 1986: 100).

Development of comprehensive, non-institution-specific measures of L2 listening proficiency has lagged behind development of measures of oral proficiency, such as the Oral Proficiency Interview (OPI) developed by Educational Testing Service (ETS), and reading comprehension, such as the Computer-Based Reading Comprehension Proficiency Test by the American Council on the Teaching of Foreign Languages (ACTFL). This lag seems counterintuitive, as well as educationally imprudent, if it is true that: (1) developing proficiency in extracting intended meaning from the flow of spoken L2 discourse is, indeed, the keystone of L2 acquisition; (2) American business firms and governmental agencies are in dire need of the services of proficient listeners of both the widely taught and less commonly taught foreign languages; and (3) teachers and administrators of English as a Second Language (ESL) need to identify and remediate the poor English listening skills of large numbers of the non-native school-age population. The scarcity of listening comprehension proficiency measures is beginning to be offset, however, and the computer will likely play a greater role in listening proficiency testing in the 1990s as a result of the recent and rapid advances in computer technology, in general, and speech technology, in particular.

This paper describes a project, the purpose of which was to conduct early-stage research and development into designing prototype computer-based tests (to run on IBM personl computers) of listening comprehension in English as a second language and in French as a native language (L1). Another objective of the project was to formulate prototype items that would be suitable for testing of L2 listening comprehension proficiency, using the ACTFL generic listening guidelines and Richards' (1985) taxonomy of listening skills. Before launching into the specifics of the prototype development effort, the advantages of computer-assisted testing will be presented, the initial attempts by ACTFL to develop computer-based tests of proficiency in reading comprehension using the ACTFL proficiency guidelines will be described, and a brief depiction of the speech digitisation process will be sketched.

The Development of Computer-Assisted Tests of L2 Proficiency

The advantages of computerised adaptive testing

Both ACTFL and ETS have acknowledged the importance of proficiency testing, and have supported research to establish guidelines for describing language proficiency (see Dandonoli, 1987; Liskin-Gasparro, 1984). The ACTFL organisation has also supported efforts to produce tests to measure L2 proficiency, using the ACTFL guidelines as a framework for test development (see Appendix A for a listing of the ACTFL generic listening guidelines).

Early on in the process of producing standardised measures of L2 oral proficiency, ACTFL considered the potential of the computer to assist in the proficiency assessment process. According to Ward (1984), the potential benefits of computerised testing range from ensuring individualised assessment to allowing for efficient measurement of one or more dimensions of an individual's achievement for proficiency-assessment purposes (e.g. in reading or listening comprehension). Computers also offer a relatively inexpensive, reliable, repeatable, secure, and standardised alternative to the traditional one-on-one L2 proficiency test, particularly for the kinds of tests which can be mass administered (e.g. a listening comprehension proficiency test). One particular kind of computer-assisted test, the *computerised adaptive test* (CAT), is analagous to the Oral Proficiency Interview, in that it 'tailors' the test to a particular examinee's competence. According to Madsen (1991: 238–9), a computerised-adaptive test:

> accesses a specially-calibrated item bank and is driven by a statistical routine which analyses student responses to questions and selects items for the candidate that are of appropriate difficulty. Then, when a specified standard error of measurement level has been reached, the exam is terminated.

As Tung (1986: 27) points out, the design of a computerised adaptive test offers the possibility of creating a more efficient and positive testing experience for the test takers because:

> the test items administered by a CAT program are determined on the basis of continual estimates of each examinee's ability. Items that are inappropriate for the examinees are not assigned. This may produce desirable affective effects on the examinees, who may discover that the test items are always challenging but never much beyond their capabilities.

A computerised adaptive test is, in addition, one that is more secure since the answers are input directly into database files, access to which can be restricted to users with designated passwords. The security, reliability, and efficiency of CATs has aroused the interest of both L2 test developers and the consumers of test data, and has sparked a good deal of research and development into their design and application, especially in the areas of reading and listening comprehension (see Dunkel, 1991).

Initial attempts to develop computerised tests of proficiency in reading and listening comprehension using ACTFL guidelines

Recognising the potential benefits of computer-assisted testing of foreign language proficiency, ACTFL began development of a computer-based reading comprehension proficiency test in French in the mid 1980s, completing the project in 1988. A criterion-referenced test of global functional language ability in French, the ACTFL Reading CAT uses the ILR/ACTFL (Interagency Language Roundtable/American Council on the Teaching of Foreign Languages) rating system. Dandonoli (1987) describes the prominent characteristics of the ACTFL reading proficiency test as the following: it is criterion-referenced; it presents items that are indicative of the performance of specific tasks; it is structured to follow particular themes, rather than consisting of isolated items; and it reflects the four-phase structure of the Oral Proficiency Interview in that it includes a 'warm-up', 'probes', a 'level check', and a 'wind-down'. Dandonoli (1987: 82) describes these four phases as follows:

(1) *Warm-up*: During the warm-up the examiner attempts, as much as possible in a testing situation, to put the candidate at ease. During this time, the tester (or the computer) can obtain a preliminary indication of the level of the candidate's ... understanding ability.
(2) *Level check*: This phase is used to determine the level at which the candidate functions most comfortably and consistently in the language. It serves to demonstrate what the candidate is capable of. During this phase the tester (or the computer) establishes a base line rating for the candidate.
(3) *Probes*: Probes ask the candidate to attempt to function at a level beyond her or his tentatively established base level. This phase provides the examiner (or the computer) with an indication of the 'ceiling' of the test-taker's ability, i.e. the level at which the candidate's language performance breaks down. The level check and probe phases are iterative processes. If the probes show that a candidate is able to perform at a probe level, the process of level check and probe recommences until the candidate's ceiling is found.
(4) *Wind-down*: During this phase the examiner (or the computer) returns the difficulty of the test to the level at which the candidate sustained preformance accurately, allowing the examinee to leave the testing situation with a positive sense of accomplishment. In non-adaptive tests, an examinee often 'works to failure' and leaves the testing situation feeling frustrated and dissatisfied.

Initially, ACTFL had hoped to present the reading passages as well as the items via computer, but because many of the passages included accompanying photographs, illustrations, and diagrams that proved difficult to display on standard IBM PC equipment (i.e. an IBM PC/XT machine), it was decided to utilise printed materials for presentatation of the reading passages and to use the computer for presentation of the test items and scoring of responses. The *MicroCAT Testing System* (Assessment Systems Corporation) was used to develop, administer, score, and analyse the computerised tests. As Dandonoli (1989) notes:

> MicroCAT contains stand-alone sybsystems for development, examination, assessment, management, and conventional testing. The development subsystem includes the capability to enter and edit items, generate special character fonts (including those reading from right to left), creating tests using pre-defined templates, and creating customized tests with the Minnesota Computerized Adaptive Testing Language.
> The examination subsystem administers the tests to examinees either singly or through a local area network. The assessment subsystem is used to analyze test items using conventional statistics as well as by estimating IRT [item-response theory] parameters using either the one- or three-parameter model. The management subsystem allows monitoring of tests

when used as part of a local area network, while the conventional testing subsystem governs the creation and analysis of conventional (i.e. non-adaptive) paper-and-pencil or computer-administered tests.

When ACTFL began development of the computerised adaptive reading comprehension test, the organisation recognised that foreign language tests in the receptive skills of both listening comprehension and reading comprehension were needed; however, the limitations of microcomputer floppy-disk technology made it impractical to think of using speech technology to develop a microcomputer-assisted test of L2 listening proficiency in the early part of the 1980s. The process of digitising, storing, and retrieving speech for audio-cueing of test items is a memory-hungry one, and it was possible to store only about three minutes of speech on a floppy diskette in the mid to late 1970s. In the early 1980s, however, two major advances in microcomputer and speech technology made the design of a microcomputer-based listening comprehension proficiency test not only imaginable but actually realisable: the development of speech digitising microchips and the availability of multi-megabyte hard disks for storage of the digitised speech (Dunkel, 1991).

The process of digitising, storing, and retrieving speech for audio-cueing of test items

During the 1980s, microcomputer-based speech technology emerged from its stone age with the development of powerful speech digitising microchips — e.g. the NeXT computer's 10 MIPS Motorola 56001 Digital Signal Processor (DSP). In simplest terms, speech digitising chips convert human sounds, input via a microphone, a compact disc (CD), or a traditional audiotape recorder, into digital information that can be stored on magnetic on laser-optical disks. By reversing the process (i.e. by reading the stored, digitised data on the disks and feeding it through a speaker or a headset), high quality human voice is reproduced and can be used to create various types of listening exercises containing spoken discourse at the level of words, phrases, and short statements/questions, or at the more extended level of conversations and minilectures. The quality of the voice output is excellent. In fact, the NeXT Computer System's DSP chip can generate CD-quality stereo sound (i.e. 44.1 kHz, 16-bit two-channel digital audio).

As microchips capable of digitising segments of prerecorded or *ad hoc* recorded speech were evolving, the storage capacity of microcomputers was increasing by leaps and bounds. Mega-storage hard cards and laser-optical disks became commercially available and increasingly commonplace, making possible the storage and retrieval of the memory-hungry voice files created with the digitising chips. The storage capacity, for example, of the NeXT computer's 256 megabyte read/write/erasable optical disk — a text-storage capacity equivalent to 300 to 400 books — has made the creation, storage, retrieval, and revision of digitised speech files a relatively simple process.

As a result of the constant research and development in the field of microcomputer-generated speech during the past decade, it is quite likely that audio-enhanced computer-assisted testing, and computer-assisted language learning (CALL) as well, will become the norm, rather than the exception, in the twenty-first century; one might say that CALL users are perched to leave the era of the 'silent' computer and enter the age of the 'talkies', just as our grandparents or great-grandparents made the transition from silent films to talking motion pictures. It is also likely that testing of L2 listening comprehension proficiency will come to include, as a matter of course, a digitised speech component and not just an audiotape component, as is the case with present-day tests such as the Test of English as a Foreign Language (TOEFL) and the Comprehensive English Language Test (CELT). In fact, development efforts at Brigham Young University (BYU) and The Pennsylvania State University (PSU) have already demonstrated the feasibility of designing and implementing computer-assisted adaptive listening tests. The BYU English as a Second Language Computerised Adaptive test (YESCAT), for example, contains both listening and reading-grammar components. The upgraded commercial version is known as COMPUTEST: ESL (Madsen, 1991).

The Development of a Prototype ESL Listening Comprehension Test

The remainder of this paper describes the research project begun at The Pennsylvania State University during the 1987–1988 academic year with federal funding provided by the International Research and Studies program of the United States Department of Education (DOE) to build a prototype ESL listening comprehension test, using speech digitising technology. The objectives of the ESL part of the project, and the basic application (i.e. program) logic and file structure of the test are described for the benefit of those interested or engaged in computerised test development, implementation, or use. Discussion of some issues related to the writing of the listening items is also touched upon.

The primary objectives in the ESL prototype development project (see Ariew & Dunkel, 1989) were the following: (1) to determine the hardware configurations and software applications needed to create and implement a computerised-adaptive listening comprehension test that would run on readily available IBM-PC equipment (e.g. an IBM-PC XT); (2) to design an appropriate application logic and file structure for the prototype; (3) to build an initial pool of test item types using the generic ACTFL listening guidelines (Appendix A) and Richards's (1985) taxonomy of listening skills (Appendix B). In sum, the overall goal of the DOE project was to determine whether a prototype computer-based ESL listening comprehension proficiency test could be designed for implementation on IBM personal computer (PC) hardware that would create, store, and retrieve digitised speech for audio-cueing of the test items.

PC hardware configuration and software applications for the ESL prototype

The following hardware was used to develop the application:

CPU — IBM XT/286
Memory — 640 KB RAM with 2 megabytes of extended memory
Operating System — DOS 3.3
Disk Capacity — 80 megabyte Seagate hard disk, 1.2 MB high-density floppy drive and a 360 KB floppy drive
Graphics Interface — IBM extended graphics monitor and extended graphics board
Sound Interface — IBM Voice Communications Subsystem and Operating System
Miscellaneous Hardware — IBM Proprinter 24 dot matrix printer, speaker, microphone, headset, tape drive, graphics equaliser, potentiometer, and mouse

The application program (i.e. the listening comprehension CAT) was developed using the following vendor software products:

dBase III Plus — an interpreted relational database language used in the application to store the results of each test taker's performance
IBM Interpreted Basic
PC Mouse Plus
PC Paint Plus
PC Paint Gallery
IBM Voice Communication Options Board and *Toolkit* software
Microsoft C

The design of an application logic and file structure for the prototype listening CAT

The prototype application can be employed by three types of users: test taker, test supervisor, and test designer. The test taker sits at the computer listening to the segments of speech and to questions about the utterances, reading the possible answer choices displayed on the computer monitor, and pressing a number key and then the ENTER key to indicate to the computer a response to a question. The test taker also has to provide demographic data at the beginning of the test, such as the number of years of experience with English, age, occupation, field of study, and other descriptive information.

The test supervisor may or may not be present during testing. If the test supervisor is present, he or she may assist in starting the application and handling the databases of student responses.

The test designer is the individual who enters the text and graphics that are displayed with each question and creates the portions of speech that will be played during the test. The test designer can also decide on the order of test questions given during a test. The order includes an algorithm that conditionally modifies the level of questions asked depending on the test taker's score at various points or proficiency levels in different parts of the test. The test designer can also analyse the test results using various functions of dBase III Plus.

Application Logic

The application consists of three modes of operation: Test mode, Design mode, and Analysis mode. The purpose of the Test mode of operation is to probe the test taker's English listening comprehension skills. Since the projected pool of test takers will possess diverse levels of listening skills, the test will have to tailor the questions to the test takers to allow the most meaningful and valid measurement of the test takers' skills. The difficulty of the test questions will be a function of the test taker's English listening skills and the success the test taker has achieved at various points during the test. The purpose of the Design mode of operation is to assist the test designer in creating, modifying and deleting tests and portions of tests such as questions or answers from the application file structure saved on disk. Lastly, the Analysis mode will allow the test results to be accumulated after the application has been completed and used by a number of test takers.

The test taker and the test supervisor use only the Test mode portion of the application, while the test designer can use the Design mode and Analysis mode of the design specifications. An overview of the three modes of operation and the various programs that comprise the three modes is necessary for a full understanding of the prototype test and its operation.

(a) Test Mode

Test mode is the portion of the application program that executes the listening comprehension test. The testing begins when the test taker or supervisor enters the word 'TEST' on the DOS command line. Test mode begins by displaying the First screen, which prompts the test taker to provide demographic information, such as, 'How many years have you studied English?' The test taker completes the fields and presses the ENTER key which results in the display of the directions in written and spoken form. A headset is used to listen to the speech during testing. After reading the directions, the test taker responds to a prompt by pressing any key to start the test.

The ESL form of the prototype is divided into three main divisions: (1) Detecting/Making Appropriate Responses to Questions Heard, (2) Recognising Synonymous Statements, and (3) Comprehending Dialogues/Conversations. The test begins with either a question, a statement, or a short monologue or dialogue produced by a native speaker. This is followed by another speaker who asks a question about the information just presented. In the Detecting/Making Appropriate Responses to Questions Heard section, for instance, the novice-high listener is asked to determine whether the response to a question heard is an appropriate or inappropriate one. For example, the test taker hears the question, 'How old are you, Mary?' and then hears the response: 'I live in New York'. The response is an inappropriate one. (A conversational situation, such as a visit to a doctor's office or to a restaurant is first established, and then several questions relating to the situation are posed.) The Detecting/Making Appropriate Responses to Questions Heard format crosses various levels of proficiency and yields different types of items depending on the proficiency level. An item in this section about a car accident, for example, asks the intermediate-high-level listener the question, 'When did the accident occur?' On the screen are displayed four answer choices:

(1) On Highway 101.
(2) She's out of danger.
(3) At around midnight.
(4) During a snow storm.

Of the four choices, the appropriate response is 'At around midnight'. (For additional examples of item frameworks and formats, see Ariew & Dunkel, 1989; Dunkel, 1991)

In general, after presentation of each speech sample, a list of answers from which the test taker has to select is displayed on the monitor. (The answers range from two to four choices, with two choices for the lower levels of proficiency, and four for the intermediate through superior levels.) The program then waits for the test taker to respond by typing an answer on the command line and pressing the ENTER key. The finalised program needs to respond to ten proficiency levels: novice-low, -mid, and -high; intermediate-low, -mid, and -high; advanced; superior; advanced-plus; and distinguished. To date, items for four of the ten levels have been designed.

At the initial levels of proficiency (novice-low through intermediate-low), the test taker may ask for a repetition of the question/statement/dialogue since the ACTFL guidelines acknowledge that beginners must often ask for repetition of information from speakers. For test takers at the upper levels of proficiency (intermediate to distinguished), no repetition will be allowed, and if the test taker does not respond after a predetermined period of time, a prompt is displayed stating that the test taker must answer within ten seconds. If the test taker does not do so within the allotted time, the answer is recorded as incorrect, and then the next question is displayed. Furthermore, at the bottom of every answer/question screen, there is a key that can be pressed to exit the test should the examinee wish to do so. If the test taker presses this key, a prompt appears, warning that the test will end if (s)he presses the key a second time. If the key is pressed again, the testing session is terminated; if the ENTER key is pressed, the test continues until the test taker's optimal level of listening proficiency is established with the aid of the testing algorithm. When the test has been completed, the test results are written to the appropriate dBase files and the last screen is displayed.

(b) Testing Algorithm

The testing algorithm is driven by testing rules that are provided from the Design mode portion of the application. The intent of the rule structure is to provide a way to tailor the selection of test questions which will not require changes in the application code. Further clarification of the semantics and syntax of the design are presently being established and will be inserted into the application at a later date. The algorithm will likely introduce another file type called Rule files and would require additional functions to be included in the Design mode portion of the application. At present the prototype is being driven by a mechanical algorithm set arbitrarily to a percentage 'success/failure' rate for items undertaken. The algorithm needs further refinement and should incorporate a model of Item Response Theory (IRT) into the design of the adaptive aspect of the test, and test development efforts beyond the stage of prototyping should include IRT as an integral component of the adaptive algorithm (see Madsen, 1991; Tung, 1986).

(c) Design Mode

The design mode is the portion of the application used to create, change and delete files in the file structure. It is used to add new tests, change, and/or delete tests. Design mode not only allows modifications to which questions are presented in which tests, but also allows modifications of each question by facilitating changes to the Voice file names in the Question record used for a test question. In a similar manner, the Display mode can also be changed from text to graphics, and the answer displayed can also be changed. This flexibility in modifying the user interface allows the testing of program logic using text mode, and the altering of the user interface to a bit-mapped graphics interface without changing the program logic. Furthermore, since the design is not specific to the language used or the contents on the screens, the design can be used for any language written in the Roman alphabet. The function of the Design mode also allows non-programmers to modify the tests without the assistance of a programmer. It should be noted that a test can also have screens of both text-only and text-and-graphics interspersed within the same test.

Design mode operates in the following way: the test designer types 'DESIGN' from the DOS command line, and the Design mode main menu is displayed. The test designer selects the proper function desired (e.g. #1 to select PC Paint to create graphics screens; #2 to record or play a Voice file; #3 to back up the system hard disk; or #4 to start dBase III Plus), and the data entry or sub-selection for that function is displayed. The test designer either completes the data entry screen or makes a selection from a function sub-selection.

Upon pressing ENTER, the test designer changes the appropriate file structure file, or is presented with a data entry panel if selection #1 (to select PC Paint to create graphics screens) is chosen. Upon successful completion of the data entry panel, the test designer has a choice of continuing with more changes or quitting and returning to the Design mode main menu. Another choice from the Design main menu is to quit and return to the DOS from the main selection panel. Each of the data entry panels in the Design mode portion of the application will provide appropriate error checking and the reporting of successful actions completed on the file structure.

(d) Analysis Mode

The Analysis function is currently under development. dBase III Plus has been found to be sufficiently robust to provide all the analysis functions needed to analyse the data collected during subject testing. dBase can accrue statistics such as the number of items attempted and correctly/incorrectly answered per level, and so forth. In addition, dBase maintains the file structure of the application.

File Structure

The file structure of the application provides a skeleton that integrates the various application programs. The files that are read and written by the application are not apparent to the test taker; however, the test designer must have a thorough understanding of the file structure. The test designer can use the Design mode functions to create, change and delete the various application files. Currently, five types of files have been identified as necessary to implement the application. The file types are:

— Voice files
— Test files
— Question files
— Graphics files
— dBase files

The following sub-sections contain details of the use, the internal format and the program functions that operate on the file types.

(a) Voice Files

Voice files contain the digitised representation of the speech phrases used by the voice communications board. A microphone must be attached to the voice communications board when invoking the Voice create function. Voice files are created by invoking the Design mode portion of the application and selecting the appropriate selection in the Design mode main menu to create or change a Voice file. After the Voice create program is invoked, the speech for the current question is recorded (via microphone or audiotape input), and stored in a Voice file, which is a DOS file and can be called up by the application during the test for playing the speech. Knowledge of the internal format of Voice files is not necessary at the application level. The Voice files are kept on the hard disk and can be accessed fast enough by BASIC to provide uninterrupted speech; thus, no extended memory is needed for storing the Voice files during the execution of the application.

Voice files can become quite large even for short durations of speech. For the present project, the average amount of disk space consumed for one minute of speech was 155 KB, plus or minus 40KB. This indicates that about 12 megabytes of disk space will be needed to store about an hour's worth of Voice files.

(b) Test Files

Test files are created, changed, printed, and deleted from within the Design mode portion of the application. The Test files contain the information needed by the Test portion of the application to execute a test. Specifically, a Test file is a sequential DOS file and contains the names of the Question files that can be accessed, the number of questions that can be used from each Question file, and the record numbers to be used from each Question file.

Test files can be created, changed, printed, and deleted by the test designer by making the proper selection from the Design mode main menu. After the test designer successfully selects a function from the selection menu, a data entry screen will appear. A separate data entry screen is used to create and change the current Test file. Upon successfully completing the data entry screen, the test designer presses ENTER and the operation on the current Test file is completed. At this point, the test designer is returned to the Design mode main menu.

(c) Directions Files

Directions files contain the information that the test taker needs to understand the type of item that will be presented and the response-input format (e.g. 'Press key #1, 2, or 3 to indicate the correct answer') that will be used. Within a set of items for a given level of proficiency, there may be a number of different directions keyed to the type of items being presented.

(d) Question Files

Question files can be created, changed, and deleted by the test designer from within the Design mode portion of the application and contain the information needed by the Test portion of the application to execute each question in the test. Specifically, a Question file is a random DOS file that contains twenty records. Each record contains four fields indicating the display mode of the current question, the Text or Graphics file name of the answer portion of the current question, and two fields containing the names of the two Voice files of the current question.

Question files are created, changed, and deleted by making the appropriate selection from the Design mode main menu. If the test designer chooses to change a Question file, then a data entry screen will appear. Upon successfully completing the data entry screen, the test designer presses ENTER and changes on the Question file are completed. The test designer is then returned to the Design mode main menu.

(e) Graphics Files

The Graphics files contain the graphic images necessary to 'paint' pictures on the screen that are stored in BSAVE format. These pictures are used to support comprehension of utterances at the lower levels of proficiency, as deemed appropriate, and may be incorporated into the answers to items. Test takers at the lower levels of proficiency are presented a greater number of graphics images during their testing session, as it is assumed that they will need more assistance in comprehension than higher-level test takers. The graphics images are created and modified by the test designer using PC Paint Plus and a mouse. The first implementation of the application uses only a few graphics screens created with 'clip art' from PC Paint Picture Gallery, which interfaces with the PC Paint Plus software; the remainder of the screens use only text to display the test answers and directions.

(f) dBase Files

dBase III Plus files are created automatically by the program at the end of each test and contain the demographic data of the test taker and the test score (i.e. proficiency level). dBase files are created by the final program (TestEND.BAS) in the structure. This program is called from the Test-driver program (TestDRVR.BAS) after the testing of the test taker has been completed, and passes the test taker's demographic data and test score data to the Test-end program (TestEND.BAS). The Test-end program then writes all the data to a dBase file using dBase III Plus. An analysis of the dBase files will include a statistical compilation of the test takers' scores, an indication of proficiency level, and demographic information. In addition, a compilation of each test taker's responses will allow for item analysis of the test questions, for assessment of the reliability indices of individual questions and the test as a whole. These latter functions will be performed within the Analysis mode.

Building an initial pool of prototype test items

Within each of the three main test divisions — (1) Detecting/Making Appropriate Responses to Questions Heard, (2) Recognising Synonymous Statements for Statements Heard, and Comprehending Dialogues/Conversation — the ACTFL listening guidelines were used to guide preparation of the items as far as possible. In addition, Richards' (1985) Taxonomy of Micro-skills in Conversational Listening were used to guide item writing. Although the ACTFL guidelines and Richards' taxonomy guided some aspects of the item writing, during preparation of the prototype items, it became clear that there is a pressing need for the creation of a model that captures the essence of developmental listening proficiency, that is, a model that relates input factors (e.g. linguistic simplifications and elaborations), listening tasks, learner variables, and socio- and psycholinguistic considerations influencing information processing. The availability of such a model would be of great assistance to those engaged in the writing of listening proficiency test items that relate to the various stages of listening comprehension development, e.g. as outlined in the ACTFL listening guidelines (Appendix A).[3]

Conclusion: Is It Feasible to Design and Implement a Listening CAT on PC Hardware

BYU's computerised adaptive listening comprehension test is already fully operational, and the one-year PSU project has also clearly demonstrated the feasibility of creating a CAT of L2 listening comprehension proficiency as a possible alternative to the traditional format of the audiotape cum paper-and-pencil listening test; however, during the course of conducting the Penn State project, it became clear that a good deal of further research and development into present-day and emerging technologies, as well as listening CAT construction and validation (see Stansfield, 1986) will need to occur before the full potential of the computer and speech technology can be tapped to design and deliver a test of L2 listening comprehension proficiency. Building a standardised metric of listening abilities in the foreign languages of common and less common use, as well as in English as a second language, is an exceedingly time-consuming and complex task, calling for the assembled input of designated experts in the disciplines of computer science (i.e. programmers, graphic artists, hardware/software experts), educational psychologists (i.e. those trained in testing and measurement), linguistics (i.e. both theoretical and applied), second language acquisition and pedagogy, cross-cultural communication, and even media production. Interdisciplinary team effort, both of an inter- and intra-institutional nature, will be required to bring to fruition the implementation of an L2 listening proficiency CAT.

It is anticipated that the microcomputers of the 1990s will have speech-generating processors built into their architecture, (much as the NeXT computer of today has). The inclusion of speech processors in system architecture will obviate the need to build and patch elements of disparate systems together to create a hybrid system that accepts, stores, and generates voice output. It will eliminate the need to fashion or use components that could pose problems of non-compatability with respect to the various software packages and hardware 'add-ons'. The IBM system used for the PSU-DOE project was a hybridised system, which contained numerous add-on boards (e.g. the voice communications board, and the extended graphics board), various vendor software packages (e.g. PC Paint and dBase III Plus), and non-IBM hard disks (e.g. the 80 MB Seagate hard disk). While the test does, indeed, run on such an amalgamated system, it is felt that a more integrated speech delivery system (e.g. the NeXT system) would pose fewer potential problems of compatibility and would eliminate possible system errors and crashes. It would, above all, simplify the development effort needed to create and implement the test. A system that comes equipped with speech input/output capabilities (e.g. the Macintosh or the NeXT systems) should prove more suitable and friendly environments for test development and delivery. IBM PC systems do not incorporate speech input/output as an integral, hard-wired component. This situation may change in the future, but for those beginning audio-enhanced PC-based test development, it would seem advantageous to build the test on a system that has a speech-digitising processor built in, and that has advanced graphics capabilities also hard-wired in the system.[4]

Notes to Chapter 12

1. It has been noted that the fastest growing segment of the school-age population in the United States is the English as a second language populace, with current estimates of the total number of students ranging up to 6.6 million students (U.S. Congress' Office of Technology Assessment, 1987).
2. To help determine the effectiveness of L2 training programs, measures of L2 proficiency are sorely needed, as asserted by Clark & Johnson (1982). These authors suggest that in the absence of 'external-to-program assessment instruments, oriented in both format and content to determining the student's ability to function appropriately in real-life language use settings, evaluation of the effectiveness or lack of effectiveness of the [foreign] language programs being conducted at individual institutions, or on a group basis, within the United States generally will continue to be both extremely difficult and of doubtful accuracy and validity' (p. 27).
3. Craig Chaudron, Grant Henning, and the present author are recipients of Mellon Collaborative Research Fellowships from the National Foreign Language Center at the Johns Hopkins University for development of a model of listening comprehension proficiency that is compatible with computer testing applications.
4. The IBM audiovisual connection (AVC) system for the PS2 module now also provides speech and image digitisation and storage. Its potential for use in CAT development should be explored.

Appendix A

ACTFL Listening Guidelines: General Description

Novice-Low — Understanding is limited to occasional words, such as cognates, borrowed words, and high-frequency social conventions. Essentially no ability to comprehend even short utterances.

Novice-Mid — Able to understand some short, learned utterances, particularly where context strongly supports understanding and speech is clearly audible. Comprehends some words and phrases for simple questions, statements, high-frequency commands and courtesy formulae about topics that refer to basic personal information or the immediate physical setting. The listener requires long pauses for assimilation and periodically requests repetition and/or a slower rate of speech.

Novice-High — Able to understand short, learned utterances and some sentence-length utterances, particularly where context strongly supports understanding and speech is clearly audible. Comprehends words and phrases from simple questions, statements, high-frequency commands and courtesy formulae. May require repetition, rephrasing and/or a slowed rate of speech for comprehension.

Intermediate-Low — Able to understand sentence-length utterances which consist of recombinations of learned elements in a limited number of content areas, particularly if strongly supported by the situational context. Content refers to basic personal background and needs, social conventions and routine tasks, such as getting meals and receiving simple instructions and directions. Listening tasks pertain primarily to spontaneous fact-to-face conversations. Understanding is often uneven; repetition and rewording may be necessary. Misunderstandings in both main ideas and details arise frequently.

Intermediate-Mid — Able to understand sentence-length utterances which consist of recombinations of learned utterances on a variety of topics. Content continues to refer primarily to basic personal background and needs, social conventions and somewhat more complex tasks, such as lodging, transportation, and shopping. Additional content areas include some personal interests and activities, and a great diversity of instructions and directions. Listening tasks not only pertain to spontaneous face-to-face conversations but also to short routine telephone conversations and some deliberate speech, such as simple announcements and reports over the media. Understanding continues to be uneven.

Intermediate-High — Able to sustain understanding over longer stretches of connected discourse on a number of topics pertaining to different times and places; however, understanding is inconsistent due to failure to grasp main ideas and/or details. Thus, while topics do not differ significantly from those of an Advanced-level listener, comprehension is less in quantity and poorer in quality.

Advanced — Able to understand main ideas and most details of connected discourse on a variety of topics beyond the immediacy of the situation. Comprehension may be uneven due to a variety of linguistic and extralinguistic factors, among which topic familiarity is very prominent. These texts frequently involve description and narration in different time frames or aspects, such as present, nonpast, habitual, or imperfective. Texts may include interviews, short lectures on familiar topics, and news items and reports primarily dealing with factual information. Listener is aware of cohesive devices but may not be able to use them to follow the sequence of thought in an oral text.

Advanced-Plus — Able to understand the main ideas of most speech in a standard dialect; however, the listener may not be able to sustain comprehension in extended discourse which is propositionally and linguistically complex. Listener shows an emerging awareness of culturally implied meanings beyond the surface meanings of the text but may fail to grasp social-cultural nuances of the message.

Superior — Able to understand the main ideas of all speech in a standard dialect, including technical discussion in a field of specialisation. Can follow the essentials of extended discourse which is propositionally and linguistically complex, as in academic/professional settings, in lectures, speeches, and reports. Listener shows some appreciation of aesthetic norms of target language, or idioms, colloquialisms, and register shifting. Able to make inferences within the cultural framework of the target language. Understanding is aided by an awareness of the underlying organisational structure of the oral text and includes sensitivity for its social and cultural references and its affective overtones. Rarely misunderstands but may not understand excessively rapid, highly colloquial speech or speech that has strong cultural references.

Distinguished — Able to understand all forms and styles of speech pertinent to personal, social and professional needs tailored to different audiences. Shows strong sensitivity to social and cultural references and aesthetic norms by processing language from within the cultural framework. Texts include theater plays, screen productions, editorials, symposia, academic debates, public policy statements, literary readings, and most jokes and puns. May have difficulty with some dialects and slang.

Appendix B

Richards' (1985) Taxonomy of Listening Skills

Micro-skills: Conversational Listening

1. ability to retain chunks of language of different lengths for short periods;
2. ability to discriminate among the distinctive sounds of the target language;
3. ability to recognise the stress patterns of words;
4. ability to recognise the rhythmic structure of English;
5. ability to recognise the functions of stress and intonation to signal the information structure of utterances;
6. ability to identify words in stressed and unstressed positions;
7. ability to recognise reduced forms of words;
8. ability to distinguish word boundaries;
9. ability to recognise typical word-order patterns in the target language;
10. ability to recognise vocabulary used in core conversational topics;
11. ability to detect key words (i.e. those that identify topics and propositions);
12. ability to guess the meanings of words from the contexts in which they occur;
13. ability to recognise grammatical word classes (parts of speech);
14. ability to recognise major syntactic patterns and devices;
15. ability to recognise cohesive devices in spoken discourse;
16. ability to recognise elliptical forms of grammatical units and sentences;
17. ability to detect sentence constituents;
18. ability to distinguish between major and minor constituents;
19. ability to detect meanings expressed in differing grammatical forms/sentence types (i.e. that a particular meaning may be expressed in different ways);
20. ability to recognise the communicative functions of utterances, according to situations, participants, goals;
21. ability to reconstruct or infer situations, goals, participants, procedures;
22. ability to use real-world knowledge and experience to work out purposes, goals, settings, procedures;
23. ability to predict outcomes from events described;
24. ability to infer links and connections between events;
25. ability to deduce causes and effects from events;
26. ability to distinguish between literal and implied meanings;
27. ability to identify and reconstruct topics and coherent structure from on-going discourse involving two or more speakers;
28. ability to recognise markers of coherence in discourse, and to detect such relations as main idea, supporting idea, given information, new information;
29. ability to process speech at different rates;

30. ability to process speech containing pauses, errors, corrections;
31. ability to make use of facial, paralinguistic, and other clues to work out meanings;
32. ability to adjust listening strategies to different kinds of listener purposes or goals;
33. ability to signal comprehension or lack of comprehension, verbally and nonverbally.

Micro-skills: Academic Listening (Listening to Lectures)

1. ability to identify purpose and scope of lecture;
2. ability to identify topic of lecture and follow topic development;
3. ability to identify relationships among units within discourse (e.g. major ideas, generalisations, hypotheses, supporting ideas, examples);
4. ability to identify role of discourse markers in signalling structure of a lecture (e.g. conjunctions, adverbs, gambits, routines);
5. ability to infer relationships (e.g. cause, effect, conclusion);
6. ability to recognise key lexical items related to subject/topic;
7. ability to deduce meanings of words from context;
8. ability to recognise markers of cohesion;
9. ability to recognise function of intonation to signal information structure (e.g. pitch, volume, pace, key);
10. ability to detect attitude of speaker toward subject matter;
11. ability to follow different modes of lecturing: spoken, audio, and audio-visual;
12. ability to follow lecture despite differences in accent and speed;
13. familiarity with different styles of lecturing: formal, conversational, read, unplanned;
14. familiarity with different registers: written versus colloquial;
15. ability to recognise irrelevant matter: jokes, digressions, meanderings;
16. ability to recognise function of nonverbal cues as markers of emphasis and attitude;
17. knowledge of classroom conventions (e.g. turn taking, clarification requests);
18. ability to recognise instructional/learner tasks (e.g. warnings, suggestions, recommendations, advice, instructions).

References

ACTFL Proficiency Guidelines (1986). Hastings-on-Hudson, NY: American Council on the Teaching of Foreign Languages.
ARIEW, R. & P. DUNKEL (1989) A prototype for a computer-based listening comprehension proficiency test. Final report to the U.S. Department of Education international research and studies program.
BACHMAN, L. F. & S. J. SAVIGNON (1986) The evaluation of communicative language proficiency: A critique of the ACTFL oral interview, *Modern Language Journal*, 70: 4, 380–390.
BELASCO, S. (1981) Aital cal aprene las lengas estrangieras, Comprehension: The key to second language acquisition. In H. WINITZ (ed.) *The Comprehension Approach to Foreign Language Instruction*. Rowley, MA: Newbury House.
BLOOM, L. (1970) *Language Development: Form and Function in Emerging Grammars*. Cambridge, MA: MIT Press.
BROWN, R. (1973) *A First Language: The Early Stages*. Cambridge, MA: Harvard University Press

CLARK, J. & D. JOHNSON (1982) *A Survey of Materials Development Needs in the Less Commonly Taught Languages in the U.S.* Washington, DC: Center for Applied Linguistics.

CONGRESSIONAL OFFICE OF TECHNOLOGY ASSESSMENT (1987) Trends and status of computers in schools: Use in chapter I programs and use with limited English proficient students. Washington: COTA.

DANDONOLI, P. (1987) ACTFL's current research in proficiency testing. In H. BYRNES & M. CANALE (eds), *Defining and Developing Proficiency Testing.* Lincolnwood, IL: National Textbook Co., 75–96.

— (1989) Computer-assisted testing of L2 reading and listening proficiency. Paper presented at the 23rd annual conference of the Teachers of English to Speakers of Other Languages, San Antonio, TX, March.

DUNKEL, P. (1991) Computerised testing of nonparticipatory L2 listening comprehension proficiency: An ESL prototype development effort. *Modern Language Journal*, 75, 64 73.

— (1986) Developing fluency in L2, *Modern Language Journal*, 70: 2, 99–106.

KRAMSCH, C. (1986) From language proficiency to interactional competence, *Modern Language Journal*, 70: 4, 366–372.

KRASHEN, S. (1982) *Principles and Practice in Second Language Acquisition.* Oxford, England: Pergamon Press.

LAHEY, M. & L. BLOOM (1977) Planning a first lexicon: Which words to teach first, *Journal of Speech and Hearing Disorders*, 42, 340–350.

LISKIN-GASPARRO, J. E. (1984) The ACTFL proficiency guidelines: A historical perspective. In T. V. HIGGS (ed.), *Teaching for Proficiency: The Organizing Principle.* Lincolnwood, IL: National Textbook Co.

LOWE, P. (1986) Proficiency: Panacea, framework, process? A reply to Kramsch, *Modern Language Journal*, 70: 4, 391–397.

MADSEN, H. (1991) Computer-adaptive testing of listening and reading comprehension: The Brigham Young University Experiment (pp. 237–257). In P. DUNKEL, (ed.) *Computer-Assisted Language Learning and Testing: Research Issues and Practice.* New York: Newbury House.

MicroCAT Testing System (1987). St Paul, MN: Assessment Systems Corporation.

MILLER, G. (1978) The acquisition of word meaning, *Child Development*, 49, 999–1004.

OMAGGIO, A. (1986) *Teaching Language in Context: Proficiency-oriented Language Teaching.* New York, NY: Heinle and Heinle.

RICHARDS, J. C. (1985) *The Context of Language Teaching.* New York, NY: Cambridge University Press.

RIVERA, C. (ed.) (1984) *Language Proficiency and Academic Achievement.* Avon, England: Multilingual Matters.

SCHULZ, R. (1986) From achievement to proficiency through classroom instruction: Some caveats, *Modern Language Journal*, 70: 4, 373–379.

STANSFIELD, C. W. (ed.) (1986) *Technology and Language Testing.* Washington, DC: Teachers of English to Speakers of Other Languages.

TUNG, P. (1986) Computerized adaptive testing: Implications for language test developers (pp. 11–28). In C. W. STANSFIELD (ed.) *Technology and Language Testing.* Washington, DC: TESOL.

WINITZ, H. (ed.) (1981) *The Comprehension Approach to Foreign Language Instruction.* Rowley, MA: Newbury House.

13 Answer Analysis, Feedback and On-Line Reference Help in CALL with Particular Reference to German

NIC WITTON
Macquarie University, Sydney, Australia

Introduction

This paper begins with a review of prior developments in CALL for German and then presents two programs of quite different kinds developed by the author. The first deals with German verb forms, but is not merely yet another drill and practice program. It allows the student to respond using a whole sentence and to compose the sentence making full use of German's relatively free word order. This is made possible by the program's answer judging capabilities. Furthermore, it combines the advantages of an expert system with those of an authoring package. This is accomplished by the use of an authoring module which allows the teacher to determine the language material to be used in the program, and also prompts the teacher for the grammatical information required by the answer judging routines. These routines enable the program to carry out a precise analysis of student responses and to provide feedback specific to these responses, in regard not only to verb forms, but also word order. Although the program is not communicative in its approach, it does not represent a commitment to grammar-translation as a main teaching strategy. It is intended to meet a need, felt mainly at university or college level, for relatively sophisticated programs which can help students reach an understanding of the linguistic systems of the language being studied.

The second program is a computerised German–English dictionary for students learning to read German for academic purposes, but it too goes beyond this basic function. Since it can accept the input of inflected word forms, which are analysed using algorithms similar to those of the first program, it can not only display a dictionary entry for the word being sought but also provide a grammatical analysis of the inflected form entered. Ambiguous forms are handled by interactive routines which ask the user questions about the word's syntactic environment in order to arrive at a correct analysis. Through these routines and through the program's explanations of how analyses were arrived at, the use of this tool becomes a valuable learning experience.

Review of CALL development for German

CALL (Computer-Assisted Language Learning) and, in particular, CALL in German have been well represented over the whole period of the development and expansion of CAI (Computer-Aided Instruction). The mainframe instructional systems in the U.S., such as the German language programs of *PLATO*, *TICCIT* (Hendricks *et al.*, 1983), etc., are well documented (John, 1984; Underwood, 1984: 41–42). The advent of the microcomputer brought about a burst of software development in CALL on both sides of the Atlantic: Higgins & Davies (1985: 9) list five projects in progress at British universities and colleges of higher education at the end of the 1970s. By contrast, the development of CALL in West Germany was still at the beginning stage around this time (Jung, 1985: 77ff.) and has been slower to develop. The prevailing attitude seems to have been one of cautious appraisal (Rüschoff, 1984: 26).

However, the project 'Mikrocomputer in der Spracharbeit' undertaken at the Goethe-Institute, Munich, did develop a series of programs (available commercially through Langenscheidt publishers) for the Apple II. These are similar to programs developed elsewhere in the early 1980s.[1] They make extensive use of graphics and include vocabulary programs, authoring programs for multiple-choice and other tests and for a cloze-type exercise, a travel quiz on Germany, a guessing game, etc. (Berger, 1985: 112–113). Two examples are *HANSI* (Schumann *et al.*, 1985) and *MORGENS GEHT FRITZ ZUR SCHULE* (Schäpers & Schäpers, 1984). The former program deals with the prepositions associated with certain verbs and adjectives, which are practiced via a game where the learner manipulates the controls to guide an owl carrying a nut to the appropriate nest, avoiding sundry obstacles. This program is typical of many early CALL programs where the game element predominates in what is really a rote learning exercise. In the latter example, the daily adventures of Fritz are used to teach the appropriate case for nouns following prepositions in German.

It provides analysis of the case forms entered by the student and has feedback and tutorial backup, but the language material used is integral to the program and cannot be varied by the teacher to suit, say, adult learners.

Advances in technology have provided the opportunity for incorporating audio and video media into interactive CALL programs (Howlett, 1986). Though the future in regard to interactive videodisc has already arrived in a number of places, especially in the U.S. — e.g. the German 'Gateway' course of the *VELVET* project (Rowe, 1984: 45) or the German programs of the MIT Athena Project (Kramsch *et al.*, 1985) — programs are also being developed for German elsewhere using audio cassette and videotape/cassette. Rüschoff (1985: 97–98, 1986: 208) describes listening comprehension exercises developed using a Tandberg audio cassette recorder controlled by a microprocessor (see also Last, 1984: 94ff.) and coupled with a microcomputer: the cassette recorder plays a short dialogue and then a question relating to this appears on the screen. Once the student types in an answer, the fast and accurate accessing system of the cassette recorder enables branching feedback to be provided in audio form. Students can also request backup information in written or audio form. This and other CALL programs developed at the Bergische University's Audio-Visual Media Centre in Wuppertal, West Germany, make use of written follow-up tasks which serve, amongst other things, to integrate the individual CALL work into wider classroom activities (Rüschoff, 1985: 99–100; 1986: 208–209). Beyond the cassette recorder, the student can now make use of an audio card allowing instant access to digitally recorded sound files stored on the hard disk. Audio cards also allow students to record and play back their own productions of the target language.

At the University of New South Wales (Sydney, Australia) comprehension programs in German have been developed using dedicated interactive videotape equipment. Students are shown sequences of film followed by multiple choice questions. Depending on the student's answer, the system can branch to any section of the tape (Bruce Matthews, Director of Technical Services, personal communication). Non-dedicated microcomputer control of video recorders is of course also possible via hardware controllers (Dahl & Luckau, 1985: 14). A number of authoring programs for various computers are also available.

The use of authoring programs for traditional CALL exercises has become widespread due to the amount of time required to produce reasonably sophisticated CALL programs of one's own and because they are quicker and easier to use than authoring languages (see Kenning & Kenning, 1983: 12; Underwood, 1984: 87ff.). An innovative example is the *DASHER* package (Pusack, 1983), which allows the student to enter a full sentence answer. Differences between this answer and the one expected by the teacher are indicated by 'pattern markup' —

dashes or other symbols replacing the relevant letters — but the program is not designed to analyse or explain errors made by the student, nor does it allow for major variations in word order. The popularity of authoring programs is reflected in the fact that the British CALL authoring packages *STORYBOARD*, *CHOICE-MASTER*, *VOCAB*, etc. are now being produced in MS-DOS versions (in six languages).[2] The Langenscheidt package INTERAKTIVES TESTPAKET (Schumann & Breitsameter, 1985) is now also available for MS-DOS machines. Mention should perhaps be made here of an inexpensive mainframe CALL authoring program and authoring language, EMU,[3] developed in Melbourne, Australia, by Sussex & Burr. It accommodates colour graphics and foreign character sets, can be interfaced with audio recorders, can monitor the progress of individual students and can be implemented on a variety of computers (see also Tuman, 1983: 61).

Other inexpensive authoring programs (both for the Macintosh) are *MACLANG* by J. Frommer, Harvard University and *PRIVATE TUTOR SYSTEM* (PTS) by S. Clausing, Yale University. Bickes & Scott (1987) describe how the latter program was used at the University of Western Australia to develop CALL materials integrated with a course using the Langenscheidt textbook *Deutsch Aktiv*. Pictures from the textbook are easily incorporated and PTS fully exploits the Macintosh's 'pull-down menus', making it 'suitable for use by mature learners who prefer a learner-controlled approach to language learning' (Bickes & Scott, 1987: 5). A further authoring program for the Macintosh (DRILL) is described in Blake & Duncan (1985).

A CALL Program in German with Full-Sentence Input

Background

The first of the two microcomputer programs to be presented here seeks to combine the advantages of an authoring program with those of a dedicated expert system. The latter type of program is complicated to design and to write, but can provide a high degree of help and information specifically tied to the learner's input — as, e.g. in the *TUCO* German programs in use at Ohio State University (Hope *et al.*, 1985: 31–32) — while authoring programs normally cannot. Authoring programs on the other hand are easy for teachers to use, requiring no programming knowledge on their part, and — unlike dedicated expert system programs where the language material is built in — allow them to provide the material to be presented to their students. A further aim in the design of the present program was to allow the student to enter a full German sentence with free choice of word order. Dedicated programs normally limit the student to gap-filling (the input of a single word or phrase) because of the complexity involved in providing diagnosis and feedback on more than one type of sentence element.

The idea of writing a CALL program in German to allow full-sentence input from the student yet still carry out detailed error analysis, to provide explanatory feedback and background information and — while dealing principally with the morphology of the German verb system — to be sensitive to basic features of German sentence structure, arose during a demonstration of a CALL exercise on French verb forms which was made using the authoring program *DASHER*, discussed above. The main point which stood out was the need to be able to cater adequately for acceptable variations in word order. For example, if the expected answer was (in English) *I watch TV in the evening*, the program would not accept *In the evening I watch TV*. It also seemed highly desirable to not merely 'pattern mark' deviations from the expected answer, but to provide detailed analysis of the student's response and explanatory feedback. In the demonstration referred to above, the only backup information available to the student was a sample sentence.

One must of course expect a trade-off between the ease of use for the teacher of an authoring program and the level of analysis and explanatory feedback which it can provide. The program to be presented here bridges this gap by utilising an authoring module which requires far more information from the teacher than merely a cue, an example response in German and vocabulary or other information for the student.

Part of this information comprises the constituent elements of the example response sentence: the particular verb form (divided into finite and non-finite constituents such as auxiliary and past participle or full verb and separable prefix), the 'verb complement' and 'free adverbials',[4] pronoun subjects/objects and noun (phrase) subjects/objects. It is the data stored in this form which enables the program to handle variations such as the one illustrated in the *I watch TV in the evening/In the evening I watch TV* example mentioned above. Having stored these as discrete elements, it can identify them — using its matching routine (see below), if necessary — wherever these elements occur in the student's response.

The capability of recognising elements wherever they occur is of particular importance in a German CALL program because of the fundamental differences in the arrangement of sentence elements in German and English. For example, in English, the sequence of subject before finite constituent of the verb constitutes a declarative clause (Halliday, 1985: 74), whereas in German it is solely the positioning of the finite constituent of the verb as second element in the sentence which does this (Schulz & Griesbach, 1970: 393). German also has greater freedom in the choice of the first element in the sentence. While English heavily favours the subject and it is least likely that the direct object of the verb will occupy initial position (Halliday, 1985: 45), almost any sentence element can come first in a German sentence, including the direct object (Hoberg, 1981: sect. 2.2.2). An example from a newspaper may illustrate this point:

> Eine unendliche Folge von Zusammenstößen...hatte Carters Sicherheitsberater Brzezinski vor wenig mehr als zehn Jahren vorausgesagt; ... Sowjets wie Amerikaner reizt die Aussicht darauf heute nicht mehr. (*Die Zeit* 7/15/88: 3)

In English (keeping the object first, as in German):

> An unending series of conflicts ... Carter's security adviser Brzezinski had predicted only a little more than ten years ago; ... Soviets and Americans alike the prospect of this no longer attracts.

It is highly desirable that a CALL program in German with full-sentence input should allow students the freedom to make use of this aspect of the language. Students can also be reminded of it if the teacher places an appropriate item other than the subject in the first position in the example response. The program will still accept a student response with the subject first but will present the teacher's version for comparison.

Other information provided by the teacher comprises details relating to the verb form of the particular sentence: the tense, mood and voice required, details regarding the auxiliary verb (if one is involved), the infinitive and other basic forms of the lexical verb and, if no auxiliary is involved, a paradigm of the required tense/mood. This information enables the program to carry out specific error analysis on the verb forms in the student's response and also to give feedback which is keyed exactly to the error made. In addition, general background information is always available to the user (see below).

Something the teacher does not have to provide and which authoring programs often call for is a list of anticipated errors. These are taken care of as types by the analysis module, thus avoiding the need for the teacher to anticipate them for each individual sentence. Types of errors covered include word order (discussed in more detail below), wrong agreement, incorrect use of tense, mood or voice, use of the wrong auxiliary, of an inappropriate imperative form, treating a strong verb as if weak and vice versa, use of incorrect vowel alternation in strong verbs, etc.

The operation of the program may perhaps best be illustrated by following a sample student response through the various processing stages. Students can be asked to provide a response to a question in German or translate an English sentence, using a particular tense. The program supports all the German tenses (indicative and subjunctive, active and passive). The teacher can also provide vocabulary hints or other information for each sentence. To illustrate some of the features of the program, let us imagine an exercise where the student is asked to use the pluperfect indicative in translating a sentence from a story already treated in class:

On Wednesday, the bus had stopped in front of my house.

The example response is:

Am Mittwoch hatte der Bus vor meinem Haus gehalten.

and the student responds with:

Mittwochs, der Bus ist gehaltet bei mein Huas.

In the next four sections, the workings of the program will be described with reference to the above example of a student-generated response.

Error analysis

The first check the program makes is for the expected finite constituent of the verb (here: the auxiliary *hatte*). Not finding it, it carries out a check for other auxiliary forms and finds *ist*. This results in the following message to the student:

The verb 'halten' forms its past compound tenses with 'haben' (not with 'sein').

The student is then presented with the following menu:

Do you want to

(1) Replace a word or phrase in your sentence with another?
(2) Retype your whole sentence now?
(3) See how the Pluperfect Indicative is formed before changing your sentence?
(4) See all the forms of the auxiliary needed to form the Pluperfect Indicative of 'halten' before changing your sentence?
(5) See the principal parts of the verb 'halten' before changing your sentence?
(6) See General Information on the German Verb System before changing your sentence?

Let us assume that the student chooses Option 1 and decides to replace *ist* with *hat*. This results in the message:

The Pluperfect Indicative of 'halten' is formed with the Past Indicative of 'haben' as the auxiliary verb.

Your form 'hat' is not the Past Indicative, but the Present Indicative.

The same menu as above is again presented. If the student is not sure of the terminology used in the message, explanations with examples can be consulted by choosing Option 6. This time the student substitutes the correct form *hatte* and the program indicates that it is correct.

The next item checked for is the past participle. The student's form *gehaltet* now results in the message:

The verb 'halten' is a strong verb not a weak verb.

Do you want information on how to form 'strong' past participles?

The student answers 'yes' and the following information is displayed:

Your sentence: Am Mittwoch hatte der Bus gehaltet bei mein Huas.

The Past Participle of a Regular 'Strong' Verb is formed by adding a prefix ('ge-') and a suffix ('-en') to a special stem of the verb:

e.g. INFINITIVE   PAST PARTICIPLE
     Stem + en   ge + Stem + en

     singen   (to) sing   gesungen   (has) sung
     fahren   (to) drive   gefahren   (has) driven
     schlafen (to) sleep   geschlafen (has) slept
     schreiben (to) write   geschrieben (has) written

Note: Some 'strong' verbs have the same stem vowel in the Past Participle as in the Infinitive. Most do not.

If the student cannot remember the form of the particular verb, it can be looked up under Option 5.

Although not demonstrated in this sentence, the program checks for wrong agreement between verb and (expected) subject and also picks up errors which are related to the use of the German grapheme 'Eszett' (ß). Two examples of feedback on the latter, where the student's form diverges from the expected form 'haßt' are:

1. (Your finite verb form: 'hasst')

'Double s' is always spelt: ß unless there is a short vowel immediately preceding AS WELL AS an 'e' immediately following. Then it is spelt: ss

e.g. aßen   iß   ißt   essen

ließen	laß	läßt	lassen
beißen	beiß	beißt	bissen
Straße			Tasse

2. The stem ('hass-') of your verb form: 'hasset' would be correct if the ending were correct.

   That is to say, the 'double s' form: 'ss' is correct for the ending you have used, however ...

   The ending: 'et' is incorrect.

   When looking at the information on the next screen, please pay particular attention to the Notes section.

(The program then supplies detailed information on how various types of German weak verbs form their present tense).

After the form of the verb has been checked, the program turns its attention to the arrangement of the constituent elements of the sentence. The first element in the sentence is checked first. This is necessary, since the positioning of the finite constituent of the verb as first or second element in the sentence has the same importance in German in determining the sentence type (Helbig & Buscha, 1975: 499) as the relative order of subject and finite constituent of the verb has in English (Quirk & Greenbaum, 1973: 170). In the sample student response there is, however, no element which exactly matches the expected initial element *am Mittwoch*. At this point, a matching routine — described in the next section — is invoked.

Matching

Even though the student input is guided, there are obviously going to be variations from the expected response. Simple examples are typographical errors such as the transposed letters in the sample student's *Huas* for *Haus*, or spelling errors such as the failure to observe the German custom of capitalising nouns. Since German is an inflecting language, there will also be errors in case endings such as the sample student's *mein* for the expected *meinem*. Whole words may be missing (as in the sample student sentence's *mittwochs* for the expected *am Mittwoch*) or non-expected vocabulary may be used (e.g. *bei* for *vor*). A further problem is presented by certain German prepositions which can appear in either a contracted or expanded form, e.g. 'in the' could be either *in dem* or just *im*. If the student types in something completely incomprehensible, the program reports that it could not find anything like what it was expecting and then presents the student with the menu reproduced above under the heading 'Error Analysis'.

To deal with the less drastic variations, the program contains a special matching routine which attempts to find correspondences in the student's sentence for the constituent elements of the example response. It begins by looking for a match of the initial letter of the element being sought, allowing for errors in capitalisation. If the element is a phrase rather than a single word, it first tries the initial letter of the first word in the phrase but can, if no match is found, try to match the initial letter of each subsequent word. When an initial letter match is found, the two words are compared, allowing for letters which are transposed, missing (e.g. *sh* for *sch*) or additional letters (e.g. incorrect doubling of consonants). If the words match (within a set tolerance), the program works backwards and/or forwards from that word to match the other words in the phrase — allowing for missing or different words, the above-mentioned contracted or expanded forms of prepositions and one or two other special cases such as articles. In the sentence under consideration, the program will successfully match *am Mittwoch* with *mittwochs* and *vor meinem Haus* with *bei mein Huas*. It would not, however, match *am Mittwoch* with, e.g. *am Dienstag* and in such cases, after the rest of the sentence has been dealt with, it merely displays for the student the expected elements it has not been able to match, together with the unmatched portions of the student's response. The student may well have used an acceptable alternative and, if not sure, would need to check with the teacher.

When a match has been found, the original cue and the student's response sentence appear on the screen, and then the student is given the opportunity of making a change:

Do you want to

(1) make some change in: 'mittwochs'?
(2) see a suggested replacement?

The reason for offering this choice is that students can very often provide the correct answer once their attention is drawn to the fact that an error has been made in a particular word or phrase. Even when they are unable to do so, students using the program have been observed trying repeatedly to correct the error themselves, rather than opting for the second choice. This is all the help the program can offer in respect to sentence elements other than the verb, as specific feedback is limited to verb forms.

Our student replaces *mittwochs* by *am Mittwoch*, so that the response sentence now reads:

Am Mittwoch der Bus hatte gehalten bei mein Huas.

Note that the program automatically removes extraneous commas, such as the one the student had originally put after the first element. Before matching, it also removes the sentence-initial capitalisation, unless it is on the first letter of a form of *Sie* or of an (expected) noun. In cases of doubt, it asks the student. For example, if the student's response begins with *Ihre* and the expected response contains both a form of *ihr-* ('her/its') and of *Ihr-* ('your'), it will ask the student if the first word is intended to correspond to English 'your'.

Having a firm first element to go on, the program now turns its attention to the arrangement of the other elements of the sentence. This aspect of its analysis capability is described in the next section.

Word order

The program is sensitive to the placing of those elements of the German sentence which regularly occupy fixed positions:

— the finite constituent of the verb,
— the non-finite constituent of the verb (infinitive, past participle, separable prefix),
— verb complements,
— personal pronouns.
(Helbig & Buscha, 1975: ch. 3.2; Schulz & Griesbach, 1970: E 60ff.)

The positioning of these elements, with the exception of the first, can sometimes be context dependent (Helbig & Buscha 1975: ch. 3.2; Schulz & Griesbach, 1970: E 60ff.). When variations from the basic positions occur in student responses, the program advises that these are 'marked' — not incorrect — options within the system. However, since the position of the finite constituent of the verb determines the sentence type — polar (yes/no) question, statement, command/request, (or subordinate clause) — it is always fixed (Helbig & Buscha, 1975: Ch 3.2; Schulz & Griesbach, 1970: E 60ff.). The program now supplies the following feedback in relation to the positioning of the verb constituents *hatte* and *gehalten* in our student's sentence: *Am Mittwoch der Bus hatte gehalten bei mein Huas*.

> In a statement-type sentence or an information question the finite part of the verb (here: 'hatte') should be the second element in the sentence, i.e. it should come after: 'Am Mittwoch'.
>
> Unless an element is added as an afterthought or is to be highlighted by being placed outside the Verb Bracket,[5] the non-finite part of the verb (here: 'gehalten') should be the last element in the clause or sentence.

Since this sentence contains no personal pronouns and no verb complement, it only remains for the matching routine to deal with the deviant form of the student's free adverbial *bei mein Huas*. The positioning of free adverbials and noun subjects/objects is always context dependent and the program makes no comment on these.

General information

Apart from the feedback information provided after error analysis and exemplified above, the student can access general information on the morphology of the German verb system as a whole or on the form required in a particular sentence, before or after attempting an answer. The top of the screen always presents the following options:

Question n of 10   HELP (Information)   — Type X and press Enter
              HELP (Instructions)   — Type Y and press Enter
              STOP   — Type Z and press Enter

If the first option is chosen, the following menu appears:

[Information Options]

1. Names of Tenses and how each is formed (incl. Indicative, Subjunctive, Passive, Imperative)
2. Full Verbs: Present and Past Forms (Indicative and subjunctive)
3. Auxiliary Verbs: Present and Past Forms (Indicative and subjunctive)
4. Specific Information on the Verb Form in this sentence.
5. Return to doing exercise.
6. Stop doing exercise altogether.
   Please type in the number of the option you want and press <Enter>

Options 1–3 offer some 25 screens of general background information on terminology and German verb formation, with examples in German and English, while the fourth offers information directly relevant to the task in hand. If this latter option is selected in relation to our sample sentence, the student is then asked:

Do you want to

(1) See how the Pluperfect Indicative is formed?
(2) See the principal parts of the verb: 'halten'?
(3) Return to the Information Options List?

The choice of Option (1) results in the following information being displayed:

The Pluperfect Indicative is formed with the Past Indicative of 'haben'/ 'sein' as the auxiliary verb plus the Past Participle of the main verb.

Examples:	Es hatte ... geholfen.	It had helped
	Er hatte ... mitgemacht.	He had joined in.
	Es war ... verschwunden.	It had disappeared.
	Sie war ... abgereist.	She had left on a trip.

In general, verbs which don't have a direct object and also express a change of location or change of state/condition form their Perfect and Pluperfect Tenses with 'sein'.

'sein' and 'werden' also form these tenses with 'sein'.

If the tense required does not use an auxiliary verb (i.e. present or past tenses), the student has the option of seeing, for example, all the present indicative forms of the lexical verb. The choice of Option 2 results in the following display:

Infinitive:	halten
3rd Singular Present:	hält
3rd Singular Past:	hielt
3rd Singular Perfect:	hat ... gehalten

The comprehensive feedback and general background information features provided by the program have been designed so that most students can work problems out for themselves. It is this aspect of the program which is intended to promote cognitive learning. The program is an example of a 'strong drill' which 'challenges the students' grasp of principles and teaches through helpful correction of error' (Hope *et al.*, 1984: 17). In a communicatively oriented course it could be utilised at the stage which lays the foundations for the ability to communicate ('Stufe B: Grundlegung von Verständigungsfähigkeit,' Krüger, 1981: 22).

Computerised Dictionary and Word Form Analyser for Readers of German for Academic Purposes

Background

This program makes use of a similar degree of analytic capability but applied to a completely different area of CALL. It represents a tool for the student who only needs a reading knowledge of German — usually for study and research in other fields — and takes the form of a computerised dictionary combined with a word-form analyser. The latter module of the program achieves, by somewhat different means and on a microcomputer, the reverse of the output of the *MOLEX-Generator* developed for mainframe use in the Institut für deutsche Sprache, Mannheim (Kolvenbach, 1980). When the basic form of a word is entered, the *MOLEX-Generator* generates all the inflected forms of that word. It does this by combining lists of forms. The basic form list keys each entry to a word class and inflection class code. For example, the entry for the German verb *fahren* is: 'fahren (V 130).' A paradigm list then supplies the various stems of the verb class 130, each followed by a series of numbers, e.g. 'fuhr 43 44 45 46 47 48.' Each of these corresponds to an entry in an inflection list, e.g. 44 is the ending *-st*. This ending is followed by a code showing that it is 2nd person singular, past tense, indicative mood, active voice (Kolvenbach, 1980: 64). One of the applications of the program is the compilation of a full-form lexicon to serve as the basis for the morphosyntactic description of texts. Another is to generate all the forms of a particular word to aid in searching for occurrences in the Institute's computer corpora (Kolvenbach & Teubert, 1983: 43).

In the program to be presented here, the input is the inflected form of a word and the output is the basic form. A morphosyntactic analysis is also performed, but not on the basis of manually prepared lists.

Most universities offer reading courses in German for students and researchers who need to be able to read German books and articles in their field. Anyone who has taken one of these courses will know that until a considerable amount of experience has been built up, most of the reader's time is spent not on reading but on searching through the dictionary. Dictionary use is complicated by the fact that German is an inflecting language and very often the form of a word on the page is different from the basic form which is listed in the dictionary. The noun *die Masse*, for example, is singular and is listed under this form; *die Busse*, however, is plural and is listed under *Bus*. To take a less simple example, a student coming across *das Aufgefundene* in an archaeological article will recognise it as 'the' preceding a noun, since German obligingly capitalises its nouns, but will not be able to find this noun in the dictionary since it is a nonce formation: an adjectival noun made from the past participle of the verb *auffinden*. Often, even when the dictionary search is successful, insufficient grammatical knowledge may prevent readers from recognising the function of the form of the word they have in front of them. And sometimes the same form can have different functions, so that it is the syntactic environment which determines which function is realised in a particular case: for example, the form *begrenzte*, like its counterpart in English ('limited'), can function either as a verb or as an adjective. In some circumstances, problems such as these can take some time to solve or can cause the meaning of a text to be misconstrued.

The present program was especially designed to aid such non-proficient readers. Its purpose is to free them to a great extent from the time-consuming and often frustrating search for words and forms in the dictionary and the grammar book. The program differs from a computerised dictionary *per se* in two ways: first, it accepts inflected forms of words, so that the user need not know or try to deduce the usual dictionary form of the word. Second, after displaying the dictionary entry for the word, it can provide a precise morphosyntactic analysis of the particular (inflected) form of the word keyed in by the user. There is also a reference grammar. Figure 13.1 gives an idea of the major components of the program.

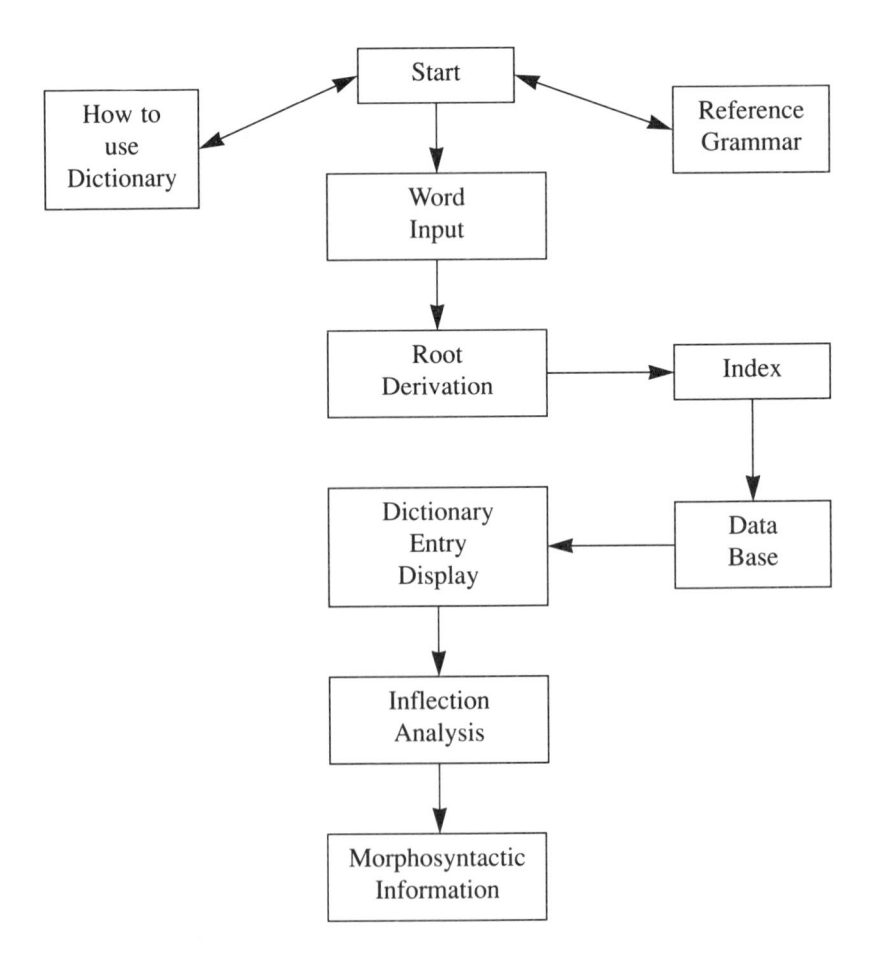

FIGURE 13.1

Lemmatisation

The key fields of the records in the database contain the lemmata (here: roots) of the words in the program's lexicon. When the user enters a word, the program first checks against the index to see whether it is, in fact, the same as the root form. This is often so for singular nouns, e.g. *der Putsch*, where *Putsch* is the root form to which inflections are added. If the user has entered a root form, the program can proceed directly to the display of the dictionary entry, the data for which is held in the corresponding record in the database. If not, the root must be derived from the inflected form which the user has entered.

In German the root can be modified by prefixes, infixes and/or suffixes as well as by stem vowel variation. Examples are the past participle prefix *ge-*, which can also be infixed as in *aufgefunden*, the *zu* ('to') of the infinitive, which can be infixed, as in *aufzufinden*, and suffixes such as the comparative *-(e)r* and superlative *-(e)st*, which are similar to those in English (e.g. 'lar*ger*', 'lar*gest*'). Vowel variation includes modification by Umlaut, e.g. *Vater* ('father') changes to *Väter* ('fathers') in the plural (like English 'mo*u*se/m*i*ce'). Umlauting also occurs in verbs, adjectives and adverbs. Another type of vowel variation is vowel alternation, which is also a feature of English, e.g. 's*i*ng/s*a*ng/s*u*ng.' Finally, there is the capitalisation of nouns formed from adjectives or verb forms, which was illustrated above, and the modification of the roots of nouns, verbs and adjectives by the addition of inflectional endings of various kinds.

The program proceeds by removing letters which could be endings from the inflected word entered by the user, at the same time checking for umlauting. After each removal, it checks the result against its index of roots. Vowel alternation is handled by 'pointer' records in the database whose key fields contain the root with the alternate vowel and which 'point' to the main record. There are subsidiary routines to deal with the prefixes, infixes and capitalisation phenomena mentioned above. When a match for a root is found in the index, the program uses information from the database to display a dictionary entry for the word.

Homographic roots, e.g. *führ-*, which could come either from the verb *fahren* ('go/drive') or the verb *führen* ('lead'), are flagged in the database. If the user enters the inflected form *führe*, for example, the program advises that it could come from either of the two verbs, and the two dictionary entries can be viewed in turn. Apart from the dictionary meanings, the user can also call for an analysis of the forms (see below) to help decide which of the two lexemes is the one which best fits the context of the text being read.

Lexicon

If the word being sought is not in the database, the program cannot, of course, supply a dictionary entry for it. However, this limitation is not as fundamental as might appear at first glance. This is because of the way the words included in the database have been selected. The selection has been made using the results of computer word-counts of large and varied text corpora — in particular that of Erk (1972–1982) and, to a lesser degree, that of Siliakus (1974). Erk's corpus comprises a selection of three texts of equal length from each of 34 different subject areas in both the humanities and the sciences, totalling 250,000 words. His word list includes all words with an absolute frequency of 10 or greater and totals approximately 2,500 words. According to Erk, this is sufficient to cover over 80% of the vocabulary of relevant texts (Erk, 1975: 7). The coverage may even be better, considering that users also often know technical vocabulary in their field and soon learn to recognise the German forms of 'international' words (e.g. *die Philosophie*).

Database

The primary function of the database is to provide the information for the German–English dictionary entries which are displayed on the screen. These comprise a headword, basic grammatical information and the most common of the word's possible meanings, each illustrated by an example sentence in German with an English translation. The display for the verb *auffinden* looks like this:

BASIC FORM: AUFFINDEN   TYPE: verb
OTHER BASIC FORMS: findet ... auf, fand ... auf, hat ... aufgefunden
MEANING: To locate, discover

> ohne die genaue Lage aufzufinden
> without locating the exact position

Press E for Form Analyser
Press X for Options List
Press Spacebar to continue using the Dictionary

This is a relatively simple entry as there are no further meanings. Entries can extend over several screens, in which case the user can page backwards and forwards.

The 'Basic Forms' are those which are needed to reconstruct any desired form of the word. If the word is a noun, they are the nominative and genitive singular and the nominative plural case forms. With adjectives and adverbs they are the positive, comparative and superlative degree forms. With verbs, as above, they are the infinitive and the third person singular present, past and perfect tense forms. For users with some knowledge of the language, this may be all that is needed for them to be able to identify the form of the word in question; others will perhaps wish to use the 'Form Analyser' — i.e. the module of the program which provides an exact morphosyntactic analysis of the form of the word. This module contains analysis routines which, among other things, use these basic forms and also additional information from the database in order to achieve a virtual 100% accuracy rate (as one would expect from a program operating on a known lexicon). This additional information includes the flagging of irregular verbs and of verbs whose present tense singular or plural has the same form as their past participle (e.g. *belehrt* or *marschiert* and *verfahren* or *begeben*).

Morphosyntactic analysis

This analysis of the form of the word can be requested by the user after viewing its dictionary entry. It is not a 'brute force' process using manually prepared lists of individual forms, endings and their associated morphosyntactic characteristics, as in the case of the *MOLEX-Generator* cited above. The initial step is similar, in that the pointer records (see above) in the database parallel the *MOLEX-Generator*'s paradigm list. However from then on there is virtually no individual coding of forms. The analysis module is divided into sub-modules, each dealing with a particular word class (nouns, verbs, etc.). These are further divided, each section dealing with a particular inflection. If necessary, these are further subdivided, e.g. in the case of verbs, to deal with different subclasses (such as strong/weak). Thus whole classes (or subclasses) of words can be dealt with by algorithm on the basis of the normal formation rules for German inflections. (Lists are only used for some very few highly irregular forms.)

To take a simple example: if the user enters the word *folgte* ('followed'), the program first removes the *e* and the *t* in order to derive the root *folg*, finds the corresponding record in the data base and displays the dictionary entry for the verb *folgen*. If a form analysis is requested, the analysis module knows from the 'basic form' information in the record that the verb belongs to the class of weak verbs which form their past tense by adding *-t* plus various endings to the root. The subsection of the module dealing with this inflection of this class of verbs then provides the relevant message regarding the form *folgte*, namely, that it can be either first or third person singular of the past tense of the verb *folgen* and either indicative or subjunctive. This information is accompanied by illustrative examples in German and English.

A more complicated example is that of *Aufgefundene*, mentioned earlier (see 'Background' and 'Lemmatisation' sections above). The message for this word is as follows:

> Regarding your word 'Aufgefundene':
>
> It has the adjective ending -e but the capital letter shows that its main function is that of a noun.
>
> It is derived from the verb 'auffinden.'
>
> The -ge- and the -en ending of the stem show that it is the past participle (Engl.: '-ed/-t/-en').
>
> Compare: der Vor*ge*lad*e*n*e*   das Ab*ge*schaff*ene*
>   the summonsed (person)   the (thing/s) abolished
>
> If you want further information to assist in determining what function is indicated by the adjective ending -e, select option E from the options offered below.
>
> Press E for specific information on the adjective ending,
> Press D to see dictionary entry again,
> Press X for Options List
> Press Spacebar to continue using dictionary.

If the user selects option E, he/she is presented with the question and table as seen in Figure 13.2.

Because the combination of the endings on these determiners (articles, demonstratives, possessives, etc.) with the endings on adjectives in a German noun phrase signals the function of the phrase, the answer to the above question enables the program to deduce the possible function or functions of the adjectival noun *Aufgefundene* in the sentence the student is reading. (There are further screens to deal with other determiners and their endings.) The choice of column 1, for example, results in the message:

> Your adjectival noun: 'Aufgefundene' is singular.
> It is also Nominative (subject of verb, or complement of verb like 'sein')
>
> Compare:
> Dieser interessant*e* Bericht ist erst kürzlich erschienen.
> This interesting report has only recently appeared.
> Es war von diesem wichtigen Ereignis der einzig*e* Bericht.
> It was the only report of this important event.

Does the phrase containing your adjectival noun: Aufgefundene begin with one of the following words?

1	2	3	4	5
der	die	das	alle	eine
dieser	diese	dieses		keine
jener	jene	jenes		meine
jeder	jede	jedes		deine
aller		alles		seine
mancher		manches		ihre
solcher		solches	solche	unsere
welcher		welches	welche	unsre
irgend-		irgend welches	irgend- welche	euere eure
derselbe	dieselbe	dasselbe		Ihre
derjenige	diejenige	dasjenige		
einiger		einiges		
folgender		folgendes		
sa"mtlicher		sa"mtliches	sa"mtliche	

If so, type in the number of the column in which the word occurs.
If not, press <RETURN>.

FIGURE 13.2

Interactive Routines

The above question put to the user is one example of the interactive routines used by the program to solve the problem of inflectional forms which, out of their syntactic context, are functionally ambiguous. These routines put specific questions to the user regarding the syntactic environment of the word being analysed. The program is thus utilising both its 'knowledge' of German morphosyntax and the (non-artificial!) intelligence and analytical capabilities of the user in order to solve the ambiguity. To further illustrate how these routines work, let us take the example of *begrenzte*, mentioned above under 'Background.' This word-form could be (i) a past tense form of the verb *begrenzen* or (ii) an adjective formed from the past participle of this verb. The interactive routine firstly makes the novice reader aware that the form is potentially ambiguous. When the ambiguity has been resolved with the reader's help, the normal analysis routines take over once more. This interactive routine goes as follows:

> In your text, is 'begrenzte' being used
>
> (1) as an adjective
> e.g. Das hier *behandelte* Projekt war interessant.
> The project discussed here was interesting.
> (2) as a finite verb
> e.g. Der Beitrag *behandelte* ein neues Projekt.
> The article discussed a new project.
>
> Please type 1 or 2 as appropriate.

If it is functioning as an adjective, the subsequent interaction and analysis is similar to that shown above in relation to the adjectival ending on *Aufgefundene*. If it is a verb, the program provides the information that it is past tense, either subjunctive or indicative and either first person or third person. Examples with English translations are provided to help the user decide which is applicable to the text at hand.

Reference grammar

The on-line reference grammar contains a section on German inflections for readers, organised to show the various functions a particular inflection can have. It also contains sections on the inflectional systems of German adjectives, determiners, nouns and verbs.

Interactivity, Student Control and Individualisation

The two programs described above fall fairly clearly into Higgins' two program types: 'magister' and 'pedagogue' (Higgins, 1983: 4). The dictionary program — like the pedagogue of ancient times — is available at the beck and call of the student and represents a tool. However, as can be seen by the kind of detail given in the grammatical analyses reproduced above and by the way in which the questions are put to the user in the interactive routines, the program is indeed more than just a reference tool, i.e. a dictionary where the user need not know how to derive the basic form of an inflected word and a grammar which is 'always open at just the right place' (Hammond & Simmons, 1987: 100). The manner in which it presents its information and interacts with the user gradually imparts insights into various aspects of the morphosyntactic system of German.

The user is thus acquiring knowledge and understanding of the German language while making use of the tool. The user also has control over the way the program is to be used: purely as a dictionary, as a dictionary cum word-form parser, as a reference work or any combination of these.

The verb form and word order program has alleviated the more forbidding attributes of the 'magister.' Though it still largely determines the manner in which this particular body of knowledge is to be acquired, the program affords the student a large measure of control: The student can select the level of exercise from those made available by the teacher, decide on which exercises to do and in which order and can at any time stop the exercise, change to another or ask for information. When an exercise is completed, the student has the possibility of repeating if so desired. If this option is chosen, the items are presented in a different order. Once the verb form in a particular sentence is correct, the student can ask to see the example response and so shortcut the checking of the other sentence elements and the word order. While the program is obviously suitable for self-study, practical experience in the classroom has shown that it is also effective when used by small groups of students. Many learn effectively together with (and from) their peers while co-operating in using the program (see also the discussions in Göbel, 1985: 73–74; Piper, 1986). The control which the student has over the material to be worked through, combined with the program's interactivity and its answer-judging, feedback and on-line information features, provides a powerful cognitive learning environment.

Individualisation is a consequence of the program's being data driven, the data being provided via the authoring module. Thus, depending on the level of language material entered by the teacher, exercises can present simple tenses in simple sentences, or more complicated ones with or without the use of the subjunctive or the passive and involving different sentence types (subordinate clauses, questions, etc.). Here the teacher is in control and can adjust the complexity of the exercises to cater for any level from elementary to advanced or can create exercises in response to the needs of different learner groups or individuals.

Conclusion

In foreign language learning at an advanced level there is a place for the study and practice of the grammatical systems of the language, particularly for those students who see the acquisition of the requisite knowledge and the achievement of accuracy as a worthwhile goal. Though the emphasis in CALL is now mainly on communicative applications and its image has had to recover from its early association with primitive drill and practice software, one should be wary of 'throwing the baby out with the bathwater.' Programs like these, provided they are sophisticated enough to provide the means by which students can reach an understanding of what they are doing, can very usefully be integrated into courses aiming at the comprehensive study of a language.

Notes to Chapter 13

1. For an extensive annotated list including CALL programs in German, see Higgins & Davies (1985: 109–139).
2. Through co-operation between Wida Software and Eurocentres. Available from Eurocentres/MBA. P.O. Box 7, Wetherby, Yorkshire, LS23 7EP, U.K.
3. The original name of the package was *Mentor*. Contact address: Horwood Language Centre, University of Melbourne, Parkville, Victoria 3052, Australia.
4. 'Verbergänzung' — see Schulz & Griesbach (1970: 323ff., 398ff.); 'freie Adverbialbestimmung' — see Helbig & Buscha (1975: 514ff.).
5. The verb bracket ('verbale Klammer') comprises the finite and non-finite constituents of the verb, which normally enclose other elements of the German sentence (Drach, 1940: ch.XII–XIV). In an unmarked declarative clause the verb bracket encloses the whole clause except for the element in initial position (Drach, 1940: ch. XII–XIV).

References

BERGER, R. (1985) Mikrocomputer im Lehren und Lernen einer Fremdsprache. In Langenscheidt Redaktion (ed.), *Computergestützter Fremdsprachenunterricht: Ein Handbuch*, 109–14. Berlin: Langenscheidt.

BICKES, G. & A. SCOTT (1987) CALL exercises for a German beginners' course, *Babel: Journal of the Australian Federation of Modern Language Teachers' Associations*, 22: 3, 3–7.

BLAKE, R. & B. DUNCAN (1985) CALL for the Macintosh, *CALICO Journal*, 3: 1, 11–15.

DAHL, R. C. & P. F. LUCKAU (1985) VIDEODEUTSCH: A computer-assisted approach to verbal and non-verbal cultural literacy, *CALICO Journal*, 2: 4, 13–19.

DRACH, E. (1940) *Grundgedanken der deutschen Satzlehre* (repr. 1963). Darmstadt: Wissenschaftliche Buchgesellschaft.

ERK, H. (1972) *Zur Lexik wissenschaftlicher Fachtexte: Verben — Frequenz und Verwendungsweise*. Munich: Hueber.

— (1975) *Zur Lexik wissenschaftlicher Fachtexte: Substantive — Frequenz und Verwendungsweise*. Munich: Hueber.

— (1982) *Zur Lexik wissenschaftlicher Fachtexte: Adjektive, Adverbien und andere Wortarten — Frequenz und Verwendungsweise*. Munich: Hueber.

GÖBEL, R. (1985) Mikrocomputer und Fremdsprachenlehrer. In Langenscheidt Redaktion (ed.), *Computergestützter Fremdsprachenunterricht: Ein Handbuch*, 67–76. Berlin/Munich: Langenscheidt.

HALLIDAY, M. A. K. (1985) *An Introduction to Functional Grammar*. London: Edward Arnold.

HAMMOND, J. & C. SIMMONS (1987) The cognate language teacher: A teaching package for higher education. In G. CHESTERS & N. GARDNER (eds), *The Use of Computers in the Teaching of Language and Languages*. Proceedings of a Conference held at the University of Hull, April 22–23, 1987. Claverton Down, Bath, Avon: CTISS, University of Bath.

HELBIG, G. & J. BUSCHA (1975) *Deutsche Grammatik: Ein Handbuch für den Ausländerunterricht*. Leipzig: VEB Verlag Enzyklopädie.

HENDRICKS, H., J. L. BENNION & J. LARSON (1983) Technology and language learning at BYU, *CALICO Journal*, 1: 3, 22–30, 46.

HIGGINS, J. (1983) Can computers teach?, *CALICO Journal*, 1: 2, 4–6.

HIGGINS, J. & T. JOHNS (1984) *Computers in Language Learning*. London: Collins.

HIGGINS, J. & G. DAVIES (1985) *Using Computers in Language Learning: A Teacher's Guide*, 2nd revised & enlarged edition. London: CILT.

HOBERG, U. (1981) *Die Wortstellung in der geschriebenen deutschen Gegenwartssprache*. Munich: Hueber.

HOPE, G. R., H. F. TAYLOR & J. P. PUSACK (1984) *Using Computers in Teaching Foreign Languages*. Orlando: Harcourt Brace Jovanovich.

— (1985) Der Einsatz von Computern im Fremdsprachenunterricht. In Langenscheidt Redaktion (ed.), *Computergestützter Fremdsprachenunterricht: Ein Handbuch*, 7–76. Berlin: Langenscheidt.

HOWLETT, G. S. (1986) Interactive audio/video hardware configurations, *CALICO Journal*, 4: 1, 39–50.

JOHN, D. G. (1984) Computer assisted instruction in German, *Canadian Modern Language Review*, 41: 1, 53–62.

JUNG, U. O. H. (1985) Angewandt-Linguistische Aspekte des Einsatzes von Computern im Sprachunterricht. In Langenscheidt Redaktion (ed.), *Computergestützter Fremdsprachenunterricht: Ein Handbuch*, 77–92. Berlin: Langenscheidt.

KENNING, M. J. & M-M. KENNING (1983) *An Introduction to Computer Assisted Language Teaching*. Oxford: Oxford University Press.

KOLVENBACH, M. (1980) Das morphologische Lexikon (MOLEX) des Systems PLIDIS, *Mitteilungen des Instituts für deutsche Sprache*, 7, 60–6.

KOLVENBACH, M. & W. TEUBERT (1983) Der MOLEX-Generator: Probleme der Nominalflexion, *Mitteilungen des Instituts für deutsche Sprache*, 8, 43–54.

KRAMSCH C., D. MORGENSTERN & J. H. MURRAY (1985) Designing materials for the language lab of the future: An overview of the MIT Athena language learning project, *CALICO Journal*, 2: 4, 31–4.

KRÜGER, M. (1981) Übungsabläufe im kommunikativen Fremdsprachen-unterricht. In G. NEUNER, M. KRÜGER & U. GREWER (1981) *Übungstypologie zum kommunikativen Deutschunterricht*, 17–28. Berlin: Langenscheidt.

LAST, R. (1984) *Language Teaching and the Microcomputer*. Oxford: Blackwell.

PIPER, A. (1986) Conversation and the computer: A study of the conversational spin-off generated among learners of English as a foreign language working in groups, *System*, 14: 2 (Theme Issue: Computer-Assisted Language Learning: A European View), 187–98.

PUSACK, J. P. (1983) *DASHER: An Answer Processor for Language Study*. Iowa City: CONDUIT.

QUIRK, R. & S. GREENBAUM (1973) *A University Grammar of English*. Harlow, England: Longman.

ROWE, A. A. (1984) Interactive language simulation systems: Technology for a national language base, *CALICO Journal*, 2: 3, 44–7.

Rüschoff, B. (1984) The integration of CALL materials into the overall curriculum, *CALICO Journal*, 1: 4, 26–8.
— (1985) Der Mikrocomputer als Werkzeug des Sprachlehrers. In Langenscheidt Redaktion (ed.), *Computergestützter Fremdsprachenunterricht: Ein Handbuch*, 93–101. Berlin: Langenscheidt.
— (1986) The 'Intelligence' of intelligently programmed adaptive CALL materials for self-study, *System*, 14: 2 (Theme Issue: Computer-Assisted Language Learning: A European View), 205–10.
Schäpers, A. & R. Schäpers (1984) *MORGENS GEHT FRITZ ZUR SCHULE*. Munich: Verlag für Deutsch.
Schulz, D. & H. Griesbach (1970) *Grammatik der deutschen Sprache*. (8., neubearb. Aufl.) Munich: Hueber.
Schumann, J. & J. Breitsameter (1985) *INTERAKTIVES TESTPAKET*. Berlin: Langenscheidt.
Schumann, J., Th. Schumann & H. Krohn (1985) *HANSI*. Berlin: Langenscheidt.
Siliakus, H. (1974) *German Word Lists: Basic Vocabulary for Arts and Social Sciences*. Adelaide: University of Adelaide.
Sussex, R. & L. Burr (1983) A System of Computer-aided Instruction. Mimeographed introductory notes. Melbourne: University of Melbourne.
Tuman, W. V. (1983) Boris and MENTOR: The application of CAI, *CALICO Journal*, 1: 1, 59, 60–1.
Underwood, J. H. (1984) *Linguistics, Computers and the Language Teacher: A Communicative Approach*. Rowley, Massachusetts: Newbury House.
Die Zeit: Wochenzeitschrift für Politik, Wirtschaft, Handel und Kultur. 7/15/88, Hamburg.

Index

Accent, 67, 248, 249, 252, 254
Acceptance of computers in society, 21
Accessibility Hierarchy Hypothesis, 132-133, 142, 150
Acoustic analysis and features, 245, 251, 255, 259-263, 267
Acquisition
— computer-based research in, 4-6, 127-152, 201-211
— correlated with cognitive and affective factors, 24, 52
— first language, 112-113, 211
— implications for teaching, 247, 268
— internalizaton in the course of, 16, 48, 97, 140, 150
— order of, 129-132, 247-248
— related to
  comprehension in, see Comprehensible input
  conversation and listening, 119, 274
  interaction with environment, 15, 20, 48, 50
  focusing, 245, 248
  instruction, 112, 141-144, 254
  interaction with computer, 157-174, 259, 315
    c.f. acquisition of programming languages, 113
Affective considerations, 13, 16, 52, 81, 248, 252, 276
Animation, 18, 49, 62, 140-141, 149
ANOVA, 145-147
Answer-judging, 7, 49, 58-61, 71-73, 96-97, 145, 294, 315
— accept alternative answers, 7, 49, 60, 295, 298, 299, 298, 303, 308
— analysis of learner input, 61, 68, 71, 113, 276, 294-295
  error diagnosis, 49, 70-73, 82-84, 112-113, 145, 284, 297-306

  input matching, 72-73, 145, 298, 302-305, 309
  pattern marking, 3, 60, 71-73, 145, 296-298
  recognizing input, 60, 94, 159
Arabic, 123, 252, 255
Artificial languages 113, 183
Artificial intelligence, 7, 10, 25, 31, 34, 40, 67, 208, 246
Assistance, see Help
Attitudes toward computer-mediated
— adventure games (e.g. move-based simulations), 156-160, 169-173
— exploratory CALL, 15
— games, 5
— writing tools, 80-89, 94-99
Audiolingual method, 12-14
Audio interface, 26, 34, 49, 57, 62, 244-293, 296-297
Audio-visual method, 244, 248
Augmented transition network or ATN, 6, 209, 211, 216, 227-230
Aural/auditory recognition, 248, 252-258, 267, 282, 287
Authenticity, 6, 7, 15-18, 32-33, 48, 54, 70-71, 181, 183, 188, 251, 260, 264; see also Text, authentic
Authentic labor 22, 26, 55
Authoring tools, 7, 50, 57, 63, 68-74, 113, 136, 294-299, 315
Autonomy in learning, 12-23, 55, 63, 73, 86, 98, 263, 315

Behaviorism, 2, 11-12, 14, 16, 21, 31, 34, 38-39, 48, 112, 248
Branching in response to user input, 16, 24, 59-62, 296
Bulletin board(s), see Communications software; also E-mail

319

CD-ROM, 17, 34, 71
Children, 52, 79
— analysis of children's speech, 112-113, 189-190, 209-211, 274
Chinese, 4, 86, 158, 250, 252, 259-261
Cloze, 18, 20, 27, 44, 53, 59, 161, 295
Cognitive, *see also* Induction and inferential learning
Cognitive-academic language proficiency, 4, 110-111, 121-124
— models, 15, 48, 68, 130, 249, 306, 315
— processes, 4, 12, 16, 53, 72-74, 134, 169, 173-174, 247-248, 255, 257, 265, 272, 313
— styles 24, 50
— variables, 16, 24, 52, 248
Collaborative learning 28, 55, 99, 110, 116-117, 123, 245, 249, 253, 263-268, 315; *see also* Peer interaction
Communication with computers, 2, 14, 30-34, 49, 54, 59-60, 96
Communication around computers, 2, 4, 14, 19, 21-23, 28-30, 55, 61, 64, 68-69, 74-75, 79, 83, 96, 110-125, 137, 156-157, 170
Communications software, 21, 29-30, 280, 288; *see also* E-Mail
Communicative
— methodologies, 12, 52-53, 256, 288, 306
— contexts, 12, 121
Communicative CALL, 22, 40, 43, 48, 112-113, 315
Competence, linguistic, 15, 16, 70, 121, 134, 152, 273, 276
Comprehensible input, 15, 54, 112-116, 133-137, 140, 151
Comprehension-based approach, 133-134, 140, 150, 274
Comprehensive English Language Test (CELT), 279
Computerized-adaptive testing, 275-283, 288
Concordancing, 17, 27, 208, 265
Content-based materials and curricula, 5, 19, 22, 24, 52, 54-55, 68, 111, 113, 157, 245-253, 258-264, 268
Context-embedded/reduced, 121-124
Control over medium, 4, 12-28, 32-34, 48-49, 53-61, 134, 144, 249, 253-257, 297-306, 312-315
— learner directed, 12, 14, 23, 27-28, 33, 49, 52-54, 57-62, 73, 253, 255, 300-306, 310, 312, 315
— program directed, 8, 11, 20, 61, 116, 134-136, 150
computer-managed instruction (CMI), 24
lockstep instruction, 3, 13, 23, 66, 132
Conversation, *see* Communication with and around computers
Cooperative-learning, *see* Collaborative learning
Corpora, 5-7, 17, 181-192, 205, 307, 310
— analyzed corpora, 5-7, 181-194; *see also* Natural language; *also* Parsers, accuracy of; *also* Text, analysis of
Correction,
— self-correction, 4, 96-97, 220
— negative effect of on acquisition, 112
Cryptograms, 21
Cueing student responses, 298, 303
— audio, 278-280
— morphological, 182
— prosodic vs. phoneme level, 254
— situational/linguistic, 121
— visual, 138, 149, 255
Cultural considerations, 22, 52, 54, 62, 70, 259, 288
Curiosity, stimulation of in learners, 15, 17, 159
Curriculum, integration of CALL into 4, 12, 38, 44, 155, 174, 246-247, 254, 257, 272, 274, 296, 316
— integration into writing curricula, 79, 81, 84, 99, 100

Data, computer-assisted
— analysis, 4, 6, 24, 144-147, 154, 277, 281, 284-285, 287
— manipulation, 6, 16-17, 22, 25, 30, 69, 145, 210, 231-233, 245, 249-257, 265, 268
Databases
— associated with a particular program, 31, 187, 249, 309-311
— comprising natural language 3, 5-7, 15-19, 21-22, 25-26, 70-71, 75; *see also* Corpora; *also* Natural language;

also Spoken language
—systems for managing, 6, 21, 207-242, 280-288
Decision-making, *see* Control over medium; *also* Problem-solving
Deductive learning, 16, 20, 48, 51-52, 149-150, 255; *see also* Rules
Dependency-tree analysis, *see* Grammar, models of
Desk-top publishing, 21, 30
Diagnosis of errors, *see* Answer judging
Dictionaries, *see* Help, dictionary
Difficulty
—of CALL lessons, 25, 45, 50, 53-54, 121-123, 129-133, 151, 158, 162, 170-173, 248, 276-277, 281, 315
—order of, 130-132
Discovery learning, *see* Exploratory learning
Discussion, *see* Communication in and around CALL
Ditidaht, 252, 255, 262, 264
Drill-and-practice, 12, 14, 16, 33-34, 39, 48-49, 55, 59, 61, 64, 112, 294, 297, 306, 315

E-mail, 29, 69, 74-75
English as a foreign language (EFL), 52, 244
English as a Second Language (ESL), 1, 3-4, 17, 19, 22, 24, 29, 30, 80, 83-86, 88, 98-100, 116, 121, 127-128, 134-135, 156, 247, 262, 274-275, 279-280, 282, 288
English for specific purposes (ESP), 157-158, 173
Error analysis (study of student error types), 25; *for on-line analysis of error, see* Answer judging; *also* Feedback
Evaluation,
—of effects of mode of instr, 4
—of courseware, 2, 40-44, 49, 57, 110, 155-156, 158, 246, 249
—of computer-based writing analysis, 80-100
Expert-system, 3, 6, 7, 25, 31, 67-70, 294, 297
Explanations, *see* Feedback
Exploratory learning, 2, 14-18, 26-29, 33-34, 55, 59, 61, 89, 157-158, 169, 187, 249, 252-255, 264-265

Facilitative learning, 55
Feedback (computer-based), 44, 56-62, 294-316; *see also* Branching
—anticipatory interaction, 7, 49, 54-55, 60-62, 70-73
—explanation, 7, 27, 33, 49, 55, 88, 96, 112, 137-140, 149-151, 262, 295-298, 301
—exposure to collected variants, 248
—facilitative information, 17
—leading students to correct answers, 7, 49, 62, 84, 94, 303
—response via voice synthesis, 67, 276-277, 287
—text analysis, 3-4, 94-97
—wrong-try-again, 112
Feelings, expression of, 13, 28, 30-31, 246
Field dependence/independence, 24, 51-52
Fluency, conversational vs. cognitive-academic, 121, 124
Focus
—of learner attention, 4, 25, 27, 56-57, 95, 97-100, 134, 137, 140-152, 249-253
—program focus (on content or skill), 44-45, 50, 52-53, 55-56
Focusing (approximating from global to specific), 245, 248, 255
Form-function relationship, 202; *see also* Structure Function
—of language, 47, 52, 182, 185-187, 190, 201-206, 209-210, 215-220, 225, 237, 273, 276, 307, 312-314
—communicative, 12, 48
Functional
—materials, tasks, and activities, 21-22
—syllabus, 52

Gaelic, 252, 255
Games, 19-20, 28, 39, 44, 56, 59-60, 174, 295
—Adventure, 4-5, 18-19, 27, 29, 33, 55, 61, 155-174, 295
—Puzzles, 18-21, 59
—simulations, 13-14, 28, 30, 39, 55, 59-61, 67, 116-120, 122-123
move-based (MBS), 5, 18, 156-174
real-time (RTS), 156

Gap filling
  —fill-in-the-blanks, 19, 298
  —chart completion, 250
Generative CALL, 25, 70-71
German, 5-7, 122, 201-209, 221-227, 231, 235, 237, 294-315
Grammar, *see also* Competence; *also* Deductive learning; *also* Structure
  —acceptability vs grammaticality, 183
  —accuracy, vs fluency 97, 112, 151, 277, 315
  —errors in, 60, 84, 87, 94, 97, 231
  —models of, 16, 47-48, 112, 182-183
    dependency-tree analysis, 185-187
    phrase-structure grammar, 185-187; *see also* Structure, phrase
    systemic-functional, 190
    grammar-translation, 294
  —teaching and materials, 19, 25, 27, 29, 33-34, 39, 52, 112, 116-119, 123
Graphics, 6, 57, 59-60, 62, 187, 239, 245, 250, 280-281, 284-289, 295, 297
Grice's Maxims, 31

Hangman, 44
Hearing-impaired, 79, 244, 263
Help (on-line), 17-18, 27-28, 54, 58-59, 61-62, 137-138, 297, 303, 305
  —Atlases, 18
  —dictionaries, on-line, 17-18, 22, 137-138, 151, 191
    of abstract words 82, 94
    of morphemes, 224
    German-English 306-315
Hints, 6, 23, 49, 54, 61-62, 300
  —efficacy of, 158-159, 172-173
Humanism, 2, 6, 11-34, 48
  —Human-facilitated process approach, 98
  —Human factors, 73-75
Humor and absurdity, 32-33
Hypermedia, 17, 26-27, 257

Immediate constituents, 185-190
ILR/ACTFL rating system, 276
Imaging principle, 258-262
Individual differences, 2, 13-16, 23-25, 34, 50-52, 56
Individualised instruction, 23-25, 48, 51, 56, 72, 80, 84-85, 99, 275, 296-297, 314-315
Induction and inferential learning, 6, 12, 16, 20, 48, 51, 52, 149, 255; *see also* Cognitive processes
Inferences, drawn by
  —computers from available data, 70-73, 206-207, 217
  —linguists from corpora 183, 217
  —students from feedback, *see* Inductive; also Cognitive processes
Integrative/instrumental motivation, 51
Intelligence, strategic, 3, 75
  —learner intelligence: *see* Inferences
Interlanguage, 128-129, 132, 201-202, 207, 211-213, 216-217, 229, 230, 237, 247, 264
Intonation, 190, 244, 257, 259
Introversion, 51-52
Item response theory (IRT), 277, 283

Japanese, 27, 52, 122, 123, 252, 259
Joystick, 25, 57

Key word search, 22, 31, 40, 57, 72-73
Keys, cursor or arrow, 27, 33
Korean, 86, 252, 255

Laboratories or labs
  —language, 21
  —computer, 28, 80, 144, 245, 250-268
Languages not listed by name in this index, 252
Laser-optical disks, 278-279
Learner variables, 50-52, 55, 287; c.f. Style, learning
Lexis, *see* Vocabulary
Listening comprehension 6, 55-56, 71-72, 114, 137, 252-267, 273-291, 296; *see also* Richards' Taxonomy of Listening Skills
Listening Comprehension Proficiency Test (ESL), feasibility of, 280
Literacy programs, 75, 79
Local area network, 277-278

Machine-readable text, 5, 17, 181-192
Machine translation, *see* Translation, machine
Magister-pedagogue dichotomy, 14-15, 40, 61, 314-315

INDEX 323

Mainframe, 84, 87-88, 295, 297, 307
Management of instructional systems, 50, 56, 67-74, 277
Markedness, 4, 132-133, 147-150, 304
Mastery learning, 16, 140
Matching exercises, 245, 249, 266
Mazes, 18, 20
Meaning, *see also* Help, dictionary; c.f. Rules, rule-oriented
—discerning meaning, 21-22, 144, 203, 274, 307
—expression of, 13-14, 34 121-123
—meaning-oriented instruction, 4-5, 134-152
—meaningful practice, 22, 49, 246
—meaningful revision, 4, 30, 83-99
—negotiation of, 30, 66, 73, 114-121, 137
Mechanical practice, 32, 48-49, 112
Memorization, 130, 247, 249, 259, 265, 268; *see also* Retention
Memory considerations, 18, 278-280, 285
Metalanguage in instruction, 43, 112, 148-151; *see also* Rules, rule-oriented
Monitoring, self-, 4, 96-97, 99
Morpholological, *see also* Syntax, morphosyntactic features, 52, 55-56, 182, 189, 204, 206, 210-213, 216, 218-230, 235, 237, 298, 305
—analysis, 224
Motivation, 2, 10, 12, 18, 20, 22, 51-52, 66-67, 81, 83, 156
Mouse, 6, 25, 57, 262, 280, 287
Multi-tasking, 68
Multiple-choice in CALL, 32-33, 61, 282-283, 295, 296

Natural language, 3, 12, 15, 22, 32-33, 67-68, 70, 82, 84, 99, 113-116, 130, 182-184, 208, 244, 252, 255
—analysis of, 82, 181-200, 201-240; *see also* Speech, analysis of; *also* Text, analysis of; *also* Parsed corpora
Networks, communications, 30, 57, 78-79, 277-278
Neurological variables, 248
Non-native learners,
—of English, 22, 99, 115-116, 273, 275
—of other languages, 202-209
Non-threatening ambiance, 14-15, 81, 94

Notional-functional, 52-53
Nyangumarta, 252, 255, 266

Options for learners, *see* Control
Oral proficiency, 143-145, 274-276
Oral practice, 256, 268
Orthographic phenomena, 185, 188-191
Orthographic representation 257, 265-266

Pace in CALL, 66, 247
Paralinguistics, 257
Parallel distributed processing, 15
Parallel Function Hypothesis, 129-132, 149
Parsers and parsing, *see also* Augmented Transition Network; *also* COALA; *also* Critique
—accuracy possible with analyzed corpora, 186, 188, 191
COALA 204-205, 211, 218, 229-230
Critique, 94, 96, 99
diagnosis of error, 71
German lessons, 311
—in expert systems, 31, 68
—problems in parsing homographs, 224, 226, 309
—recognizing constituents, 190, 202-204
—rules in, 70, 84, 189, 202, 204, 237, 239, 311
—stochastic optimization system of, 183
—techniques in, 33, 315
Patterns vs. rules, 16, 47, 245, 248, 253
Pedagogue, *see* Magister-pedagogue dichotomy
Peer interaction, 14, 28, 30, 83, 115-116, 121, 247, 264, 315; *see also* Collaborative learning
Perception exercises, 248-256, 259
Perceptual Difficulty Hypothesis, 130-132
Phonation, 255, 259
Phonemic phenomena, 246, 250-254, 257
Phonetic phenomena, 244-268; *see also* Phonetic Database (PDB)
Phonology, 7, 55, 247-248, 252, 255-256, 267-268
Phrase-structure grammar, *see* Grammar, models of
Problem-solving, 2, 5, 14-15, 18-22, 27-29, 34, 53-54, 59, 114-125, 134-135,

157-158, 171-174, 249, 254, 259, 306-307
Process approach to writing, 3-4, 22, 30, 79-100, 110
Productivity tools, 2, 15, 21-23
Programmed instruction (PI), 12, 14, 16, 17, 23, 112
Proficiency, adjustment of software to, 6, 16, 25, 50-53, 60, 140, 158, 249, 254, 258, 268, 273-289, 308
Pronunciation, 246, 249-250, 254, 257, 262, 267
Prosodic phenomena, 252, 254, 267, 268
Psycholinguistic considerations, 247, 287
Psychomotor variables, 248
Pull-down menus, 297
Punctuation, 82, 90, 185, 188-189, 191

Readability, 82, 93
Reading, 18-20, 25, 27, 39, 48, 53-59, 57, 134-141, 144, 148-152, 265, 274-279, 281-282, 295, 306-315
—comprehension of relativization in, 130-152
—reading aloud, 202; *see also* Scanning; *also* Skimming
Realism, *see* Authenticity
Recognition activities (Kemmis), 55
Reflection/impulsivity, 24
Relativization, *see* Reading, comprehension of
Responsibility, *see* Autonomy in learning
Retention of what is learned, 14, 16, 53; *see also* Memory and Memorization
Richards' Taxonomy of Listening Skills, 275, 280, 287
Role play, 13, 33
Rote learning, 295
Rules
—role of in language learning, 15, 47-48, 62, 112-113, 129, 140; *see also* Deductive learning
—rule-oriented, vs. meaning-oriented, 4, 134-136, 140-144, 147-151; *see also* Metalanguage in instruction

Salience, 137-140, 148-150, 184
Scanning text with a scanner, 19, 71-72
Scanning while reading 19, 134, 136, 141, 144

Scrabble, 20
Search-and-replace, 29
Segmental phonological level, 246, 252-255, 260, 268
Self-access, 12
Self-actualization, 13-14
Semantic phenomena, 47, 52-53, 95, 113, 137, 143, 149, 182, 191, 202-205, 208, 223, 237, 239, 283
Sentence-combination, 141, 149
Sequencing instruction, 15-16, 23, 52, 61, 129, 132
Simulations, *see under* Games
Situational syllabus, 52, 54
Skagit, 252, 255, 257
Skimming in reading, 57, 134, 136, 144
Social aggregation and transaction, 22, 27-29, 137
Societal consciousness and acceptance of computers, 21
Sociolinguistics, 54, 247, 252, 254, 264, 287
Sociophonetics, 247, 257
Software
—convenience in using, 2, 14, 23, 25-28, 34, 112, 208, 211, 240
—inadequacy of, 13-14, 34, 74, 277
Spanish, 26, 32, 33
Speaking, skill of, 30, 58, 253; *see also* Speech
Speech, *see also* Spoken language
—analysis of, 113, 189-190, 201-268
—pathology, 245, 262
—recognition, 26, 33, 67
—spectral representations of, 259-262
—synthesis, 26, 67-68, 244-245, 249, 262-264, 268, 275-289
Spelling, *see also* Parsers, problems in parsing homographs
—activities, 55
—check programs, 21, 73, 82, 208, 239-240
—dealing with misspellings, 60, 90, 94, 301
Spoken language
—Transcribed corpora, 181-182, 185, 187, 189-191, 201-202, 209-211, 217-221
—Database of sounds, 6, 245-268; *see also* Phonetic Database

INDEX

Spreadsheet, 21-22, 249
Strategies
—for learning, 13-14, 20, 24, 50, 53, 57, 130
—for solving problems, 20, 29, 159, 257
Structure
—constituent, 55, 203-205, 217, 225, 227
—discourse, 57, 82, 205
—language, 47, 56, 99
—morphological; *see* Morphological features and analysis
—phrase, 47, 130-132, 140, 184-189, 203-240; *see also* Grammar, models of, phrase-structure
—sentence, 90, 95, 298
—underlying (i.e. tree), 182, 185-192, 232-233
Structural
—approach, 52, 140
—frequency, 52, 82, 131, 148, 237
—linguistics, 12
Structuro-global audio visual methodology, 248
Style, cognitive learning, 24, 50, 52, 55; c.f. Learner variables
Style checkers, 21, 82
Syllables in phonology, 253, 259, 264-267
Syllabus in relation to CALL, 43, 49-54, 184
Syntax,
—analysis of, 99, 113, 182-192, 201-242, 300-306
—checkers, 21, 82
—features of, 47, 52-56, 130-132, 205, 208, 213-214, 221-225, 283, 295, 307, 313
—morphosyntactic analysis, 201, 306-314
features, 52, 211, 214
Systemic-functional grammar, *see* Grammar, models of

T-test, 146-147, 162-172
Task-oriented materials, 22-23, 28, 66, 249, 256, 268
—communicative tasks (vs. linguistic ones), 114-125
Test of English as a Foreign Language (TOEFL), 24, 86, 279

Testing, standardization of, 6, 273-275, 288
Text, *see also* Corpora
—analysis of, 2-6, 80, 82-100, 181-194
automatic coding, 182, 201, 205-206, 211, 216, 217, 229
manual coding, 5-6, 26, 90, 182-186, 201-211, 215-226, 229-237, 307, 311
reconstructing original data from coded forms, 186, 264, 310
—authentic, 17, 252-259, 310
—storage of, 279; *see also* Scanning text
—manipulation and reconstruction, 18, 20-21, 29, 44, 49, 53, 55, 59
Tolerance/intolerance, 51-52
Tonal languages, 259-261, 267
Toolkit approach to CALL, 70-71
Total Physical Response, 20
Touchscreen, 25, 57
Transcription exercises, 264-268
Translation
—exercises, 299-300
—(as a) help option, 18, 26, 310, 314
—machine translation, 183, 208
Trivial Pursuit, 20
Turkish, 252, 255
Tutorials, 19-20, 27, 34, 39, 54-55, 59, 63, 244, 296

Umpila, 252, 255
Understanding, constructive (per Kemmis), 55
Universal constraints on relativization, 130-131

Variety in language, 53-54, 158, 191-192, 201-204, 209, 245, 247-248, 254-255, 260-261, 264, 268, 297-298, 302, 310
Video, interactive, 18-19, 26-2, 32-34, 49, 57, 62, 257, 259, 264, 296
Vocabulary/lexis, 5, 15, 17-19, 44, 47-48, 53-56, 97, 112, 137-138, 144, 151, 157-162, 167-169, 173-174, 202-240, 256, 295, 298-311
Vocal production modeling, 264, 267
Voice setting, 252-255
Voice-driven typewriters, 183

Waveform, 253, 257, 259, 264, 266, 267
Whatsits, 117
Windows, 17, 25-26, 62, 135-136, 213
Word Processing, 4-5, 17, 21-22, 29-30, 55, 79-82, 84-85, 87, 95-100, 110, 116-120, 208, 245, 247, 250
Word order, 55, 72, 204, 207, 218, 237, 294, 297-299, 304-305, 315
Word-frequency, 53, 185, 231, 310

Writing, computer-assisted, 3-4, 18-19, 22, 29-31, 48, 53, 58, 79-100, 113, 245, 247, 249-250; *see also* Process approach to writing

Xhosa, 6, 252, 255, 259, 266

Yoruba, 252, 260

Index of Computer Software and Hardware Systems

ACTFL Computer-Based Reading Comprehension Proficiency Test, 274
Andrew+ operating environment, 68, 71
ANIMATED GRAMMAR, 140
Apollo DN300 system and Aegis editor, 144-145
APRIL system of parsing, 183
Athena Project, 3, 32-33, 68, 75, 296
AWK programming language, 145

BASIC, 57, 113, 285
—IBM Interpreted, 280
Bernoulli Cartridge and IOMEGA mass storage device, 145
Brown University Corpus, 181-182, 184-186, 191
BYU ESL Computerised Adaptive Test, YESCAT (BYU), 279

C programming language, 57
CHAT (Codes for the Human Analysis of Transcripts) 210-211, 225
Chatterbox, 55
CHOICEMASTER, 297
CLAM (Computerised Line Access Monitor), 69, 71
CLAN, (Child Language ANalysis), 210-211
COALA system 202-241
COLOSSAL ADVENTURE, 156-162, 169-174

COMPUTEST:ESL, 279
Critique (IBM), 3, 80-99

DASHER, 296, 298
dBase III Plus, 280-288
Deutsch Aktiv, 297
Domain Analysis Based Instruction System (DABIS), 71
DomainPC interface software, 145
DRILL authoring program for Macintosh, 297

ELIZA, 31
EMU, 297
ENGTUTE, 71
ESSENTIAL IDIOMS, 19
EUROPEAN NATIONS AND LOCATIONS EUROPEAN, 19
EXCALIBUR, 3, 67-71

FAMOUS SCIENTISTS, 19
FRENCH VIDEODISC, 33

German "Gateway" course in VELVET, 296
Gothenburg Corpus, 184-187, 191

HANSI, 295
Hayden Speller, 239-240
HyperCard, 26

INDEX

IBM, system in general, 275, 277, 288-289
— 3081 Mainframe, 84
— XT/AT, 127, 251, 280
— extended graphics monitor and board, 280
— Proprinter, 280
— Voice Communication Options Board, 280
International Computer Archive of Modern English (ICAME), 181
INTERAKTIVES TESTPAKET, 297
Invent a Monster, 114
IPAEDIT, 264
IPALABEL, 249

KANJI CITY, 27

Lancaster Spoken English Corpus, 182
Lancaster-Leeds Treebank, 184, 187-191
Lancaster-Oslo/Bergen (LOB) Corpus, 5, 181-192
LARSP, 210
LASERIPA, 249, 278
LDB (Linguist's Database), 187
LOGO, 113
LONDON ADVENTURE, 18-19, 27, 33
London-Lund Corpus, 181
LUCY, 31-32

MacIntosh, 239, 249, 289, 297
MacLang, 57, 297
McPlus, 239
MEdit, 208, 239-240
Memoscriber, 144
MICRO SPEECH LAB (MSL), 251-267
MicroCAT Testing System, 277
Microsoft C, 136, 280
Microsoft Word, 239-240
Minnesota Computerized Adaptive Testing Language, 277
MINT, 113
MOLEX-Generator, 307, 311
MONTEVIDISCO, 32-33
MORGENS GEHT FRITZ ZUR SCHULE, 295
Motorola 56001 Digital Signal Processor (DSP), 278
MSLEDIT, 253-257, 264
MSLPITCH, 259-262

MSLSORT, 257
MSLSPECT, 259, 262
MultiFinder (Multitasking Finder), 240
MYSTERY HOUSE, 19, 156

NeXT Digital Signal Processor, 278
Nijmegen Corpus, 184, 186-187, 191

Oral Proficiency Interview (OPI), 274

Pascal programming language, 57, 113, 140
PC Mouse Plus, 280
PC Paint Gallery, 280, 287
PC Paint Plus, 280, 284, 287-288
PFS:Write, 87-89
Phonetic Database (PDB), 252-267
PILOT, 57, 113, 205
PLATO, 24-25, 30, 295
Polytechnic of Wales (PoW) Corpus, 184-190
PRIVATE TUTOR SYSTEM (PTS), 297
Prolog, 240

REFLEX, 239-240
ROBOT ODYSSEY, 19
Robotropolis, 19-20

Sanyo Memoscriber, 144
SCIENTISTS, 19, 251
SPSS, 24
STORYBOARD
SUPER CLOZE, 27
SUSANNE Corpus, 184-185, 191-192
SYSTAT (version 3), 145-146

Tandberg, 296
Tempo, 239-240
Texas Instruments, 145
TIANMA, 250
TICCIT, 295
TOSCA, 209
TUCO, 297

UNIX 4.2/4.3 BSD operating system, 69, 75

VARBRUL, 248
VCScreen, 136
VELVET project, 296

VISI-PITCH (Kay Elemetrics), 244
VISIBLE SPEECH AID (VSA), 244, 259, 263
Vitamin C, 135
VOCAB, 297

Writer's Workbench (WWB), 82-85

Youngman's SMLR multiple regression program, 160